NEW FRONTIERS
FOR YOUTH DEVELOPMENT
IN THE TWENTY-FIRST CENTURY

NEW FRONTIERS
FOR YOUTH DEVELOPMENT
IN THE TWENTY-FIRST CENTURY

REVITALIZING & BROADENING
YOUTH DEVELOPMENT

MELVIN DELGADO

COLUMBIA UNIVERSITY PRESS

NEW YORK

COLUMBIA UNIVERSITY PRESS

Publishers Since 1893

New York   Chichester, West Sussex

Copyright © 2002 Columbia University Press

All rights reserved

Library of Congress Cataloging-in-Publication Data

Delgado, Melvin.

New Frontiers for youth development in the twenty-first century:
revitalizing and broadening youth development / Melving Delgado

p.cm

Includes bibliographical references and indexes.

ISBN 978-0-231-12280-1 (cloth : alk. paper) — ISBN 978-0-231-12281-8 (pbk : alk. paper)

1. Social work in youth–United States. I. Title

HV1431 .D444 2002

362.7'0973–dc21

Casebound editions of Columbia University Press books are printed
on permanent and durable acid-free paper.

Printed in the United States of America

c 10 9 8 7 6 5 4 3 2 1
p 10 9 8 7 6

To Denise, Laura, and Barbara
they never cease to inspire and support

CONTENTS

PART 2 NEW FRONTIER SETTINGS 159

ACKNOWLEDGMENTS

I n acknowledging the contributions of numerous individuals and organizations who have made the writing of this book possible, I want to start with the Boston University School of Social Work. Dean Wilma Peebles-Wilkins once again played an important role by encouraging me to write the book; Suzanne Logan provided administrative support throughout the writing process; and several research assistants were instrumental: Celina Miranda and Mary Colleran assisted with literature reviews and the undertaking of the three case studies that appear in the book; and Girma Asfaw and Ben Cook assisted with literature reviews.

Individuals in a number of institutions were helpful in helping to construct the case studies. At the Miami Museum of Science: Jennifer Santer, director of grants/codirector of *SECME RISE*; Jennifer Schooley, director of the *IMPACT* Upward Bound Project; Ted Myers, director of museum education; and Willy Louis Charles, Niki Reaves, and Maria Hernandez. At the Mexican Fine Arts Center Museum: Carlos Tortolero, museum director; Yolanda Rodriguez Pacheco, *WRTE* general manager; and MariCarmen Moreno, assistant director of the Yollocali Youth Museum. At the New England Aquarium: William S. Spitzer, director of education; Julie Anne Crump, supervisor of out-of-school programs; Cindy Cheney, senior supervisor of Boston programs; and Stephanie Wagner, coordinator of the teen program.

Finally I want to thank Peter Correia, executive director of the National Research Center for Youth Services, and Donna Woonteiler, managing editor of *CYD Journal*, for their support.

PART 1

THE PRACTICE
OF YOUTH DEVELOPMENT

No amount of skill or care on the part of those engaged
in youth development work will eradicate the problems
of underserved youth. Racism, drugs, violence, poverty, and
lack of resources are root problems that will not
disappear quickly. What we can do, however, is
demonstrate the value of these young people and
empower them by providing choices for better
decisions about relations in schooling and
"doing the right thing."
—T. Martinek, in the epilogue to
Youth Development and Physical Education

Youth development is both a wonderful and an elusive paradigm. This
paradigm is inclusive to the point where virtually no activity is excluded. This can be rewarding and damning at the same time. Part 1
specifically seeks to provide the reader with a map of the territory to
help develop a better understanding of the multifaceted aspects of
youth development and the tensions inherent in this field of practice.
This part of the book will also raise questions that must be actively addressed in order to maximize the potential of youth in American society. Special attention will be placed on marginalized youth because of
their unique needs and the challenges practitioners' face in reaching and
engaging them.

1 / SETTING THE CONTEXT
FOR THE PRACTICE OF YOUTH DEVELOPMENT

NEW DECADES, new centuries, and new millennia bring forth great anticipation, hope, anxiety, and searches for new perspectives. The entrance to the twenty-first century presents the United States with numerous challenges such as remaining competitive in an increasingly global economy, reversing the growth of undervalued groups, and creating a workforce with the requisite competencies for employment in the information age (Bouvier and Grant 1994; Edelman 2000; Haveman and Wolfe 1994; Linn 1998; McCabe 1999; Murdock 1995). Those three arenas, as well as others not mentioned, are highly interrelated, and youth are critical to each if this country is to make strides toward achieving significant social and economic goals.

Today's youth will have a significant role in bringing about changes in technology, demography, economy, and politics (Boyle 2000d). Whether they will be prepared for the task is another question—one based on the society's views and actions toward youth. Major investment of time, capital, and commitment must be made in youth in order to answer this question in the affirmative (Haveman and Wolfe 1994). There is a realization that a "benign neglect" approach is simply not good enough to ensure that this country can continue to prosper as the new millennium develops.

The Committee for Economic Development (1997: 1) well summed up why the United States cannot afford to neglect segments of its youth population if it hopes to make significant economic and social progress:

A skilled, productive work force is essential to the economic growth and international competitiveness of the United States. Failure to utilize our nation's diverse work force means lost national output. At the same time, it leaves workers struggling to earn wages that enable them to support themselves and a family. The nation can ill afford the consequences, from costly welfare dependency to skyrocketing prison populations, when the job market fails to absorb all segments of the population effectively. To ensure both prosperity and social progress, the United States must extend opportunities to develop produce careers to all young persons entering its labor market.

Discussion about the status of today's youth elicits a wide range of responses, most of it being a negative assessment of youth's "at-risk" status (National Research Council 1993; McWhirter et al. 1993). Educational scores and attainment (or lack of it), drugs, juvenile crime, and lack of respect for authority are topics that frequently—even usually—come up in any assessment of youth (Besharov 1999; Morley and Rossman 1997). In academic, community, government, and policy arenas, there is little disagreement: youth-related issues and needs must be seriously understood and addressed (Furstenberg et al. 1999; Rollin 2000). The Carnegie Council on Adolescent Development (1989: 11) stated this clearly: "We call upon all those deeply concerned about young adolescents' future, and the future of this nation, to begin now to create the nationwide constituency required to give American young adolescents the preparation they need for life in the 21st century."

Setting a context is about setting a foundation. This chapter provides a map for this book: why the book is needed, its potential for practice and professional education, and definitions of key concepts and terms. In addition, this chapter orients the reader to the importance of youth development in the arenas of education, recreation, and human service. Youth development, however, cannot be separated out from the society in which it occurs. There is little question that youth development as a form of practice is here to stay for the immediate future. While the length of that stay will depend on how the practice is operationalized, supported, and evaluated, and how many adherents it can count upon, its potential for transformation is already well recognized.

SOCIAL PERSPECTIVES ON YOUTH

Much can be said about how society views youth. Society's views play an instrumental role in how youth is perceived by adults and how youths, both male and female, see themselves. As might be expected, there is no unified view of youth in this society. Youths are usually referred to as perpetrators (criminals), hedonists (drug users, addicts, promiscuous), victims (unemployed, abused, neglected, etc.), or prodigies (Griffin 1997; Males 1996, 1998; Rook 1998) (the view of youth as a consumer group I will deal with separately).

These perspectives either categorize youth as a drain on national resources, a group to be feared, or as having qualities that "ordinary people" cannot emulate (that is, prodigies are seen as "outstanding," having near perfect grades and test scores, as "volunteers," or as incredible athletes). A historical reliance upon a deficit perspective has resulted, not surprisingly, in a dearth of programs and services that contribute to healthy development of youth (Hahn 2000; Nixon 1997).

Adults, however, have not escaped the consequences associated with a deficit perspective. The pervasiveness of this perspective makes a shift in viewing youth from a positive viewpoint that much more challenging for the field of youth development. Although there is an increasing body of scholarly knowledge on youth from an asset perspective, it pales in comparison with the literature focused on a problem perspective.

A perspective on youth as consumer takes a narrow view of the group and identifies them as a $105 billion-a-year market (Youth Markets Alert 1999) that can be influenced in what products it purchases (DNR 1999; Find/SVP Market Reports 1998; Hill 2000; Market Europe 1998). Youth as consumers of business on the Internet are expected to account for $1.3 billion in revenues from on-line sales by the year 2002 (Howe and Strauss 2000). Adolescents have, on average, $84 a week in disposable income ($56 of their own money and $28 of family money), and the average pre-teen spends $13 per week (Cable World 1999). These figures add up to $94 billion a year of youths' own money and $26 billion of their families' money (Cable World 1999). The adolescent sports market, to cite one recipient of youth dollars, takes in more than $246 million a year (*Footwear News* 1999).

Youth comprise a significant, growing, and distinct U.S. market (Howe and Strauss 2000; Zabel 1999). The introduction of "strategic philanthropy," whereby companies give away items to schools in exchange for opportunities to display their corporate names, is a new dimension to marketing to youth, complementing the usual approaches through mass media. It graphically illustrates the importance of this market group.

Not surprisingly, an increasing number of books deals with the marketing of products to youth (Acuff and Reiher 1997; Lopiano-Misdom and Luca 1997; McNeal 1992, 1999; Vecchio 1997; Zollo 1999). Youth-targeted marketing has been approached from many perspectives; it is, for example, estimated that girls aged thirteen to nineteen spend $9 billion annually—on fragrances, cosmetics, and other beauty products (European Cosmetic Markets 1994; *Women's Wear Daily* 2000), food (Littman 1998), movies (Youth Markets Alert 1999), cameras (*Discount Store News* 1999); sporting events (Urresta 1996), beverages (Barboza 1997; Russo 1998), theaters (Betley 1995; Miller 1996), cars (Konrad 1999), music (Minority Markets Alert 1999), and libraries (Dimick 1995), to name but a few. The role of media in creating markets among youth, particularly adolescents, has not been overlooked (Currie 1994).

Another perspective takes a dramatically different viewpoint, seeing youth as an asset—a group that can be embraced for current and potential contribution to society (Barton, Watkins, and Jarjoura 1997; Garbarino et al. 1992; Heath and McLaughlin 1993b; Hein 2000; Kyle 1996; Lerner 1995; Males 1998; Rook 1998; Way 1998). This view sees youth in a position to help rather than to receive assistance (Checkoway 1999). It empowers youth, and this focus—away from problems such as drug abuse, crime, and pregnancy to one of enhancing potential—is much more than a change in semantics (Family Youth Services Bureau 1998; Hein 1999): it represents a dramatic potential shift in paradigms. A switch to such a perspective would offer tremendous rewards for society, not to mention youth and their families (Drake, Ling, and Hughes 2000; Finn and Checkoway 1998; Pittman 2000a, 2000b). However, such a shift is not possible unless we embrace the paradigm that specifically sets out to achieve this goal. The founder and director of the Youth Development and Research Fund (2000: 1) stated it eloquently: "Basically, what decision makers are telling us is that there is little value placed on the potential contributions of . . . young adults. In-risk young adults have become undervalued by society and overlooked in policy." A tremendous amount of resources and careers, unfortunately, have been invested in portraying youth as "problems" for society (McKnight 1995).

Bell (1996) argues that the prevalence of adultism ("disrespect for the young based on the assumption that adults are better than young people, and entitled to act upon young people without their agreement") must be recognized if society is to make effective progress in having youth as equal partners. The fundamental belief that adults know what is "best" for youth often interferes with the development of a genuine dialogue about youth participation and direction of youth programs. When adults subscribe to this belief, the true potential of youth development cannot be achieved.

A shift in paradigm from deficit to asset would result in an equally prominent change in the social norms pertaining to the role of caring in social relations and interactions (Rauner 2000: 10):

Advocating community responsibility for the care of the next generation implies an ethic of care that crosses the realms of morality, culture, and reason, and represents no division between the private and the public. A worldview organized around care argues for an ethic that stands beside, and reinforces, the work ethic of individual responsibility that is dominant in our culture. It is the vision of a life organized around commitments and shared responsibilities in which interdependence, mutuality, and nurturance are seen as public, as well as private, virtues. This is caring as a social norm.

WHAT IS YOUTH DEVELOPMENT?

There is confusion concerning what is meant by the term *youth development*. The federal government, through its Family and Youth Services Bureau (the Administration for Children, Youth, and Families) summed up the confusion quite well (The Exchange 1998: 1):

> The youth development concept often is described as amorphous or cloudlike. The vision is pretty, but hard to grasp. There is no place to call for the handbook that says, "Just complete the following ten easy steps to implement youth development in your community." And so people struggle: youth service professionals, policymakers, and funding sources. They know what they want to accomplish; they just wish someone would tell them. Unfortunately, there are no easy methods for converting the youth development concept from words to action.

Roth et al. (1999: 272), summing up the state of the search for a definition of youth development, wrote, "A parsimonious definition of youth development programs has been elusive . . . most simply, youth development programs can be understood as age-appropriate programs designed to prepare adolescents for productive adulthood by providing opportunities and supports to help them gain the competencies and knowledge needed to meet the challenges they will face as they mature." Thus we can see that one of the biggest challenges facing the field of youth development is deriving a consensus definition. One that, incidentally, can draw together various constituencies.

The barriers present in preventing a unified and comprehensive approach to youth development are far greater than agreeing to a "simple" conceptualization of the concept (Linetzky 2000). The primary challenges associated with operationalizing youth development are social, economic, and political in nature (The Exchange 1998): (1) Proclivity for political expediency—lack of willingness to devote considerable financial resources toward achieving change; (2) Competition for resources—youth are not a powerful voting block and are therefore relatively easy to ignore; (3) Low public value placed on youth services—youth staff, for example, often bear the brunt of this low priority, minimal efforts being made to provide them with training and competitive salaries; and (4) Immediate vs. long-term results—priority being given to short-term results and profits, with a focus on problem-reduction rather than enhancement.

These barriers interfere with obtaining a consensus definition. However, it does not mean that a general definition is not possible—one that is both broad and sufficiently flexible to allow local circumstances to decide how it is used in practice.

There is a misconception in the field that youth development can only effectively transpire within a "formal" youth-development program. Nothing could be farther from the truth. Youth development is not confined to any one setting. It can happen in families, communities, and among peers (Murphy 1995b). It is not restricted to place or to adults being the "developers."

The field of youth development is still in its infancy—which speaks well for its potential to grow and transform itself. "Growing pains" are natural to development (we expect youth to meet and surmount challenges; why can we not expect the same from the field?). Challenges are inherent in any form of practice that has yet to achieve maturity, and feelings of excitement and dread can coexist in the field (adrenaline can result from both excitement and anxiety). There are so many questions: Who can be legitimized to practice? Who decides what the requisite competencies are to practice effectively? It will be noted throughout this book that there is confusion about what is meant by the term *youth development*. Nevertheless, with debate, commitment, and no doubt some hurt feelings, confusion can be clarified.

I will introduce an analogy. For me the term *youth development* conjures up images of "focus groups" (it seems everyone in human services has either led or been a part of a focus group), and the use of focus groups represents a very distinctive methodology and qualitative analysis. People questioned about their focus-group experience report a dramatically wide range of group characteristics: number of participants, number of questions asked, composition of the group, time allotted to meetings—all these vary. If we stick to a definition of what "experts" identify as necessary for a group to qualify as a "true" focus group, then very few participants or leaders have ever been part of one (Krueger 1988). Youth development, I believe, is similar to my focus-group analogy.

The youth-development field of practice has become a catchall for any and all forms of youth-related services. It is almost as if there is a total absence of theory and scholarship on the subject, which is certainly not the case. On the one hand, the broad nature of the concept—youth development—has its appeal, since: it allows many staff and organizations to say they practice youth development. When, on the other hand, a narrow definition is used, the practice is restricted to a chosen few—those fortunate enough to have the competencies and resources to qualify. The answer to the question of what is in the best interests of the field will vary according to who is "authorized" to make the reply.

As youth-development principles and practice are addressed in chapters 3 through 7, they are distinctive: they capture a process, philosophy, and approach. The American Youth Policy Forum (1995: 1) identified two premises that, they said, need to act as a foundation and guide for youth-development practice:

> Youth development is an ongoing process in which young people are engaged and invested. Throughout this process, young people seek ways to meet their basic physical and social needs and to build the competencies and connections they need for survival and success. All youth are engaged in the process of development. Youth development is marked by the acquisition of a broad range of competencies and the demonstration of a full complement of connections to self, others, and the larger community. Confidence, compassion, commitment and character are terms commonly used to express the attitudes and behaviors that determine whether and how learned competencies will be used.

These two premises serve not only as a foundation but also as a guide for operationalization. Within this paradigm there is, however, sufficient flexibility for it to be brought to life at the local level.

Paradigms need to be broad. Narrow paradigms invariably fail to capture the imagination of practitioners or public. True. some paradigms effectively limit themselves to select contexts and environments, but sweeping paradigms are energizing, offer hope where hope is limited, and reach out to engage as many practitioners as is possible. However, we must note that this flexibility is not so broad as to allow *any* form of youth-focused service to be called youth development.

This book is about *contextualizing* youth development practice. It would be a serious mistake for the field of youth development to standardize practices in such a way as not to build in sufficient flexibility—enough to allow for considerations such as a variety of settings and activities and what I call the core factors—cognition, emotion, physical, moral, social, and spiritual. The paradigm must allow for issues of gender and sexual orientation, race/ethnicity, and emotional and physical challenges. Such "lenses" influence how youth see their world—a world that may well be toxic and therefore detrimental to youth achieving their potential. This book is cognizant that we walk a thin line between, on the one side, capturing as many practitioners as possible with the youth-development net and, on the other, not sufficiently limiting the paradigm's boundaries.

GOALS OF THE BOOK

This book seeks to ground the reader in current youth-development thought and tensions. At the same time, it seeks to expand the vision of what youth development can be and where it can be practiced. The field is dynamic, and to reduce it to a list of concepts, principles, and activities may seem to be an arduous task; nevertheless, such listing will be essential to my effort to "ground" the paradigm.

The book addresses five goals. It seeks (1) to provide a state-of-the-art description of youth development—its rewards and challenges; (2) to provide an expanded view of settings in which youth development can take place; (3) to consider what I have called "new frontier settings" and analyze the rewards and challenges they offer; (4) to provide an in-depth picture of day-to-day operation in new frontier settings; and (5) to provide a series of recommendations for work on this new frontier—aimed at enhancing the prospects of success and minimizing the obstacles.

Readers will be able to develop a comprehensive view of youth development at macro, mezzo, and micro levels. The macro perspective outlines the broad social forces that impact youth; the mezzo examines youth development at community and organizational level; and at micro level we look at specific cases. The latter perspective makes extensive use of interviews with youth-development staff working in new frontier settings.

YOUTH DEVELOPMENT IN NEW FRONTIER SETTINGS

A definition of new frontier settings for youth development has to take into account the turn-of-the-century challenges facing youth in the modern world. New frontier settings can be defined as community sites that have a primary focus on education, information, and/or recreation and that lend themselves to programming for youth (there is, for example, a whole new intensity of interaction between zoos and youth). These new frontier settings do not have to serve youth exclusively; they can be accessible to all age groups, but in them youth patronage is not stigmatized. Youth-development programming will not significantly alter such a site's mission in society but will enhance some aspect of it.

For many people, settings such as museums, libraries, zoos, and aquariums are places that we might visit once a year. They are places to pass through, not stay in—places where not too many people imagine themselves working or studying at. I, for one, knew no one who worked in a zoo. But the recent evolution of youth-development programs has thrust such sites into a prominent position in the field. Such settings can now, much more than in the past, be viewed as high-profile places for youth to visit, study in, and even work at.

All of these settings bring youth into contact with professionals who do not have a history of this type of involvement in community, unlike social workers, psychologists, recreational specialists, and educators. This exposure to a "new" type of professional has its challenges and rewards for everyone involved. Although youth development can take place in any type of setting, historically it has been limited to certain types of youth agencies and after-school settings. This book examines commonalties and differences between new frontier settings and urges the importance of accessibility for youth.

The new frontier settings covered in this book, while having many elements in common, are different from each other in significant ways. Youth development in libraries differs considerably from youth development in zoos. Libraries focus most youth-development activity indoors, with special emphasis on literacy; zoos, on the other hand, generally take youth participants outdoors, and since their programs involve animals as well as humans they require youths to develop a range of animal-oriented competencies. Libraries can be found in almost all communities and generally are one of the few settings where youth and adults coexist, whereas far fewer communities have local zoos or aquariums, which limits the possibilities for youth-development programming. Libraries—a traditional nonstigmatizing environment—in certain circumstances employ staff who have fluency in multiple languages, which is a particularly important offering in communities where few residents have English as their primary language, and in such situations, communication skills will tend to stress verbal and nonverbal interactions. In zoos, on the other hand, communication skills rarely involve languages other than English, but youths working in zoos and aquariums must develop communication skills involving the public and in working with animals (Harmon 1999). While aquariums often show many similarities with zoos, most youth-development activities at aquariums take place indoors.

The book's discussion of different new frontier settings addresses four key elements of accessibility: (1) geographical; (2) psychological; (3) cultural; and (4) operational. *Geographical* accessibility is a critical, although not the sole, element in increasing the reach of youth development. It is a rare community that has an abundance of museums, zoos, and aquariums (although few communities do not have a public library), and it is crucial that youths be able to get to such settings. In cities, this means that these facilities be on public transportation routes and in suburban and rural settings it means provision of transportation.

Psychological accessibility relates to how comfortable youths feel in attending a setting—being at ease, feeling accepted, not stigmatized, and physically safe (Gambone and Arbreton 1997; McLaughlin, Irby, and Langman 1994; Pittman 1999b). For example, can youths feel comfortable at a museum, a place that usually targets adults? *Cultural* accessibility relates to settings providing youth with experiences that are validating in terms of ethnicity, race, social class, and gender. Does the setting seek, for example, to enhance a nonwhite youth's self-image or does it seek to undermine and replace that image with a Eurocentric identity? *Operational* accessibility is to do with the times when a program is offered. Do the hours facilitate or hinder youth participation? Settings that severely limit days and hours of operation systematically screen out those who cannot be there during scheduled times. For optimal accessibility, all four forms of accessibility must be present.

THE NEED FOR THIS BOOK

The field of youth development is now facing many challenges, and it will face more in the immediate future. One of those challenges is who—what profession—will step forth to claim this practice as their own. Hellison et al. (2000: xii) note that the lack of a home for youth development opens up a potential for university departments of physical education to fill this vacuum:

> Right now, youth development is without a home in most universities. Schools (colleges, departments) of social work don't really focus on youth development nor do schools of education. Departments of recreation and/or leisure studies as well as programs in therapeutic recreation have shown some interest, but physical education in higher education . . . could step into the breach, thereby expanding opportunities for the employment of graduates.

In this book I want to push the boundaries of where practice can "legitimately" take place. My predisposition for community to play a central role in practice necessitates that I consider places, or "settings," that have multiple roles and functions and that they be considered "practice worthy." My desire to find new settings is a journey without any definite destination or timetable, and it invariably results in new discoveries. This book is an unscheduled stop on this journey.

The subject matter—new frontier settings—first emerged in the process of my writing a book on the use of the arts, humanities, and sports (Delgado 2000a). In the process of researching and writing that book, I came across settings that were undertaking what I considered to be innovative approaches to youth-development practice. Since detailed description of those settings did not fit into that book, the information was gathered and stored until now.

My enthusiasm for new places that can broaden youth-development practice will be contagious, I hope, and open for readers new sites for youth development in their communities. I hope that the energy, drive, and commitment that readers bring to this effort will help them surmount any barriers encountered along the way.

The field of youth development has already received considerable attention in print. Numerous foundation reports have been issued on the subject, and books on various aspects of youth development have been published. However, the amount of writing about the ground covered in this book is very limited. Most previous publications, although of immense importance, focus on a narrow aspect of youth development or are very broad in nature. Youniss and Yates (1997) focus on community service and social responsibility in youth; Rauner (2000) uses the construct of caring to ground youth-development practice. The broadly based works (e.g., Lakes 1995 and Lerner 1995) set the stage for the philosophical foundation for youth development.

My *New Arenas for Community Social Work Practice with Urban Youth: Use of the Arts, Humanities, and Sports* (Delgado 2000A) is the closest to this one in subject matter; however, my earlier book is specific to certain activities (arts, humanities, and sports), is focused on urban youth that are primarily of color, and did not address new frontier settings. This book, broader in scope, does not limit itself to urban areas or youth of color, and it represents a newer vision that will appeal to a new and broader audience. It can be considered complimentary to *New Arenas*. As to the future, the ever-expanding arena of youth development will bring with it increased scholarly attention and an increasing number of books—a key indicator of the field's growing prominence.

The practice of youth development has tremendous promise, yet in some cases the field has relied on activities that spark neither the interest nor the imagination of today's youth. New frontier settings offer great potential for learning and fun when compared with traditional youth activities. Youth-development organizations, therefore, have a great deal to learn from such settings on how to plan and market programs and activities. However, people working in new settings can also benefit from the countless years of history and wisdom of their traditional counterparts.

WHO SHOULD READ THIS BOOK?

The broad nature of this book's subject matter will make it useful to many different professions. Not only those traditionally involved with youth development—for example, those in social work, education, recreation, and psychology—but people working in libraries, museums, aquariums, and so on will find the book relevant. The book can be used as a supplemental text in professional education programs as well as by youth-development practitioners. In social work, the book can be used in graduate-level practice classes that provide a "positive" view of youth (e.g., human behavior and the social environment). For people in macro practice the book will show how youth-development activities are used in programming; it can also be used in planning/program development and community-practice courses.

I am a social worker, and this book naturally draws on this perspective, but the broad nature and importance of youth development makes it necessary that a wider view be taken. There is little question that the youth-development field cannot be the exclusive domain of any one profession. The field touches on so many practices and disciplines that to take a single professional focus would be to do it an injustice. I have made great effort to draw on the literature and experiences of other professions. This encompassing approach also serves to bring together professions that, while they may all deal with youth, are not accustomed to working together.

The book draws on a wide variety of sources, scholarly as well as popular. Youth development does not belong only to scholars, and the topic's popular appeal naturally lends itself to coverage by the popular media. To ignore this source of material would constitute a serious bias and would significantly detract from the book's usefulness.

THE STRUCTURE OF THE BOOK

This book consists of three parts, divided into sixteen chapters and an epilogue. The eight chapters of part 1 set the context and present up-to-date thoughts about youth-development issues in the United States. Part 1 serves a foundation for the remaining chapters in the book. The eight chapters of part 2 are devoted to examining issues, challenges, rewards, and "New Frontier Settings" that are currently using youth development principles and approaches, with chapter 15 providing especially detailed case studies. In part 3—the epilogue—I offer some reflections on youth development practice.

I use case illustrations and case studies throughout. By tying theoretical constructs to real-life situations I hope to help readers to see how theory can be operationalized.

The twenty-first century holds much promise for the field of youth development, particularly as the concept gets broader exposure and acceptance. The number of undergraduate and graduate education programs offering degrees in this field will no doubt continue to expand, and in so doing increasing the number of "formally" trained staff. Increased scholarship and research in youth development will serve to inform programs across the United States, regardless of geographical locale. Youth development will find itself being a subject of discussion in field agencies, academic settings, and in government circles.

However, as advocates for this form of practice push a youth-development agenda at local and national levels, the increased recognition of youth development will experience greater scrutiny and criticism. This book hopes to better prepare practitioners, academicians, and policymakers to recognize the rewards and challenges that lie ahead. If youth development takes on a "system change" focus, opposition to this paradigm will grow (see chap. 3). Not that academics and practitioners must actively seek to "depoliticize" this paradigm, but if the field is politicized, we must be prepared for a backlash.

I believe that a political approach to youth development is inevitable, so the field must systematically and strategically prepare itself for an extreme reaction. This reaction will manifest itself in a variety of ways, including the types of programs and activities funders are prepared to support under the youth-development rubric. This book hopefully will fill a variety of gaps in the field, and do so in a way that encourages partnerships between professionals, youth, and communities. The true meaning of youth development can be achieved only through partnerships, particularly those that have youth play increasingly critical and decision-making roles.

Those committed to the field of youth development must walk a thin line between being "realistic" and being "visionaries." We must continue to dream the impossible dream while keeping our feet firmly on the ground. We need to inspire youth and each other to maintain a steadfast devotion for a better world, yet understand that setbacks are a natural occurrence in this line of work.

2 / CHALLENGES AND REWARDS FOR YOUTH IN THE TWENTY-FIRST CENTURY

THE BEGINNING of the twenty-first century finds the United States at a critical crossroads concerning how we prepare future citizens and workers. The globalization of the economy, increasing the need for the country to interact with the expanding international scene, necessitates having a workforce that can meet the new challenges. For the necessary resources of time, energy, and money to be devoted to youth there will have to be a major change of political will. Today's youth will bear the ultimate responsibility of helping the nation make the transition (Kyle 1996); the success of this transition, however, depends on how the nation addresses the needs of this age group, and how it mobilizes the group's assets. Failure to do so will effectively render that entire generation voiceless in shaping the future.

This chapter does not delve into the myriad of statistics highlighting the needs of youth: this has been well documented in countless books and articles and government and foundation reports. It will suffice to say that serious challenges related to education, participation, and the health of youth must be successfully addressed in order that the nation better the living standards of all who live here. In the words of DeJesus (2000: 2):

We know that the process of becoming a responsible adult starts long before these youth reach our programs. Further, we know that we cannot address sixteen to twenty-one years of neglect in six months. Nothing short of a serious intervention strategy will address this. To mount this rescue, to take on the mission, we will need sufficient resources and a policy supported by the popular will. We must give this the highest priority. However, we know this is not, and probably will never be, an issue of major concern for this country's decision makers. The only time . . . we see major investment in at-risk youth is after major social disturbances. . . . Are we ready to pay the price?

Long-term commitment to redressing years of neglect, unfortunately, decreases the appeal of a major initiative for a nation unaccustomed to doing so. Marian Wright Edelman (2000: 35), a renowned advocate for children, well sums up this point:

> The United States is the sole superpower in the waning twentieth-century world. We stand first among industrialized countries in military technology, in military exports, in Gross Domestic Product, in the number of millionaires and billionaires, in health technology, and in defense expenditures. But we stand tenth in our children's eighth-grade science scores, sixteenth in living standards among our poorest one-fifth of children, seventeenth in low birth-weight rates, eighteenth in infant morality, twenty-first in eighth-grade math scores, and last in protecting our children against gun violence.

Haveman and Wolfe (1994) concluded, based on their study of the effects of investment in children, that the chances for children's success can be significantly improved if they are viewed as human capital. Society's social investment in children, in turn, can either enhance a child's likelihood for success, if sufficient resources and planning is paid to an intervention, or, decrease the likelihood, if there is minimal investment of resources and planning.

Practice that systematically involves youth, peers, families, community-based organizations, and communities holds great appeal for practitioners, for "ordinary" citizens, and for families and communities (Brown 1995; Delgado 2000b; Garr 1995; Olasky 1996; Wuthnow 1995). This form of practice has the potential to make a significant return on investment for the general public because of its broad reach across boundaries—a return that, incidentally, has an impact on other areas of a community's life. Nevertheless, the voices of youth have generally not been actively sought out; nor has their active participation in major community institutions been sought. Until such developments occur, youth will continue to have a marginal status in this society—a "time bomb" that will explode within the lifetime of many of us.

YOUTH CULTURES

"Youth culture," as a construct, has been around for a long time. The 1950s saw an increase in the number of studies with a focus on youth culture

(Wulff 1995), and the term *youth culture* has been traced back to Talcott Parsons. Wulff (1995) notes that Parsons's focus, however, was squarely on white, male, middle-class, youth and their quests before achieving adulthood, and it was not until the 1960s that a youth-culture perspective captured the public's imagination.

Interestingly, the literature on cultural competence has generally taken one of two main approaches: either that of ethnic/racial and gender/sex or the socioeconomic approach. Taking the latter perspective, particularly when it is part of a human-service agenda, is understandable, but it tends to neglect "youth" as a culture unto itself. The merging of these two perspectives holds great appeal because it can be an important step toward a more holistic view of youth.

Youth culture is frequently viewed from a marketing perspective, as we saw in chapter 1; that is, How best can we sell a product or service to a youth audience? A lot of time, money, and resources are allocated to better understanding youth as consumers—their buying habits and so forth. But in youth-development literature, the subject of youth culture is generally (although there are some notable exceptions) absent (Heath and McLaughlin 1993). The "youth culture" perspective effectively broadens how we view youth as constituting an identifiable group, rather than as a group made up of many subgroups that do not have much in common. Such a unifying perspective raises the political capital of this age group in a society that well understands the power of a constituency.

A youth-culture perspective places youth in the position of being a subculture that actively resists the dominant culture, engendering symbolic meanings to actions, language, and so on—although in this case the subculture has been created by adults. Valentine, Skelton, and Chambers (1998: 13) point out that "young people were understood to either negotiate with, or oppose, the dominant ideology, or to subvert dominant meanings by actively appropriating and transforming those meanings. The creation of new subjective meanings and oppositional lifestyles were interpreted as a cultural struggle for control over their lives." The study of youth as a cultural phenomenon examines behavior and attitudes not from a deviant perspective but from one that seeks to understand meaning and motive without assigning a deficit label. Youth subculture can more commonly be understood as the "way" youth view themselves, and not the way adults view them (Garratt 1997). The temptation to assign a "deviant subcultural" label may be too great for many adults to resist, but such a label further alienates youth from the dominant culture by signaling to them the low status they are assigned by society (in this case, adults).

Marginalized identities can be reshaped into "positive identities" through the interaction of youth in shaping their perceptions of themselves and others (Austin and Willard 1989; Leadbeater and Way 1996). This change necessitates that youth and adults engage in a dialogue and a willingness to enter into partnerships for bringing about desired changes. Activities that cater to youth either because youth themselves have initiated and shaped them or by adults with a keen understanding of what youth want and how they view themselves can fulfill multiple functions. They can (1) actively engage youth in prosocial behavior; (2) provide structured activity that keeps them out of risk-taking behaviors; and (3) reinforce identities that are not marginalized and therefore are empowering. No activity can focus on only one of these functions: youth are important, and activities must fulfill multiple goals that are both internal and external to youth. Youth-development programs are in strategic positions to pursue these goals.

When applied to urban youth of color, a marginalized group in this society, culture transcends the traditional meaning generally ascribed to ethnicity and race. Youth culture, as a result, serves to unify various distinctive groups into one group—one that has more commonality than it has differences related to ethnicity/race and gender. The forces that reinforce this group identity can be powerful. Music and dance styles are excellent examples of how a youth-cultural perspective can result in standards of behavior and dress and influence values in the process (Decker 1994; Deyhle 1998; Einerson 1998; Gaunt 1998; Giroux 1998; Lipsitz 1994; McClary 1994; Muellar 1994; Tasker 1999; Thornton 1996; Walser 1998). A number of scholars have viewed music and dance as mediums through which, in addition to their function in bringing together youth from different backgrounds, ethnic and racial identities are formed and reinforced (Deyhle 1998; Tasker 1999).

Ferrell (1993, 1997), Phillips (1999), Cooper and Chalfant (1984), and a number of other scholars interested in urban youth culture have examined graffiti as a cultural phenomenon. They contextualize youth culture for marginalized urban youth, art being the method and language used to convey the youth "voice" to society. Attempts by society (adults) to control the behavior of youth is just that: social control. Phillips (1999: 23) makes an important point:

> The antisocial nature of graffiti makes its analysis an inherently social endeavor. Graffiti it's all about people. It's about relationships, and indi-

viduals and motives. As a researcher, you need to get a hold of a social situation on the ground in order to understand the story presented on its wall. It may be visible to adults, but not obvious.

Phillips's comments apply to all other elements of youth culture. Culture is about context. Without context, symbols, language, and actions become meaningless. Youth culture is very much about the visible and what may appear to be obvious to other youth.

Youth culture as a construct is overarching and serves as a rubric for capturing many different youth subculture groups (Garratt 1997). Although there is more than one "youth culture" (youth, after all, are far from being a monolithic group) the commonalties of age help to shape perceptions, group identity, and behavior. That said, however, they are not sufficient to represent all groups as one. A youth-cultural perspective broadens the concept of culture and allows us to view youth as consisting of many different subgroups, each with a distinctive personality, set of values, and view toward adults and society. Such a perspective allows us to individualize rather than lump youth together because of their age.

Thornton's (1996) study of youth culture and music coined the term *subcultural capital* as a means of capturing how music—in this case, clubs—shape youth behaviors, attitudes, and perceptions. Thornton has defined subcultural capital as extracurricular activity and knowledge that cannot be obtained through formal educational channels such as schools. A view of youth as a cultural group, as a result, can help organizations to shape programming and services targeting this age group (Skelton and Valentine 1998). Commonalties are not lost in taking into consideration group differences—both between and differences within.

Ferrell (1997) argues that youth often seek cultural space as a means of asserting their individuality. However, it is important to note that culture itself is a dynamic construct, and one very similar to youth development in many regards. *Culture* is ambiguous and very hard to place boundaries around. It means many different things to different people. Its definition is highly politicized. It exists and is influential in shaping perceptions, values, attitudes, and behaviors.

Taking a youth-culture perspective to help youth-development practitioners and scholars to better appreciate the voice of youth is not an easy task, and one that the increased number of youths makes even harder, as any front-line staff member will attest. It seems that just when adults learn the meaning of a new term, another replaces it. Learn the lyrics of a popular song or the name of the hottest group and it is already history. The importance of understanding youth for adults is matched by the challenge of "staying on top of it"; nevertheless, it is not possible to practice youth development without grounding the paradigm in a youth-cultural context—a context that is not absolute and that can differ considerably within and between communities.

DEMOGRAPHIC PROFILE AND TRENDS

An in-depth understanding of youth development in the twenty-first century requires a working-level knowledge of demographics, both the current profile and the projected one. Demographics help society to structure education and services, and one does not have to be a demographer to better understand and use demographics in youth programming. This section examines the current demographic picture and makes note of projected trends for youth in the early part of this century that will serve as a foundation from which to organize youth-development programs and activities.

A global economy requires a global perspective of demographics. No sector of the world is totally isolated from the rest, and any understanding of demographic trends in the United States will be enriched by an understanding of global demographic trends, particularly those in nations that historically have supplied immigrants to the United States.

Three interrelated factors influence demographics: (1) birth rates; (2) death rates; and (3) immigration rates. The interplay of these three factors can result in dramatic, and often sustained, demographic trends, as will be seen in the case of California (Hayes-Bautista, Schink, and Chapa 1988). Birth rates are highly correlated with the percentage of a population that is of childbearing age. Mortality rates are influenced by factors such as the number of elders in a group, the extent of violence resulting in death, and the prevalence of life-threatening diseases. And in any given geographical area, the difference between in-migration and out-migration can result in a net gain, a net loss, or no change. Any effort to examine demographic trends, particularly those involving youth, must take these three factors into account.

WORLD YOUTH

First I want to take a global perspective. It is estimated that if world childbearing rates rise to 2.5 children per childbearing woman, the world's population will increase to 11.2 billion by 2050 and surpass 27 billion by 2150

(Market Europe 1998). This of course implies huge increase in the global youth population—one unprecedented in the history of the world. The vast majority of this increase expected in southern Asia and Africa. There are currently 2 billion people under the age of twenty years in developing areas of the world; 400 million of these are adolescents aged fifteen to nineteen years. In the year 2000, the world population was an estimated six billion, half of whom were under the age of twenty (Bronfenbrenner and White 1993).

It is estimated that two-thirds of the world's population will be living in cities by 2025, with more than one hundred cities having 5 million or more residents (Berg 1999). A highly urbanized world population combined with an increase in the median age from 25 (1995) to 36.5 years (2050)—an aging population—will present unparalleled challenges. One challenge will be how to balance the needs of age groups.

Immigration trends involving people from non-European countries have had significant impact on the composition of many of this country's urban areas, particularly those that historically have served as a port of entry into this country. New York City, for example, has experience a dramatic increase in the number of immigrants of color (Foner 1987a, 1987b). Without immigrants, New York City's population would have declined between 1990 and 2000.

More than one-half of New York City's residents were born outside of the city, with more than 2.5 million originating in other countries and more than 1 million originating in other sectors of the United States (Tierney 1997). Recent estimates point to more than 100,000 documented newcomers arriving in the city every year, an increase of more than 66 percent from that of a decade earlier (Goetz 1997).

The racial composition of New York City has changed dramatically as a result of immigration and high birth rates, with Latinos (primarily Puerto Rican and Dominican) and African Americans each accounting for 2 million residents (55.3 percent of the total) in 1995; Asian Americans accounted for 630,000 (8.7 percent) (Halbfinger 1997; Haslip-Viera and Baver 1996; Jones-Correa 1998; Torres-Saillant and Hernandez 1998).

Several major ethnic shifts occurred in the last decade of the twentieth century: Russians, for example, increased from 81,000 in 1990 to 229,000 in 1999; Mexicans increased from 35,000 in 1990 to 133,000 in 1999; Dominicans increased from 230,000 in 1990 to 387,000 in 1999 (Hernandez and Torres-Saillant 1996). Among the Asian groups, people from India, Pakistan, and Bangladesh increased from 67,000 in 1990 to 146,000 in 1999 (Lambert 2000).

YOUTH IN THE UNITED STATES

The demographic profile of youth in the United States is dynamic. In the past ten years distinct trends have emerged, and they are expected to continue unabated well into the twenty-first century. Leading up to the mid-1970s, a decline was experienced, but since then the number of adolescents has steadily spiraled upward. In 1993, adolescents (i.e., those aged ten to nineteen) accounted for 35,807,000 of the U.S. population (almost 14 percent). It is projected that the group aged from ten to twenty-four years will rise to 65 million in 2020 and be 80 million in 2050 (20.8 percent), at which time it will level off (National Research Council 1999). The age group covers a wider span, but it is evident that the proportional increase will be significant.

The U.S. Census Bureau projects that in the 2000–2010 period the number of youths thirteen to nineteen years of age will double in size, at two times the rate of the overall population, peaking between 2006 and 2010 at 30.8 million. One estimate of school-aged youth (five to seventeen years) will increase by 10 percent by 2006. By 2020, youths (ten to nineteen years) will increase from 34 million in 1992 to 43 million (Kellogg Foundation 1998).

It is widely estimated that by 2050 a majority of U.S. residents will be people of color, numerically surpassing white non-Latinos (Kolasky 1997). If current trends continue, the percentage of the population consisting of people of color will go from approximately 28 percent to slightly more than 50 percent in the fifty-five years between 1995 and 2050. This trend, coupled with an overall increase in the age of the population, will have a dramatic impact. The terms *browning* and *graying* have been coined to label these two trends.

The current and projected number of youths in the United States shares both similarities and significant differences with the baby boom of the post–World War II generation (National Center for Policy Alternatives 1997: 2):

> And much like their parents who never knew a world without television, "Gen-Y" kids won't know a world without computers. On the other hand, the educational system isn't ready for them: analysts note that there is no building boom for schools to match that of the Baby Boom generation. And they fear the gap in technology and education between Gen-Y haves and have nots could have a dramatic impact on the nation's economy in the 21st century.

Information technology is important for this generation. Youth development programs must address this element (see chapters 9 and 12).

YOUTH OF COLOR IN THE UNITED STATES

It is of critical importance when studying demographic data and trends that every effort be made to be specific about groups and subgroups. Youth of color represent a group that has statistics different from the overall picture. Within the youth-of-color group are many subgroups—African American, Asian, Latinos, for example. Each of these major subgroups consist of further subgroups: Latinos, for example, can be, among others, Cuban, Dominican, Mexican, Puerto Rican, or El Salvadoran. Each such subgroup has a distinctive demographic profile.

A focus on youth of color (African American, Asian, Latino) reveals an even greater rate of growth than that overall. In 1980, white non-Latino youth accounted for 74 percent of all U.S. children under the age of fifteen; in 1990, more than 33 percent were of color, and it is projected that by 2050 this group will surpass white non-Latinos (52 percent compared with 48 percent) (National Research Council 1999).

The projected increase in the number of youth of color must not, as is customary, be viewed only from a deficit perspective—that is to say by citing only the number of youth of color without a high level of formal education, who are in prison, are pregnant, or who are on public assistance. Youth of color are projected to increase their presence in the nation's colleges and universities; with enrollments in institutions of higher education projected to increase by two million (to nineteen million) over the next fifteen years, students of color will account for 80 percent of this growth (Wilgoren 2000). Students of color (African American, Asian, and Latino) will represent 37 percent of the nation's students in colleges and universities by 2015, up from 29 percent in 1995.

In some states (California, Hawaii, and New Mexico) and Washington D.C., white non-Latinos will be a minority by 2015. Texas is projected to join this group after 2015 (Wilgoren 2000). California is widely expected to become the first big state in the country to have a population predominantly of color (Hawaii and New Mexico already have such a population composition) (Purdum 2000: 1). Approximately 7.5 million Latinos live in California, or one-third of all Latinos in the United States. Almost one-third of California's Latinos are under the age of eighteen (Martinez 1999). Latinos in the City of Los Angeles, for example, constitute a majority of the residents (Davis 2000). California population projections to the year 2025 indicate that the white non-Latino proportion of the state will decrease from 52.6 percent in 1995 to 33.7 percent in 2025, with Latinos increasing from 20.6 percent to 43.1 percent (Davis 2000). The increase in the number of people of color (primarily Asians and Latinos) is fueled by immigration and high birthrates.

⌒

The challenges and rewards for youth in the twenty-first century can only be guessed at. Nevertheless, if youth-development programs and funders take a strategic perspective, trends related to economics, technology, politics, and demographics will have to be considered. Strategic planning does not guarantee what the future will look like, but it does increase the odds on getting things right. Demographic trends are greatly influenced by labor-supply needs, economy, dominant political ideology, and technological advancements. Thus demographic trends should be looked at through a broad set of lenses; that way, global forces as they relate to local circumstances can be better understood.

Demographic trends are predicated on key factors remaining constant (even though we know that few things in life remain constant). Calculated guesses are not out of order for either practitioners or academics, and the development of demographic profiles—be they best-case, worst-case, or neutral scenarios—can help the nation better plan for the future. The data presented in this chapter highlights the increased numbers of youth (particularly urban-based youth of color) predicted for this country and the world.

If the past is our best guide, there is little hope that youth will make significant progress toward the goals postulated by youth-development programs (Delgado 2000a: 49). But as I have observed elsewhere, "a failure to maximize current resources to prevent or intervene early on in an adolescent's life can effectively serve to doom millions of youth in the twenty-first century. Such a short-sighted approach will result in an even greater portion of the nation's gross national product being devoted to later-stage intervention, and seriously reduce the quality of the nation's work force" (49).

If the nation refuses to think of youth as social capital, preferring to view them as a "capital drain," then the twenty-first century will witness tremendous upheavals as millions upon millions of youth become disconnected and in so doing become a major internal-based liability. But we must continue to hope and to plan. A youth-development paradigm is predicated upon a hopeful view of the future. It attracts practitioners who are optimistic, and it is rare to find staff in a successful youth-development program that have a negative view of youth, their communities, and their future.

3 / YOUTH DEVELOPMENT: ORIGINS AND DEFINITIONS

THE TURN of the century saw a tremendous amount of attention being paid to the youth-development field at the national, state, and local levels. A thrust toward expanding this field of practice utilizing youth and community assets as an integral part of an organizing paradigm has appealed to youth, residents, practitioners, academics, policy makers, and funders (Baines and Selta 1999; Delgado 2000b; Kirby and Coyle 1997; Kurtz 1997; Lakes 1996; Lerner 1995; Rollin 2000).

A youth-development paradigm has received worldwide recognition for its potential to transform the lives of youth. The United Nations has advocated youth development as an effective strategy for achieving both youth and community potential (World Sources Online 1999). In this country, too, combining youth and community development has been strongly advocated. The involvement of communities in youth development represents the latest thinking on the subject and effectively broadens its potential for change at family and community level (Curnan 2000b).

Broadening the concept of youth development to include family or community serves to ground it and give it context, as well as give it a vehicle with limitless possibilities. A definition of youth development that is further expanded to include themes of social and economic justice, making them central to the paradigm, increases the practice options for both organizations and practitioners. Brown et al. (2000: 38) write:

> Our lives are full of opportunities to combat injustice. If Community Youth Development is to make any mark on our world, it must embrace this challenge. This is our common work—not just the work of the so-called 'underprivileged,' or the work on behalf of the under-privileged, people of color, or youth. Exposing and examining power relationships . . . is a critical and necessary first step in changing them, and in transforming our communities.

Such an expansion of the understanding of what is meant by youth development, however, is a challenge for students, practitioners, and academics. It not only expands the types of activities involved, but also the number of settings for them, public as well as private (Collins in press). The definitions of youth development identified in this chapter either explicitly or implicitly encompass community and its various manifestations. The field of youth development can no longer limit itself to a select number of settings, and new ones have emerged during the 1990s (hence the term *new frontier settings*).

The new settings offer much promise for the field. They take the concept and principles of youth development into places that historically have not been thus engaged. Expansion necessitates the involvement of all the major settings and institutions youth come into contact with, and achievement of such a goal will entail encountering numerous barriers and challenges.

Before the subject of new frontier settings can be thoroughly explored, it is necessary to develop an in-depth understanding of the origins of youth development and how it is defined in the field. Unfortunately, no universal definition exists. This chapter will define, explore, highlight, analyze the field and recommend a new definition for it—one that is both broad and contextualized.

This new definition is needed to continue the expansion of youth development into new and exciting areas of practice. The new arenas will, incidentally, provide opportunities for enhancement of community as well as youth capacities (*Commerce Business Daily* 2000; U.S. Newswire 2000; World Sources Online 1999). These new arenas will bring with them increased recognition for the value of youth development and a corresponding increase in resources. They must be cultivated and supported by the field if their potential is to be fully realized.

THE ORIGINS OF YOUTH DEVELOPMENT

The etiology of a paradigm can rarely be traced to the work of one individual, organization, or a particular year. Paradigms, by their very nature, owe their creation to many people, practitioners as well as scholars. However, there is general agreement in the youth-development field that the work of Werner and his colleagues stands out in its early influence on the movement (see Werner 1989; 1990; Werner and Smith 1977, 1982, 1992).

The work of Werner et al. is widely credited for laying the foundation of youth development as it is conceptualized and practiced today (Baines and

Selta 1999). Their research, based in Hawaii, with children from disadvantaged backgrounds was ground-breaking. They found that many such children were not only able to surmount their socioeconomic obstacles but were also able to thrive. These findings led to stressing the importance of resiliency and environmental protective factors. The conceptualization of youth development as consisting of two separate (internal and external) but interrelated spheres has continued up to the present time. How these two spheres are defined and operationalized varies considerably, as this book demonstrates; however, there is little debate over the conceptualization itself.

Resiliency factors (internal to the individual) usually consist of cognitive abilities, imagination or creativity, having an engaging personality, a sense of purpose and direction, an ability to establish and meet goals, an ability to form positive relationships, and a sense of spirituality. These factors, it must be stressed, are highly interrelated and at times it may be arduous, if not artificial, to separate them (chapter 5 specifically addresses these core elements). Consequently, resiliency—a multifaceted construct—can be put into operation in a variety of ways depending on context or local circumstance and is greatly influenced by sociocultural considerations.

Environmental protective factors (external) serve as a critical buffer for youth living in nonoptimal living conditions (family, school, community). External factors, too, are highly interrelated and difficult to separate out. While many individuals have subsequently helped shape the conceptualization of youth development, the work of Werner and colleagues laid the foundation and it influences current research on the subject; the study of neighborhood and how it can enhance or diminish youth competencies is a case in point (Furstenberg et al. 1999).

The Search Institute (1997, 1998) has underscored the importance of society identifying and enhancing the assets youth possess, advocating the need to incorporate a strength perspective in youth-based initiatives. The Search Institute has also conceptualized assets into internal-based and external-based. Each group consists of four general types. Internal are commitment to learning, positive values, social competencies, and positive identity; external are support, empowerment, boundaries and expectations, and constructive use of time.

Although the field of youth development has embraced assets as a cornerstone of any strategy and activities, it is important to pause and note that the presence of assets or negative factors in the lives of youth do not guarantee success or failure, According to the Search Institute

(1998): (1) assets are not a panacea; (2) circumstances do not dictate destiny; (3) a lack of assets does not equate with a doomed future; and (4) engagement in risky behaviors does not automatically result in a doomed future. Assets, while increasing the likelihood of success, do not guarantee success.

A JOURNEY IN SEARCH OF A DEFINITION

I have struggled with how to arrive at a comprehensive definition of youth development that both captures the excitement and potential of the field for achieving positive change in society and lends itself to incorporating dynamic changes. The metaphor of a journey is apt and can help the reader develop such a definition. A journey often has a distinct destination; however, the amount of time to be taken on the journey, the number of stops and detours needed before arriving at the destination, can vary from traveler to traveler. Some travelers will rejoice in exploring at every opportunity. These individuals seek to pause, observe, reflect, comment, and learn every step of the way. Other travelers are more interested in getting to their destination as quickly as possible. Stops are few and far between. Destination for them has greater significance than the journey.

Providing an answer to the question, "How is *youth development* defined?" is similarly varied. No two practitioners or academics in the field see and define youth development in the same manner. In this matter of definition, no one is right and no one is wrong. The destination on this journey is to arrive at a definition of youth development. The slow and deliberate traveler places emphasis on the process of getting there; the expedient traveler places greater emphasis on getting there as quickly as possible. The prospect that these two travelers might cross paths, like two ships in the night has great appeal. The slow, prodding traveler can pick up the pace; the expedient traveler can slow down without losing sight of the destination. Such a meeting of minds is possible if there is willingness to compromise, but all stakeholders must be willing to agree to a core definition of youth development. There will then be opportunities to add "attachments" to best capture particular circumstances—attachments that may stress, for example, one or other social arena: family, peers, schools, community. Others may place greater emphasis on considerations such as multiculturalism, gender, sexual orientation, or disabilities.

WHAT IS YOUTH DEVELOPMENT?

What does youth-development programming usually mean? Do academics differ from practitioners in how they view it? Do youth differ from practitioners? Answers to these questions are needed in order to ground the reader into this field of practice (Project Map 1997). Youth development encompasses a philosophical stance, goals, process, and outcomes. Youth development is a process, not an event. In essence, youth development often reflects a wide range of occupations that share a common goal or purpose (Murphy 1995b). Consequently, any effort to capture a process is far more difficult than capturing an event. This can be frustrating for all involved. A rush toward quantification of outcome measures may well result in losing sight of how we got there, or the lessons learned in the process.

Even though youth development is a moving target, it does not mean we can stand by idly and not make an honest and concerted effort at hitting that target, defining it and putting it into operation (Roth et al. 1998). The future of the field depends on achieving this goal. Hence, (1) it is important to push the boundaries of what is typically thought of as a youth-development setting (covered in chapters 6 to 17); (2) it is also important to push the boundaries of the essential core elements, approaches, and considerations (see chapters 4 to 6); and (3), while there is a wide range of interpretations of what is meant by youth development resulting from major philosophical differences and emphasis, it is important that the concept be "attached" to youth and not to the organizations that serve them (Pittman 1991). The challenge is made ever greater when youth development can take on many different forms and names without being labeled *youth development*.

Murphy (1995b: 13) identified one of the key tensions and contradictions of defining youth development:

Defining youth development work as exclusive, that is defining youth development work as related but distinct from teaching, child care, counseling, social services, is not easy. However, efforts to include everyone within the definition of youth development work will undermine efforts to define the field. If youth work is to be considered a field, youth development workers . . . will have to define youth work in comparison to the other major professions that work with youth.

The boundaries of what can be labeled as youth development are ever expanding; "youth philanthropy" is one example. Youth philanthropy is defined by the Kellogg Foundation (1999: 4), a key force in this approach, as follows:

> Youth philanthropy gives young people the power to make decisions, experience with a full range of leadership opportunities, achievement of social skills and improved community-youth relationships. In achieving this, youth and adults learn about and from each other, establish genuine relationships, and make an investment in the future of the community. Involving youth in philanthropy connects young people with the important local issues, increasing their self-esteem and building ownership and pride in the community. Through this experience, the young people participate in their own development while contributing to the development of the community.

Youth philanthropy borrows from a number of paradigms and approaches such as leadership development, community development, multi-culturalism, team building, and youth development (Kellogg Foundation 1999).

The creation or enhancement of what Taylor (2001) calls positive behavior settings brings a dimension to youth development that will increase in importance as the youth-development paradigm gains greater currency. Youth development can occur in any setting and not just those specifically devoted to serving youth. However, every effort must be made to avoid using the words *youth development* as a label for every after-school or youth program (McKenna 2000). Each sector of society must share in the responsibility of achieving the goals usually associated with youth development. We must not let adult stakeholders have the final say and exclude youth—the most important stakeholders. Youths themselves not only have the most up-to-date perspective on their needs, they also have a keen appreciation of their talents, hopes, and dreams. Any viable definition of youth development must have their input and their influence.

The translation of theory into practice is never easy. The application of youth-development principles and practices within the juvenile justice system, for example, is not without its challenges. As Taylor (1996: 2) writes:

The contrast between youth development theory, which defines and supports the quest of all adolescents to become healthy adults, and the realities of juvenile incarceration is extreme and disturbing. Youth development theory emphasizes growth and expansion, and symbolizes society's positive expectations. In turn, juvenile justice is too often characterized by inconsistent laws, policies, and enforcement rates, and the systematic oppression of young people.

The theoretical perspective that underpins youth development will no doubt challenge practitioners in bringing this form of practice into day-to-day operation. Chalmers (2000: 24) writes: "Youth development and strengths-based perspective are popular concepts now with people who work with youth. Too often they resemble intellectual exercises more than tenets for good practice. As is frequently the case, the translation from theoretical musings to practice can be quite difficult."

DEFINITIONS OF YOUTH DEVELOPMENT

The emergence of the concept of youth development should not be confused with historical commitments to serve youth. The YMCA, the Boy Scouts, boys' and girls' clubs, and settlement-house movements have played significant nonstigmatizing roles in reaching out to youth. However, unlike youth services, youth development, as a paradigm and concept, is a relatively recent phenomenon.

The term *youth development* is enjoying greater use in practice involving youth in the United States (Networks for Youth Development 1998a). The concept of youth development has existed in the professional literature in the United States for at least thirty years (NTIS 1971). However, it was not until the 1980s and 1990s that this concept as it is more commonly used gained greater currency.

The role of youth advocates cannot be overestimated in making youth development a viable paradigm for practice. Researchers and scholars followed them (which is not unusual), helping the field to develop conceptual models to describe and explain the potential of youth development to transform lives. Nonetheless, the role and appeal of youth themselves as advocates has been refreshing for the field of youth services, with youth development being but one dimension of it.

A number of scholars, government offices, foundations, major youth-serving organizations, practitioners, and youth themselves have embraced the concept of youth development. They have created definitions or identified a set of factors to inform this practice. And yet, while definitions, in the conventional sense, are in short supply, guidelines and key factors are not. These "definitions" and elements of youth development all touch upon a set of values, principles, and beliefs that not only stress process but outcome as well.

VOICES OF PROFESSIONAL ASSOCIATIONS AND ACADEMICS

A number of associations have played critical roles in shaping how youth development is defined and practiced in this country. According to the National Assembly (1994: 11) the term *youth development* can be defined as "purposefully seeking to meet youth needs and build youth competencies relevant to enabling them to become successful adults. Rather than seeing young people as problems, this positive development approach views them instead as resources and builds on their strengths and capabilities to develop within their own community." To succeed, youth must acquire adequate attitudes, behaviors, and skills (Sagawa 1998; Scales and Leffert 1999).

The National Clearinghouse on Families and Youth (1998: 1) defines youth development as

> a policy perspective that emphasizes providing services and opportunities to support all young people in developing a sense of competence, usefulness, belonging, and power. While individual programs can provide youth development activities or services, the youth development approach works best when entire communities offer youth development opportunities. This can occur when a community as a whole agrees upon the standards for what young people need to grow into happy and healthy adults and then creates a continuum of care and opportunities to meet those needs. Youth development also is about strengthening families and communities and involving young people in those efforts.

The role of community in setting standards and expectations stands out in this definition, as does the importance of a continuum of resources devoted to youth.

The American Youth Policy Forum (1995: 1) defines youth development as "an ongoing process in which young people are engaged and invested. Throughout this process, young people seek ways to meet their basic physical and social needs and to build competencies and connections they need for survival and success. *All* youth are engaged in the process of development." Nixon (1997), too, defines youth development as a process in which all youths engage over time in order to meet their needs and build competencies. The Search Institute (1998) advocates a "youth development asset" model that emphasizes enhancing strengths rather than focusing on reducing risky behaviors. Youth assets (forty in total) fall into two main categories, as noted above: external and internal. The institute's model explicitly identifies community as an important dimension. Other definitions and models generally do so implicitly.

Baines and Selta (1999) define youth development as an

> ongoing process in which young people are engaged in building skills, attitudes, knowledge, and experiences they feel prepare them for the present and the future. The youth development process is smoothed and youth development outcomes enhanced when adults (as individuals and professionals) work with young people to help them set and monitor their course and work with youth and each other to ensure that the course options are plentiful, positive and varied.

Their definition borrows substantially from that of Pittman and Irby (1998). The emphasis on the role of adults in this process sets this definition apart from many of the others presented in this chapter.

Lakes (1996: 134) ties youth development to the promise of democratic action and non-school-based programs:

> Yet, youth development practices, in my view, work best when kids and adults engage in participatory decision makings and practical democratic actions away from schools. Nonprofit organizations are best suited to attracting students voluntarily, willingly, and noncoercively in projects. . . . Remember, too, that young people's commitments to their neighborhoods strengthen when the democratic foundations of citizenship are doable and realizable, as a praxis rooted in problem-solving for community change.

Youth development as conceptualized by Lakes (1996) is closely connected to youth decision making. However, its potential can only be realized in settings that are not autocratic and where adults do not refuse partnership with youth. Schools, with some notable exceptions, are one of the least youth-empowering settings in this society (for the role of schools in youth-development programs, see chapter 6).

The National Youth Development Information Center (1998: 1) defines youth development and positive youth development as: "A process which prepares young people to meet the challenges of adolescence and adulthood through a coordinated, progressive series of activities and experiences which help them to become socially, morally, emotionally, physically, and cognitively competent. Positive youth development addresses the broader developmental needs of youth, in contrast to deficit-based models which focus solely on youth problems." This definition stresses the need to expand interventions beyond conventional social services, and to do so in a manner that is holistic. Specific core elements of youth development are enumerated.

Bronfenbrenner and White (1993), although specifically not providing a definition of positive youth development, nevertheless identify twelve principles for practice: (1) "Being there"—the importance of adults in youth lives; (2) Affection—formation and enhancement of enduring affection; (3) Activity—action through engagement of adults and youth; (4) Reciprocity—youth need to receive and give back; (5) Challenge—actions must progress in difficulty over time to expand to growth and maturing of youth; (6) Stability and continuity—sustained activities over an extended period of time; (7) The developmental power of parents—parental involvement, support, and guidance; (8) The developmental power of adults outside the Family—these adults help sustain, supplement, enhance, and substitute, when necessary; (9) The developmental power of peers—engagement of peers in joint activities with age-mates and with youth who are younger and older; (10) The developmental importance of altruistic actions—service to others and community; (11) Activities with objects, symbols, and ideas—knowledge and skills in working with objects, symbols, and ideas that will help prepare them for adult roles; and (12) The importance of linkages between settings—collaboration between community institutions is essential because the goals associated with youth development cannot possibly be carried out by one entity.

Although Bronfenbrenner and White have not provided the reader with a formal definition of positive youth development, they do prescribe the areas that must be addressed in their vision of positive youth development. As with others mentioned in this chapter, positive youth development is an all-encompassing paradigm, with multiple targets, time lines, and levels of intervention. Roth, Brooks-Gunn, and Foster (1998: 425–26) define positive youth development as "the desired outcomes for our nation's youth. Positive youth development encompasses all our hopes and aspirations for a nation of healthy, happy, and productive individuals. It recognizes that preventing problem behaviors is not all that is needed to prepare youth for their future."

The W. K. Kellogg Foundation, a major national foundation that has played an instrumental role in the field of youth development, has stressed the need for an expansion of youth development to also include community within this paradigm. In the Kellogg view, as quoted by Baines and Selta (1999: 26):

> Youth development has to be explicit and intentional. More importantly, the practice of positive youth development . . . is emerging as one of community involvement, community ownership, community mobilization, and youth involvement. This approach is less interested in holding agencies responsible for the well-being of our children and more interested in creating the whole "village" by changing conditions in the community which fosters healthy youth development.

The Child Welfare League of America (1995), although not specifically providing a working definition of "Positive Youth Development," identified eight core elements of this type of practice: (1) Embrace of total youth involvement; (2) Creation of a healthy and safe environment; (3) Promotion of healthy environment; (4) Learning by doing; (5) Creation of community partnerships; (6) Realization that independence takes time; (7) Valuing individual strategies; and (8) Building-in feedback and self-assessment.

The National Collaboration for Youth (1999: 3) defines positive youth development as "a process which prepares young people to meet the challenges of adolescence and adulthood through a coordinated, progressive series of activities and experiences which help them to become socially, morally, emotionally, physically, and cognitively competent." The "positive" definitions address the broader developmental needs of youth—in contrast to deficit-based models, which focus solely on youth problems—and prescribe a set of activities, or approaches, that embrace youth playing a central role in decision making.

Hahn and Raley (1997) note that there must be multiple levels in any definition of youth development—that the process must lead to human growth and development. This process is interactive and lends itself to youth participants maturing as decision makers. Hahn and Raley also identify a philosophical orientation to social development and community. Youth development can transpire only within a broader context that goes far beyond a focus on individuals. An individualistic society tends to focus almost exclusively on individuals. Youth development, on the other hand, represents a much broader set of lenses (see chapter 6). Finally, a programmatic framework must be explicated: one that stresses a vision, holistic approaches, staff support, caring and committed staff, multi-institutional collaborations, positive relationships between adult staff and youth, youth-focused activities, and youth ownership and involvement (empowerment).

Catalano et al. (1998) conclude, not surprisingly, that "Positive Youth Development" is not yet well defined by the field. This is based on their meta-analysis of evaluations of positive youth-development programs. They identify ten key goals promoted in positive youth-development programs: bonding; resilience; social, emotional, cognitive, behavioral, and moral competence; self-determination; spirituality; self-efficacy; clear and positive identity; belief in the future; positive behavior and opportunities for prosocial involvement; and prosocial norms (healthy standards for behavior). These goals guide positive youth-development programming across the United States.

Pittman (1991) identifies five arenas youth development must address to be successful: (1) Health (physical and emotional); (2) Personal/social (interpersonal); (3) Knowledge, reasoning, and creativity; (4) Vocational (preparation for future employment); and (5) Citizenship (contribute to the greater good). Pittman (Academy for Educational Development 1991: 8) also makes a similar observation to that made by Hahn and Raley (1997) about the need for a more encompassing definition of youth development:

> A single, commonly used definition does not exist. Instead, discussions often resolve around what we wish youth to be or not to be. . . . Our definition regards the reduction of risky behaviors and existing problems as important. But, it asserts that competence and string connections to the larger society are essential and invaluable in preparing youth for the challenges of adulthood. Indeed, it is not enough to develop strategies to prevent dangerous things. . . . We must be equally adamant about stating and enabling goals that we wish young people to achieve.

The American Youth Policy Forum uses a "youth promotion" construct and defines it as "efforts specifically designed to bring about clearly defined positive outcomes, or designed to foster the development of skills and competencies in young people" (Halper, Cusack, Raley, O'Brien, and Wills 1995: 1). Promotion, in this instance, stresses the premise that youth have innate competencies that need to be supported and enhanced rather than developed. A focus on developing competencies, however, does not mean that youth-development interventions must only stress skill acquisition. Competencies require a foundation that has as its base a distinctive set of values, attitudes, and knowledge.

Lawrence (1998: 9) uses the construct of "positive youth development" rather than just youth development: "Positive Youth Development is an approach to working with youth that operates from the premise that all youths engage in a developmental process by which they seek to meet their needs and build competencies. The model suggests that the way to assist youths in achieving positive outcomes from the process is the design of environments and services that emphasize strengths, asset building and youth/adult relationships." The future of positive youth development, according to Catalano et al. (1998), is very much dependent upon meeting three significant challenges: (1) Creation of shared definitions of the key constructs; (2) An ability to document the effectiveness of the intervention; and (3) Development of an in-depth understanding of why enhancement of capacities also prevent risk-taking behaviors and problems.

The National Network for Youth created the Community Youth Development (CYD) paradigm for youth in the early 1990s (Jarvis, Shear, and Hughes 1997; National Network for Youth 1997). Interestingly, a book titled *A Community Youth Development Program* was published in the early 1950s (Havighurst et al. 1952). Their concept of community youth development, however, focused more on how to help youth in need and how to mobilize local resources to accomplishing this goal.

A central premise of the National Network for Youth's conceptualization of CYD is the importance of cultivating community partnerships in service to youth, particularly those involving youth and adults. Youths, after all, grow up in communities, not programs (Bremby 1998). The National Network for Youth (Hughes 2000: 7) defines community youth development as "a new philosophical, sociological, and educational movement which harnesses the power of youth to affect community development and, similarly, engages communities to embrace their role in the development of youth."

This perspective, as the name change implies, brings community to the forefront of the discussion of what constitutes youth development. It further grounds this form of practice within the community—as a source of strength, purpose, a vehicle for achieving change, and as a focus of change (Guest 1995). Hughes and Nichols (1995) stress that community youth development must be inclusive of all youth and should not be limited to those "at-risk" or in treatment. This concept encompasses prevention, early intervention, and rehabilitation, and to succeed it requires a focus on youth and family, school, and community, with the latter playing an influential part in creating and facilitating the creation of activities.

CYD implies a "political" agenda grounded in a social- and economic-justice context. In Dominguez (2000: 16) we read:

> While Youth Development (CYD) requires the provision of programs that meet developmental needs and involve neighborhoods in developing resources for the development of those needs, CYD goes one step further by involving youth in community building activities that foster social empowerment. CYD looks to funnel the politicizing experience that disenfranchised youth experience when they realize that ethnic/racial and cultural group membership differentiates them from those that have privilege over them. CYD seeks to transfer information needed by youth in order to access opportunities and mobilize for change. Community Youth Development requires the activation of youth toward civic participation geared to coalition building and political participation that challenges the growing levels of inequality and capital concentration that leaves minority communities impoverished and isolated from each other. Through this process, youth build a sense of personal efficacy and a belief that social change is possible. They gain access to opportunities towards positive youth outcomes and develop a stake in the socio-economic development of their own communities.

Dominguez's analysis of community youth development has transformed the conventional view of youth development from one focused on youth to one examining key social, political, and economic forces on youth, their families, and community. When CYD is embraced by practitioners, the approach is social-change oriented, and this creates tensions between providers and funders. The social-change agenda raises the social- and economic-justice dimension of youth development, youths themselves playing active and central roles.

Penuel (1995: 1), like Dominguez, highlights a social-change role for youth development: "In taking youth as resources as a new metaphor for relating to and understanding youth as resources to the community, the question of youth development becomes less one of how to preserve the social order but rather of how to involve youth in changing the social order." A community youth-development perspective fits well with Penuel's statement on social order.

Probably the two most compelling, as well as among the shortest, definitions of youth development come from Hugh Price, CEO of the National Urban League, and the 4-H organization. Price states pithily: "Youth development is what we do for kids on a good day." Youth development must be an ongoing process with "good" days being every day; it is predicatedon enriching and empowering the lives of youths in a process that benefits an entire community. The 4-H definition sees youth development as "a process of mental, physical and social growth that takes place within a community and is affected by the customs and regulations. The process of growing up and positively developing one's capacities happens where young people have quality experiences in their living" (Michigan State University 2000: 1)—a definition that foregrounds process within a community context.

VOICES OF PRACTITIONERS

How practitioners define youth development is very revealing. A document produced by the National Collaboration for Youth (1996 7, 13, 19, 25, 31, 37) provided a vehicle for six practitioners to reflect on what youth development meant to them. Each emphasized a different aspect; however, a core set of elements is evident in how these practitioners conceptualized and defined youth-development practice. Their perspectives also highlighted the importance of process and outcome.

Sandy Stevens, a branch manager at the Boys and Girls Club, Scottsdale, Arizona, said he viewed youth development as a vehicle for youth having fun and finding a creative outlet for their energies and passion: "My profession is youth development. When I work with a kid, it is not just, 'How are you?'

How was your day?' It is constantly thinking about how am I going to make this kid special. How am I going to change this kid's life today? That is youth development: How am I going to do make that person feel good? It is an ongoing process."

Paul Watson, an executive director at San Diego Youth and Community Services, California, thought of youth development as an opportunity to identify and marshal community resources and create collaborative partnerships in service to youth: "There are many community development projects around the country, but youth are usually an afterthought, They are not involved with the planning, designing, and implementation of programs. . . . My passion is to create equal partnerships, so together young people and adults can strengthen communities."

Joi Smith, a program director at Big Sisters of Central Indiana, Indianapolis, saw youth development as an opportunity to connect adults with youth through mentorship: "We are giving young people the opportunity to participate in something that is good, positive and fun. It's not complicated. Sometimes our challenge can be helping volunteer mentors know that taking time out of their lives to see the kids on a regular basis does not mean spending money. They are impacting their lives by just caring about them. They need to recognize the little successes."

Christopher Egan, a camp director for Camp Fire Boys and Girls for the Eastern Massachusetts Council, Boston, stressed the importance of building self-esteem, character, and self-confidence: "Everything we do is built around the goal of helping kids to develop. We help kids develop self confidence and self esteem, help them understand that they are not defined by their environment, but they have the ability to strike out on their own. . . . We make it safe for kids to take risks and expand their horizons."

Angela Key, a clinical case manager with the Damamil Program, Boys and Girls Homes of Maryland, Baltimore, saw youth development as a way of tapping youth strengths: "A positive youth development perspective helps youth to move away from child rescuing and helping poor people with problems. . . . I see so much hope. . . . I think what I like most about them is that they teach me, too . . . there is more than one thing that defines whether [teen moms] are a success or failure."

Laura Heaney, division director of Child Care Services, YMCA, at Columbia-Wilmette, Portland, Oregon, viewed youth development as an opportunity to discover the special gifts of youth and build upon them by actively listening to them: "We need overall guidelines for youth work that help staff to recognize and support each kid's unique development in out-of-school hours. . . . You have to sit and listen to them. They will tell you what they want and need to say. . . . Kids will tell you in a heartbeat if you take the time to listen. If you want to earn the respect of kids and help them, you have to step into their world."

VOICES OF YOUTH

In this chapter on definitions, youth, too, needs its say. Youths are, after all, the ultimate beneficiaries of the paradigm and its resources. Youth participation and empowerment is essential in developing a more complete definition of youth development—which is not to say that, for adults, communicating with youth is easy; there is inequality in status between youth and adults, staff and participant (Banks 1997; Coleman, Catan, and Dennison 1997).

The comments of seventeen-year-old Robert Cline, although not directed at a definition of youth development, raise this matter of the need for youth to have a voice (Cline 1998/99: 10):

Adults need to know that they are being affected every day by the absence of youth opinions. I asked my peers: "What do you think the consequence is for leaving youth out of societal activities?" The common answer was: "You'll end up with more rebelling youth." What would it be like if we gave youth an opportunity to have a place in society? The amount we can give is phenomenal. We are at our peak of creative ability when we are younger. We are also at our peak of risk-taking ability. If we were to hone these attributes of creativity and risk taking in this society, we could achieve so much."

Rasheed Newson, a nineteen-year-old, states (Cline 1998/99): "Don't be afraid to give control over to the youth, take a deep breath, say a short prayer, and get out of the way. . . . One reason youth volunteer is because, at their best, volunteer opportunities allow youth to be in control, to make decisions. Unfortunately, the lives of youth don't allow them that kind of freedom. They go to school as they're told and shuffle from classroom to classroom at the sounding of a bell. How often does anyone go to them with major decisions and say, 'What do you think we should do?' "

When I visited youth-development programs in various states across the country, I was given the following spontaneous definitions. Youths were asked individually, not in groups, in order to minimize group influence on the answers. Interestingly, few respondents needed to pause and think before answering. I told them I was writing a book on youth development and that the book would not be complete without their input. The intent was not to produce a systematic survey of all youth, but simply to get random youth reactions to the paradigm. The sources are not named individually—only by city.

⌒

Atlanta, Georgia: "To me youth development means having a place to hang out with friends and not being afraid for my safety."

"Positive youth development means having adults believe in my abilities."

"Youth development brings out the best in my artistic talents and provides a place where I can show them off."

⌒

St. Louis, Missouri: "Youth development means that I have a place to go to where it is safe, I can be myself, and have fun, too."

"What is youth Development? It is a program that helps me better prepare myself for the world!"

"Youth development helps me better understand myself and those around me."

⌒

Austin, Texas: "Youth development allows young people to gain control over their lives."

"Youth development is all about serving each other, our families, and community."

"Youth Development brings me into contact with caring adults who can help me gain a better life."

⌒

Miami, Florida: "Youth development is just that! It helps youth develop into caring and responsible members of the community."

"Youth development not only helps me but also my family. We all have needs and strengths."

"Youth development has helped me better understand my roots and the rich cultural roots that I have" (statement translated from Spanish).

⌣

New York City: "Youth development provides me with something constructive to do and keeps me away from the trouble in my family and community."

"Youth development gives me an opportunity to learn about youth who are from different backgrounds, in an atmosphere that encourages learning about each other."

The above statements capture a variety of views on youth development. Short and often to the point, the statements bring to the fore the individual needs and perspectives of youths of both sexes from different ethnic and racial backgrounds. The socioeconomic circumstances also varied, although respondents were primarily low-income. In many ways, the statements point more to the importance of the present than to eventual transition to adulthood (a characteristic that did not surprise me). The importance of competencies was mentioned several times, as was the importance of having a place to go to that they could call their own.

COMMON THEMES AND THREADS

Definitions of paradigms often seek to be descriptive and prescriptive at the same time—no small challenge. Youth development, if it tries to do this—to address both in great detail— will ultimately fail in that task. The descriptive aspect will not fit neatly into what is commonly expected of a definition—a short and concise statement of meaning and clear boundaries. The prescriptive aspect, in turn, seeks to be broad, encompassing, and sufficiently detailed to give direction. This aspect of youth development takes on the qualities of a laundry list—one that, in listing activities, can easily go on and on.

In bringing together distinct yet complimentary themes, I want to present a unified vision of youth development. All constituencies must see elements of what they value in the definition. In addressing both descriptive and prescriptive aspects of youth development, the definition will sacrifice depth and detail; youth development, however, is too rich a paradigm to allow it to be reduced to a simple definition—the lowest common denominator. Any effort to reduce it to a simple definition will not do justice to this paradigm—for a paradigm is, among other things, a way of looking at life. Youth development, in essence, is a process of human growth and development, a philosophical orientation to social and community development, and a framework for delivering youth-focused services (Edginton and deOlivera 1995). All these three aspects are of equal importance in bringing this paradigm to life in the daily lives of youths.

Youth workers and youth-serving organizations must be willing to subvert their interests in favor of the field of youth development. In Murphy's (1995b: 13) words:

> Youth work is strongly identified with youth-serving organizations. So much so, in fact, that it is not clear whether youth workers see themselves as part of a field or as staff of a particular organizations. If youth work is to be considered a field, youth-serving organizations will have to make organizational identity subordinate to field identification and professionalization issues. These organizations will have to acknowledge and encourage the interorganization movement of staff to support their development.

To make youth development a widely recognized field of practice, with a consensual definition, language, and formal credentials, will necessitate a major commitment from the major stakeholders.

An analysis of descriptions of youth development, most of which have already been mentioned in this chapter, uncovers seven main themes: (1) an inherent belief in the self-worth of youth, regardless of their competencies—cognitive, emotional, social, spiritual, and physical; (2) stress on the importance of cultural heritage; (3) the importance of youth exercising control over their lives; (4) a holistic perspective of assets and needs—cognitive, emotional, physical, moral, social, and spiritual; (5) belief in the possession by youth of innate capacities (Blum 1995); (6) an understanding that it takes a whole community to carry out youth development and that no one institution has the total responsibility or ability to do so (Feely 1995; Guest 1995); and (7) long-range commitment—this latter being essential because the goals are long-term.

AN ENCOMPASSING AND CONTEXTUALIZED DEFINITION

Rather than develop a new term for youth development (e.g., something like *youth capacity enhancement*) I have elected to go back to the roots of the original concept and broaden and contextualize the meaning of youth development for practice. I feel strong reluctance to project a new term because doing so would perpetuate what is currently happening in the field—the ever-evolving shift in meaning regarding what youth development is and in the comprehensiveness of the paradigm. A definitive definition of youth development is too important to rest solely on the shoulders of a single individual or association. A summit of key stakeholders—including youth—will be in order to accomplish this immensely important task.

Youth development as conceptualized and implemented in this book views youth both as partners and central figures in interventions. These interventions systematically seek to identify and utilize youth capacities and meet youth's needs. They actively seek to involve youth as decision makers and tap their creativity, energy, and drive; and they also acknowledge that youth are not superhuman—that they therefore have needs that require a marshaling of resources targeted at youth and at changing environmental circumstances (family and community). Positively changing environments that are toxic and antithetical to youth capacity enhancement requires the use of a wide range of strategies—tailored to fit local circumstances—ranging from advocacy to consciousness raising and political mobilization.

That is a working definition. The orientation that it articulates, explicitly and implicitly, tries to bridge the divide between conventional views of youth development, which focus almost exclusively on the individual, and those that take a distinctive line such as "positive," "community youth," "youth promotion," and "youth developmental assets."

This definition has special significance for youth development specifically targeted at youth historically viewed as at-risk—those at risk for a variety of social problems and devoid of assets or strengths. That is not to say that the definition is not universal, but that its saliency for marginalized youth cannot be easily ignored. When applied to marginalized youth (see chapter 7), the political features of the definition carry far-reaching significance. Changes at family and community level are critical in maintaining the integrity of a youth-development paradigm. Youth cannot fulfill their potential without changes in these two domains.

Youth development in a middle-class or upper-class community may share many of the goals and activities of this approach with youth who are poor or working-class. However, activities involving the latter must seek to empower youths, their families, and communities while addressing social- and economic-justice issues. Practitioners in these communities cannot ignore the forces of classism and racism. Programs and activities, as a result, may well look substantially different between the two economic sectors. This should not only be expected but be required. As is noted in several of the definitions cited above, a youth-development paradigm must be flexible and take context into account. Thus, an encompassing and contextualized definition of youth development is necessary. In more day-to-day terms, the field of youth development can make significant advances through the adaptation of a consensus definition of youth development, establishment of core competencies and standards, and establishment of some form of certification as to who can call themselves "youth development specialists." The latter is now often associated with professional status, and all of the rights and privileges associated with it.

The nature of the field of youth development—broad, ambitious, ambiguous—lends itself to staff being obtained in a variety of ways. Regardless of the approach to practice that is used, the rewards for practitioners in the field are limitless, as pointed out by the National Collaboration for Youth (1996: 2). "Whether a career in the youth development field is studied for, stumbled on by chance, or discovered as a second career, once on the job, there are opportunities for vertical and lateral movement within agencies and agency to agency. What ties individuals in the field together is a commitment to providing productive and healthy environments for young people to grow and develop." Youth, in effect, are the glue that holds together the disparate elements.

The professionalizing of the field has various manifestations. The professionalization of language is one example. Language serves to "legitimize" the field of practice by identifying and promoting a set of key concepts. It also serves to elevate a particular form of practice and those who profess to practice it; and it increases political legitimacy that can be translated into increased funding and support (Murphy 1995a).

Caution, however, is in order if the field moves toward professionalization. Professionalism has historically been used to keep people out, and the standards used have often involved achievement in formal education as a criterion. Such criteria may effectively keep out excellent staff—people with requisite competencies and attitudes but no university-level credentials. I am not sure that that will ultimately benefit the field and position it strategically in the twenty-first century. Youth need and want role models that they can relate to. This necessitates that organizations be sufficiently flexible to hire the "right" person for the job, The right person may not have a university degree but with training, supervision, and consultation, may accomplish the aims of the program.

⌒

The multiple role that definitions play in helping practitioners design interventions and delineate boundaries for practice is well accepted in professional practice. Definitions, as a result, provide a foundation. Youth development requires a definition that seeks to bring together various social and political constituencies and systematically build upon the work of others in the field. A consensus definition of youth development will result in the creation of a "shared identity" that benefits all in this field of practice (Pittman and Zeldin 1995). However, no definition can possibly be all-inclusive. This chapter hopefully has captured the excitement of youth development as well as the frustrations inherent in defining this form of practice. Needless to say, there is tremendous need to adopt a consensus definition.

Delgado (2000a) raised the possibility that a consensus definition of youth development based upon assets (strengths) can, in addition to helping youth, their families, and communities, be instrumental in bringing together practitioners from different disciplines as well as participants and communities. A common definition serves as a unifying force across disciplines; it may even result in a common language for youth development. A problem-focused definition does not lend itself to coalition building because it increases the likelihood of differences of opinions about what constitutes a problem. The answer to this question may well rest upon funding, in the case of community-based organizations. However, a focus on youth and community assets, for example, is not predicated upon historical definitions, turf, and funding considerations. Coalitions and partnerships can prove very powerful in moving a youth-development agenda forward, nationally and internationally.

The Center on Youth Development (2000) estimated that it will cost $144 billion to ensure that all U.S. youth have access to appropriate developmental supports and opportunities. Based on this formula, it would cost $2.55 per hour per youth for twelve hundred hours per year to help youth transition into productive and socially responsible adults. This investment can then translate into a gain of $10.51 for every dollar invested. The financial difference is significant unto itself, and the social benefits go far beyond any dollar amount.

If youth development is to remain an inspirational but vague paradigm, it will cost the field dearly in its quest to increase funding of programs. The need to concretize—and just as importantly, to evaluate results—is essential in galvanizing support across various constituencies, particularly those that set policy. Pittman (2000a: 39) stated this challenge eloquently:

Imagination is a powerful thing. One of the biggest failings of youth development advocates (myself included) is that we fail to capture the imagination of policy makers, funders, the public, and even parents. These decision-makers have difficulty imagining what youth development is. . . . Why? We are just too vague. . . . "Youth development" may be creeping into the public lexicon. But it is not yet into the policy dictionary.

Vagueness makes the important job of selling youth development as a viable alternative to conventional approaches arduous, at best, if not impossible. Nevertheless, this challenge must be addressed head-on. Nothing short of this goal is acceptable.

The "people" versus "places" balance is one that will result in youth-development initiatives stressing the interactive ramifications of infrastructure development and individual development (Greenberg 2001). Blyth (2001: 227), however, makes an important observation: "No single framework or diagram can single-handedly help communities revitalize their efforts on behalf of children and youth." That said, society must provide the "non-negotiables of youth development"—basic supports and opportunities needed to achieve positive long-term outcomes for youth (Avenilla and Singley 2001).

4 / YOUTH DEVELOPMENT: APPROACHES AND CONSIDERATIONS

A NUMBER OF crucial considerations must be addressed before programming of youth-development activities can be planned and implemented. These considerations, however, strike at the heart of many of the issues that we encounter daily in this society: they are like lenses that color our vision and influence our expectations and actions (Murphy 1995b). Adults rarely touch on such subjects since there are few arenas where they can be discussed openly. Issues related to culture, gender, age, sexual orientation, and disabilities are often deeply rooted in the many social- and economic-justice issues that this country struggles with—either to ignore them or address them. Many of these issues have been a part of the country's history since colonial days. They can easily be totally ignored, and often are; and in the development of youth programs, it seems, as if they do not even exist. That is why I have written this chapter.

Youth organizations have to walk a very thin and difficult line between welcoming all youths who seek to attend and strict adherence to rules that apply to everyone (McLaughlin and Heath 1993). The first of these policies seeks to personalize youth participants, their assets as well as their needs; the second places emphasis on group conformity. To what extent do we reinforce individual identity at the expense of group identity? The answer to the question can come only from the local level. A youth-development program that stresses conformity will look dramatically different from one that stresses the importance of individuality, although rules and regulations can be found in both types.

This chapter will not be an exhaustive examination of these two areas, but I do hope it will ground the reader in the essential challenges involved in bringing youth development to life in community organizations. These challenges, while not unique to youth development, are rarely addressed in other forms of practice. I would like to see it be acceptable to talk about them in a youth-development context. This does not mean that a consensus is necessarily possible, either among staff or between staff and youth. One reason why these issues are rarely discussed is because agreement may not be possible. Nevertheless, day after day these issues are influential in all aspects of youth-development work. They cannot be ignored or relegated to secondary status.

A REVIEW OF APPROACHES

For most helping professions, the quest for new conceptual models and frameworks for practice with youth is a never-ending goal—one fraught with excitement, debate, and tension (Catalano et al. 1998; Delgado 2000a; Lakes 1996; Lerner 1995; Males 1999; Perkins 1997). The quest for new models, for innovation, is essential if significant progress is to be made. But the development of new approaches causes tension in a field between the old guard and the new.

Penuel (1995: 1) well summed up these challenges and contradictions for youth development:

> The challenge of youth development in the U.S. is indeed difficult. Youth in particular are faced with an array of contradictory messages about themselves and their generation. Youth are at once burdens on the society and the hope of the future. They are criticized for their apathy, but are given few social responsibilities. They are supposed to conform to adult expectations, but their opportunities for decision-making are limited by many social practices. Regardless of competence, youth are constructed in our society as immature and manipulable for the purposes of development. There is, however, another way of responding to youth. Youth can be respected by adults as resources to and collaborators in their communities.

These contradictions facing youth make the tasks of youth development that much more difficult.

Rauner (2000: 135) stresses the importance of interconnectedness and caring in youth development:

> To become the caring citizens we need them to be, young people need to have made real the vision of the interdependent life organized

around public, as well as private, caregiving responsibilities. They must see the adults whom they admire devote themselves to willed fidelities and
intentional caring, beyond self-focused achievements and pleasures, They must see care made the serious work of public life, rather than a private lifestyle choice. They must grow up in a true community, where they can both expect the constancy and trust of caring and know that such responsibility will be expected of them.

Several aspects of youth development need to be specifically addressed. These aspects address youth-development approaches and language that must be articulated for the paradigm to achieve its incredible potential. Youth development cannot be successfully divorced from cultural diversity, age, gender and sexual orientation, and abilities. These areas get at the crux of what youth development *is*, regardless of the definition used.

CULTURAL DIVERSITY

Cultural diversity presents both rewards and pitfalls. In order to talk about the concept of diversity and what it means for youth-development practice in the United States, Terry (1999: 5) came up with a fitting metaphor: "a neutral compound." He writes:

> Another way to phrase this is to say that diversity is a neutral compound that can be sculpted to many forms. Diversity, by itself, leads us nowhere. It is what we do with diversity that counts. It is how we perceive its importance and role in our organization, communities, and culture that will determine what we will do with it. Diversity is an asset or liability, depending on how you view it.

Thus, a cultural-diversity perspective needs to validate and encompass many different elements, cultural heritage being but one, albeit a highly influential one (Murphy 1995b).

The increased racial and ethnic diversity of youth in this country (the percentage of youth of color is rapidly increasing; see chapter 2), combined with gender-specific needs and programming and a changing economy, has implications for the field of youth development. Demographic, technological, and economic changes necessitate the use of new, more "relevant" models (Delgado 1999; Furstenberg et al. 1999).

Zeldin (1995: 5) places culture in an ecological context:

> Development occurs within and is profoundly influenced by environmental contexts. Environments include physical, cultural, philosophical, and social dimensions. Good practice, therefore, demands that activities be in safe places and made accessible to those most in need of assistance. It requires that places respect the cultural traditions and lifestyles of all participants. A youth development paradigm is one example of an emerging perspective on how best to address the needs and capacities of youth in this country.

Zeldin cites Crockett (1997), where it is pointed out that a social and cultural context, in addition, help shape what it means to be a youth in this society by dictating social roles and prescribing what are "acceptable" activities.

Such a context also serves to determine the importance of caring at a family, community, and societal level (Murphy 1995b; Rauner 2000).

Walsh (1999: 27) presents a multifaceted view of culture, and includes disabilities in it:

> There is no more powerful way to appreciate, understand, and have compassion for the strengths, skills, and effects of another person then to really be with them on equal terms. And there is no more important way for you to build an appreciation for diversity among the youth you work with than to create an inclusive program. Many important and effective programs—such as rites of passage for African-American youth, gay and lesbian clubs, etc.—are built upon the proven methodologies of helping children and youth understand, appreciate, and love who they are. Children and youth with disabilities are members of these communities, as well as the disability community, and need to be included.

A broad definition and understanding of culture serves to capture the dynamic nature of the construct and grounds youth-development strategies and activities in ways not possible under a narrow definition.

Ethnicity and cultural background represent a critical dimension of individuality in youth (Camino 1992; Koss-Chioino and Vargas 1999). A youth-development paradigm *must* take culture into account in programming. Local factors that influence programming and mandate flexibility include socioeconomic status, ethnic/racial composition, gender, age, and disabilities.

The National Research Council (1999: 52) identified a racial divide between youth of color and their white non-Latino counterparts as a major issue that youth and society will face in this new century:

> With this increase in diversity, coupled with worldwide patterns of increased mobility and migration, cooperative relations among different racial and ethnic groups are essential to the nation's future. Yet there is growing evidence to suggest that white youth and youth from ethnic minority groups hold deeply divergent views on how to relate to each other. The harmful results of this racial divide among youth are becoming more apparent as demonstrated by an alarming increase of adolescent hate crimes, organized hate groups, and overt expressions of racial intolerance.

This divide must not be minimized.

As is discussed later (chapter 6), youth-development programs seek to build competencies—health, social, emotional, cognitive, spiritual, and moral (Millstein, Petersen, and Nightingale 1993; National Collaboration for Youth 1998). But for these core elements to have meaning, youth development must take into account the cultural background and context of youth (Lerner 1995). Cultural here refers to youth culture both in general and by heritage. Youth culture can be a very powerful socialization mechanism but it is often overlooked in constructing youth programs (Skelton and Valentine 1998).

Such grounding of the youth-development construct is imperative in the design of goals, activities, and strategies. Delgado (2000a: 89) cautions staff about the critical need to address the racist aspect of culture and its impact on youth: "Youth programs need to be keenly aware of how the ethnic/racial backgrounds of participants can severely limit relationship-building. . . . Youth themselves, after all, are not beyond harboring racist sentiments and stereotypes." Successful programming cannot leave it to chance that youths surmount racist barriers on their own. Adults can fill an important leadership role in this area. They can help youths to identify the many subtle, as well as not so subtle, ways that racism manifests itself, and provide effective strategies that youths can use to combat racism and minimize its effects.

Developing critical thinking skills is one step in this direction.

Positive youth identity in youth of color cannot be accomplished without development of pride in ethnic identity (Catalano et al. 1998; Delgado 2000a; Hill et al. 1994; Koss-Chioino and Vargas 1999). Ethnic identity as a construct consists of various factors, most notably self-identification as a group member, a sense of belonging, and positive attitudes toward one's group (Phinney 1990). It also includes a grasp of cultural history and traditions. Successful transition to adulthood cannot be successfully accomplished without a strong ethnic/racial identity, particularly for youths who are marginalized (Montero-Sieburth 2000; Phinney and Kohatsu 1997). This self-pride forms the essential core of progress toward youth-development goals.

Youth-development programs are in a unique position to promote in youths an in-depth, positive understanding of who they are. Participation in these programs will result not only in better self-understanding but also in better understanding of those of a different cultural background. The development of positive intercultural relationships must be a goal, either explicit or implicit, of youth-development programs (Osher and Mejia 1999). This can be accomplished only through setting purposeful goals.

I find that the most successful youth-development organizations are those whose missions actively embrace social-justice, participation, and community-change themes while stressing practice based on principles of cultural competence. An example is ROCCA, based in Massachusetts, whose activities show what is possible in a good program. Their series placed a high value on culture (Ban et al. 1999: 14): "Offering culture-specific and multicultural celebrations and classes. Targeting young people and adults in community outreach. Reaching out and partnering with many different groups of people, both within . . . staff and volunteer populations, and in the larger community. Learning about trauma from war, religion, and acculturation. Recognizing differences. Hosting discussions. Promoting and supporting leadership." Activities do not have to be "special initiatives." They can take place through the natural course of events; in other words, they do not have to take place during a celebrated month, like October for Latinos or February for African Americans.

Delgado (2000a) argues that activities such as the arts and humanities make excellent vehicles for youth of color to discover or rediscover their past—a past that as a result of racism has been distorted by society and has robbed them of positive role models, significant achievements, and appreciation of their groups' places in world history. Such activities can have a powerful transformative experience in the lives of youth of color, as Delgado (2000a: 13) testifies:

> My interest in using the arts and humanities . . . to outreach and serving urban youth of color started in the early 1990s when I was principal investigator on a federal substance abuse prevention grant. . . . I was able to witness firsthand the power of development-focused activities for reaching, engaging, and transforming youth . . . when relevant to the life of urban youth. "Self-esteem" was enhanced by an emphasis on cultural heritage and pride and reaffirmed the importance of ethnic identity.

Youth development can have an influential role in helping youth of color gain a prominent position in this country. However, before competencies can be developed, youth of color must gain a positive self-identity. This is the foundation—the core.

THE AGE FACTOR

Age is a not inconsequential factor in this field of practice (Schilling and Martinek 2000). Youth development historically has focused on the latency age groups and adolescents (Quinn 1999; Wahl 1995). Adolescents, however, are probably the most serviced group because they present the greatest security threat to communities and schools. This is unfortunate. Any systematic bias for or against a particular age group impacts how the field conceptualizes services, and research and scholarly literature will also reflect the bias.

The importance of precision in what is meant by the term *youth* goes far beyond semantics, as Wahl (1995: 19) noted:

> A broad term, "youth" refers to a range of ages and stages depending on who is talking. For some, it is the end of middle childhood—eight or nine years-old through early, middle and late adolescence—eighteen or so. For others, it refers to school age and for others it goes back to early childhood. The imprecision about age is fairly benign. But the generic nature of the term permits unintentional exclusion of some groups and

imputations about others. The term "developmentally appropriate health care services," for example, has been coined to reflect the importance of age within the youth category.

Wahl's points have important implications, and youth development must become more specific on this subject. The United Nations defines youth as being between the ages of fifteen to twenty-four; Commonwealth countries say between the ages of fifteen and twenty-nine (World Sources Online 1999). In the United States, the term *youth* generally refers to those from age ten or eleven years up to twenty. Fassler (1998) has argued that youth capacities do not start or end at a certain age; for example, they do not magically appear in early or middle adolescence.

The age of the participants in a program and their cognitive, social, physical, moral, spiritual, and emotional capacities of course determines how development principles are operationalized (Michigan State University 1997). Scales and Leffert (1999), based on their review of the literature on developmental assets, found that age is a key factor in the moral reasoning of youth, and participant age thus becomes much more than a descriptive variable that is addressed only in record keeping and evaluation. It has far reaching implications for all aspects of youth development.

Youths are not "adults in waiting": they are capable human beings with abilities that must be enhanced or fostered (Administration on Children, Youth, and Families 1997). They have immediate challenges and needs that must be addressed in the present; that is, they are not being primed for adult roles. If the immediate challenges are addressed, the transition to adulthood will take care of itself. These challenges, however, have a lot to do with the age of the participant.

Weinberger's (2001) synthesis of the research on the brain (specifically, the frontal cortex) is relevant here. Youths under the age of twenty do not have full development of the frontal cortex and thus do not have the "biological machinery" to inhibit impulses. Adults, parents, and others, however, impose limits on youth behavior. It is immensely important that this age factor be considered in conceptualizing youth-adult relations.

GENDER AND SEXUAL ORIENTATION

The importance of gender and sexual orientation is well recognized in the human-service field. Sex and gender influence perceptions, behavior, and opportunity, and have a strong interactional dimension. Issues around gender-specific programming are complex and wield a tremendous amount of influence on day-to-day operations; they get a good share of attention in staff meetings and conferences. Sexual orientation, however, although important, does not receive equal air time.

Enhancement of capacities to aid youths in their transition to adulthood is often the goal that is most frequently mentioned in the youth-development field and in professional literature. Youths must be aware of and prepared for the challenges of the transition (Canada 1998; Gilligan 1982; Gilligan et al. 1988; Pipher 1994). If youth-development practice is oblivious to how gender and sexual orientation influences context and behaviors, it will not be able to advance.

However, gender-related considerations are not new to the field (Hansot 1993; Heath and McLaughlin 1993a; Scales and Leffert 1999). In 1991, the Carnegie Council on Adolescent Development (Nicholson 1991) issued a working paper on gender issues and youth-development practice. This report addressed several key questions: How similar or different are girls and boys at early adolescence? What is the history and current status of youth organizations when it comes to gender? What gender issues affect the informal education and enrichment offered by youth development programs? What are the implications of our current understanding of the effects of gender for planners of youth development programs? What difference does it make whether youth development programs are offered in mixed-sex or single-sex settings? What are the priorities for research in understanding the significance of gender in youth development programs? To this day, these questions have not been satisfactorily answered. Much more scholarship is needed.

In this book, gender is treated as a distinct factor that plays out throughout all aspects of a program, including the hiring of staff and how activities are conceptualized and carried-out. For girls, gender issues are a key factor in education (Orenstein 1994) and programming decisions (Henderson and King 1998). Henderson and King (1998: 16) noted: "Recent research . . . points to the ways that many girls lose self-esteem and confidence during adolescence. These changes are noteworthy because . . . professionals may need a different context to understand girls' lives today compared to the past if we want to play a role in their positive development. Further, we cannot assume that the risk issues that boys face are the same for all girls." However, a study by Erkut et al. (2000) came to a different conclusion. They found that early adolescent Puerto Rican boys and girls generally had high self-esteem and that there were no gender differences.

Recent attention on the early onset of puberty among girls ties the construct of gender to age (Belkin 2000). If girls are increasingly entering puberty at a younger age, this needs to be factored into programming decisions, particularly those involving mixed-gender groups of the same age. Whether there is, in fact, an onset of earlier puberty in girls is a matter of debate (Kolata 2001a, 2001b), but youth programs should take the matter seriously.

It would be irresponsible for a youth-development program involving girls not to address body image, particularly for girls of latency and adolescent age. Elementary school is widely considered to be the place where girls start to develop a sense of what is "good" and "bad" about their bodies; middle school is the place and time for girls to start dieting. Proper nutrition takes on added significance as part of a program that stresses discussion of body image, social pressures, and knowledge of body changes during puberty (Shartin 2001). Eating disorders overwhelmingly affect girls (90 percent of the total number of cases), which has important implications for youth-development activities in this area.

Gender-specific activities do not fall neatly into discrete categories since youth-development programs are greatly influenced by other considerations (e.g., geographical, age, race/ethnicity). Gender is, however, a key factor in how activities are selected for a program. Stereotypical activities, involving girls in cooking and active, physical games for boys, are outdated (although a fairly recent study based in New York City found that such activities were still alive and well in many programs. [Academy for Educational development 1997]).

Several authors note the importance of context in the making of choices for individual and group activities. In the following example, the factors involved include gender (girls), socioeconomic class (poor and working-class), and race (African American). Gaunt (1989) examines the game of double-dutch (jump roping) played by African American girls and the integration of black ideals in the songs used in the game. Willard (1989) focuses on skateboarding, which creates a sense of shared space and shared history among youths, primarily males.

Based on a review of the literature, Delgado (2000a) found three important differences in programming for stressed mixed (male and female) groupings and gender-specific activities: (1) Activities that are gender-specific facilitate the emergence of issues difficult to address in mixedgroups; (2) Gender-specific programs for girls tend to focus on sexual behavior and preventing problems such as teenage pregnancy;

and (3) Gender-specific programs for boys stress activities that are present-oriented (sports, dealing with peer pressure) and that will keep them out of trouble. Programming for girls stressed future roles in motherhood; unfortunately, leadership-role activity tended to be for males.

Gender roles are much influenced by cultural background: they dictate attire, communication patterns (verbal and nonverbal), ways of relating to the opposite sex, division of labor, and so forth, and cannot be ignored by staff (Heath and McLaughlin 1993b). Hansot (1993), however, strongly advocates that youth organizations endeavor to look "beyond the matter of gender mixing" in order to create ways of achieving cross-generation learning contexts for both sexes. Contexts that will provide youths with exposure to a range of gender-specific behaviors from which they can learn are much in need. Such activities should involve adults of both sexes.

Gender-specific programs have both supporters and critics. Delgado (2000a: 250) writes: "If programming activities are to provide youths with experiences that will better prepare them for living with the opposite sex it is a worthwhile goal. However . . . there is much to be said for single-sex programming, particularly for girls. . . . Creation of a 'sense of family,' which is often one of the goals of programming, necessitates having both boys and girls co-activity involved."

When we turn to how sexual orientation is dealt with in programming, we find that much work must be done. Mallon (1997), in one of the few publications specifically addressing sexual orientation and youth development, addresses strategies that can be used to welcome gay, lesbian, and bisexual youths into programs and to enhance the competencies of heterosexuals in relating to sexual orientation that is different from theirs. Misperceptions and fear-based attitudes are sometimes found in youth-development programs (Sanford 1999). Acceptance and celebration of gay, lesbian, bisexual, and transgender youth is not often reported in the professional and program-related literature. Program staff may argue, spuriously, that programs are welcoming of "all" youth regardless of sexual orientation; in some cases, they go so far as to say there are no gay, lesbian, bisexual, or transgender youth in their program and therefore the issue does not need to be addressed. Undeniably, the subject causes uneasiness in youth, staff, and parents.

The national debates about gays in the Boy Scouts of America and the U.S. Supreme Court decision backing that organization's right to exclude gays serve as reminders of the sensitivity of the subject (Boyle 2000a, 2000b,

2000c). Interestingly, the Girl Scouts do not discriminate against lesbians, their ability to embrace rather than exclude being traced to Girl Scout fundraising from nonexclusionary institutions, outside of mainstream religious channels.

Numerous things can be done to work on the issue. The subject of sexual orientation can be included in a program's policy statement where it addresses issues of nondiscrimination. Activities and discussions about sexual-orientation stereotypes can be developed. Written materials for gays, lesbians, bisexuals, and transgender youths can be made prominently available. A program might help youths to come out, although this process is complicated and requires serious thought and discussion (Boyle 2000a, 2000b 2000c). A warm and supportive environment can do wonders for youths struggling with this decision.

There is a cultural dimension to the sexual-orientation issue. Merighi and Grimes (2000) document how young gay people of color encounter particular problems and obstacles while coming out to family members. Because of ethnic, racial, and cultural background, youth of color who are gay may not feel comfortable coming out in a youth-development program because of family considerations. This decision must be respected.

However, having a "safe" place where homosexuality is accepted is very important. Mallon (1997: 601) specifically relates this to youth-serving organizations:

> In youth development with gay, lesbian, and bisexual youths and their families, recognizing the importance of supportive social networks is vital. Reflecting the social isolation faced by many gay, lesbian, and bisexual persons, close interpersonal ties are often limited or constrained. Intimate relationships with parents, siblings, children, and friends may become compromised and incomplete. Many gay, lesbian, and bisexual youths and families need assistance in healing current relationships and/or in developing new relationships to reduce their sense of isolation, achieve their goals, and enhance their well-being.

Program staff must not totally neglect this subject based on an assumption that there are no gays in the program and that the subject is therefore irrelevant. Even in a case where that assumption is correct, program youth will come into contact with those of a different sexual orientation. Their interactions with homosexual youths, therefore, must be addressed in the program, to whatever extent is mandated by local circumstances. The question then becomes one of degree, not one of whether it is addressed at all. Mallon (1996: 606) says, simply and eloquently, that the best way to serve gay, lesbian, and bisexual youth:

> is to provide them with the same types of supports and services that other adolescents need. Young people need organizations that offer them opportunities to take healthy risks, places where they can make real choices and contributions, and possibilities of forming lasting relationships. . . . It requires that adults pay as much attention to the environments that they create for youths as they do to the context of what they teach. . . . We must stop trying to fix youths, conceding instead that the key to youths is development, not repair.

YOUTH DEVELOPMENT AND DISABILITIES

The subject of disabilities has advanced in the last twenty years to become what can be considered a movement. Disabilities have gone from being a social issue into being a rights issue. The passage of the Americans with Disabilities Act in 1990 brought with it not only an increased awareness of people with disabilities but a legal mandate to eliminate barriers to their participation in society. French and Swain (1997: 203) note: "In ideological terms, the movement has developed and promoted a social model, in which disability is understood as a social rather than an individual condition. Disabled people have shifted the focus to the barriers faced in a society geared by and for non-disabled people. These barriers pervade every aspect of the physical and social environment."

Casting disabilities in a social context strengthens the view that society must eradicate barriers to people with disabilities achieving their potential (Nisbet 1992). When applied to youth development, the opportunities thus afforded to help youths with disabilities making the transition to adulthood cannot be squandered. The youth-development field must do some serious soul-searching as to how inclusive it is of youths with physical, cognitive, and emotional disabilities.

Few families do not have a family member with some form of disability. The rights and privileges of individuals with disabilities are now part of the national landscape, and the subject can no longer be limited to programs and services specifically established for individuals with disabilities. Universal access is just that—universal. Walsh (1999) acknowledges that despite recent progress in the area of disability rights, much work remains to be accomplished. This work goes far beyond providing physical accessibility. Attitudes about youths with disabilities—their level of competency—has not kept up with the progress in providing physical access. As part of the recent advances, integration of youth with disabilities into mainstream educational programs has greatly gained momentum. Effort, attention, and resources has gone into making classrooms and schools better fitted for students with disabilities. However, the same cannot be said of after-school programs. Fink (2000: xv) writes: "The lives of youngsters with disabilities do not end when they exit their classroom, and their participation in a wide variety of youth programs and recreational settings is becoming a fact of life in many communities. Yet this latter subject has drawn little focused attention from scholars, journalists, or even the family members of the participants."

Poertner and Ronnau (1992), writing about resiliency, focus specifically on youths who are emotionally and physically challenged. Youths with disabilities can be valuable and contributing members of society, but this can be accomplished only if society is prepared to recognize their strengths and if such youths are given the potential for continued learning and personal growth. We must create an atmosphere that accepts and celebrates all, regardless of cognitive, emotional, and physical challenges. This would benefit all youth. All of the core elements in youth-development programs (see chapter 5) can be tapped in providing services that include youths with disabilities.

To what extent is the field a part of this movement to include people with disabilities? It is very much open to question. Youth with disabilities very rarely take part in youth-development programs open to *all* youth. Segregated programming seems to be the norm. All too often, the literature focuses on programming for "typically" abled youth. But youths with disabilities, too, have strengths (Patterson and Blum 1996). They, too, possess assets that must be enhanced. Segregated into educational programs for people with disabilities, they have few opportunities to learn and play with "typical" youth (Fink 2000).

Accessibility should not be narrowly defined as physical. In many ways, physical accessibility is the least challenging task for youth-development programs. The most challenging is psychological accessibility. How are these youths to be accepted by "typical" youth and staff? Programs must seriously examine bias against those with disabilities and actively explore ways of involving such youths in all aspects of programming. Program modification is in order, however; modification is far more acceptable than exclusion.

The peer networks of youths with disabilities often consist of similarly situated youth. Self-esteem issues, not surprisingly, are often present. Peers can greatly influence self-esteem of group members. Delgado (2000a: 112) writes: "Self-esteem . . . cannot be separated from the influence of peers. Those youth that are an active, supportive, and positive peer support system are more likely to also have positive self-esteem. Thus, the increase in self-esteem is closely tied to activities involving groups of peers." Families of youths with disabilities, too, would benefit from having their children in a youth-development program. Youth-development programs can help the families to learn new strategies for assisting their children and help them to create opportunities for them in their communities.

Inclusion of youth with disabilities will present program staff with challenges. How to make the setting physically and psychologically accessible? What specialized training must staff obtain? How do programs address the subject of disabilities as part of the curriculum? How do we do so without reinforcing stereotypes?

Fink (2000)identified seven areas in which programs could foster greater and more meaningful integration of youth with disabilities: (1) The tailoring of activities to individual capacities (i.e., simply participating is insufficient); (2) The promotion of social interactions (competency in social relations is as important for youths with disabilities as it is for others; creating friendships for all participants needs to become an important priority); (3) Honest acknowledgment of differences (diversity must be understood to be broader than ethnicity and cultural heritage; the existence of multiple levels of ability is a part of diversity); (4) The widening of options for all participants (greater variety in program activity increases the likelihood of wide participation); (5) Increased opportunity for leaders to share (encouragement of communication by experts on inclusion will inform others); (6) Increased and more direct, open recruitment of youth with special needs (the more the merrier; increased numbers of youth with disabilities reduces isolation within a program, as does the hiring of staff with disabilities); (7) Flexibility in sports rules (rules are never cast in stone, and changing them to increase meaningful participation by youth with disabilities is preferable to excluding some members of a program from certain activities).

The youth-development field needs to think seriously about what role is it preparing youth with disabilities for as they enter adulthood. Is it preparing them to become adults with disabilities or adults who happen also to have disabilities? Youths with disabilities participating in youth-development programs cannot and should not be prepared to assume adult-with-disability roles; they must be prepared for adult roles, just like other participants. They just happen to have some form of disability, just as we all happen to be ... whatever: male, female, tall, short, African American, white, gay, straight. The list goes on and on.

PARTICIPATION: INVOLVING YOUTH IN DECISIONS

The term *participation* is often used in the field of human service; few programs totally exclude the term from their mission statements. Participation, which can be defined in many different ways, is well described as "a process of involving people in decisions that affect their lives" (Checkoway 1998: 767). Such a definition provides programs with a tremendous amount of latitude on how participation is to be operationalized. The literature has a multitude of frameworks that can guide practitioners in conceptualizing participation. It is best viewed as a continuum: at one end there is no participation, followed by minimal participation, or tokenism; at the other end is power to make decisions and control outcomes (Arnstein 1969; Burke 1979; Checkoway 1998; Sonenshein 1998).

Checkoway (1998), in an excellent analysis of youth participation, developed a five-part framework for viewing youth involvement in community-based initiatives. This framework places emphasis on decision making and the role of youth in these efforts: (1) Youth action groups (organizing for social and political action); (2) Youth-development agencies (involved in enhancement of capacities); (3) Neighborhood development (programs developed by youth that target their community); (4) Neighborhood-based initiative (integral connection between youth and neighborhood); (5) Citizen action (like the youth action groups, organizing for social and political action).

Viewing such a framework, we may ask: How meaningful is such activity? The tensions between process and outcome are not restricted to the youth-development field, but in this field, as with other initiatives that strive to empower and build upon assets, process takes on as great, if not greater, value than outcome. However, when it comes time for evaluation, funders invariably look toward outcomes as indicators of a program's success. In Delgado (2000a: 248), I came out on the side of process: "Practitioners must weigh the final outcome ('product'), with the importance of 'process.' . . . It would be wise for practitioners to conceptualize this dilemma along the lines that a 'product' without meaningful process is nothing more than an artifact." If process is meaningful, then positive outcome will follow. However, the opposite is not possible. Meaningful outcome without corresponding emphasis on process is meaningless.

Youth development simply cannot take place without active and meaningful involvement of youth in all aspects of programming. Participation is central to any activity undertaken within a youth-development perspective. Further, this participation must not be restricted to "input." Active and meaningful decision making must be the criterion used to measure youth-development success (Hahn and Raley 1997; Smilowitz 2000). Thus ways to measure participation must be developed as a central part of any formal program evaluation. Moreover, participation must be evaluated in a manner that is not artificial, such as relying on attendance records.

Activity design in this area must be flexible. Decision making for a group of five year olds will look dramatically different from that for a group of fifteen year olds. The former, however, can still be involved in decision making if they are encouraged to make the rules for an activity, this rule making being facilitated. The older group, on the other hand, may not need any facilitating. The younger children may also be given activities that promote cooperation, such as in pairing or in small groups (Michigan State University 2000). Gender, particularly in mixed-gender groups, may require staff to play a more active role, making sure that one gender group does not dominate the other.

Newcomers to this country who come out of cultural traditions where youths do not have an active voice within the family (as in the case of the author, who is Puerto Rican) will not participate in decision making as much as the native born. Although the process of acculturation may eventually take hold and thrust them into a comfort level regarding decision making, this evolution may place them at odds with their family, which may still view them as "voiceless." Help in negotiating these two worlds is needed in order for them to benefit from participation.

Adult involvement in youth-development programs is not only unavoidable but essential (LaMonaca 2000). However, the role of adults needs to be carefully thought out and monitored, as it was in the Kellogg Foundation's Youth Philanthropy initiative (Kellogg Foundation 1999: 6):

It is recommended that adult involvement be limited, allowing youth members to feel a sense of freedom to create without the potential imposition of adult ideas and influence. If the process is to work, youth must be completely in control of their own program. The adult roles throughout the programs are to act as mentor and facilitator, assisting the members during the allocation of funds and in the development of volunteer and community service projects. It is crucial to have adults oriented toward servant leadership, helping the young people realize their vision and work through the process, as opposed to having adults who are oriented toward finding fault, criticizing, and "doing for youth."

The Kellogg Foundation was very eloquent in how they cast the role of adults in their youth initiative. Adults need to be a guiding presence without exerting undue influence on the process—difficult as that might be. Adults play a role in creating a program climate that is encouraging, "being there" when needed, without being pushy. Adults are rarely comfortable with such roles, and special attention should be paid to this aspect of a program. Programs should screen staff with this in mind. Many, many years have gone into the forming of adults' opinions about youth, and it will take more than an in-service training workshop to erase such views.

Youth development and empowerment are closely related (Huebner 1998). According to the United Nations (World Sources Online: 2), youth development can be defined as

the development for the youth and by the youth. For this purpose, young people are to be empowered. They are empowered when they feel that they have or can create choices in life, are aware of the implications of those choices, make an informed decision freely, take action based on that decision and accept responsibility for the consequences of that action. Empowering young people means creating and supporting the enabling conditions under which young people are empowered.

The U.N. definition, by focusing on the role of empowerment, highlights the delicate role that adults must play. As in the Kellogg Foundation statement on decision making, adults and youth are indispensable partners in youth development. The relationship requires adult flexibility in role definition, a willingness to engage in process, and a determination about what is best for both youth and community. In this case, youth dictate the goals and how they can be operationalized (Bogenschneider 1996).

Huebner (1998), in summarizing the literature on empowerment and adolescents, notes three basic ways that the empowerment of youth can come about: (1) through the sharing of information (the withholding of information conveys a message of untrustworthiness); (2) through the creation of realistic autonomy (with teaching about rules and boundaries); and (3) through examination of the role of staff (emphasizing the importance of process).

Pittman (2000a: 34), quoting Barry Checkoway about "participation" sometimes in fact being business-as-usual in "sheep's clothing," sees a problem: "There is a tendency in the youth development field to accept all notions of youth participation and to embrace all forms of practice. Some of what passes today as 'youth participation' actually may be a new form of agency service delivery in disguise." This tendency must be guarded against. Youth participation in fact must be explicitly referred to in the mission statement of an organization; and it must be operationalized in a way that is observable and measurable. An often-used strategy that helps ensure that youth participation is not tokenism is having youth members of an organization's board of directors (National Assembly 1998). However, youth must not occupy such seats without being able to make informed decisions. They need a firm basis, and must be prepared to accept the responsibility that goes with the opportunity to exercise power. This requires soul-searching by adults, who have to come to grips with the difficult real-life task of sharing power.

THE PLACE OF PREVENTION IN YOUTH DEVELOPMENT

Murphy (1995b: 10) addresses the basic differences and commonalties between prevention and promotion-based approaches to youth:

> An issue discussed is the relationship between prevention and youth development, which includes service, support, and opportunity. The United States, unequivocally, has adopted a prevention model of programming that aims to reduce the incidence of problem behaviors. The limitation of prevention, however, is that it narrows the perspective

about what youth can accomplish and what youth need to achieve positive outcomes.

The recent attention on youth resiliency and strengths has been influential in increasing the attractiveness of youth development as an arena for practice (Bernard 1997a, 1997b, 1993a, 1993b, 1993c, 1987; Blum 1998; Bogenschneider 1996; Rutter 1987 1993). Bernard (1997b: 13) comments on the lasting appeal of the term *resilient*: "While many terms were used early-on to describe these survivors and thrivers, the term 'resilient,' implying springing-back, has stuck and is used to describe successful adaptation, growth, and development despite exposure to severe stress and adversity." Some practitioners define resiliency as the ability to display competence despite adversity (Gordon and Coscarelli 1996). The term has also been used with reference to youth with disabilities (Kysela et al. 1996; Patterson and Blum 1996). Much of the attention paid to resilience comes out of the work undertaken by prevention programs targeting drugs, violence, and pregnancy (Gabriel et al. 1996; Smokoski 1998). Werner and Smith (1992), in their classic research on resilient and nonresilient youth in Hawaii, found that resilient youth were more likely than their nonresilient counterparts to engage in extracurricular activities.

The field of prevention has embraced the constructs of resilience/protection and risk, grounded in ecological and developmental contextualist theories, and this in turn has informed the youth-development paradigm (Bogenschneider 1996; Catalano et al. 1998; Larson 2000; Mundy 1986; Perkins and Villarruel 2000; Rake and Patterson 1996). Moore and Glei (1995), for example, developed a "positive well-being" index that uses multiple measures of positive development.

The Moore and Glei index consists of two measures. One focuses on the avoidance of multiple forms of risk; the other focuses on determinants of positive development. Risk is a complex concept and can entail any or all of the following activities: exploration, imagination, establishing new relationships with peers, achieving new levels of autonomy, establishing new identity and values (National Research Council 1999).

The field of prevention has made significant strides in the last ten to twenty years. Funders, most notably the federal government and major foundations, have placed increasing emphasis on development of model programs and more research has been undertaken in this arena. There is also wider acceptance of moving away from narrowly focused programs that look only at one risk-taking behavior (Catalano et al. 1998: 18):

> Research showed that many of the same risk and protective factors predict diverse adolescent problems . . . that problem behaviors are correlated with each other . . . and typically cluster within the same individuals and reinforce each other. . . . These findings suggested the need for more comprehensive or "non-categorical" approaches for preventing a broad range of youth problems. . . . Like youth development practitioners, prevention scientists became increasingly dissatisfied with a single-problem approach to prevention.

Historically, prevention programs have generally been categorically funded to address specific social problems. This rather narrow focus has limited a broader enhancement perspective. Youth, as a result, are not looked at holistically. Many of the social problems facing youth in socially and economically marginalized communities are not separated from each other—an unrealistic perspective that seeks to compartmentalize behavior. Youth, in turn, get the impression that only certain types of risk-taking behavior are important—a message that may not be sent explicitly but that is nevertheless perceived.

Beck (1999) traces the evolution of prevention programs from problem-specific to a current-day holistic perspective. Benard (1997b), Dryfoos (1991), Husock (1993), and Nobles and Goddard (1992) stress the importance of broadening prevention initiatives.

The lessons learned from years of funding prevention initiatives have resulted in a broadening of this perspective to more enhancement-focused goals, and have therefore blurred the distinction between prevention, in the conventional sense, and youth development (Catalano, et al. 1998: 19):

> All of these developments led prevention scientists to call for a broader focus in prevention interventions: The identification of important connections between risk and protective factors and youth outcomes; the evidence that problem behaviors share many common antecedents; the evidence that the number of risk and protective factors to which a youth is exposed strongly affects the youth's likely outcomes; the importance of factoring age-appropriate task demands and processes

into prevention program design; and documentation that early initiation of problem behavior is itself a predictor of poor outcomes.

Bond (2000) looks at the field of prevention as entering its adolescent identity period and notes that the field's potential can be realized only through taking a broad perspective. Honig (2000) argues for the use of prevention initiatives focused on the family, school, and neighborhood. This entails thinking about prevention across systems (domains) and through the lifespan. Jason et al. (2000) advocate for interventions to target the community-wide level. Uhl (2000), on the other hand, cautions the field not to oversell itself in ever-expanding its spheres of influence.

The prevention field has likely fed many staff members into youth-development programs (I have no data to substantiate this point, however). Staff with prevention backgrounds bring a wealth of experience and knowledge to the field—a crossover that has further blurred the distinction between the two fields. The prevention field, like its youth-development counterpart, has started to target peers and adults in multiple domains such as family and school (Coie et al. 1993; LoSciuto et al. 1999). This trend, in combination with a more holistic view of youth and their assets and needs, also serves to blur distinctions between the two paradigms.

Prevention efforts have largely focused on at-risk youth—youth who, based on a set of socioeconomic criteria, were considered to be at higher risk of engaging in antisocial behavior. In prevention programs, risk characteristics are foregrounded; they are given prominence in recruitment and programming. Assets (strengths) are relegated to the background. Sometimes such significance is given to the the at-risk perspective that programs simply ignore assets.

The concept of risk, like that of assets or strengths, must be thought of as a continuum from very strong to very weak; but strong or weak, it is well to remember it is still a risk (Bembry 1998). Blum (1998), too, makes this point when commenting on how risk and resilience as a conceptual model has successfully captured the imagination of researchers and program planners over the past decade. Resilience, however, implies resistance to threat, but it must be conceptualized as a graded phenomenon. Cumulative risk can overwhelm the most resilient child.

Paying particular attention to the weight of an asset or risk provides important information for programming. Thus, the mere presence of an asset or risk is not sufficient for purposes of programming. And a focus on risks and assets must not be solely focused on individuals. An environmental perspective is needed to better understand the significance of these factors in the lives of youth (Baines and Selta 1999; Bogenschneider 1996; Santiago 2000; Stanton-Salazar 2000).

It is important to note that a risk does not have to be the opposite of an asset factor. Volunteering and engaging in community service is widely considered an asset; however, failure to volunteer or engage in community service is not a risk factor. The conceptualization of these two constructs can be completely different.

The parallels between youth-development and prevention programs are striking to the average practitioner and observer. According to the U.S. Department of Education (1994), characteristics of effective prevention programs are: (1) they actively seek to respond to youth needs and interests; (2) they are comprehensive in scope; (3) they promote positive development and resiliency; and (4) they actively reach out to youth who are at-risk and do so through involvement of families and communities.

Funders create very formalized methods for gathering information that is problem-specific (that is what they consider to be important). Documentation tends to focus on, for example, rather common problems such as an ability to abstain from sexual intercourse or criminal behavior. Keeping youth out of trouble becomes a priority. This is also relatively easy to measure. Most methods for gathering data are quantitative in nature. Qualitative methods, as a result, are either ignored or relegated to secondary importance.

The deemphasis on assets is also very troubling from a conceptual and practice viewpoint. Bogenschneider (1996) goes on to argue that an asset perspective or paradigm may encounter obstacles in mobilizing parents and significant community stakeholders to mobilize in service to community. Risks/problems/issues seem to capture the imagination and attention more than do resiliency, assets, and strengths. They certainly do for the media. A resiliency perspective assumes that youth have an innate capacity to grow and mature. This capacity is natural and observable to both adults and other youth. It becomes a question of how can their capacities be enhanced? This perspective necessitates that programs gather information that is holistic and focused on positive actions and achievement rather than emphasizing narrow and specific problem behaviors. It would be an incredible step forward in the field of youth development to develop categories of resiliency that have the same level of depth, intensity, conceptual acceptance, and legitimacy (expertise, institutional, ethical, and consumer) that deficit-oriented categories now enjoy (Pittman 2000a, 2000b).

Pittman, one of the earliest advocates of youth development, goes on to note (2000a: 55): "I would retire with a small sense of accomplishment if this new knowledge and evidence could be used to help define and demonstrate the elements of effective programming and sound practice for developing fully prepared youth." A focus on resiliency allows youth to celebrate their talents and what they bring to programs. It also facilitates youth coming because of their talents rather than having their "common" problems be the organizing element behind their participation.

✑

Much progress has been achieved in bringing the field of youth development into the twenty-first century (Larson 2000). A number of organizations, practitioners, and funding sources have combined to increase the visibility of this field as a legitimate practice arena. But if this form of practice is to make it through the next decade, it will have to make a lot of progress. Youth development tends to mean all things to all people; appealing as that may be, the challenges ahead necessitate that some degree of consensus be achieved (McKenna 2000).

The topics addressed in this chapter are those that influence how youth development is practiced across this country. If youth development is to better prepare youth to transition to adulthood, it must do so in a highly diverse society—one that consists of people with disabilities, people with cultural customs that differ from those of the dominant culture, people whose sexual orientations is other than heterosexual. We cannot walk away from these subjects because they are unpopular and cause uneasiness. The youth-development field can play a leading role in how these subjects are addressed.

Recent attention on how resiliency and risk factors influence youth development is exciting (Booth and Crouter 2001). These factors are extremely complex and difficult to disentangle from a host of other factors; nevertheless, a conscientious effort to better understand and incorporate strategies to enhance resiliency and diminish risk factors holds much promise for the field of youth development. Resiliency and risk factors cannot be totally divorced from the considerations addressed in this chapter. Age, gender, sexual orientation, ethnicity/race, and emotional, physical and cognitive challenges all serve to contextualize resiliency and risk. Neighborhood effects on youth, for example, will not be uniform across all age and gender groups (South 2001). Neighborhood conditions might wield a greater influence on young women than on young men (Spencer 2001; South 2001). Thus, a dynamic and contextualized perspective is needed to better put into practice the principles, domains, and core elements that the following chapters explore.

5 / YOUTH DEVELOPMENT: PRINCIPLES AND CORE ELEMENTS

WHAT IS meant by youth development? So far, this book has probably raised more questions than it has answered on that score. Multiple definitions that are sufficiently broad do not make it easy to grasp what this paradigm is all about. Yet theoretical concepts play an increasingly important role in defining and operationalizing a youth-development paradigm—something that will be noted throughout this book. The importance of theory has not received the attention it deserves from practitioners.

Theory should not be the exclusive domain of academics; practitioners, too, need to own and help shape it (Dosher 1996: 11): "The word theory is too often viewed as an esoteric word that has no practical meaning. In fact, theory is of the utmost practical importance because theories are distillations of our knowledge and understanding of the world. Theories represent the general principles drawn from a body of facts and observations. Without them, we could not learn because we would have no means to provide a coherent structure to our observations." This chapter therefore draws extensively upon theoretical concepts in helping to ground key core elements of youth development. Principles for youth-development practice can serve a unifying function for practitioners in their quest to make sense out of a confusing situation. Principles, through the purposeful categorization of information and the subsequent planning of activities, help practitioners to focus (Adams 2000) and thus see the field's potential to transform lives. A set of the most common types of principles is presented. These principles can be added to or dropped depending upon local circumstances; either way, they capture the essence of youth development. However, consensus on youth-development principles and philosophy involves a set of expectations and pressures. As Murphy (1995b: 24) writes: "Adoption of a youth development philosophy will put new demands on staff as they will have to strengthen their existing competencies consistent with new expectations. In a similar fashion, a youth development philosophy will put new demands on organizations as they will have to strengthen their staff development strategies, or create new ones, to enable staff to learn, sustain, and excel in their work."

Identification and use of core elements that can be used in guiding the selection and construction of youth-development activities is a natural extension of practice principles. These core elements (cognitive, emotional, health, moral, social, and spiritual) form the basis for programming and they help practitioners to prioritize the goals of their programs. Elements can be chosen in many combinations, and local circumstances will dictate how they are put into effect.

This chapter provides an appreciation of how the core elements actually influence programming. There is no lack of ways for bringing them to life since numerous activities can both develop and enhance them. Competencies—skills—in the core areas are necessary for youth to successfully transition to adult roles (Carnegie Council on Adolescent Development 1989; Catalano et al. 1998). An understanding of the interrelationship between principles and core elements serves to contextualize youth development and provides a foundation for examining other essentials of youth-development practice.

A word of caution is in order at this point. The paucity of literature and studies focused on younger-age groups is very troubling. It seems almost as though the field of youth development, maybe as the result of funding pressures, has neglected to better understand the needs of younger children in regards to youth development programming. Much work must be accomplished in this area if we are to conceptualize youth development across the lifespan, rather than for a particular age group.

THE IMPORTANCE OF PRINCIPLES

I am fond of principles. For some practitioners, principles are too vague, too subject to interpretation, but they have aided me in applying theory to circumstances—to situations that were not taught at graduate school, addressed at professional conferences, or written about in the professional literature. Anyway, I welcome any tool that will help practitioners to address the ambiguity that is often inherent in the field of human services. New ethnic and racial groups, for example, are now present across the United States; however, no course on cultural diversity or multicultural practice can possibly prepare a practitioner for all newcomers to a community. As practitioners, we simply cannot be left to our intuitions for help in the field, and principles of practice are sufficiently detailed to supply help in managing ambiguity without being so specific as to handcuff creativity. The principles of practice represent the best of all possible worlds.

Practice principles should play an influential role in carrying forth the paradigm into the field (Pittman and Zeldin 1995: 2): "Defining practice principles is integral to the effectiveness of any organization but critical to effectiveness of those organizations approaching work with youth and families from a development rather than a problem perspective; and, linking principles to practice within an organization or to standards of practice across organizations is a challenging and sometimes controversial task."

Pittman and Zeldin (1995) argue that it is not possible, let alone advisable, to think one has clarity about youth-development practice without pausing to identify its key premises and principles. Failure to do so will result in wasted energy, frustration, and at best an incomplete definition. Pittman and Zeldin advocate a process of dialogue that will examine the premises and principles that practitioners believe in.

Principles provide practitioners with important direction and guidelines for conducting practice (Adams 2000). In addition, principles act as a natural bridge between abstract theoretical concepts and real issues in the field. Principles integrate knowledge (experiential and theoretical), values, and assumptions. They can play an instrumental role in shaping practice across different geographical, organizational settings and population groups. It is not, in fact, possible to practice youth development without a set of principles, although they may be either explicitly or implicitly stated. Many of the more common youth-development principles are in many ways not unique to youth-development practice (Delgado 2000; Heath and McLaughlin 1993b; Lakes 1996; Youniss and Yates 1997). The stress on strengths, community assets, participation, empowerment, cultural heritage, and community service can be found in most definitions of community capacity enhancement (Delgado 2000b). Capacity-enhancement practice systematically identifies, mobilizes, and incorporates indigenous community resources (formal and informal) into an intervention.

Youth development can easily be placed in the broader conceptualization of community capacity enhancement, although youth development is, of course, age-specific. The University of Washington School of Social Work (1998) identified fifteen descriptions of youth-development programs and core elements. In this list, youth development (1) promotes bonding; (2) fosters resilience; (3) promotes social competence; (4) promotes emotional competence; (5) promotes cognitive competence; (6) promotes behavioral competence; (7) promotes moral competence; (8) fosters self-determination; (9) fosters spirituality; (10) fosters self-efficacy; (11) fosters clear and positive identity; (12) foster belief in the future; (13) provides recognition for positive behavior; (14) provides opportunities for prosocial involvement; and (15) fosters prosocial norms. Their list was based on an extensive review of the literature, interviews, and other sources. Delgado (2000A) identified fourteen principles for programming that targets use of the arts, humanities, and sports. These principles focus on a set of activities that lend themselves to use with urban, marginalized youth of color. To be effective, programs must

1 Seek to deepen creativity, provide critical tools for negotiating developmental stages, and provide multiple avenues for the processing of cognitive information
2 Emphasize innovative, dynamic, and comprehensive approaches to serving youth
3 Provide youths with opportunities to succeed and contribute to their community
4 Build on youth assets and what youths value
5 Have multiple clear, high, and realistic expectations for participants
6 Provide youths with a sanctuary wherein they can generalize their learning—and in a fun manner
7 Be voluntary and provide youth with decision-making powers in shaping programming
8 Be built on quality staff and programming and a willingness to invest resources in support of staff
9 Emphasize positive intergenerational mentoring relationships
10 Actively seek to involve parents and other people significant in the lives of participants
11 Require long-term institutional commitment and seek to be comprehensive
12 Serve as vehicles for delivering conventional services to youth, if necessary in unconventional settings and at unconventional times.
13 Systematically involve other organizations (formal and informal)
14 Stress the importance of interethnic/racial relations among participants by preparing them to live in a multicultural world

These descriptions address the importance of systematic thinking on a subject that is immensely and increasingly complex. Some readers or their organizations will undoubtedly have their own sets of principles. When the principles between practitioner and organization are similar, there will be few misunderstandings, differing expectations, or tensions. When the opposite is the case, unfortunate consequences can be expected. Obtaining clarity regarding principles is an essential first step in any form of youth development. Time spent in examining principles before engaging in practice is time well spent. It is also advisable to have youth participants identify the principles that should guide a program. These principles, in the youths' own words when possible, can be compiled, distributed, and put on display.

Youths can also be helped to identify a set of principles that can guide their lives—a process that can be enlightening. The author has found this activity to be very effective in highlighting group differences based on gender and cultural background.

THE CORE ELEMENTS—FROM THE PHYSICAL TO THE SPIRITUAL

Many foundations, government agencies, professional associations, and academic reports have focused on identifying and detailing core elements, or constructs, of youth development (Carnegie Corporation 1989; Catalano et al. 1998; National Collaboration for Youth 1998). These core elements form the basis for the creation of strategies and activities. Although the strategies and activities vary according to setting (see chapter 7), the core elements are, as the term states, central to youth development. Youth development uses these elements as a foundation.

The Carnegie Corporation (1989) identified five characteristics that fifteen-year-olds must possess to become effective human beings. Such a youth should (1) be intellectually reflective; (2) have a direction toward a lifetime of meaningful employment; (3) be a good citizen; (4) be caring and ethical; and (5) be healthy.

Meyer (1999) used the term *life skills* for such coping behaviors and attitudes. No intervention can prevent youth from encountering challenges in life, but skills can help them weather the storms. Little (1993) conceptualizes resiliency-based youth-development programs as consisting of four dimensions: (1) Development of life-skill competencies; (2) Connections of youth to caring adults (involves mentoring, tutoring, community service, leadership development); (3) Character development (decision making, values, honesty, integrity); and (4) Confidence building (hope and self-esteem; setting and meeting goals). These four aspects of programming prepare youth for successful functioning in a variety of domains. Core elements can be found in each of these dimensions, with core elements cutting across different dimensions.

Larson (2000) focuses on the importance of initiative, a construct associated with capacity for autonomous action in positive youth development. It involves multiple core elements. Creativity, leadership, altruism, and civic engagement are outgrowths of initiative. This construct is grounded in a Western cultural context—one that has a capitalist-driven central ideology. One can argue that striving for autonomy is itself based on a Western value, and may well conflict with the cultural values of youth from nondominant cultures: the perspective of such cultures may stress interdependence or dependence. We can thus see that contextualization is a key to helping programs decide how core elements are to be integrated and prioritized in their activities.

Economic self-sufficiency, a goal often associated with being a successful adult, cannot be achieved without a constellation of core elements being present (Santiago 2000). Self-esteem, self-efficacy (an ability to set and achieve personal goals), and positive identity require a range of core elements. Possessing a sense of identity and self-definition, for example, does not rest with one core element; nor does it take place in one domain of influence, such as the family (Hudson 1997). When constructing indices to rate program success, a comprehensive approach that ties together multiple core-elements should be taken—an approach that, incidentally, makes the job of youth development that much more challenging and rewarding.

Youth development does not occur independently of environment; it is best thought of as a positive adaptation to surroundings (Blum 1998; Bandura 1979; Harter 1987; Perkins and Villarruel 2000; Sameroff and Chandler 1975). Such an interactive and dynamic process brings together the concepts of resilience, competence, and development (Bandura 1979; Blum 1998). Supportive environments tap into resiliency factors, which in turn develop competencies. These competencies enhance youth development through the life cycle. Too great a focus on the individual misses this interactive dimension and simplifies the complexity of the constructs covered in this chapter. Staff therefore need to develop a consensus definition of what "community" means to the program (see chapter 6). Further, an organizational effort should try to identify community assets. Since it is unlikely that any organization has a consensus definition of community assets, achievement of such a goal will be difficult.

Benard (1997: 17) discusses how a resiliency perspective influences all elements and aspects of youth development:

Resiliency research also has elucidated the nature of effective developmental supports and opportunities. It has shown that healthy development is an ongoing process—of meeting basic developmental needs through caring relationships, high expectation messages, and opportunities for participants. It challenges the youth development—and prevention and education —fields to move beyond a focus on program and what we do, to an emphasis on process and how we do what we do; to move beyond a fixation with content to a focus on context.

Benard's challenge to the field—a tall order—cannot be disregarded.

Although some writers emphasize certain core elements over others, or leave some out altogether, the six core elements listed above—health, emotional, social, cognitive, moral, and spiritual—are routinely identified in the literature. How they are operationalized of course depends on local definition and contextualization. Although each core element is distinctive in its own right, they have aspects that overlap. A holistic perspective is needed, but each will be discussed separately to help readers comprehend their importance. When the core elements are thoroughly grounded in gender, sexual orientation, ethnic/racial, and physical and cognitive abilities, a true appreciation of how they complement and reinforce each other can then be made.

The social domains are also distinctive yet overlapping: youth, family, school, peer group, and community (Beck 1999; Feely 1995; Guest 1995; Hernandez, Siles, and Rochin 2000; Hughes and Nichols 1995; Wahl 1995). The interrelationship between core elements can be extensive, as in the case of activities targeting cognition. Bembry (1998: 30) writes:

The interrelationship of education and other program objectives include: how math increases the ability to problem solve and how problem solving relates to the ability to resolve conflicts; how through reading and demonstration a person can increase their knowledge and skills about an area of interest; and how communicating in writing and learning a foreign language increases a youth's ability to function in a multicultural society.

THE COGNITIVE

Cognition is a central core element of youth development. The conventional view would have cognition-related goals resting in school or preschool programs, but it is foolhardy to associate cognition only with formal schooling. In the words of Beyth-Marom and Fischhoff (1997: 111): "Adolescence is a time of choices. It involves gaining autonomy, assuming responsibility, and making choices about health, family, career, peers, and school. The ability to confront these decisions effectively is essential to teen's well-being." Cognition needs to be viewed much more broadly venue in order to appreciate its role in helping youth achieve maximum potential.

Cognition is an integral part of programming and activities. More often than not, its role is implicit, since the teaching of academic (problem solving/decision-making) subjects, if labeled as such, may be off-putting to youth. Unfortunately, this society often places too much emphasis on cognitive abilities, which translate into "smarts," "IQ," "academic achievement," or "intelligence." Cognition, however, is too important to be so narrowly defined

Howard Gardner's (19983) pioneering research on multiple intelligences is an excellent example of the importance of not taking a narrow view of cognition. As is the case with multiple intelligences, a definition of intelligence would include inter- and intrapersonal intelligence, spatial, musical, linguistic, bodily kinesthetic, and logical-mathematical intelligence. Each of these aspects needs to be developed and enhanced in schools, but schools, unfortunately, typically focus on linguistic and logical-mathematical to the exclusion or minimization of the others (Zeldin, Kimball, and Price 1995).

Rauner (2000) notes that cognitive goals can be achieved through community service, particularly when it is sponsored and supervised by schools. Service learning can enhance problem-solving skills and critical thinking, two important aspects of cognition.

Catalano et al. (1998) have conceptualized cognition as a two-part core element: (1) as an ability to apply reasoning skills, and (2) as an academic and intellectual achievement. Cognitive competence (W. T. Grant Consortium on the School-Based Promotion of Social Competence 1992: 136) has also been defined as "the ability to develop and apply the cognitive skills of the self-talk, the reading and interpretation of social clues, using steps for problem-solving and decision-making, understanding the perspective of others, understanding behavioral norms, a positive attitude toward life, and self-awareness."

The latter definition of cognition broadens this construct to cover acquisition of subject content matter and the active process of knowledge acquisition. This process is not, however, restricted to academic learning. It is well understood that an adolescent's view of the world (social cognition) differs from that of an adult, and this affects decision making (National Research Council 1999) (emotional state, too, influences decision making, which supplies an example of overlap, or interrelationship, between two core elements).

Increased self-esteem may result from increased cognitive competence (Beck 1999). However, cognitive competence may be difficult, if not impossible, to achieve without a grounding in cultural heritage. The interrelationships between cognition, self-esteem, and cultural heritage necessitate the use of activities that creatively involve youth in exploring their cultural heritage while developing "academic" skills. This requires that careful thought go into the creation of an activity. An example might be researching the origins of certain cultural traditions or artifacts and developing an exhibit. Another example might be writing and producing a play on a historical event of significance in the life of an ethnic/racial group. Conventional academic skills play an active role in both of these activities (analytical, communication, study habits, research).

The need to create alternative solutions and create change in frustrating, possibly dangerous, situations requires competencies that can best be thought of as cognitive (Corwin 2000; National Youth Development Information Center 2000). These skills provide youth with tools to help them negotiate difficult situations with peers and other significant people in their lives. We can thus see that a cognitive core element is not restricted to "academic" subject matter, and since successful transition to adulthood often rests on cognitive competencies, this is no small matter.

Schustack et al. (1994: 48) report how cognition lessons learned in an after-school computer-oriented youth-development program transferred over to the school domain: "Many focal areas in our program are related to the knowledge and skills taught in traditional schools. We have a strong focus on the basic skills of reading, writing, and mathematics, as well as on geography and science. There is overlap with school learning in some of the content of the instructional play materials as well." Although the authors stress the transfer of cognitive skills to schools, the new-found competencies can also be used in all other social domains. Their description of the successful benefits of a math activity illustrates the importance of an activity integrating more than one element.

Cognitive skills help prepare youth for life in society (Hudson 1997). However, vocation is only part of what life is about. The W. K. Kellogg Foundation's initiative combining youth development and job readiness illustrates well how these two goals are complementary and can be achieved through creative use of community partnerships (Richmond (2000). This is not to say that youth-development programs must eschew any form of academic activities that have a vocational goal. The "new frontier settings" described later in this book rely extensively on vocation-related activities to recruit and engage youth.

Many conventional and unconventional sources can be tapped to help youth-development programs address this core element in activities. Cognitive skills grounded in a community context take on special meaning for participants. The well-known Children's Television Workshop provides another example of an unusual resource. The television team developed materials and activities for use in after-school programs, and their experience can serve as a lesson for all youth-centered programs. One activity focused on math skills but carried over to social relations. As Martin and Ascher (1994: 18–19) describe it:

> The kits . . . provided many chances for children to practice cooperation. Particularly in the math games, children often evolved cooperative group practices, especially after they had played a game long enough to develop sound strategies. Children often shared strategies with each other, explaining why one would work more successfully than another. The object of the games shifted from winning to playing well, and children teamed up to beat the game rather than each other.

These social skills, particularly those involving peer-to-peer relations, are developed naturally in the process of carrying out an activity if staff also seek to foster within-group social relations. A cognitive and social core element combined to make this activity's impact far greater than it may appear on the surface.

THE EMOTIONAL

Play word association with the word *adolescent* and it will not be long before the word *emotional* emerges. Emotionality is ever-present in everything youth do. Sometimes this element is thought of as "mental health" (Peterson et al. 1997). (I think the same thing could be said about adults; however, youth seem to have a corner on the market where this word is concerned.)

The core element of emotion is generally broken down into several categories in youth-development practice. These might be ability to (1) empathize; (2) display appropriate emotions; (3) control anger; (4) identify and label feelings; (5) motivate oneself; (6) inspire hope in one-self and others; (7) delay gratification; (8) establish and maintain relationships; (8) establish self-worth; and (9) tolerate frustration. These abilities, not surprisingly, are interrelated and may be present in varying degree (Beck 1999; Goleman 1995; Meyer 1999; W. T. Grant Consortium on the School-Based Promotion of School Competence 1992). Such a list of highlights this core element's multifaceted nature. It impacts on relationships, self-worth, cognition, and perceptions, as well as hopes for life. The complexity of this core element—its pervasiveness—necessitates that programs be ever-vigilant for ways to help youth develop emotional competencies, both for the transition to adulthood and to help them in current situations (Hudson 1997).

Salvey and Mayer (1990) developed a five-part framework for categorizing emotional competence in youth: (1) awareness of one's emotions; (2) managing emotions; (3) motivating oneself; (4) recognizing emotions in others; and (5) handling emotions. These aspects highlight the interactive nature of this core element. Programs need to need to build activities that enhance these competencies. Motivating oneself, for example, taps into what Larson (2000) describes as "initiative," and motivation (or lack of it) is complex and may well be influenced by the experiences a participant has had in the past. For a youth who has been encouraged and supported, even when having failed at a task, the willingness to take chances will be different than that for someone who has not had encouragement and support. A youth-development program may have to use different strategies to have the latter participant take a risk on an activity.

The core element of emotion easily illustrates that the core elements are interrelated. Recent research shows the interactions between emotions and decision making, for example, and how adolescents differ from adults. The National Research Council (1999: 11) reported that

> emotions affect how people think and behave and influence the information they attend to. When people are experiencing positive emotions, they tend to underestimate the likelihood of negative conse-

quences to their actions; when they are experiencing negative emotions, they tend to focus on the near term and lose sight of the big picture. Both adolescents' and adults' decision-making abilities are influenced by emotions. However, there is evidence that adolescents experience more intense emotions than adults, which suggests that they may process information differently and therefore make different decisions then adults do.

This core element also plays an influential role in helping youth better understand family, their role in this domain, and how family/youth interactions carry over into other domains. Interestingly, youth-development programs often seek to help youth to practice with what they have learned in other aspects of their lives. Family, for better or worse, depending on circumstances, is a domain that can benefit from youth becoming more in touch with their emotions. A family-systems perspective, as a result, is helpful in guiding staff about the consequences of youth participation on their families.

Addressing an emotional core element also serves to address other core elements—cognition, health, social, moral, and spiritual. Many practitioners would argue forcefully that avoidance of the emotional element in programming for adolescents would effectively render interventions fruitless.

PHYSICAL HEALTH

Optimal health is of prime importance in the lives of youth if they are to meet their challenges (Giarratano-Russell 1998; Noack and Kracke 1997). Optimal health not only covers physical status but also possession of knowledge, attitudes, and behaviors regarding well-being (Henderson 1998; Hudson 1997; Millstein, Petersen, and Nightingale 1993; National Youth Development Information Center 2000). Blum (1998 ties in health promotion specifically to the identification and mobilization of resiliency factors. In determining how health is conceptualized and how health-enhancement behavior is carried out day by day, sociocultural context is highly influential.

Millstein, Petersen, and Nightingale (1993) stress the importance of health promotion. They define health in the broadest sense, including physical, psychological, social, and environmental aspects. These authors go on to argue (1993: 7) that any program focused on adolescent health must necessarily be grounded in context:

The recognition that individualized programs are most effective in the context of societal and community change greatly complicates the implementation of health promotion programs. Such a perspective requires not only commitment by individuals to make adolescents a priority, but also cooperation and coordination of complex bureaucratic institutions . . . by not limiting the responsibility for adolescent health to one person or one institution, we make multiple responsibilities for promotion to occur.

Context determines how health and other core elements are conceptualized and addressed (Farmer, Krochalk, and Silverman 1998; Noack and Kracke 1997; Villarruel and Lerner 1994a). Health of families, for example, has an impact on youth and their willingness to seek services (Galambos and Ehrenberg 1997). Failure to understand the contextualization of health results in the imposition of values that may not only be foreign to participants but that may systematically undermine their cultural traditions.

Health promotion, like youth development, is most effective when defined in a broad and highly contextualized manner (Lerner, Ostrom, and Freel 1997). Health promotion, therefore, needs to be comprehensive and ambitious (Earls 1993; Earls, Cairns, and Mercy 1993; Hingson and Howland 1993; Maggs, Schulenburg, and Hurrelmann 1997; Millstein, Petersen, and Nightingale 1993). This greatly enhances the possibilities for community-wide involvement. Feetham's (1998: 325) definition of health promotion touches on its applicability for use in multiple arenas:

Health promotion is a multidisciplinary concept that is on a continuum ranging from disease prevention to optimal health and that emphasizes physical capabilities and social and personal resources. Most causes of mortality and morbidity in children and adolescents are a result of behavior and lifestyle and technically could be prevented through behavior change. . . . Health promotion activities are the primary means of achieving this change.

Note that this health-promotion perspective stresses capacities rather than deficits.

Youths of course undergo rapid and dramatic physical changes—changes that take on greater prominence they enter the late latency and adolescent periods (Belkin 2000). There is a tremendous need to provide youth with information about these changes. It is important, however, not to focus exclusively on the "physical," as they are occurring or about to occur. It is important to mention that the standards used to measure these physical changes relate to the norms of the groups youth belong to and not the norms of the dominant culture (an approach that, incidentally, must be used with all age groups and for all activities—gender, ethnicity/race, disabilities, and sexual orientation).

Leisure studies, especially in the area of sports, have increased in popularity the last two decades, both nationally and internationally (Roberts 1983). These studies have generally shown the importance of gender, race/ethnicity, and socioeconomic class in determining how youth use free time. Fine (1989) has taken the position that leisure activities need to be conceptualized by their capacity to mobilize resources ("provisioning theory"). The more successful the activity, the greater the efficient use of resources. Resources refer to materials, time, and space, and programs need to provide sufficient resources (material and symbolic) in order to maximize their inherent potential for benefits—instrumental and expressive.

Henderson and King (1998)—specifically addressing gender—note that recreational programming for females cannot be predicated on the same risk issues as those faced by males. Recreational programming cannot ignore that negative self-images for girls are possible because of this society's sexism.

Recreational programs cannot pass up the opportunity of addressing core elements in addition to physical development. The challenge becomes how to make a sporting activity, for example, a meaningful experience for both males and females—an experience that goes beyond physical exercise and teaches a lesson that can be tapped into in later life. For example, a sporting activity may involve youth from different ethnic/racial backgrounds; lessons on communication styles (verbal and nonverbal) can be extremely useful in helping youth develop friendships across groups. Grimmette (1998) includes a reminder that physical exercise and fitness activities need to keep a focus on fun and be consistent with the lives of youth.

Sallis (1993) stresses the importance of proper diet and physical activities as essential ingredients in any health-promotion effort. Availability and proximity play determining roles in access to health foods and physical exercise for youth (Elliott 1993; Millstein 1993; Sallis 1993). The prevalence of obesity among youth and families of color is tied to cultural traditions and the lack of availability of certain foods (Barboza 2000). Proper diet and physical activity, however, need to build upon local values and beliefs, and exercise does not have to take place as part of structured and organized play.

But in a program youths do need to be engaged in some form of activity and to have access to proper snacks and food. There is good reason for having health promotion in the youth-development paradigm. It's a good fit. Frank (1998: 28) makes an important observation about nutrition: "Youth face short-term risks resulting from their daily eating behavior and the long-term chronic disease risks reflecting years of eating habits." Health promotion stresses enhancement of knowledge and skills and it has participants playing an active, rather than passive, role (Millstein, Petersen, and Nightingale 1993).

Physical development through use of play, organized or unorganized, can result in development of other core elements such as cognition and socio-emotional development (Kaufman 1994; Sallis 1993). It can also take place through a wide range of activities; structured sports are but one type (Delgado 2000a). Sports play an important role in the lives of most youths, not only through active participation but also through them being fans of local and national teams (Beedy and Zierk 2000; Gerzon-Kessler 2000; Solomon and Gardner 2000). Sports, nevertheless, may not be the "right" approach for all, and physical activity can take shapes and forms other than formal competition. Flexibility in designing activities in these realms is essential, taking into account local circumstances, access to resources (e.g., parks and recreational centers), and the safety concerns of youth and their parents (Hingson and Howland 1993).

MORALITY

It is not possible to address the subject of morality without being prepared for an intense debate as to what kind of behavior can be considered moral or immoral. Few enter this subject area without trepidation (Rollin 2000a). Morality, according to Dreyfus (1972: 68), refers to the "code of behavior adopted by a people. It refers to the appropriateness of specific behaviors in relation to other people and the responsibility one assumes for his actions." The development of a sense of morality and a value base that encourages youth to think morally as an integral part of their lives is often mentioned in the literature (Connell and Aber 1999). Moral development is not restricted to any one domain or arena. Yet it is undeniable that it is influenced by cultural context.

Interestingly, it is not as if the subject of youth morality has captured the attention of the general public, particularly in relation to organizations such as the Boy Scouts of America and their reluctance to include gays (Boyle 2000a, 2000b, 2000c). "Morality" has stoked the nation's swing toward punitive social policies, with youths being tried in adult courts and sent to adult prisons (Delgado, forthcoming b). Hart, Atkins, and Ford (1998: 514) argue that "the emphasis of current social policy on isolating, segregating, and punishing adolescent transgression obscures from the public view both the genuine moral strengths of adolescents and the opportunities that the developmental process offers for fruitful interventions with youth." Hart, Atkins, and Ford, while identifying the importance of morals in youth, also take a strength perspective and advocate for opportunities for youth to enhance this core factor. Moral identity through political and civic engagement benefits not only youth but also their community and society.

Parks (2000) specifically mentions the mentoring of young adults aged twenty-plus as they search for "means," "purpose," and "faith." This age group has generally been overlooked. Like their younger brothers and sisters, they, too, have needs and challenges requiring targeted initiatives and strategies.

The core element of morality has been operationalized as an "ethic of caring," as a "disposition to respond to others and the world as worthy of engagement" or a "sense of caring for others"; as empathy; as respect for differences, and as an ability to differentiate between right and wrong; also as a strong sense of the importance of social and economic justice for all (Ander 1996; Rauner 2000). Each of these aspects of moral development is a noble one, and seeking to achieve any of them is a life-long journey, for adults as well as for youth. Moral development can be present in any number of activities without bearing the official label—*moral*—and youth-development programs must seek to integrate this core element in such a manner that it is not lost in the carrying out of an activity, or that it is not thought of as being only part of a religious setting or program.

Hart, Atkins, and Ford (1998) identify moral identity as a self-consistent commitment to lines of action benefiting others—a construct and an essential goal for youth and community. Moral identity is not restricted to any one type of youth or community (ethnic, racial, economic class). All adolescents have the capacity to form moral identities. Opportunities to do so, however, vary, and may depend on the social support provided by adults. A moral identity, however, is essential in order to be successful as an adult.

The context in which youths find themselves plays an instrumental role in how moral development transpires day to day, in community or in a youth-development program (Anderson 1999). Inner-city youths will see issues of social and economic justice as prominent in their lives (Stevenson et al. 1997). Youth of color may see respect for racial and ethnic differences as critical in their day-to-day survival. The psychological impact on youth living in a racist and hostile environment results in the development of coping strategies that can be viewed pathologically if taken out of context. Stevenson et al. (1997: 197–198) write: "To resist one's social oppression and stress is more essential and therapeutic to one's identity development than swallowing one's anger and ignoring societal discrimination." Girls will place emphasis on gender-related social justice because of how sexism severely limits their ability to maximize their potential. Youth with disabilities may have access issues. Context shapes priorities for youth. It also shapes responses that need to be viewed and understood from a contextual perspective.

Einerson (1998) explored moral language development in young girls and the role that popular culture plays in their lives. Preadolescent and adolescent girls are said to be the largest U.S. market segment for popular music; it follows that music can be a window through which we can better understand how girls construct morality and moral behavior and explore identity. It further follows that music can be an important vehicle for transmitting moral messages to this group (messages that can be positive or negative, depending on the music group's leanings). Music can be used as an activity to strengthen the core element of morality in a youth-development program. Gender and moral development are thus interrelated.

Moral development is closely tied to many of the other core elements. Interpersonal relations (social) cannot help but be affected by whether we tolerate differences or celebrate them. A fundamental belief in equality, regardless of ethnicity, gender, sexual orientation, disabilities, and so on necessitates certain actions on the part of youth when encountering individuals who are significantly different from themselves. These actions are informed by a code of conduct or set of informal rules governing interpersonal public behavior that youth subscribe to in their daily life (Anderson 1999). If this code of conduct is predicated on all people being equal—not judging someone by the color of their skin, for example, but by their character—this results in a set of behaviors that is accepting of others.

The need to participate and help shape civic life and community services can easily be considered as a moral core element (Hudson 1997). This aspect of involvement is called by various terms. "Good citizenship practice" (Connell and Aber 1999) and "community service" (Yourniss and Yates 1997) are the ones most commonly found in the literature. In order to help shape civic life, youth need to have an understanding of a community's history (Hudson 1997). There are countless ways in which youth can practice this core element (Checkoway 1998; Curnan 2000a); for example: volunteering at local centers, carrying out community-based projects as a group, tutoring at local schools, mentoring, and helping to construct community gardens, sculptures, playgrounds, and murals (Delgado 2000b).

Leming (1997: 1) addresses the role of schools in teaching moral and civic virtues and the inherent challenges of doing so in this society:

> Today, the American people once again find themselves concerned about a perceived moral and civic crisis in our republic. This is not a new concern for the American people, just as it is not new for the American people to turn to the schools at such a time. If there is a persisting theme in our history, it has been the important responsibility that the American people have accorded to the schools to strengthen our republic by fostering virtue in youth . . . what methods does one use to teach values in a society that places a priority on the development of individuality and personal autonomy, but when is the development of children's rational facilities as applied to questions of moral and civic virtue insufficient to the task of providing a virtuous people?

A respect for diversity can also be considered a moral core element (National Youth Development Information Center 2000). Youth-development programs must endeavor to develop youth competencies in working across diverse groups (see chapter 4). Diversity—in this case of gender, abilities, sexual orientation, socioeconomic status, and ethnicity/race—will test youth abilities to relate to and work with groups different from themselves. It will also test the communities served by youth-development organizations and adults involved in programs.

THE SOCIAL ELEMENT

The social core element is central to any form of youth-development work; it could even be argued that it is all social in nature (for example, anxieties about, say, competencies can be considered to have a social component). However, in this area youth-development programs tend to focus on a specific set of social and relationship goals (Hudson 1997). The level of success attained by youths in meeting the social challenges involved will influence their relationships with family, peers, work colleagues, and community. Relationships and youth are inseparable, and rarely is youth talked about in a context of aloneness (Marshall and Stenner 1997). The essential challenge for youths is that they maximize their potential for growth through positive social interactions (Brown, Dolcini, and Leventhal 1997; Caplan et al. 1992; Catalano et al. 1998). The translation of social decisions into corresponding effective behavior is a natural consequence of growth (Elias et al. 1994). Youth-development programs must seek to prepare youth for a wide range of social interactions (Hudson 1997).

A social core element can be defined as a set of skills that enhance youth ability to achieve social and interpersonal goals. Needless to say, such a definition involves the other core elements. The integration of core elements is essential in any social core element construct (Caplan et al. 1992; Catalano et al. 1998; Elias et al. 1994; Meyer 1999; Weissberg, Caplan, and Sivo 1989). The very word social signifies the importance of a broad approach to applying this construct to practice. Both professionals and nonprofessionals in the field recognize the importance of this core element, whether the environments of the youths they work with are urban, suburban, or rural. However, relationships are particularly important in peer-centered programs (Brown, Dolcini, and Leventhal 1997).

The ability to establish and maintain social relationships is often a key indicator that an individual is healthy; this is true regardless of age (Connell and Aber 1999). Price (1999: 295) summed it up by saying: "The crux of everything in youth development is relationships." Price went on to address the importance of social competencies for staff as well as youth participants: "Because successful youth programs function like families, drawing youth into activities that enable them to move beyond the dead-end or deadly experience, staff in these programs function as family members, caring adults, helpful older brothers and sisters, concerned aunts and uncles, and grandparents. They assume, in effect, these roles."

Character attributes that can be fostered by working with this core element include ability to establish positive relationships with peers and adults; self-discipline; empathy; possession of a sense of humor (particularly the willingness to laugh at oneself); assertiveness training, communication skills (verbal and nonverbal); the ability to correctly read social cues; flexibility;

the ability to question decisions; refusal skills; ability in stress reduction; ability to both ask for help and to give it (Bembry 1998; Catalano et al. 1998; Konopka 1973; National Youth Development Information Center 2000; Walker and Dunham 1994).

The broad reach of this core element gives it significance in all aspects of life. New friendships outside of a peer network based on school or neighborhood are a not unusual outcome of participation in a youth-development program. Social networks are expanded as common interests are discovered, and the skills associated with developing and maintaining these new relationships carry over into other arenas. Social skills related to engaging youth of dissimilar backgrounds (see chapter 4) are a valuable dimension of this core element.

But a cautionary word is necessary about families—a social unit that this country tends to romanticize. Families may not facilitate expansion of social networks—may not like it when youthful family members try to transcend their usual set of peers. For young people, this can make social relations across groups difficult to achieve.

THE SPIRITUAL

The subject of spirituality is rarely addressed in the field of practice. It is even more rarely addressed in academic arenas (Beck 1999). As Dreyfus (1972) comments, the subject of spirituality is often combined with religion and morality, which in fact are very different perspectives. It is easy to confuse these areas.

Spirituality, of course, plays an influential role in a countless number of people's lives. Cervantes and Ramirez (1992: 104) define spirituality as "a transcendent level of consciousness that allows for existential purpose and mission, the search for harmony and wholeness, and a fundamental belief in the existence of a greater, all-loving presence in the universe," and that is how spirituality is thought of in this book. The definition brings out the need for a goal that transcends the here and now. The core element of spirituality has a cultural component, and the definition provided by Cervantes and Ramirez will not sound not alien to many ethnic and racial groups in the United States (c.f., the Native American beliefs about nature and the role religion plays in the lives of African Americans). The cultural perspective will help to contextualize what spirituality means to a community.

Spirituality, it should be emphasized, is much more inclusive than religion. One can be spiritual without being religious. Religion usually refers to a specific religious faith, practice, and values (Pate and Bondi 1992). There is, of course, no denying the close relationship that spirituality has with religion, and no denying the historical role of ministries in youth-development practice (Atkinson 1997; Rollin 2000a; Zuck and Benson 1978).

Fine and Mechling (1993) speak very positively about religious organizations' long experience in youth work. Commenting on the absence of religion and religious organization in the public discourse on youth programs for at-risk youth, they write (1993: 142): "This secular bias is completely understandable, given the symbolic demography of the baby boomer generation, but the bias may be leading parents and youth workers of the 1990s to neglect a sort of organization that already understands the importance of group identity, moral education, and constructive uses of peer cultures." Wallace and Williams (1997), in a review of research studies, found that youth who are religious are less likely to engage in drug use and sex than youth who are not religious.

If spirituality is given a heavily religious connotation—making it in many ways synonymous with religion—it will be difficult to implement the core element of spirituality in any place other than a house of worship. This is not to say that important youth-development work has not been undertaken by the religious traditions. Importance of relationship, caring, and respect for others has strong theological linkages (Roehlkepartain, and Seefeldt 1995), but in my view a holistic approach best fits youth-development work.

Spirituality can be fostered in a variety of ways in youth-development programs. These include efforts to help youths develop beliefs in a higher power or authority, the creation of opportunities for internal reflection and meditation, explorations of spiritual belief systems: these all address a spiritual core element (Catalano et al. 1998). Much of what can be classified as spiritual can also be seen as part of the moral core element. "Moral reasoning," "moral commitment," "moral order"—these are examples of how this core element merges with the other (Benson, Donahue, and Erickson 1990; Donahue and Benson 1995; Meyer and Lausell 1996; Stark and Bainbridge 1997).

Practitioners should not be afraid of incorporating this core element into activities because of its complexity.

Shear (2000: 24–25), addressing this challenge, writes:

How can we as youth workers reclaim the sacred in youth work without stepping into the murky quicksand of dogma and debate? We have four interrelated tasks: To develop fresh definitions of spirituality and spiritual development. To create a metacontextual design that supports the discovery of new meaning. To design an appropriate learning system that demonstrates the spiritual development and discovery process. To layout a roadmap that practitioners can follow.

Writers on youth development have seen a variety of roles for spirituality. Everson (1994) views it as a resiliency factor. Kessler (2000) associates it with assisting youths with friendships, acquiring effective communication skills, stress management, problem solving, health, and achieving personal and social responsibilities. Moore (2000) stresses the role of spirituality in helping youth rediscover and reclaim cultural and linguistic roots: spirituality has played an important historical role in the cultural beliefs of many groups, and identity and cultural meaning are integrally related to spirituality. Spirituality in a family context grounds youth in an operating unit, provides them with a common symbolic language for interactions, and provides them with a sense of future direction. Spirituality can be an excellent vehicle for the development of competencies. Loury (1999) views this core element from a social-capital perspective, stressing the benefits of church attendance, which he associates with youth staying in school longer. Hughes ( ) integrates spirituality into the construct of hope and the role it plays in providing youth with a vision of their future.

The importance of principles in helping practitioners cannot be overly stressed. That youth development has to be contextualized to take into account local circumstances (issues, resources, goals) increases the importance of having a set of practice principles. It is important to remember that principles are not meant to restrict practitioners; rather, they give us the freedom to individualize practice.

The core elements addressed in this chapter serve as a foundation from which programming and activities can be developed. The six elements identified, while arbitrary to a certain degree, can serve a vital role in practitioners' conceptualization of goals for youth development. All youth-development programs consciously address all or most of these six core elements, emphasizing some, relegating others to secondary importance. The activities chosen to address these core elements will vary across programs and domain (family, school, peers, community). That is to be encouraged.

Finally, some of the core elements discussed here are controversial. To what extent should youth-development programs seek to initiate newcomer youth to the culture of the United States? Do they seek to function like the settlement houses of the nineteenth century or do they venture into other areas? The theme of sexual orientation, for example, cannot be separated from moral or spiritual core elements (although the Boy Scouts of America sought to do in their exclusion of gays). Readers must come to terms with their values and biases as they program their activities.

6 / YOUTH DEVELOPMENT DOMAINS: FAMILIES, PEER GROUPS, SCHOOLS, AND COMMUNITY

THE PRACTICE of youth development often entails the creation of strategies and activities that focus on a particular domain or arena—family, peer group, school, or community-at-large. The field consequently has grown in complexity as the number of domains considered to be a legitimate part of the paradigm has increased. The importance of reaching out to influence these domains can be expected to increase (Larson 2000; Perry, Kelder, and Komro 1993).

Bogenschneider (1996: 136) notes that the field's growth of knowledge has presented a new challenge: "Our knowledge of youth development has expanded at a faster pace than our articulation of the theoretical perspective for applying this knowledge in ways that benefit youth and families." Practitioners thus will need to develop competencies in more than one domain. Youth, too, are challenged to be involved across domains.

The professional literature has identified the four domains listed above for targeting by youth-development programs: families, schools, peer groups, and community. These domains obviously do not exist in isolation from each other. Peer groups, for example, can exist in both schools and communities. In these two different settings, they may be similar in composition or totally different. Programs may target one of these domains, a combination of them, or all of them, depending on how youth development is conceptualized.

This chapter describes the four domains and highlights how programming is operationalized according to domain. Special attention is paid to how these domains overlap and the value of programming across domains. The more comprehensive a strategy is, the greater the likelihood that it will have real impact.

The National Research Council (1999), in a synthesis of studies on adolescence, concluded that a youth's development is shaped by a variety of domains and contexts—most notably, family, schools, peers, community,

community-based organizations, health organizations, child and juvenile justice systems, and the media. The impact of these different contexts can enhance youth competencies or severely hinder youth's potential for growth and achievement. The question is not whether they are influential but to what extent and direction are they influential—positive or negative? How a youth-development program focuses its strategies is very much determined by how it conceptualizes the influences of particular domains (Blyth 2001; Connell and Kubisch 2001; Greenberg 2001; Taylor 2001).

Scholars have used different terms to describe and analyze the domains. Duncan and Raudenbush (1999) refer to them as "extrafamilial contexts." Connell and Aber (1999) call them as social mediators, or linchpins, between community, youth-development process, and the socially desired outcomes associated with a youth-development paradigm; the success of these mediators in shaping youth competencies can vary from community to community. Connell and Aber take their analysis a step further by questioning how social mediators themselves are influenced. Bronfrenbrenner (1986) calls these mediators "microsystems."

The term *developmental pathways* is often used to conceptualize and describe the major systems involving youth development (Administration on Children, Youth, and Families 1997). These pathways (family, peers, schools, community, and society) can either have positive or negative impacts on youth. The interactions between them can be dynamic and reciprocal; they can also vary enormously from youth to youth. Staff must take them into account.

A synthesis of recent research on the importance of settings (another word that is used for domains) has shown the complexity and importance of these arenas (National Research Council 1999: 63):

> This research on settings suggests that certain implicit social norms, resources, and networks in affluence or higher resource settings that are often taken for granted (such as good schools; recreational and sports programs; safe homes and social centers; private health care; attitudes toward the value of work, education, community service, and parenting; and beliefs about future career and employment opportunities) constitute positive assets that have profound impact on the ways in which youth prepare themselves for their adult lives. Conversely, the absence of these assets creates significant gaps in the social support and opportunity structure for youth as they experience important transitions in becoming adults.

That is, settings strongly influence youths' futures: they can either enhance youths' chances in life or place them at risk for failure.

The variety of approaches to enhancement of youth capacities will be based on how a program conceptualizes these capacities (Masten 1994; Smokowski 1998). Family, schools, peers, and community can be seen as either protective of the life of youth or as a stress factor. Rarely will all four domains be one or the other. Youth-development programs must first assess these arenas and then make an informed decision about interventions. Programs can specifically seek to reduce vulnerability and risk. They can also promote positive outcomes by reducing the number and strengths of stressors. Programs can increase resources specifically focused on facilitating adaptive outcomes. Finally, programs may seek to mobilize protective processes.

These four approaches do not have to be mutually exclusive, of course. They can be present in youth development to varying degrees and in various combinations. If youth development is thought to occur within multiple contexts or domains, then it will require multiple partnerships (Bogenschneider 1996; Coie et al. 1993; LoSciuto et al. 1999). These partnerships must systematically be based on the lives of youth participants and not just on what is politically expedient and looks good on a funding proposal (Walberg, Reyes, Weissberg, and Kuster 1997a).

YOUTH DEVELOPMENT AND FAMILIES

The changing nature of the American family over the last fifty years has resulted in changes in the structure of the "typical" (nuclear) family to one that is "untypical." These families, while "untypical," nevertheless make up a majority (households headed by single females; gay/lesbian households; families headed by grandparents, siblings, etc.) (Walberg, Reyes, and Weissberg 1997a). This dramatic sociocultural restructuring of the family has had a corresponding impact on the family's function as primary socialization influence on children. Youth can no longer be thought of as being almost universally raised in conventional two-parent households.

The subject of families is very complex and not without controversy. Politically, both the Left and the Right have placed families as a central component in policy debates: Where would youth be without family? Without question, family is often central in any youth-development program

(Garnier and Stein 1998). Family context has been conceptualized in many different ways, however. Coleman's (1988, 1990) conceptualization, using terms like human and social capital, fits well within a youth-development paradigm. *Human capital* refers to assets (knowledge, skills, and values) that originate within the family. *Social capital* refers to the resources that are derived from the quality of relationships among family members. This conceptualization from an asset perspective allows youth-development programs to focus on enhancing and utilizing family structure and functions to further enhance youth capacities (Feetham 1997).

Batavick (1997), drawing important parallels between youth development and community-based family support, comments on the close interrelationship between these two movements. The importance of an active and complementary relationship between family and school is relevant to use of the core elements in practice (see chapter 5). This complementarity also highlights the porous nature of the boundaries between school and home. As Redding (1998: 114) writes:

> The motivation to attend and persist in school, the desire to achieve, the discipline to do homework, the interest in reading, and the feeling of fitting comfortably into the school environment are all functions, in part, of a child's support system of parents, other interested adults, and peers. The child can redeem this social capital when necessary. As social capital declines, so does its asset value for the child.

Family as "capital," human or social, cannot be minimized in conceptualizing youth-development domains (Haveman and Wolfe 1994). The factor of family will be involved in youth-development programs even when the primary target is school, peers, or community. It may be arduous to achieve success for an individual without also addressing the success of the family (Vargas and Busch-Rossnagel 2000).

The relationship between families and other domains brings an interactive dimension to any discussion of the role and importance of family in youth development (Ander 1996; Kysela et al. 1996; Reed-Victor and Stronge 1997). Loury (1999), for example, found a positive association between family, church attendance, and the effects made by schools. A family's position within a community social network can serve as a mediator, or protective factor, for youths. An active network can extend the influence of family beyond one domain into others. An isolated and disorganized family, however, may not be in a position to influence youth development positively; it may be unable to model, set boundaries, establish rules, and act as an advocate.

Tolan and Gorman-Smith (1997) discuss families and the development of youth in an urban setting. Marginalized urban families face a particular set of challenges in launching their children into adulthood—challenges different from those faced by more affluent, generally white, non-Latino suburban youths. This particular situation highlights the influence that community context has: the sources that urban families manage to tap, or fail to tap, shapes development outcomes for youths in marginalized urban settings. In the same work, Tolan and Gorman-Smith, seeking a better understanding of the sources of stress, developed a four-type typology of stress for inner-city families. They identified (1) chronic environmental stress (this gave the baseline level of stress; it was based on specific characteristics of the surroundings such as extent of unemployment, crime, drug problems, and homelessness); (2) life events (derived from life transitions that cause direct distress—deaths, divorces, significant health problems, etc.); (3) daily hassles (minor but day-to-day stressors such as racist incidents, feeling unable to go to a store at night because of danger, avoiding sections of a neighborhood because of gangs, etc.; and (4) role strain (inability to fulfill ascribed roles such as males being unable to be the primary bread winner). A family's ability to buffer children from such stressors is an important part of aiding healthy development.

Brooks, Petersen, and Brooks (1997), like Tolan and Gorman-Smith (1997), look at youth and their families from an urban ecological perspective, proposing a strength paradigm to better understand how family structure, contexts, strategies, and legacies influence social relations and youth development. "Standard" family definitions do not work when scholars try to better understand these urban families: a deficit perspective and conventional definitions do not appreciate a lot of the diverse processes and individual efficacies that are involved here. Single-parent African American households, for example, cannot automatically be considered to put positive adolescent development at risk. Garezy (1984) found that the presence of additional caregivers or social supports played critical roles in single-parent households.

The use of predicators for youth risk-taking behaviors has received a lot of attention, both historically and recently. This attention has been mostly on predicators used to examine the effects of race and ethnicity (whites, non-Latinos, African Americans, and Latinos), income, and family structure (i.e., single-parent families) on risk-taking behaviors of adolescents. Blum et al. (2000), based on their study of adolescent risk behaviors (data from the Longitudinal Study of Adolescent Health), found, not surprisingly, that these factors do influence risk-taking behaviors; however, they accounted for less than 10 percent of the variance. Thus the presence of certain socio-demographic characteristics does not necessarily translate into negative behavior.

The contextualization of what Spencer (2001) calls "low resource" urban African American male youth and their families helps both practitioners and researchers better grasp "normative" life-course development processes and transitions for this population group. Spencer goes on to give community a prominent place in factors that help to explain socialization of African American male youth into certain roles, behaviors, and attitudes. "Low resource" African American male youths do possess productive values and are capable of establishing and maintaining positive relationships with parents. However, unless seen through a contextualized lens, behavior is judged and interpreted from a middle-class viewpoint, using a middle-class set of norms. Sullivan (2001), like Spencer, shows how contextualization of behaviors provides alternative explanations, in this case involving African American masculinity. Male roles in marginalized urban communities are not restricted to violence or sexually exploitative behaviors.

The field of youth development recognizes that the family is the ultimate mentoring domain for children and youth (Cappel 1998). When this domain does not fulfill this important function in a positive manner, the task of doing so in other domains increases in importance. Youth-development programs, however, may be the only setting where the importance of rectifying negative familial experiences can take place. This does not mean that a program becomes a parental substitute, but it does mean that a program must make a serious effort at involving family whenever possible, and providing assistance where needed. This may entail making referrals to other community-based organizations or establishing a partnership with an organization to better meet the needs of parents.

The focus on families from a youth-development perspective has evolved over an extended period of time, but even so Gebreselassie and Politz (2000: 24) write:

> Unfortunately, the importance of families in youth development has often been overlooked, despite research on youth resiliency demon-strating that even when they grow up in high risk environments, young

people are likely to have positive outcomes if their lives are characterized by the presence of caring and continuous relationships with parental figures and high parental expectations. Therefore, it is essential to take into account the family context that influences the healthy development of youth.

Initially, family was viewed contextually in order to obtain a better understanding of youth participants in a program. The involvement of family in programming was minimal, with some notable exceptions, with occasional visits by program staff to a home and attendance of family at events created by youth. As the understanding of the importance of family increased, family was no longer exclusively viewed from a contextual viewpoint and instead was actively engaged in support of youth participants. Support of youth-development goals, however, necessitated that families, particularly those of marginalized youth, needed interventions, too. This shift in perspective has resulted in youth-development programs providing a host of services intended to help families to better help their children. Family as an integral part of youth-development interventions is now well accepted in the field.

An often used goal in youth development regarding family is having youth respect and contribute to the maintenance and cohesion of the family (Administration for Children, Youth, and Families 1997). Lack of respect for family can have a detrimental affect upon how a youth is viewed by the family, and how the family interacts with the youth. If a family is not viewed positively by the youth, then in situations where this is desirable every effort must be made to increase the "status" of family. (There may be situations where this goal is unattainable, however.) Empowerment of families may be one strategy for achieving this goal. Empowerment, incidentally, is not restricted to youth participants. Empowerment strategies are increasingly being targeted at parents and seek to promote parental pursuit of their own life options (Ross et al. 1992). The self-efficacy resulting from this intervention will undoubtedly have a positive carryover into the life of youth members of the family.

How to define *family*? This is an arduous task, highly political, and very significant in helping to shape any kind of intervention. If family is defined in a narrow way, such as nuclear, then it will systematically and deliberately negate families that are more fluid and have open boundaries (Mendez-Negrete 2000). Not surprisingly, the field of youth development has had its share of struggles with this definition. Gay or lesbian couples, for example, constitute family in some practitioners' definition, but not in that of others. Defining what constitutes a family strikes at basic values in this society. Youth-development staff are not oblivious to this, and basic beliefs will no doubt continue to be challenged.

The active support and involvement of families in youth-development programs is not always accepted without mixed feelings on the part of youth and staff. Youth may well value the involvement of family in their programs; however, not *their* family—just the families of other participants. Staff, too, may experience mixed feelings since family may not always be a support mechanism for a participant. Their participation may not be welcomed and could be perceived as counterproductive to the goals a program. Nevertheless, highly successful youth-development programs have managed to involve families.

YOUTH DEVELOPMENT AND SCHOOLS

Schools are a natural domain for deployment of youth-development principles and programs. Schools are geographically accessible to communities, have physical space for activities, and have a captive audience. They also have an explicit mandate to prepare youth for adulthood. LaBelle (1981) calls schools "society's most legitimate and formal system of teaching and learning."

Schools are not only mandated to address cognitive core elements but also moral development, citizenship, and vocational preparation. Sugarman (1975: 12) writes: "Schools perform a variety of useful functions for the society in which they operate; some, but not all, of these are also useful to the pupil individually. Three functions are valuable from both perspectives: (1) developing the cognitive faculties of the pupils; (2) cultivating socially approved attitudes and modes of behaviour; and (3) training for particular vocational roles."

There are those in the field who would strongly argue that it is possible to teach youth academics and positive social values such as respect, responsibility, caring, and civic responsibility without sacrificing academics (Kohn 1991; Noddings 1992; Stiehl 2000). A choice between academic subjects and a social conscience is an artificial one—and one doomed to fail since the development of a well-educated person involves both. An emphasis on both standards-based and school-to-work transition skills should not come as any great surprise to anyone who works with or teaches youth (Linn 1998).

The role of schools in preparing youth for life—their lives now as well their future adult lives—is well accepted in this society (Linn 1998; Weissberg and Greenberg 1997). But like youth development, education needs to be grounded in local community customs and take into account local characteristics. In the words of Meier (2000: 19): "To educate today's children for tomorrow's democracy, we should insist on locally grown standards that reflect communities and celebrate differences." Increased national effort at standardizing education is the antithesis of education.

Scott-Jones's (1996) research with urban families identified five critical goals that these families had for their children (interestingly, these goals are strikingly similar to the core elements presented in chapter 5). The families' five goals were: (1) To place a high value on formal education and schooling (achievement); (2) To encourage their children to develop good social skills (social relations and socio-emotional health); (3) Good health, which included safety from psychological and physical harm; (4) To stress the importance of children developing the ability to differentiate right from wrong (moral behavior); and (5) To have their children develop a positive identity and sense of self-worth. Scott-Jones's findings reinforce the importance of youth-development programs addressing multiple core elements across multiple domains (Sagor 1996).

Seidman and French (1997) and Ogbu (1997) stress the importance of an ecological perspective for examining urban youth performance in schools. Seidman and French also argue for the creation of new organizational structures within schools, and making schools smaller in order to increase communication and relationships between teachers, students, parents, and community organizations. Ogbu (1997) stresses the need for better understanding of the coping mechanisms and strategies of youth of color (in this case, African Americans) in helping them succeed against significant odds.

Regardless of at-risk environment, when schools stress a range of competencies such as goal setting, service, problem solving, decision making, and planning, graduation rates go up significantly, compared with schools where these competencies are not stressed (Gregory 1995; Wehlage 1989). Comer (1988) stresses the need for youth to develop both socially and academically within schools (two core elements that are closely related). This can be accomplished, Comer says, through positive interactions between parents and school staff, the adults actively striving to develop a culture that is respectful and engaging of youth. To achieve a shift in cultural perspective, professional school personnel have to form a partnership with the community and youth (Boyd and Shouse 1997). McLearn and La France (1999), based on their study of African American males aged seventeen to twenty-two years, in four cities (Atlanta, Chicago, Los Angeles, and New York), found that completing high school was protection against youths' engaging in risky behaviors such as drugs and crime.

Schools cannot simply be ignored in youth-focused initiatives (Comer 1998). But neither can schools focus on only one core element—cognition (Hile 2000; Lagerloef 2000). The prominence of schools in the lives of youths and their communities necessitates that they be part of any youth-development initiative (Chahin 2000; Richardson and Nixon 1997). The empowerment of youth—meaning instilling in them the belief that they can alter their circumstances and providing them with the skills to do so—is an important aspect of youth development, regardless of definition of youth development.

Kurtz (1997) takes the view that the social context of education (meaning school) is not neutral, and education can be used as an empowering mechanism. Nevertheless, empowerment cannot take place in schools unless youth assets are mobilized (Townsel 1997). Optimal developmental outcomes have been found to occur when the learning environment gradually reduces adult control as youth desire for autonomy increases (Eccles 1991). Opportunities to exercise decision making are a central focus of empowerment goals. Some practitioners would go on to argue that parents, too, must be empowered in order for youth to be empowered in these systems.

Greene (1998) sees a role for positive youth development in schools as a strategy for reducing youth violence. The need to involve multiple domains (such as family and peers), however, cannot be neglected. Youth, based on Greene's perspective, can and should play active and influential roles in all aspects of school-based programming, including mobilization of youth assets in developing such programs as peer mediation, peer education, and peer advocacy.

Youth empowerment within an education system brings with it endless possibilities for events that might threaten the "orderly" operation of a school. Battistich et al. (2000) take a perspective that involves multiple core elements (social, ethical, emotional, and cognitive development) in their child-development project. The school setting was taken as the social domain for the creation of a system of caring community learners. Like Rauner (2000), Battistich et al. stress mutually reinforcing processes and structures to promote these core elements.

Nevertheless, from a youth-development perspective, schools (with notable exceptions such as alternative and charter schools) have not played key roles in this movement (Mercogliano 1996). Charter schools have received increased attention from policy makers and youth-development organizations because of their potential to integrate youth-development principles into the curriculum (Nichols 2000). They often are flexible in structuring educational activities and in the hiring of staff. In conventional schools, on the other hand, declines in student beliefs, values, and self-esteem have been attributed, in part, to an inability or unwillingness of the schools to meet the developmental needs of young adolescents (Wigfield and Eccles 1994).

Numerous factors—dealing with organization, structure, and process—have been cited as responsible for difficulties in working with schools. Among them are (1) Difficulty in getting classroom access to students during times set aside for academic instruction; (2) General suspicion of "outsiders"; (3) Fear of change; and (4) Disagreement with the basic tenets of youth development, particularly with regard to youth playing active decision-making roles. Any one of these factors would constitute a formidable barrier to introducing youth-development interventions in schools, and two or more would make it near impossible to do so.

Youth-development programs often acknowledge the "toxicity" of schools and encourage youth to develop problem-solving skills in helping them to negotiate this domain. In situations where youth have dropped out, or are being pushed out, of schools, efforts are made to help them obtain a GED or to get access to vocational institutes. Assistance with college admissions is not unusual. Sometimes this service is provided in-house; other times it is provided by a partnership organization.

Schustack et al. (1994) describe how an after-school computer project increased literacy in school-age participants. The program served two different but complementary purposes. It was (1) an educational support of the youth program's activities, and (2) a means of increasing the awareness of information technology, with obvious benefits for and application to school. (For more on computers, see chapters 9 and 12; computers can play a critical role in the youth-development field). However, youth-development activities are present in *some* schools, and in fact are referred to in classrooms by that term (Boyle and De Pommereau 1999). Nevertheless, as noted in chapters 4 and 5, youth development is much more than an activity or a principle; it represents a *perspective,* and that perspective must permeate all dimensions of a school program if it is to be successful in achieving its goals. Youth development involves the use of developmentally appropriate and contextualized theory to guide instructions and interactions (Spencer 2001). When schools adopt youth-development activities, it may well be in a narrow sense of the term—for example, through peer-to-peer mentoring or experiential learning through projects. Among approaches that have been successful have been those that reinforce academic achievements (awards, incentives, and public recognition) combined with placing value on (or creating a culture of) student participation, increasing student learning and motivation (Lagerloef 2000; Way, Haertel, and Walberg 1997a). However, it is a sad state of affairs when there is an avoidance of bringing youth-development principles and activities into schools in other than after-school programs.

It is widely accepted that youth development, although important and viable in youth lives, cannot get a significant foothold in schools—the community institution that has youths for the longest time period. Schools, with notable exceptions, are considered to be "non-youth-development-friendly." In some communities, experience of this attitude has resulted in community-based organizations—not all of them youth-development oriented—systematically working together to undo the harm perpetrated on youth by schools.

After-school programs lend themselves to integrating youth-development principles. Equal participation in decision making, a cornerstone of any successful youth-development program, has been well reported in the literature. Hatchy et al. (1994) describe such an endeavor in a Boston elementary school. Such a project, they say, evolves over a period of time, each year building on the previous year; and a learning context that is conducive to youth needs can occur only when all significant parties (and this can include relatively young children) have shared in the decision-making process and shared in the responsibilities resulting from those decisions.

Although after-school settings often engage in youth development as part of their programming (Beck 1999; Belle 1999; Carnegie Council on Adolescent Development 1994; Delgado 2000a), such programs are still seen as "unusual" delivery points for youth-development services because of their setting within the physical structure of a school. In spite of the setting, however, they do represent a "different" world for youth since rarely are the staff of the program drawn from the regular school program. The participants are exposed to a new set of adults—a staff with attitudes, values, and skills rarely found in highly structured and credentialed school programs. In instances where participants are not elsewhere exposed to adults who are of different racial and ethnic backgrounds to their own, this is an opportunity for this type of exposure. After-school settings provide youth with a rare opportunity to redress many of the shortcomings associated with regular school programs. Participants are provided with a structured program that combines academics with "fun" activities. In such a structure they are provided with what Beck (1999) calls "wiggle room." Youth are encouraged to engage in decision making about what aspects of an activity they wish to engage in. Autonomous space is encouraged within a structured environment. However, activities also take place within groups and enhance youth competencies in interacting with peers. The degree, to which autonomous space is needed will vary according to local circumstance; flexibility is essential (see chapter 5).

After-school settings have a long and distinguished history of providing services that have filled significant gaps in meeting the needs of youth, particularly those that are marginalized. Some scholars have gone so far as to say that the time youth spend in after-school settings is more significant than time spent in school (Gardner 1994). After-school programs have been found to play a mediating role in the lives of youth with a high number of risk factors. These programs enhance social and emotional development and reduce risk-taking behaviors (Beck 1999; Carnegie Council on Adolescent Development 1994; Perkins and Villarruel 2000; Rosner and Vandell 1994; Ross et al. 1992; Schinke, Orlandi, and Cole 1992).

Hellison and Cutforth (1997), addressing the needs of youths of color in inner cities, advocate the use of extended-day programs. The authors make eleven recommendations for state-of-the-art extended-day programs. These recommendations, although they do not specifically mention youth development, can easily be considered within the paradigm. They are: (1) It is important to view youth as resources—as people possessing strengths to be enhanced rather than as problems to be solved; (2) There is a need to focus holistically (include the emotional, social, educational, economic, etc.); (3) There must be respect for individuality, with developmentally and culturally appropriate activities; (4) Empowerment, rather than disempowerment, should be stressed; (5) The adult staff should have high and clear expectations; (6) Programs should assist youth in envisioning a positive future; (7) Programs should provide a physically and psychologically safe environment; (8) Programs should encourage participation over an extended period, keep the number of participants small, and emphasize ownership of program; (9) Programs should foster linkages between program and community, thus enhancing community capacities; (10) Programs should provide "courageous and persistent" leadership; and (11) provide opportunity for youth to develop a trusting and respectful relationship with adults. These recommendations, overlapping youth-development principles, reflect the impact this domain has on youth (Lopez, Nerenberg, and Valdez 2000).

PEER GROUPS—AN IMPORTANT DOMAIN

It is necessary to think of peer influence from a positive as well as a negative perspective. The importance and complexity of peers and peer groups in fact warrants that peers be a separate domain. Although some argue that the peer category is best seen as part of the school and community domains—the places where youths mostly come into contact with their peers-there is another good reason for treating it separately: only then will it receive the attention it deserves from practitioners and academics. Moreover, the open boundaries associated with peers groups are sufficiently different from those of the other domains, and they are more easily overlooked if peers are integrated into other domains (Brown, Dolcini, and Leventhal 1997).

It is not possible to discuss youth without also discussing the role of peers in their lives. Peers can be of any age group (i.e., age is not the only commonality that can bring a peer group together (Howes 1987); however, peer groups separated out by similarity of age tend to be the most common. It is estimated that adolescents spend twice as much time with their peers as with their parents, and in assessing the relative importance in terms of influence on the lives of youths, peers probably come in closely behind families; this is true particularly for those entering latency and adolescence. It is not out of the ordinary for youths to have between two and four "best" friends of backgrounds similar to their own (National Research Council 1999).

Contrary to common opinion, the importance of peer relationships for adolescents is not a new phenomenon. Peer friendships have long been an influential part of life (Brown, Dolcini, and Leventhal 1997). The influence of peers, however, can be either direct or indirect (passive). Thus, a youth's social network will often include a large number of age-group peers in addition to adults. Youths with disabilities may develop a peer network that includes youths who are one or two years younger than themselves. This does not detract from the benefits youths with disabilities can derive from inter-action with younger peers (Fink 2000).

There are those who believe that the competencies developed in initiating and maintaining friendships transfer over into initiating and maintaining romantic relationships. However, the influence of peers on youth goes far beyond developing competencies in the social realm. Positive friendships with peers, particularly those that involve loyalty and intimacy, can con-tribute to a positive sense of identity.

The likelihood of retaining youth in programs is often contingent upon who else is in the program (Almen 2000). Consequently, staff must be acute-ly attuned to how peer groups interact within a program. Similar peer-group considerations are also a factor to consider in recruitment (Almen 2000). Especially in the case of adolescents, an age-period where peers take on added significance, who is in a program may well become an important determinant of whether or not they join (Hartup 1993; Savin-Williams and Berndt; Patrick et al. 1999).

Much more needs to be studied in order to appreciate the influence of peers fully. Brown, Dolicini, and Leventhal (1997: 184) write: "The exceptional capacity of peers to influence both health-enhancing and health-compromising behaviors makes it imperative that we take this research agenda very seriously. In so doing, we hope that researchers will dispel simplistic myths about peer influences on adolescent health and build a firmer basis for more effective health-related prevention and intervention programs."

A review of case studies found that a network of high-achieving friends was characteristic of high-achieving students (Reis et al. 1995). It is ironic that peer pressure has generally been studied from a deficit perspective— that is, asking to what extent youth are prone to engage in risky behavior because of peer influence and pressure (Patrick et al. 1999). Academics and practitioners simply cannot ignore the strength perspective on peer pressure. A positive perspective views peers as providing an opportunity for youth to engage in reciprocity based on equality (Administration for Children, Youth, and Families 1997; Youniss 1980; Youniss and Smollar 1995).

Peer groups can also have a potentially good therapeutic effect on youths who have not had the benefits of supportive parents—for example, those who have been abused or neglected (Garbarino and Jacobson 1978). Gibbs, Potter, and Goldstein (1995) advocate that youth be effectively prepared to help one another—and, in so doing, help themselves. Peers, they say, provide a social service, benefiting society in countless unique ways.

Positive friendships can foster the creation of social supports, listening skills, mutual respect, acceptance, the giving of advice, empathy, better understanding of self (the more one gets to know others the more one learns about oneself), and relationship building skills (Cairns and Cairns 1994; Corsaro and Eder 1990; Oetting and Beauvais 1987; Werner and Smith 1992; Youniss and Smollar 1985). The outcomes of peer relationships prepare youth for social interactions in other domains such. Social competence with peers can be an indicator of future social competence.

Youth peer relations are not uniform across groups; they are greatly influenced by gender, ethnicity, race, socioeconomic class, age, and other factors. Giordano, Cernkovich, and DeMaris (1993) advance the notion that African American adolescents are not more peer-oriented than white non-Latinos. (an earlier notion had argued that they were, because of family deficits). Giordano, Cernkovich, and DeMaris raise the issue of what normative standards are being used to judge peer relationships; there is a need, they say, to better understand patterns of variations between and within ethnic and racial groups. And they go on to argue that gender becomes a key factor in peer relations; for example, both African American females and white, non-Latinas consider mutuality (sharing similar same feelings and ways of thinking) and level of intimacy to be more important as a basis for friendship than do their male counterparts.

Some youth of color have shown a strong propensity toward having friends of the same ethnicity. In a study on Chinese immigrant adolescent girls, degree of acculturation and parental support played important roles in dictating friendships (Shih 1998). Youth-development programs must take into account the racial/ethnic mix of their programs, a subject that has generally escaped attention in the literature. Balancing group composition may be distasteful to staff; however, how this balance is achieved, and the rationale used to get there, are as important as the outcome. It will take serious deliberation, but peer relations are too important to leave to chance.

How do programs identify, mobilize, and sustain positive peer influences? These questions are critical for the field of youth development, and the answers to them require an organizational culture that values peer relations—among both youth and staff. Such an organizational culture is critical to a program's success. Positive peer culture does not just happen—it needs to be planned and created deliberately. The benefits can be profound for both staff and youth. An organization that successfully fosters positive peer relations can also have a positive impact on other organizations, through interaction with them.

IT TAKES A COMMUNITY . . .

Denner, Kirby, and Coyle (2000) argue that communities can and should be expected to be a part of youth-development programming. their work was based on their study of professionals in the field of youth services. Villarruel and Lerner (1994a) identified four objectives for community-based youth-development programs: (1) Promotion of social competence; (2) Development of problem-solving skills; (3) Creation of a sense of autonomy; and (4) Development of a sense of purpose and future orientation. These four objectives and their various activity manifestations can guide strategy development.

Further stressing the view that youth development cannot occur without the involvement of community, the National Clearinghouse on Families and Youth (1998: 1) maintains:

The reality is that youth are a resource that communities can no longer afford to ignore. When we fail to provide youth with support and opportunities, they may grow into adults who are unemployed, who experience drug or alcohol problems, who commit crimes, and who are given opportunities to become involved in work or education that builds their skills, who receive support and protection during challenging times, who are actively engaged in service to the community become valuable contributors to the quality of community life. Engaging youth in communities simply makes sense, both fiscally and ethically.

The Kellogg Foundation (1999), too, found local community support to be indispensable in their youth philanthropy initiative. The trend toward including community thus seems to be getting stronger, gaining converts in practice, policy, and academic circles. In fact, few social scientists or practitioners would now argue that neighborhoods or communities play only insignificant roles in the development of youth (Connell and Aber 1999; Jason et al. 2000; Robinson 1995).

The contextualization of environment lends itself to examination of resources/forces that either actively undermine youth development or enhance it (Fitzpatrick and LaGory 2000; Smokowski 1998). As many writers have pointed out, any youth-development paradigm that addresses youth and their ecology necessarily must also involve the community (Burgess

2000; Chalk and Phillips 1996; Commerce Business Daily 2000; Delgado 1999; Connell, Aber and Walker 1999; Lachter et al. 1999; Duncan and Raudenbush 1998; Kellogg Foundation 1998; McLaughlin, Irby, and Langman 1994; Merrill 1999; Sipe and Ma 1998).

Historically, in youth-development interventions *community* has generally been defined as anything outside of a school system or anything that has a community or neighborhood focus (Catalano et al. 1998). This definition left much to be desired; however, mention of it here helps point to the complexities of defining community. Neighborhoods, or communities, can be defined geographically or functionally. The functional definition points to a set of social networks that may transcend geographical boundaries. Any definition that falls into the category of "If it's not X, it must be Y" begs the question of how this arena can be conceptualized.

Rauner (2000 :135–36) brings a different but important dimension to the discussion on community and youth development; namely, the role of values:

We must strive to become part of a real community, where each of us accepts responsibility for active participation in efforts to sustain our common values and promote the development of the next generation. We are a nation of associations, of neighbors. . . . We must individually and collectively choose caring—or trust, love, or any other moral source—as an organizing principle in our lives, and then together figure out what we must do to transform our world to reflect it.

BIAS: FOR AND AGAINST COMMUNITY

There has been a bias in the youth-development field against some communities, particularly urban communities, and this has fed an assumption that youth must be saved from their own communities—that a community-based intervention must actively buffer youth from the deleterious consequences of living in the community. This perspective, unfortunately, can seriously undermine the contribution a community can have in the youth-development field. I am glad to say that there has been a slow but steady move away from this view.

The literature has taken note of this debate: Unfortunately, communities, particularly those with a high percentage of youth with "at-risk" characteristics, have also been labeled at-risk themselves (Anderson 1999; Fitzpatrick and LaGory 2000). The at-risk label has effectively been used to write off communities as not possessing the requisite assets that can be marshaled in support of its youth (Delgado 2000b). Marginalized urban communities have an ecology of risk that translates into youth having to face increasing odds of failing (Fitzpatrick and LeGory 2000). However, these communities and youth are not without assets and strengths if we only set out to find them (Corwin 2000).

A lot of the literature and research on urban communities has been deficit driven. A focus on at-risk factors will generate data to identify problems; an asset-driven process will generate information on what strengths can be harnessed to tackle the problems. In the asset perspective, problems become the background; assets become the foreground. The questions become not "Are there are assets?" but "What are the assets?" These assets can be integrated and mobilized as part of a community-centered intervention (Delgado 2000b).

In most paradigms, a similar problem in conceptualization affects day-to-day relationships between community and agencies. It takes time and effort to engage in the politics of community—to *involve* a community— and this often scares off agencies, academics, and funders. When a community has a history of negative relationships with an organization, the task of reaching out and engaging the community becomes overwhelming.

THE ROLE OF COMMUNITY

There is no escaping community. But community can be seen as providing no more than context for youth-development programs; it can also be seen as a *vehicle* for such programs. It must be obvious that I favor the latter.

McLaughlin (1993: 57) strongly advocates the need for youth-serving organizations, not just those that are development oriented, to be rooted in the local community: "Each of the organizations effective in working with inner-city youth is palpably local. Each draws on local resources, sinks ties into the local community, and responds to the issues and needs particular to the neighborhood. Each sees youth in the context of their families, neighborhoods, schools, and peer associations."

Sampson (2001), however, notes that the construct of social capital has evolved over the years to broaden its territory to include individual-level resources. This evolution has taken the construct away from community and lost its original meaning. Social capital has its origins in communities and served to contextualize behaviors both within and outside of the home (Bourdieu. 1986; Coleman 1990; Putname 1993).

A shift toward viewing communities as possessing assets and as active partners in developing youth has occurred in many programs and communities. This shift in perspective has expanded the opportunities for operationalizing youth development. Kurtz (1997: 215), for example, outlines a series of assumptions that community youth development (CYD) has regarding the role and responsibilities of community regarding its youth:

> CYD is based on several assumptions: youth development is a community responsibility, and community factors can enhance or deter development; the community has the responsibility to provide conditions conducive to healthy development; youth are a key part of the community, and there is a reciprocal influence between their development and the roles they in creating healthy community conditions; and youths must be involved as full partners in the design, delivery, governance, monitoring, and evaluation of youth programs.

The interconnectedness between youth development and community development, or capacity enhancement, is inescapable. This relationship opens up the possibility of initiatives combining the two with each being inseparable from the other. Each complementary and enhancing of the other (Merrill 1999). Watkins and Iverson (1998: 182) specifically address the need for interconnectedness between youth development and community development: "Taking the concept of goodness-of-fit one step forward, one realizes that not only do healthy communities contribute to the well-being of their youths, but healthy, prosperous youth can also simultaneously make a difference within their community. Therein lies the mutuality between the concepts of youth development and community development." It is important to highlight that youth, too, can play influential roles in helping to enhance their community's capacities. In so doing, they enhance their own capacities in the process (Hart, Atkins, and Ford 1998).

The emergence of a community-building or capacity-enhancement perspective in the helping professions has proved to be fertile ground for youth-development programs. Weil (1996: 482) defines community building as "the activities, practices, and policies that support and foster positive connections among individuals, groups, organizations, neighborhoods, and geographic and functional communities." Ortiz, Hendricks, and Kudich (2000) stress the need for partnerships across groups to be an integral part of community building. Delgado (2000b) stresses the importance of identification and mobilization of indigenous assets, individual and organizational, in developing community-based programs and activities.

A youth-development paradigm has allowed practitioners to think of youth development and community development as integrally connected (Armistead and Wexler 1998; Barton, Watkins, and Jarjoura 1997; Burgess 1998; Chalk and Phillios 1996; Connell, Aber, and Walker 1999; Delgado 2000a; Donohue, Keith and Kaagan 1999; Duncan and Raudenbush 1998; Merrill 1999; Sipe and Ma 1998). It has also expanded the nature and number of settings where youth development can occur. The merging of these two constructs is an exciting development for both fields. Youth-development practice is no longer limited to select youth-oriented agencies and after-school programs. Among venues that have started to develop youth-development programs are houses-of-worship (Logan 1997; Roehlkepartian and Scales 1995), schools (National School-To-Work Learning and Information Center 1996), and the child welfare system (Choi 2000; LaMonaca 2000; Stevenson 2000).

Community can serve many different purposes in putting youth-development principles and activities into practice. It can be a context in which youth development is practiced (Delgado 1999; Smokowski 1998; it can be a vehicle for youth development in achieving significant change; it can be a target of youth development; and in some youth-development programs it is all three. It is tempting to quote the well-known book title and say "It takes a village" to capture the importance of community, but the words have run into controversy. Benson (1999: 1) observed that the slogan has been politicized and misused: "One side too easily equates the 'village' with the public sector's commitment to youth. The other side too quickly dismisses the responsibility of anyone beyond the family to care for young people. Each extreme misses the point of the phrase and, more important, the real challenge we face in caring for the young."

Certain sectors within communities lend themselves to positive human development better than others. This is a result of social processes and indigenous resources, and Lee (2001) argues that communities/neighborhoods must be conceptualized in ways that better grasp "collective efficacy" across spatially defined settings. Neighborhoods do not constitute internally homogeneous entities and they can best be conceptualized as having "patchwork patterns." Neighborhoods are dynamic and therefore need to be thought of from another dimension—the effects of exposure in providing outcomes, both negative and positive. A multilevel conceptualization of community is needed to better understand its role in youth development. Delgado (1999 2000b) applies this perspective in studying the role of non-traditional settings, community gardens, murals, sculptures, and playgrounds in urban communities.

Bembry (1998), Ramey and Ramey (1997), and Hendricks and Rudlich (2000), among others, stress the interconnection between community sustainability and its ability to sustain youth. A community that is fragmented, preoccupied with survival, and unable to care for its own is unlikely to be able to actualize the potential of its youth. Its major social, economic, and political institutions will be drawn into this struggle for survival, which seriously undermines the potential of youth development to bring about change.

Successful community development cannot occur without dependence on emerging leaders—both young and old—and the involvement of multiple sectors (Fellin 2001; Lakes 1996). Some researchers argue, for example, that mentoring (in this case, of African American youth) can be successful only if it recognizes family and community assets (Townsel 1997).

Zeldin (1995), among others, advocates for community-university collaborations as an additional perspective from the usual agency-to-agency partnerships in youth development. Collaboration between youth-development organizations and other community-based groups has to result in significant benefits if it is to justify the investment of time and energy. The benefits can be increased and more efficient service as well as less tangible outcomes such as trust, connectedness, personal support, and consensus on mission (Langman and McLaughlin 1993). The less tangible outcomes are still capital that can be used to increase material resources for programs.

Villarruel and Lerner (1994a) propose out-of-school community-based programs to help youth socialize and learn at the same time. These programs provide youth with opportunities to acquire academic skills, learn and practice social skills, engage peer in activities, and have a safe environment. Youth development programs need to contextualize activities and service and one way of ensuring so is to ground within the community. A sense of belonging, competence, and knowledge acquisition are enhanced for youth by bringing community into the world of youth development. Communities also benefit from being involved in youth development (Merrill 1999).

The National Research Council (1999: 19–20) comment that "neighborhood influences may operate differently for different age groups by gender." They write: "The child's age and gender are . . . likely to result in sharply divergent experiences that modify the impact of neighborhoods on development. Girls typically are granted less autonomy and are subject to greater parental control. Especially in low-income areas, boys often spend more time hanging out in the streets, and at younger ages." This observation draws attention to a wider point: that community is not a monolithic entity that impacts on members equally without regard to characteristics. S, For example, some communities are better equipped to help young children while others have paid more attention to adolescents.

Youth-development programs must be keenly aware of the limitations of involving youth in creating community change and raising their expectations (Checkoway 1998: 792): "Even exceptional efforts to involve young people in neighborhood development will not necessarily address the root causes of neighborhood problems. They may [however] show that traditionally underrepresented people can take hold of their surroundings and improve conditions when they participate in the process." Failure to prepare and thereby help to process the experience may turn youth off to participation in the future, which in the long run would be a disservice to them and the community. "Success" must be broken down into segments. An "all or nothing" perspective may prove counterproductive for youth, whereas an ability to understand the meaning of small victories helps to place "change" into context (McKeggie 2000). If, instead, youths learn that participation does not guarantee success but that lack of participation almost ensures failure, a valuable lesson is learned. When this lesson is combined with the awakening of a sense of long-term involvement, much good can come out of a failed effort. What youths need to learn is that involvement is a lifetime commitment. It does not, however, have to be a full-time commitment. The ebbs and flows of time, responsibility, and interests will influence the degree of participation in community-change efforts. A development of this understanding can be considered a significant achievement in any youth program (Kyle 1996).

⌒

The conceptualization of youth development as crossing domains of influence in a youth's life, starting with family and followed by school, peers, and community, offers tremendous potential for the field of youth development. Dosher's (1996: 12) comments, while specifically directed toward CYD, capture a philosophical stance in the field that stresses involvement in multiple domains: "The vision of the CYD Field is to create a just and compassionate society in which people and youth, adults and elders, can experience positive connections to family, community, the earth, and the sacred that provide a sense of belonging and gratitude for the wonder of life." Life is multidimensional; youth development should be so, too.

The expansion of intervention beyond a focus on the individual increases the potential of the paradigm to bring about societal change. The potential—exciting and challenging as well as daunting and overwhelming—is to have positive impact not only on youths but also on their families, friends, and communities. The more spheres of influence targeted by youth-development programs, the greater the likelihood that this will happen. The challenge for practitioners is almost as great as the rewards. However, as expectations of staff increase staff competencies in these multiple domains must be systematically addressed by the organizations that sponsor youth-development services.

In the field of youth development there is now little question about the involvement of community, peers, and family. The question now is how will they play out in programming? Each domain, with the exception of schools, taps into a set of staff values. These values wield tremendous influence in how the domains are conceptualized (Adams 2000). Staff and the organizations employing them must endeavor to achieve clarity about how domains are thought of and what factors enter into their definitions. Only when this is accomplished will the biased they hold come to light for discussion, debate, and action.

7 / YOUTH DEVELOPMENT: ACTIVITIES, SETTINGS, MARGINALIZED YOUTH, AND FRAMEWORKS

YOUTH DEVELOPMENT as established in the preceding chapters can take a multitude of shapes and forms. In the field of practice, such definitional flexibility lends itself to youth development taking on many forms and settings, hence, organizations and practitioners can be creative in how they design and implement activities. Local considerations can help shape the program.

However, the very range of activities often categorized as "youth development" can create challenges for the field of practice. Sometimes the question "What is *not* a youth-development activity?" is more relevant than that of "What *is* a youth development activity?" Although the answers to those questions remain elusive, this chapter provides grounding in the nature of the activities most often used in youth-development programming. It also gives an outline of the various types of organizations currently engaged in the field, and a framework for practice. Some specific planning recommendations are also included. Readers will quickly recognize the importance of core elements and the different domains in determining activities and settings.

Special attention is paid in this chapter to the development of marginalized youth.

Marginalized youths, when compared with those in the dominant culture, face significantly different challenges (both groups also face some common challenges, of course). Contextualization of youth development is therefore required to increase its relevance to local circumstances. Flexibility must be a key theme in youth development.

THE ORCHESTRATION OF ACTIVITIES

A synthesis of research and literature on adolescents and their families made by the Center for Youth Development and Policy Research set out four themes (Zeldin, Kimball, and Price 1995): (1) Youth benefit from opportunities to engage in positive and productive activities; (2) Youth benefit from supports (nurturance) and high expectations; (3) Opportunities and supports are associated with a continuum of youth outcomes, both individually and collectively; and (4) Youth benefit from support and opportunities without regard to who provides them or where the support and opportunities exit.

The orchestration of programs is likely to be complex. The National Research Council (1999: 64–65) writes: "Clearly, no single program approach will be appropriate for all adolescents: one size does not fit all. The challenge therefore becomes one of designing a range of intervention strategies that are comprehensive and interdisciplinary in nature, that are developmentally
appropriate and culturally relevant, and that take advantage of the many settings or environments in which children and adolescents grow and develop."

Murphy (1995b) defined three elements usual in a high-quality youth-development service or activity: (1) It provides youth with relevant instruction and information; (2) It provides youth with challenging opportunities (for expression, to make contributions, and with roles) and does so through collective participation; and (3) It provides youth with a place in which they receive respect and are judged by high standards—where they can be guided and affirmed by both adults and peers.

Youth-development activities can take place without bearing the official label "youth development" (an example would be youth philanthropy; see chapter 3). The range of services and activities considered under that rubric can be overwhelming (Delgado 2000a; Hahn and Raley 1999). To list but a small percentage: career counseling; literacy; community service; employment skills; cultural enrichment (racial and ethnic); after-school programs; camping; ecological education; life-skills training; arts; sports; humanities; media use; sports; leadership education; mentoring; community-based services; values clarification/education; parenting skills; internships; employment. This partial list shows a wide variety of types of youth-development activity. The variety would further multiply because of factors such as gender.

Prominent in most lists of youth-development programs are activities that deal with transition to the world of work, particularly those that stress such work experience as internships. But a growing body of literature and research is raising a word of caution. Recent studies contradict the conventional wisdom associated with youth working during after-school hours. It is estimated that approximately five million adolescents under the age of eighteen are working (Greenhouse 2001). Youth who work an excessive number of hours (twenty hours per week or more) have less energy and time for schoolwork, social activities, and athletics.

Three characteristics can often be found in a youth-development activity, regardless of setting, population-age group, or gender. Youth-development programs need to meet three primary criteria: (1) To provide academic subjects with a nonacademic focus; (2) To use active and experiential methods; and (3) To promote competencies (National Youth Development Information Center 1998).

It is important to remember that activities often are the primary mechanism for recruiting and retaining youth in programs. Activities can be considered the calling card for youth to participate in programs (Bembry 1998; Marshall 2000). In addition to addressing core elements (cognitive, emotional, health, social, moral, and spiritual), activities must engender trust, respect, integrity, consistency, and self-respect (Bembry 1998). Larson (2000) identifies several elements to be found in youth activities: they are voluntary, they involve structure and purpose, and they occur within a system of constraints, rules, and goals. Activities essentially are thoughtful, deliberately planned, and have clear, and often multiple, purposes or goals.

The Florida Tobacco Control Clearinghouse (1999) developed a twelve-part taxonomy of youth-development programs based on gender, cultural considerations, and nature of intervention:

1 Adventure-oriented programs: use of activities to develop skills and confidence through an emphasis on thrill and excitement
2 Artistic or creative programs: use of art, drama, music, and so forth to develop artistic skills and creativity
3 Athletic and recreational programs
4 Community-service alternatives: provision of structured activities that allow youth to perform a service while learning and reflecting on the learning process
5 Culturally specific programs: use of activities intended to provide youth with an in-depth knowledge of their cultural heritage (also improves bonding within and between groups)
6 Drop-in centers: activities invariably unstructured and determined by the need of those there at the time

7 Entrepreneurial alternatives: activities stress the acquisition of business skills

8 Gender-specific programs: activities with a strong gender-related goal

9 High-risk youth programs: intensive activities focus on participants' deficits

10 Mentoring programs: activities stress imparting of knowledge and skills through close relationship with a role model, most likely an adult

11 Religion-based programs: activities have a strong orientation to ward the beliefs and values of the religious organization sponsoring the program

12 Other—a catch-all category for activities with the unique goals of various organizations and communities

Larson (2000; 179) proposes a perspective on activities that lends itself to youth-development evaluation (a topic covered in chapter 8).

A useful starting point for conceptualizing and categorizing youth activities would be descriptive research that simply enumerates what types of process experiences participants typically have across different types of activities. How often do youth in swimming versus drama clubs versus service organizations have the experience of setting their own goals, developing plans, or empathizing with people from a dissimilar background to theirs? In gathering such enumeration, it would be useful to obtain parallel data for such activities such as schoolwork, work at a job, and unstructured leisure activities, in order to test whether rates of these process experiences are indeed higher during youth activities.

Zeldin, Kimball, and Price (1995), in a summary of the literature on youth activities, found that youth benefit the most when they have an opportunity to (1) actively plan community-service projects that contribute to the welfare of others; (2) acquire new competencies and are able to apply and practice them and new roles; (3) connect their experiences to school; (4) work closely and collaboratively with adults, familial and nonfamilial, and peers; and (5) participate in projects that are "real," with appropriate tasks and results.

Parker (2000; 25) raises an important aspect of activities that has not received the attention it deserves—probably because of the demands it would put on youth-development programs:

> Some programs that work with kids are one-shot deals (and one size fits all). They provide activities for kids that last for a set period of time, maybe just the summer, and then are gone. The kids come back the next summer and do the same thing. Again, these programs provide kids a safe place to go and teach them some skills, but the deal never changes—the program is always the same. . . . Programs that have an influence stick with kids and focus on the development of leadership skills. Programs that have a profound influence grow with kids and develop their content over time.

Programming that covers a wide lifespan holds much appeal. But such programs are extremely challenging to operate.

RECOMMENDATIONS

The following six recommendations regarding activities raise points that are often taken for granted. These recommendations may seem to be simplistic, but when these guidelines are not followed or seriously considered, the maximum potential of activities will not be fully realized:

Recommendation 1: Activities should not have the teaching of academic subjects as a primary goal. Initial participation in a youth-development program may stem from the general values and attitude that a youth may have about voluntary participation; however, ongoing participation is determined by how specific attitudes and expectations are met. If they are satisfied, participation continues; if not satisfied, termination occurs (Lammers 1991). Consequently, the better the understanding of what determines participation, the better the programming (Ngai and Cheuwg 1997). This knowledge can be obtained only at the local level.

No one disputes the importance of academic subjects in youths' lives, particularly with regard to their future in the marketplace and their transition to adulthood; mastery of academic content will ultimately determine employment options and interests. Thus, an ability to "mask" academic content in activities will be a key indicator of a program's success in engaging and keeping youth in a program. Elsewhere (Delgado 2000a: 86), I wrote:

> An organization's willingness to resist conventionality is an important ingredient in determining the ultimate success of its efforts. . . . Interventions . . . must stress recreational and other activities instead of conventional "talk-based" methods as a means of engaging youth. Much counseling and advice-giving can be systematically incorporated into the use of activities. . . . However, these methods cannot be expected to exist either solely, or in isolation from other forms of activities that are nonstigmatizing and fun.

That is not to say that academic subjects are not learned and mastered. However, youth do not view the activities with academics as a focus of youth-development programming. As an example, consider the painting of a mural. To do so, participants must learn math and chemistry; the latter involves drawing to scale; the former entails being able to mix paints and other types of fluids. Rarely would a youth look at the activity as a lesson in math or chemistry, but the lessons learned can be applied to situations that are not related to mural painting (Delgado and Barton 1998; Delgado 2000b; Siegal 2000).

Staff must be creative in integrating core elements such as cognition into activities—and making them fun. Age considerations will undoubtedly play a role: the younger the age group, the higher the level of integration. At one extreme, college-application workshops might be held for late-adolescents seriously thinking about college. Or there might be SAT preparation courses and tutorials. Nevertheless, staff must never lose sight of the need for "fun" to be a central part of any activity.

Recommendation 2: Activities should be based on the input and decisions of youth. Youth-development activities are never passive; they actively require participants to take an active part in shaping the activity (Lakes 1996; LaMonaca 2000; Smilowitz 2000). Activities must provide youth with an opportunity to achieve results and recognition in the process (Hudson 1997).

Bell (1996) cautions staff to avoid two costly mistakes in working with youth: at one extreme, to give in to anything youth want, and at the other, to let them know that adults really "run the show." Either extreme will result in youth disengagement. Bell (1996) goes on to suggest a method for testing whether or not a behavior is adultist: one needs to ask, "Would I treat an adult this way?" or "Would I have this expectation of an adult?" The answers will help to develop insight.

Empowerment is a key element in helping to differentiate youth-development activities from more conventional and deficit-focused activities (Barker et al. 2000; Morrison, Alcorn, and Nelums 1997; Rose 2000). The latter may seek only to reach out to and involve youth. It is the difference between merely seeking "input," "suggestions," and "thoughts" and allowing youth to determine all aspects of an activity (Linetzky 2000; National Assembly 1998; Villines 2000; Stevenson 2000).

This does not mean that adults cannot help youths to arrive at decisions; however, adults are clearly secondary in the decision-making process (LaMonaca 2000; Penuel 1995; Pittman 1999a). This does not mean that youths have no need to work closely with adults; they are still very much in need of establishing and maintaining close relationships with caring adults (Braverman et al. 1994; Freedman 1993; Hahn 1999a, 1999b; Hudson 1997; McLean and LaFrance 1999).

McLaughlin (1993; 61) stated, probably better than anyone else, the importance of adults in youth-serving organizations:

> Stability and consistency are essential to establishing a climate of trust and to making credible claims of caring and support. Young people are in desperate need of the things that adults can provide, but they learn from the street and family to trust no one but themselves. The most essential contribution that youth organizations can make to the lives of young people is to have a caring adult who recognizes a young person as an individual and who serves as a mentor, coach, gentle but firm critic, and advocate.

Adults can provide a corrective. They remain key players in youth-development programs.

Camino (2000), based on a lengthy study of youth-adult partnerships, concluded that these partnerships could and should form an integral part of any youth-development paradigm or program. Successful partnerships (1) are based on a set of principles and values that inform and direct relationships and behaviors; (2) entail delineation of a set of skills and competencies for both adults and youth; and (3) provide vehicles for implementing and achieving purposeful community social action.

Rauner (2000) stresses that, as a means of building relationships between staff and youth, activities should be nonthreatening and repetitive. Relationship building can happen for youths not taking part in a given activity: standing by and observing provides nonparticipants with a form of learning. This is often overlooked.

Youth-development programs are ideal places to foster increase in problem-solving skills. A democratic structure facilitates youth questions, debating, and evaluation of adults skills that are rarely actively encouraged in school or in families (Lakes 1995; Penuel 1995); yet they are essential in any healthy relationship, whether it be adult-youth or youth-youth based. Youth-development settings may be the only place where youth are not only allowed to but are actually encouraged to view themselves as equal to adults.

Decision making is closely tied to competencies in carrying out decisions and accepting responsibilities. Decision making can be thought of as occurring along a continuum: at one end, youth have input but do not decide; at the other end, youth simply decide. Getting to the latter comes through experience, support, and coaching. Thus decision making should never be thought of as an abdication of adult guidance or responsibility. Youth decision making must be a goal of any youth-development program. Youths must be actively involved in determining the nature and extent of their participation (Hudson 1997).

Recommendation 3: Activities develop competencies through individual *and* group-focused activities. Youths' goals involve working with many other youths. They want to, and need to, develop positive social relationships with both peers and adults. This dynamic dimension of youth development must be grounded in real-life circumstances. Groups of peers wield tremendous influence in shaping values, attitudes, and behaviors.

It is artificial to think of youth development as being exclusively focused on the individual. Youth-development practice can have an impact far beyond the youth participants. It can benefit adults and communities, too. Group activities facilitate what Fine and Mechling (1993; 135) refer to as "idioculture": "An idioculture consists of a system of knowledge, beliefs, behaviors, and customs that is shared and referred to by members of an interacting group and that serves as the basis of further interaction." Idioculture permits groups to become a social reality for participants. Group members, for example, can thus attempt friendships. If the group is engaged in positive actions (as are youth-development programs), the idioculture takes on greater prominence in shaping behaviors that will transfer into other domains.

Rarely will program goals be achieved without a combination of individual and group activities. Although these two types of activities can be complementary, they can also seek to achieve significantly different goals. Delgado (2000a) argues that programs should provide participants with opportunities to engage in both types of activity because each provides important information for staff and lessons for youth. Individual activities provide staff with the opportunity—perhaps a rare opportunity—to engage one-on-one and learn more about a particular participant. Group activities facilitate the development of competencies in working with peers, and such skills—for example, in communication, reading social cues, and teamwork—can all be transferred to other social situations.

Finally, whether activities be individual or group-centered they need to provide youth with the opportunity to be creative. There are far too few opportunities for youth to tap their creativity in a manner and setting that respects them.

Recommendation 4: The time element must be given careful consideration in planning activities. Activities and time are inseparable in youth development: one influences the other. Activities must be conceptualized in such a way that there is sufficient time to complete them the day they are initiated, or if this is not possible that an activity lend itself to being interrupted at some natural occurring point, so it can be picked up later without major disruption. It is well-known in the field that participants are often unwilling or unable to attend programs on a regular and sustained basis. Some youths have chaotic lives wherein long-term commitment to a program is virtually impossible. If such commitments are made a requirement of ongoing participation, many youths would not be able to participate.

Flexibility in attendance is essential in order to increase participation by at-risk youth. Consequently, staff must endeavor to plan activities in such a way that lessons can be learned and taken at the end of the day, even if the project carries over into other days or weeks. The core elements (chapter 5) have to be integrated into activities. Thought must be given to ensure that activities are more meaningful than just "killing time" and keeping youth safe.

When a series of core elements are integrated into an activity, attention must be paid to highlighting them. A cognitive core element, for example, can easily be integrated into the planting of a community garden (Delgado

2000b). Participants must be able to apply mathematical principles to the planning of a garden plot, and attention should be paid to how the "lessons learned" can be applied to other areas of a youth's life. To give another example, a social core element may require staff to explore communication patterns within a group activity (e.g., differences according to gender, cultural heritage, etc.) No opportunity must missed to maximize the benefits of an activity.

Recommendation 5: Activities can neatly be divided into three time categories, and ideally some of each type should be planned. There are those activities that can be planned, implemented, and evaluated the same day; there are those that are intermediate—that can stretch over a period of a week or several weeks; and there are extended activities that cover a period of several months and provide participants with an opportunity to address a long-term goal. Each of these three types of activities has a different set of goals. If carefully planned, they can systematically build upon each other.

Long-term activities are complex, require extensive planning, involve significant resources, and necessitate extensive interactions between youths and adults. Goals and activities are rarely of one type of another. Quite often the three types of activities—short, intermediate, and long-term—occur concurrently, much as in life itself. As youth competencies increase, the complexity of each of these activities can grow. Activities, for example, can be multiple and have a small group of youths working on them, requiring that they report to the larger group. Or they can involve participants from one program working with youths from other programs (e.g., cosponsoring a major event like a conference or community fair).

Kurth-Schai (1988) suggests a number of strategies to help youth assume more demanding activities over time: encouragement to be active and discretionary; have youths become active in shaping their educational experience; have them develop a willingness to share the results of their experiences with adults as well as peers; encourage participants to generate new knowledge to benefit themselves, their families, community, and society—a progression that must be sensitive to the age of participants. Age-specific challenges are essential both to motivate youths and to enhance their life-skills.

Hart, Atkins, and Ford (1998) suggest the use of community-service activities as a means of developing moral identity. Community service lends itself to achieving this objective through progress intensity (time and effort) over an extended period of time. Youth may initially volunteer on a limited basis. Later they can increase their involvement, both as to time and complexity of assignments.

Rauner (2000) conceptualizes community service as an activity for youth to participate in the "real world" and as a means of channeling the abundant amount of energy youth possess into productive goals. Since second chances at engaging youth are rare, a program's initial effort must be successful. Every effort needs to be made to maximize the impact of activities. This can be accomplished by setting realistic goals and addressing as many core elements as possible in the selection of activities.

Recommendation 6: Optimal use of activities involves addressing more than one core element: the more core elements addressed through an activity, the more natural the lessons learned. But this also entails more planning. Earlier in this chapter I cited an example of an activity that works with more than one core element—the community garden that involved the development of math skills. The integration of multiple core elements fits well into a youth-development paradigm.

Since core elements do not exist in isolation from each other, staff must give thought to which of the six core elements will be center stage and which will play a secondary role. If all core elements are integrated equally, depth is sacrificed for breadth. It is important to pause and identify the need to have clarity concerning the primary goals of an activity. If there are too many goals, the core elements addressed may lead to confusion and dilution of the activity's impact. This prioritizing aspect of youth programming is much too important to be left to chance.

McLaughlin (1993; 55) points how activities, regardless of type, can meet multiple needs, particularly for youths who are marginalized: "Even activities with an apparent narrow purpose—tumbling, basketball, or theater—address multiple needs for youth." To list but a few "services," tutoring, advice giving, information sharing, validation, encouragement, and trust can be integrated into what appears on the surface to be nothing but a "fun" activity. Activities bring youth-development philosophy to life; they embody the principles and core elements. They can also easily represent the soul of an organization, and be the lens through which to identify organizational priorities. A program's appeal rests with the nature of activities offered: they can attract youth or repel them. Activities, then, are not easily standardized; they are very dependent upon who implements them and the youth that do them—a latitude that is not only unavoidable but also essential.

THE SETTING—A BORDER ZONE

What qualifies as a "youth development organization"? Walker and Dunham (1994; 1) provide a definition that appropriately captures a sense of excitement:

> A youth development organization exists to promote the positive, healthy development of young people. Youth development organizations are different from agencies and systems that exist to provide social control, treatment, or training for young people. . . . Their mission is to provide the challenges, experiences, support, and help young people need to develop to their fullest potential. These community-based organizations work to meet the needs in the environment and enhance the learning experiences of young people. No single organization does it all.

Youth development settings can be conceptualized in a variety of ways. Conceiving them as "border zones," or places that effectively mediate between life on the streets and life in mainstream domains such as schools, peers, and community, provides an interesting perspective on the role of these organizations (Heath 1994). These settings provide youth with a "sanctuary"—a place where they are not only physically and psychologically safe but also have a respite during which they can explore, learn, play, and grow, without the stresses found in their lives "outside" (McLaughlin, Irby, and Langman 1994). Reflection, questioning, dialoguing, and imagining are essential aspects of growing up, and youth-development settings provide youths with opportunities to do these things (Shames and Gatz 2000).

Youth-development organizations can also be viewed as settings that provide "nonformal" education to youth. Nonformal education is defined as "organized, systematic teaching and learning carried on outside the formal school system" (Walker and Dunham 1994; 2). This education cannot be considered an alternative to formal education taking place in schools; instead of academic training, it provides life skills that help youths to maximize their potential as they mature. Youth-development principles and activities stress experiential methods of learning and are well fitted to this task.

The make-up of the organizational sponsoring programs plays a significant role in shaping how the youth-development paradigm is brought to life.

For example, organizations with established histories of hiring professionally credentialed staff will conceive of youth development in ways different from those of organizations who hire community residents as staff—people without formal-education degrees. The former will expect a high degree of "professionalism," which likely will be translated into behaviors concerning youth-staff boundaries, educational credentials, record keeping, work performance, and so on. The latter will expect staff to be closely connected to youth and that a in-service training will be required to bring them up to speed. Although youth-development organizations do not fit neatly into categories, this section provides a taxonomy to help readers think about organizational types.

It has been estimated that more than seventeen thousand nonprofit agencies can be classified as youth-development organizations. In terms of the amount of time spent by youths in an organized setting, youth-development organizations are second only to schools (National Collaboration for Youth 1996; Poinsett 1996). Although the field of youth development has enjoyed a long and rich history in this country, its practice has been limited to certain types of organizations such as recreational agencies, after-school programs, and youth-focused agencies such as YMCAs, YWCAs, and gender-specific clubs. These organizations have done an admirable job of fostering youth-development activities, but there are many other possible types of organization (Meyers 1998; Rattini 1998; Teachey 1999; Turner 1994). According to the Carnegie Council (1995), five types of undertake community-based youth-development programming: (1) private, nonprofit, national-affiliated youth organizations; (2) community-based organizations without national affiliations; (3) religious youth organizations; (4) adult service clubs, sports organizations, senior citizens groups, museums that specifically run youth-development programs; and (5) public-sector institutions such as the ones identified as new frontier settings in this book. Each of these types of organization includes many variations.

I want to add an additional category to that list: ethnically based, nontraditional organizations. Nontraditional agencies are community-based institutions that have as a primary purpose the selling of a product or service (Delgado 1999a). Institutions such as grocery stores, beauty parlors, restaurants, and barbershops may sponsor a sports league or team as part of their service to the community.

A broad definition of youth development goes well with an expanded array of settings and activities. Communities may have unique configurations of sites where youth development is practiced. The character of some settings will appear to be obvious, given the name of the organization, its history, and reputation. Other settings, perhaps sponsored by a small organization, may be almost invisible against the backdrop of many other programs; thus any effort to identify and assess the extent of youth-development programming in a community will prove to be a noteworthy endeavor (Shames and Gatz 2000).

It is worth asking whether there are ideal organizations wherein youth development is practiced optimally. A number of national youth organizations and the author have provided a profile of an exemplary organization for youth development (Delgado 2000A; Gambone 1993; Howard 1997; Networks for Youth Development 1998). The essential qualities involve organizational processes and structure. The organization (1) would sponsor supportive missions that specifically embrace youth development; (2) would be responsive to environmental forces (provide sanctuary); (3) would provide opportunities for youth contributions to community (encourage service); (4) would maintain high and clear expectations of youth; (6) would provide individual and group activities; (7) would create a caring and trusting relationship between youth and adults; (8) would have a diversified funding base with an opportunity for community contributions of funds, goods, and services; (9) would maintain a strong community base; (10) would sponsor programs stressing community capacity enhancement.

Langman and McLaughlin (1993) have found that youth-development organizations develop identities and reputations based on any or all of the following: identity of youth (gender, ethnicity, race, sexual orientation, focus on physical and emotional challenges); focus (sports, education, health, character development); and institutional affiliation (religious, public or private, national or local affiliation). It is safe to say that no youth-serving organization can lay claim to all of the above qualities. Achievement of exemplary status can best be thought of as a journey rather than a place where one has arrived. Organizations that are successfully carrying out their mission are ever willing to change and adapt to their environment.

We would do well here to pause and note the important role of staff in youth-development programs. It may seem to be stating the obvious, but the staff are of overwhelming importance to programs; this observation is sometimes lost in the day-to-day struggles. Jarvis, Shear, and Hughes (1999; 741) write: "It is essential that youth organizations create work environments in which staff know their contributions are valued, feel ownership for the mission and vision of the agency, learn what it means to really learn and to do so continually, and work together as partners with each other and the young people and families in the program." Although there is no disputing that youth-development programs are for youth, staff (sometimes young themselves) cannot be taken for granted. They are the glue that keeps all of the components of a program together. Staff needs therefore must be systematically assessed and tended to in the course of a program's life. High turnover rates, absenteeism, and low morale are often the symptoms of a program that is misdirected. Needless to say, youth-development principles cannot be achieved in such situations.

Fine and Mechling (1993; 138) comment on the tension youth programs face in seeking to balance general group needs with those of individuals:

> From one perspective, all children—indeed, all humans—are alike. But from an equally reasonable perspective, each child is unique. . . . Neighborhood-based, voluntary organizations for children necessarily fashion their programs for some general population, even if an important element of these programs is to try to accommodate the needs of an individual child. What is the appropriate level for making such generalizations, taking into account age, gender, ethnicity, race, social class, physical and mental disability, and even sexual orientation?

YOUTH DEVELOPMENT AND THE MARGINALIZED

Youth development is for all youths, regardless of life circumstances. However, a review of the literature and comments from the field of practice indicate that the paradigm is still very much targeted at specific types of youths—those who either display some set of risk-factors or have been identified as in need of services. The list goes on and on, but examples are youths in prison and juvenile-justice settings; youths in transition to independent living; youths who are disconnected from society and its key institutions, including family; youths with developmental disabilities; poor and working-class youths; youths who are parents; youths with severe and persistent emotional problems.

William Julius Wilson's (1999) work in urban communities has highlighted the interaction of various factors on the employment opportunities for African American males and how their perceptions of opportunity, or lack of it, have shaped their behaviors and expectations. It is indeed true that youth development has particular relevance to youth who are disenfranchised, their potential for making contributions to society having been severely limited (Delgado 2000A; Richardson and Nixon 1997). Roth et al. (1998; 443) argue this very point:

> Programs may be more beneficial for some groups than for others. To this date, this question has not been adequately addressed. Proponents of positive youth development talk about its universality—that all youth need supports and guidance to develop their assets. However, youth development programs tend to target economically disadvantaged youth. It is likely that programs offering services in more affluent communities may not be as effective because the need is not as great. At the same time, in communities with few supports, the type of program offered might have to be more comprehensive than those in communities with more supports.

McLaughlin and Heath (1993) coined the term *social death*. It refers to the perceptions of marginalized youths that their lives are devoid of meaningful employment and social mobility and that they have low self-confidence and belief in themselves. This social death can result in youth joining gangs, having children, dropping out of school, and turning to drugs. They disconnect from the positive elements of their social domains because they believe that "the cards are stacked against them" and that sustained efforts to progress are futile.

One of the most important roles of high school is preparing youths for, and connecting them to, the institutions of adult life, including colleges and universities. However, in the case of marginalized youth in urban high schools, this does not occur as much as it does in suburban and middle-class communities (Hill 1999). Critics argue that many urban schools prepare marginal youth for adult institutions such as prisons (or in the case of the lucky ones, the military), whereas, in a society that demands ever higher skills, a central function of schools should be to prepare students for gainful employment (Lerman 1999; Pouncy 1999). U.S. Schools are still severely segregated. It has been estimated that almost 40 percent of the nation's African American students, 32 percent of Latino, and 36 percent of students with limited English proficiency are educated in forty-seven large-school districts (Center for Economic Development 1995). Such segregation is a great challenge for the field of youth development.

Any effort to view undervalued youth—otherwise known as at-risk—must take a multidimensional perspective. Youth-related social problems rarely exist in singular form. Drug-abusing behavior, for example, may be closely linked to criminal behavior such as stealing, selling drugs, and poor school performance. The holistic perspective inherent in youth development lends itself well to work with marginalized youth, their families, peers, and community (Earls, Cairns, and Mercy 1993; Hernadez, Siles, and Rochin 2000; Leventhal and Keeshan 1993).

Anti-attrition philosophies are not uncommon in successful programs targeting marginal youth. This approach uses such techniques as home visits by staff, constant follow-up on school progress and review of report cards, and meeting with youth outside of program hours. Such efforts show youth participants that an adult cares and is not satisfied with just focusing on program time and activities—that the other social domains, too, are important.

Youth development focused on marginalized youth must also endeavor to address the needs of the surrounding community. The need for literacy training, for example, may exist not only among youth but among their parents as well. Efforts to increase reading, writing, and other basic skills are rarely found in well-to-do communities, but in poor and working-class communities such a service can have a wide impact beyond youth. The manner in which youth-development programs are conceptualized is very much influenced by whether youth are marginalized because of socioeconomic class and ethnic/racial background (Mora 2000).

Youth development with marginalized groups requires that careful attention be paid to issues related to identity, particularly with youth of color. Internalized feelings based on stereotypical views of them, and general distrust of them, are not unusual. Careful attention to ways that allow these youths to recapture their lost histories—their ethnic/racial identities—are critical components of programs in these areas (Delgado 2000A). The challenge becomes even greater in programs where the composition of participants is diverse and includes white, non-Latino youth. A climate that encourages all youths to better understand the roots of their identity and respects differences can be a powerful vehicle (Erkut et al. 1999).

Connell and Aber (1999; 8) make a clear distinction between the "navigational" skills of "advantaged" and "disadvantaged" youth:

Learning to navigate is relatively easy for youth who grow up in advantaged neighborhoods, where they daily witness adults who practice their roles and procedures. But many poor youth do not grow up where adults practice their mainstream roles and procedures; instead, these youth learn different kinds of navigational skills, aimed at surviving on the streets. In some ways the skills they learn are similar to combat skills in their challenges and the seriousness of their consequences—and also in their low applicability and transferability to mainstream life. This inability to navigate in mainstream circumstances puts many poor youth at a serious disadvantage in joining mainstream life, even when they have the will and opportunity.

Burton (2001), too, identifies the role of navigational skills —"survival strategies"—in helping her negotiate her Los Angeles neighborhood. She notes the importance of practitioners and researchers better understanding these competencies.

Youth-development programs are faced with the challenge of providing marginalized youth with "new" navigational skills without losing the old skills that may have served them well in the neighborhood (Anderson 1999). The old skills served to get them to the program, and they simply cannot turn their backs on them, having gotten this far. However, they need "transitional" navigational skills that can blend the new with the old. Clearly, programs in well-to-do communities do not have to worry about this.

Brown and Emig (1999) make an important point in their summary of the prevalence, patterns, and outcomes of disconnected youth. To become disconnected from mainstream institutions does not mean that the "disconnect" is permanent; it is not a life sentence, as many would have us believe. Youth-development programs can succeed in engaging these youths, and under the right circumstances (caring adults, creation of positive peer groups, resources) they can reconnect and become independent and contributing adults (Delgado, forthcoming b).

FRAMEWORKS FOR PRACTICE

Frameworks function to help practitioners conceptualize the various steps needed to activate their practice. Invariably, a framework consists of two key elements. One is theoretical and provides the practitioner with conceptual material to guide the intervention; the other I will call interactional. *Interactional* refers to politics and local circumstances—how they influence the application of theory. Theory and politics go hand in hand in any form of practice. Some practitioners and academics would argue that the two cannot be separated from "real life" situations.

Every profession has multiple frameworks for practice. This abundance has advantages and disadvantages. The use of a framework will be familiar to any practitioner with a degree of formal education; multiple frameworks, however, complicate the already muddy picture we have of youth development. It has been only relatively recently that frameworks specific to youth development have appeared in the literature. These frameworks have provided the field with important guidance in the conceptualization and operationalization of key constructs. They have also taken into account youth development's unique set of circumstances.

Astroth's (2000) development of a Vibrancy Index represents a novel, and painless, way that youth-development programs can measure organizational culture, philosophy, programs, staff, and power structure. This framework addresses elements that Astroth believes are essential for youth-development programs to practice. If used correctly, this tool will, over time, help organizations to achieve their goals.

The Family and Youth Services Bureau (Administration on Children, Youth, and Families) identified six key areas to consider in the development any youth-development framework (Family Youth Services Bureau 1998): (1) Collaboration; (2) Education of service providers, policymakers, families, and communities; (3) Creation of a shared vision for youth and community; (4) Achievement of requisite organization change to foster this form of practice; (5) Process and outcome evaluation—a must; and (6) Creation of positive images of youth in the media and the community. These key areas highlight the immensity of the task. It is important that a broad perspective be taken.

Hughes and Curnan (2000: 11) identify a need for a more user-friendly framework:

> Over the past seven years, communication about CYD [community youth development] has been limited and uneven. To start with, while elements of the approach were evident in many different settings (service learning, community schools, empowerment, and enterprise zones, and street outreach come to mind), there was no one unifying model to build upon. In addition, only a few, many of who were simultaneously learning and being called upon to articulate the approach to others held a picture of the whole. This often resulted in ideas that were neither fully formed nor set in a context that facilitated full participation. Last, the transformation of CYD principles into action has been spotty, for

principles alone don't sufficiently convey what people need to know to fully grasp the approach.

Hughes and Curnan (2000) then construct a five-part framework for action in the community youth-development field: (1) Target the groups that will benefit (communities, families, youth—with an emphasis on youth); (2) Formulate basic assumptions; (3) Formulate strategies (policy development, capacity building, and facilitative leadership); (4) Name the expected immediate outcomes (policy, field, youth, community/family); and (5) Name the expected broader impacts (on youth, individuals, community organizations, communities). This framework is an excellent jumping-off point for further development of action frameworks. It has an analytical dimension (theory) and an interactional dimension (political).

Connell and Kubisch (2001) advocate a community-action framework for community-based youth-development initiatives. Intended as a practical guide for funders, planners, practitioners, and evaluators, this approach stresses building community capacity and conditions for change, implementing community strategies to enhance organizational supports and opportunities for youth, and increasing adult supports and opportunities for youth. These perspectives, it is proposed, will improve youth-development outcomes and long-term outcomes in adulthood.

Youth-development goals cannot be achieved without active partnerships and collaborations between the organization initiating the programming and other community-based institutions, both formal and informal. The National Assembly (1997) identified seven concepts that provide a philosophical foundation for successful collaboration: (1) Shared vision; (2) Skilled leadership; (3) A process orientation; (4) Diversity (cultural, racial, ethnic, and socioeconomic) of membership in the initiative; (5) A membership-driven agenda; (6) Multiple (broad-based) sectors of support; and (7) Accountability (with specified results and outcomes).

The National Youth Development Information Center (1999) identified six elements that for success must be an integral part of youth-development activities: (1) The program must be comprehensive, with a clear mission and goals that stress youth development; (2) Staffing of programs must be by committed, caring, and professionals; (3) Activities must be youth-centered and in youth-accessible facilities; (4) There must be culturally competent and diverse programming; (5) There should be youth ownership and meaningful involvement in all aspects of programs; and (6) There should be a positive focus on including all youth, regardless of ethnicity/race, gender, and socioeconomic background. These elements can appear in various degrees, depending on the goals of a program, its resources, and the background of the youth participants.

The twenty-first century will witness the appearance of many additional frameworks for youth-development practice. Readers can adopt the one that best matches their perspective on practice or borrow elements from several.

꒰

At this point, the reader may be overwhelmed with excitement, confusion, and anxiety: youth development can be awe-inspiring because of its potential, and when working with youth, one cannot help but be caught up in the enthusiasm of youth itself. However, youth development can also be overwhelming because of its scope and its resistance to being neatly categorized into a narrow population, set of activities, or type of setting. I hope that this chapter has provided the reader with a sense of how, where, and with whom the paradigm can be practiced.

The broad scope of what is possible in the youth-development field should be encouraging for practitioners. A search for the "ideal" setting to carry out youth development may be just that—an "eternal search." There is no ideal organization or ideal set of activities: the intersection of where organization, community, and practitioner overlap can be considered the ideal at that point in time. Clearly, flexibility is the name of the game. Practice must also be dynamic; stagnation would mean not being there to maximize youth's potential.

Local circumstances such as sociodemographic composition of population, funding, organizational support, and community-organization relationships play influential roles in dictating how youth development can be conceptualized and carried out. Nevertheless, practitioners have selected the field not because it is easy and predictable; the challenges are always there, every day.

This chapter has also outlined a variety of places and activities that can be used to carry out youth-development strategies. In part 2, we now further explore "new frontiers" for youth development, bringing into the discussion other places for practice.

8 / YOUTH DEVELOPMENT: PROGRAM EVALUATION

PROGRAM EVALUATION often forms the final stage of any framework. This stage provides all stakeholders with insightful information on the impact of an intervention on the participants. Program evaluation is not new to youth development, but among the field's current set of challenges is *resistance* to evaluation. Although the human-services field over the years has tried to come to grips with the need for evaluation, the relationship with this area is almost one of love-hate.

It is clearly beyond the scope of this book to ground the reader in how best to evaluate youth-development programs, and this chapter will not even seek to identify all the obstacles one runs into in doing evaluations. While not a "tool box," the chapter will, however, provide the reader with insights into evaluation, and make a series of recommendations. This overview of evaluation of youth development highlights the multifaceted set of challenges and rewards associated with this form of practice. The practice of youth development is dynamic, and so is its evaluation.

KEY EVALUATION QUESTIONS

There is an obvious connection between evaluation and research, but the practice of research itself sometimes is questioned. What role can or should research play in promoting youth-development practice? Or, a better question: Is there in youth development a role at all for research? Most practitioners I think believe research should play a role, although there will be differences of opinion on its nature. Zeldin (1995b: 1) argues that the field cannot advance without the benefits of research:

Research is vital to shifting paradigms and for bringing new information into public discourse. It rarely has powerful impact alone, of course. How much research findings are accepted and understood always depends, in large part, on prevailing societal values, fears and hopes. Further, the power of research stems directly from the ability of stakeholders to incorporate research findings into a larger message, and subsequently the extent to which stakeholders are willing and able to disseminate the findings.

The relevance of research findings is increased dramatically when they can be explicit about specific and targeted audiences. Under such circumstances, the information they provide can, for example, influence the planning and monitoring of community-based collaborations and involve stakeholders. The discovery of new and exciting knowledge with immediate applicability is relevant not only to process but also can help evaluate the impact of a program on youth (Zeldin 1995b). Program effectiveness should be a topic near and dear to funders, administrators of programs, staff, youth participants, and community. All of these constituencies must both ask the questions and help answer them.

So-called program effectiveness can be rated in a variety of ways, sometimes by posing questions; it does not necessarily lend itself to standardized methods of measurement. This methodological flexibility can be a mixed blessing. It can present a problem not only when laying out goals and objectives but also when it comes time for evaluation itself. A result of such flexibility is that much effort, time, and resources must be directed to maintaining a detailed history of decisions made in the course of programming. Staff members when asked about evaluation will rarely share stories of excitement, insight, and how profound positive change resulted from an evaluation. More often than not, they share how the process was either alienating or meaningless—a process that entailed answering countless questions that made little or no sense to practitioners, posed by people who were not familiar with the program. This process, it is felt, takes valuable time, energy, and resources away from services to youth in need. Given this background, efforts at meaningful evaluation of programs must often first surmount such staff baggage.

Three questions need to be asked to address the heart of a program—questions that seem simple and straightforward but that in practice rarely are: (1) Does the program accomplish its stated objectives? (2) Who does it work for? (3) How can we make it better and more cost effective? These questions are common to other program evaluations; they are not found only in the youth-development field. However, youth-development programs face a host of issues that their deficit-oriented counterparts do not. All three of the areas addressed by these questions—process, outcome, and impact—present unique challenges to youth-development programs.

Ideally, each of these questions would be answered in an in-depth manner. However, the practical side of programming and evaluation dictates that compromises are needed in addressing them. One of the questions will invariably take center stage, the other two being of secondary importance, and the decision as to which is which depends on local circumstances.

EVALUATION CHALLENGES

At times it seems that the challenges associated with evaluation far outweigh the rewards; it is tempting to say that evaluation is too arduous, and therefore let us not bother to do it. But the challenges are not insurmountable, neither from a process point of view nor methodologically. And as noted by Curnan and LaCava (2000: 48), "without evaluation capacity, the movement may be destined to plateau long before it realizes its full potential." The field is receptive to the introduction of new models, particularly those that stress participation and capacity-enhancement principles. New models bring excitement to evaluation and offer hope that it will become more relevant.

Evaluations of any kind can cause anxiety in a program. Muraskin (1993: 9) writes: "Staff members may feel threatened by an evaluation because they believe that their individual performance is being scrutinized or that the program's fate hangs in the balance. They may believe that the tools of evaluation are ill suited to measure the positive changes they see occurring. The best method to overcome staff members' fears and resistance is to involve them in designing the evaluation and in interpreting its findings." Staff anxiety cannot be ignored by evaluators; the active cooperation of staff and youth are essential in any substantive effort to assess process or outcome (Zeldin and Camino 1998).

Some challenges are unique to this paradigm and its emphasis on enhancing youth assets (i.e., as distinct from stopping the onset of problems). When youth development specifically focuses on enhancement of life skills, evaluation of behavioral outcomes becomes problematic: the success of one participant may be different from another. No two youngsters are alike. The contexualization of this evaluation is essential (Meyer 1999). Leffert et al. (1996: 3) comment: "We need to move beyond the problem-focused paradigm that tries to reduce or control negative behavior through prevention, early interventions, and treatment and/or incarceration when the problem becomes severe. Although there will always be a need for these types of services, those who work with and care about young people are recognizing the power of an alternative approach, one which focuses on promoting the positive."

In terms of measuring success, a program that focuses on short-term problems and symptoms holds a distinctive advantage, compared with those seeking long-term outcomes (Morrison, Alcorn, and Nelums 1997). It can be argued that youth-development programs that seek both short- and long-term outcomes increase the complexity of an evaluation effort; increase in complexity translates into an increase in time and funds (Delgado 2000a).

A focus on problem-specific (expressed need) data is often reinforced by how government stresses the gathering of this type of information. Deficit-driven data, as a result, is readily available and relatively inexpensive to access. These user-friendly aspects are not to be minimized. However, data focused on youth assets does not enjoy the same luxury as their deficit counterparts (Delgado 2000a; Moore 1998; National Research Council 1999). Youth-development programs therefore face the unenviable task of having to generate community-asset data to compare participants with the general community. Programs in "unconventional" settings, stressing experiential education, typify these challenges. Adventure-based experiential programs do not respond well to conventional evaluation (Bocarro and Richards 1998). Adventure-based programs, although using a curriculum-based approach, are dynamic in nature and therefore subject to many changes in the course of programming. In addition, research methodology that follows usual procedures, which may be inconsistent with nonstandard programs, will not adequately capture the impact of these programs.

Evaluation has received increased attention as more programs have been funded (Roth et al. 1998). Catalano et al. (1998) found in their review of positive youth-development evaluations that four issues stand out: (1) There are relatively few follow-up studies; (2) There is a need for standardized measures; (3) It is important to have comprehensive information on programs; and (4) There is a need for strong quasi-experimental designs. The most controversial of Catalano et al.'s findings is the fourth. Very often the strongest measure of an intervention's impact can be measured only with a quasi-experimental research design. However, using this design is incredibly arduous in "real life" situations. Random assignment to intervention and nonintervention groups may be appealing in theory, but organizations are often reluctant to engage in this design because of political and ethical considerations. The mere mention of a quasi-experimental design, with random assignment of youth, can wreck an evaluation even before it starts. This extreme consequence, it must be said, is not restricted to youth development; any service provision in the human service or education field, if it entails depriving a youngster in need of services, will elicit this response. Effective evaluation of youth-development programs, while it may demand creative solutions, must also be applied with patience, flexibility, and a commitment to not disrupting programming.

The National Research Council (1999: 65) urged that for evaluation to be meaningful, expectations for youth-development programs must be realistic:

> The field needs to consider what are appropriate expectations for these programs in terms of individual-level outcomes. For example, it is clearly unrealistic to think that a single three-month community-based-after-school program will have such a profound impact that it will overcome competing deficits or problems, such as a dysfunctional home; overcrowded schools with few resources and poorly trained teachers; and impoverished and disorganized communities with few social services.

The Carnegie Council on Adolescent Development (1992) identified two critical areas for evaluation of youth—development programs: (1) Paucity of support, expertise, or both, for evaluation of programs; and (2) The need for improved approaches to evaluation (Roth et al. 1998). More specifically, the first of these criticisms refers to, among other things, inadequate record-keeping systems and management-information systems, staff turnover, and lack of specificity in outcome objectives. The second refers to a need for longitudinal studies, follow-up with participants, the gathering of data across domains, and an inability to integrate findings (theoretical and empirical) into program design.

Sengstock and Hwalek (1999: 8) comment on an aspect of evaluation that has generally escaped attention:

> Evaluating programs for children and youth is much more complex than evaluating programs for adults. The rapid developmental changes that occur in the first 16 years of life are unprecedented compared with

other age groups. Even within a specific age subgroup, programs for children and youth often include a wide variety of racial, ethnic, or cultural backgrounds, or children for whom English is a second language. People attempting to measure outcomes for the first time may not realize that measures developed for adults cannot be used for children.

Sengstock and Hwalek's observations cannot be overlooked by evaluators or funders. The same authors identify eight major areas of evaluation that need attention: (1) Multidimensionality of program outcomes (diversity of outcomes at the individual, age-group, and program levels can become very labor intense if we there is to be fairness for each of these levels); (2) Awareness of time and attention span of young people (this requires the development of questionnaires capable of answering evaluation questions that are not too lengthy or cumbersome; youths will not answer complex questionnaires as readily as adults); (3) Awareness of developmental changes in children and youth (measurements need to differentiate between changes caused by program participation and maturation); (4) There is a need to measure outcomes in a comparison group (locating and engaging a control group is challenging when there is a wide variety of youth in a program; (5) There needs to be age-appropriateness of measurement instruments (with regard to wording and taking into account the group's life experience, as well as attention span); (6) Diversity-sensitive instruments must be developed, with careful attention being paid to culture-specific methods and questions not biased toward standards of the dominant white, non-Latino culture; (7) Program versus individual (the two foci are different and one should not be used to evaluate the other); (8) Ethical issues (confidentiality and ethical practice must not be sacrificed to facilitate speedy evaluation).

La Cava (2000: 48) stresses the need in evaluation for a better understanding of process and context:

> I recognize both the strengths and shortcomings of many traditional approaches to evaluation currently being practiced. And although I understand the importance of being able to demonstrate the effectiveness of social programs and prove they work, I believe that too many promising CYD [community youth development] programs are never fully actualized or understood. Not enough attention is paid to learning about how and why they work, or understanding the contextual conditions that support or hinder their growth and development.

COMMUNITY-BASED EVALUATIONS

In a youth-development context, the question "Is a community more than the sum of its parts?" is provocative. Small and Supple (2001), like other social scientists, define *neighborhood* as (1) a physical location, and (2) having socially shared boundaries; *community,* on the other hand, refers to social relationships that can transcend geographical boundaries. Residents may live in one neighborhood, but worship, shop, and recreate in other neighborhoods. Thus, measurement of the impact of *neighborhood* on youth outcomes is based on the narrow view. The idea that community is not tied to a physical space can have either a positive or negative influence on youth and families. It certainly challenges practitioners in cases where activities are tied to a geographical catchment area; and it similarly affects researchers who are too focused on a set of geographical variables.

The increased importance of community in the youth-development paradigm warrants special attention being paid to this domain in any evaluation effort. Evaluation must be developed in such a way as to capture this influence. Sampson (2001) raises a number of methodological and theoretical challenges to studying the effects of neighborhoods on children, adolescents, and family development, not least of which is the grasping of social processes involving the collective dimensions of community life. Any community-based intervention, be it prevention or youth-development focused, will face numerous challenges (Bond 2000; Jason et al. 2000; Leukefeld and Staton 2000).

Burton (2001), discussing how ethnographic research can help social scientists and practitioners to gain insight into nuanced neighborhood and family processes, refers to "unmeasured variables." Burton argues that unidentified factors may be influencing adolescent outcomes. There sometimes is disagreement between researchers and practitioners over what aspects of community are the most critical to focus on in determining a program's success (Zeldin and Camino 1998). Not surprisingly, "where you stand" is often influenced by "where you sit." Evaluators are not in the same place as front-line youth staff, and a significant barrier is sometimes erected between the two sides.

An in-depth and precise understanding of processes through which neighborhoods influence indicators of positive and negative outcomes is seriously lacking (Avenilla and Singley 2001). The ability to capture how these processes occur and how they are similar or different across lines of ethnicity/race, gender, sexual orientation, and ability serves both to contextualize them and to inform youth-development activities and strategies. Any sustainable and methodologically sound effort at evaluating how neighborhoods influence adolescent development must be able to address at least five key issues, according to Duncan and Raudenbush (1999). These are: (1) Locating neighborhood-based measures that complement the theoretical constructs being used; (2) Taking into account simultaneous influences between youth and their ecological contexts; (3) Avoiding bias determined by "unobservable" characteristics of parents that influence the selection of neighborhood and youth outcomes; (4) Taking into account the role of family in mediating and modeling neighborhood influences; and (5) Selecting a sample with sufficient variability in neighborhood conditions (neighborhoods are not monolithic).

Time, energy, and funds have to be invested to address the challenges involved in conducting program evaluation (Curnan and LaCava 2000; Zeldin and Camino 1998). This investment is critical for advancing the field of youth development, and if made it would soon pay for itself in countless ways. These efforts must be innovative. An important factor is flexibility in how funding is obtained; this can be felt throughout all aspects of a program, including its evaluation (Linetzky 2000).

Venturing into a community cannot be done without serious thought and attention to how best to do so (Jason et al. 2000). It may, for example, involve efforts at hiring community residents to be interviewers and have them select a methodology based on their local knowledge—an approach that is rare but not unheard of. If community capacity-enhancement principles guide this evaluation effort, the investment will yield considerable capital for both community and evaluator.

The field of prevention has made important strides in applying program-evaluation principles. As noted in chapter 4, the field of prevention has moved away from a narrow focus on specific problems to a view of youth that is more holistic. It takes into account assets, individual as well as community. The field of youth development can learn from and borrow from the field of prevention—a development that would further blur the distinctions that have historically divided the two approaches. There are already some experienced evaluators who started in prevention programs who now bring their experience to youth-development programs.

One of the greatest challenges that I faced in evaluating demonstration projects—projects stressing the importance of youth and community assets of marginalized youth—was getting sufficient resources. What stands out in my memory is the role played by staff, particularly those without formal educational degrees, and residents of the communities being served— people of similar background to the youths they worked with. Although the need for evaluation is critical (and this is particularly true in a demonstration project), in the staff view the resources used in this way (time, energy, money) can "as easily" be spent on providing services for marginalized youth, perhaps on increasing the numbers a program can serve. The fear that at the end of a demonstration project, particularly one that is federally funded, a final report will be written and the program closed is not always unfounded; consequently, why bother with evaluation if the community is not to benefit? Or the report goes into a "black hole" and nothing ever comes of it. True, some scholarly publications are produced and results are disseminated at professional conferences. This certainly helps academics to gain tenure and fame, but from the community's standpoint, and particularly from the youth participants' view, life for the community continues without significant change (Curnan and LaCava 2000).

Results of evaluations must be funneled back into communities as quickly as possible. In the process of information dissemination, evaluators must never lose sight of the youths involved and their communities.

RESULTS FROM THE FIELD

Much work still needs to be done in the meta-analyses of youth-development programs (Larson 2000). However, although the practice of youth development has a relatively short history, as the number of programs has increased, findings have slowly started to emerge in the literature. The review of youth-development program-evaluation literature by Roth et al. (1998) could uncover only fifteen studies that met methodological criteria that could be considered scientifically rigorous.

There have been notable efforts at evaluating programs and performing meta-analyses of these evaluations. Larson (2000), for example, found that adolescents participating in effective organizations acquire a new operating language that corresponds with youth development principles. Kahn and Baily (1999). in their longitudinal study of "I have a Dream" programs (a sixth-grade-focused initiative in Chicago) reported that the programs were very successful in increasing graduation rates. Catalano et al. (1998) found encouraging results in their meta-analyses of positive youth-development programs across the United States. These programs were found to change youth behavioral outcomes and the prevention of problem behaviors. Roth et al. (1999), reviewing the evaluations of six programs that employed an integrated conceptualization of youth development and that offered a wide range of services and opportunities, used either random assignments (N=3) or a comparison group design (N=3). They found significant changes in attitudes and behaviors of youth.

Roth et al. (1998) found three themes in their review of fifteen youth-development programs: (1) The more elements of youth development the greater the positive changes in participants; (2) The presence of a caring adult-adolescent relationship is important, although the relationship does not have to follow the conventional one-to-one mentoring model; and (3) Programs that view long-term involvement of youth appear to be more effective than short-term programs.

An often overlooked aspect of evaluation is the need to link individual-level and community-level variables. This linkage offers great promise for the field. No longer can we argue that healthy communities enhance youth development and healthy individuals create healthy communities. The interplay between the two results in an integrative and dynamic approach to understanding youth outcomes (Connell and Kubisch 2001; Massey 2001).

Allowing youth to continue their involvement across the lifespan increases the likelihood of benefits accruing. Although such findings will not come as a great surprise to anyone in the field of youth development, they should have a profound impact on how programs are conceptualized, both from a planning perspective and for funding.

The task of developing measures of success must be accomplished before a program opens its door. In practice, funding will not be obtained until this aspect of evaluation is firmly in place, but unfortunately it is not unusual for a program to come up with measures that do not reflect local circumstances. The professional literature (pro forma in federal grants for example) often dictate what measures of success will be used in a program; however, this literature may not reflect the characteristics or circumstances of local youth. For example, measures of success based on findings involving African American youth should not automatically be applied to Vietnamese youth— a recommendation that may seem obvious but that addresses a quite common mistake. This does not mean that measures of success from elsewhere cannot be used, if they are locally modified; however, the dynamic nature of standards should be recorded and commented on as part of any formalized evaluation, particularly one that places importance on process as well as output and impact. The importance of evaluation linking process and output cannot be overestimated (The Exchange 1998). Process-related information can be instrumental in helping to explain why certain measures of success had to be modified. The lessons learned in doing this can be of immense assistance to other programs.

"Success" in youth development is not absolute, however, because it varies depending upon the levels of adversity faced by youths prior to participation. For example, survival, in the case of marginalized urban youth, is a successful level of achievement (Anderson 1999; Connell and Aber 1999; Delgado 2000a); whereas for economically and socially secure youth, success will rarely so be defined. Achievement of lofty educational and vocational goals may be what determines success for youths with a high degree of security. Connell and Aber (1999: 9) comment on the relativity involved in the term *successful*, calling it "a dynamic and relative concept that will shift in definition depending on the context in which it is employed. However, setting minimal thresholds and optimal levels on those outcomes for individuals and groups of individuals will remain important tasks in . . . the design and evaluation of interventions." Nevertheless, difficult though it maybe to accomplish, youth-development programs should establish thresholds and standards based on local circumstances and norms. These standards can be set through local involvement—that of youths themselves and their communities. It is critical in reviewing evaluations that context not get lost.

PROMISING APPROACHES TO PROGRAM EVALUATION

That a unique set of challenges is encountered in evaluating youth-development programs has not been lost on evaluators. Models specifically targeting youth development have emerged over the past decade. Ostrom, Lerner, and Freel (1995), for example, propose a model that stresses collaboration as a central strategy. It is based on a set of guiding principles: (1) Encouragement of a holistic approach; (2) Inclusion of as many stakeholders as possible in the process; (3) A focus on the actions involved in forming effective programs; and (4) The need for continuous and longitudinal evaluation.

The attractiveness of longitudinal studies for measuring the impact of youth developments is the preferred approach (Larson 2000). Longitudinal studies that are designed to measure dependent variables on multiple occasions are considered the most rigorous approach. The authors advocate the use of asset mapping as an integral part of all phases of an evaluation.

In the spirit of participation and empowerment, the field of youth-development research and evaluation has slowly embraced youth themselves playing an active role in this type of endeavor (La Cava 2000; Matysik 2000). Young people—the ultimate beneficiaries of programs—when partnered with staff and evaluators form a formidable evaluation team. This participation perspective, which stresses research, education, and social change and action, fits well into a youth-development paradigm. Matysik (2000: 19) concludes that "Community Youth Development evaluators need to provide opportunities for youth to take charge of many aspects of their own learning experience . . . such involvement results in valuable development impacts, including greater responsibility, empathy, empowerment, and positive social consequences—not only for the youth involved, but also for those schools and communities in which the projects take place."

Honig, Kahne, and McLaughlin (1998), too, report on the emergence of a theory-of-action approach. The approach emphasizes two critical tasks: (1) To identify the "invisible" assumptions on which a program is based, with an explicit effort to reach consensus on what success depends upon; and (2) A critical examination of these assumptions. The approach impacts all facets of a program, including evaluation. The authors provide a framework to organize the process (indicators, activities, underlying assumptions, assumption check, and future action).

Moore and Glei (1995) discuss the need for measures that cut across domains. This is a challenge for the field since few studies specifically gather data on risks across domains. The authors develop a "missteps scale" (focused on multiple forms of risk taking) and a "positive well-being scale" (focused on measuring positive promising results, evaluation efforts being closely tied to program goals). They stress planning *with* rather than planning *for* youth. Perlmutter, Bailey, and Netting (2000) stress the need for outcome measures to be determined by what clients want, not what funders consider to be important. This may sound easy to implement, but in practice it may prove arduous. Funders rarely have youth playing instrumental roles in determining allocation of funding; thus an adult perspective may prevail in determining "success."

Barkman and Machtmes (2000) propose a fourfold youth-development model for conducting evaluations. The authors developed this model to address four sets of problems often encountered: limited evaluation expertise (raising the importance of having a common language); the need for increased accountability (cost effectiveness); the lack of instruments that generate valid and reliable data; and the lack of user-friendly tools. The Barkman and Machtmes model uses inputs, outputs, and outcome measures on four key youth-development constructs: health, head (cognition), hands (skills), and heart (emotional/social). These constructs encompass forty-seven development skills.

⌒

The challenges facing youth development fall equally into conceptual (analytical) and political (interactional) realms. It should come as no surprise that these two realms are also a part of evaluation.

The subject of program evaluation rarely gets the attention it deserves from practitioners. Evaluation has a great following among academics and funders, however. Part of the reason for this rift can probably be traced to two factors: the importance that practitioners place on service delivery; and the small amount of input they have in the design of the methodology and the construction of questions. Time devoted to evaluation and the countless meetings associated with it takes away from time with youth—time that many staff members believe is much more important than that spent evaluating a program they already know to be successful. Evaluation of programs is not "business as usual." If decisions are made by top management and outside expert evaluators, staff being required only to answer the questions, the procedure will not endear practitioners to researchers. This is divide that does not have to exist. We should take the principles of participation we use in working with youth and apply them to staff, too. with such a democratic approach, feelings of alienation would be minimized.

Terry (2000: 5), identifying an often overlooked aspect of theory building, notes the importance of practitioners influencing theory:

> Evaluators and researchers must examine the traditional notion that "good" ideas are discovered only through academic research. Ideas as effete and socially detrimental as social Darwinism, racial inferiority (eugenics), women's lack of capacity in mathematics, and so on, were developed out of arcane academic research. Perhaps even more important for our discussion is this simple fact: acknowledging CYD practitioners as intuitive sources of "good" ideas opens broad new vistas to our quest for understanding how to better organize our communities and raise our youth.

Youth-development programs cannot perform miracles. An expectation of miracles ultimately leads to "creaming," a process through which youth with low probabilities of success are not accepted into programs. It is critical that programs do not shy away from a challenge. They should be supported in doing so by funders, stakeholders, and community alike.

However, youth-development programs must be prepared to articulate a vision, a profile, of what they are trying to achieve and who it is they seek to serve. This requires that programs maintain clarity, with as much detail as possible, about the "typical" youth they have in mind. This clarity will serve the program well when it comes time to evaluate results.

Enthusiasm for this paradigm must not be taken as a guarantee that all participants will succeed in terms of program objectives. Marginalized youth may not be able to benefit as much as others. Their progress must be measured against their own background and experience, not by standards that are unrealistic or based on norms derived from the dominant culture.

New paradigms bring with them a need for new models of evaluation. New paradigms, however, are rarely totally new, and new evaluation models can best build on previous models. It may entail modifications to existing methods or it may involve new techniques and methods of analysis. Much can be learned and borrowed from experiences of prevention programs, with practitioners and academics working closely together. There must be a willingness to admit mistakes and to accept the results of evaluation efforts. Trust must form the cornerstone of these efforts.

Notwithstanding the advances reported in this book, the importance of conducting contextualized analyses requires that even greater conceptual and methodological developments occur (Billy 2001). The challenges should not be minimized.

PART 2
NEW FRONTIER SETTINGS

We are now ready to approach the subject of new frontier settings. New frontier settings represent a natural extension of what has been said about contextualization in this book's part 1. They will challenge the field of youth development in ways unlike anything faced in the twentieth century. They will require that the field decide where youth development take place to maximize youth potential—decisions that will not be arrived at easily. Dialogue and debate will inform the decisions. Part 2 will usher the reader into the future. For those new to youth development, this trip may appear fast and furious: there are new developments all the time. For readers well initiated in youth development, the following chapters will raise hopes and fears about where the field is heading. This is an exciting time.

9 / THE EMERGENCE
OF NEW FRONTIER SETTINGS

THE EXCITEMENT of venturing into new and uncharted worlds is never for the faint of heart. Previously established approaches, procedures, and experiences may have little value in negotiating a transition such as that taking place in the field of youth development. Ambiguity is very much a part of such an endeavor, but I believe that this situation provides practitioners and academics with an unprecedented opportunity for unprecedented personal growth.

The number of possible new types of settings for youth development is limited only by our imagination—that and our ability to encourage communities to engage in such forms of practice. No one can predict where the field will go in the future—not even in the next decade. The chance to influence the direction is too good to pass up for anyone interested in the well-being of youth.

The speed of change, however, makes it difficult to get a solid grasp of youth development. Practitioners are ever too busy meeting the day-to-day needs of youth to pause and examine the latest trends and events in the field. People in academia, too, are challenged to stay ahead of changes in the field. Youth development is influenced by developments in many other fields (most recently that of information technology), which makes it that much harder to stay on top of the changes.

Today, youth development can take place in settings previously not thought of as possible sites, and those interested in youth development therefore must be flexible in how they define the field and competent to incorporate innovations into existing programs. New frontier settings do not neatly fall into particular known categories, which in part is why this book has been written. This openness as to what can be considered a new frontier setting may cause some confusion. If there is no particular type of setting that can fall into this category, then all settings can be considered new frontier—a view that is well rooted in historical factors. But sets of unique circumstance play critical roles in determining the evolutionary process of new frontier settings.

This chapter examines how some new frontier settings (museums and libraries, for example) have entered the youth-development field. It identifies some of the challenges and considerations they have faced in introducing youth programming into settings that have generally not been thought of as part of the field. The chapter also sets the stage for the other chapters in part 2.

DEFINING NEW FRONTIER SETTINGS

Although youth-development activities have generally been limited to a rather select group of types and settings, youth programming has been advocated for by places that historically have not been thought of as "typical" youth-development settings. Examples of such advocacy groupings are child welfare (Collins in press; Liederman 1995; Sheehy et al. 2000); the juvenile-justice system (Bazemore and Clinton 1997; Capowich 1995); the workplace (National School-to-Work Learning and Information Center 1996); the public assistance sector (Cohen and Greenberg 2000; Gebreselassie and Politz 2000; Knox, Miller, and Gennetian 2000); and therapeutic milieus (Glover 1995). The expansion of youth development to new frontier settings is therefore not out of the ordinary, and this background is one good reason for defining youth development in a broad and flexible manner. This encompassing perspective brings with it the flexibility to include local circumstances—namely, *community* new frontier settings and the targeting of youth with certain sociodemographic characteristics.

Since new frontier settings can take almost any form, the following definition seeks to provide a way both to identify such settings and yet not to exclude potential settings. This is no easy task. I will define new frontier settings as:

> Organizations within a community where a service is provided to the residents. This service is multifaceted and invariably has an educational and recreational dimension. To carry out its mission, the organization targets youth as assets and as a specific age-group population that will play an instrumental role in carrying out the functions of the setting. However, in so doing, youths are required to undertake some form of preparation (training or mentoring).

Various aspects of this definition can be classified as covering structure, process, philosophy (mission), and role within the community.

The rich array of settings that can be placed in the new frontier category can be overwhelming. Museums, for example, can take as their specialty virtually any subject: communication, dolls, media, war, art, computer, automobile, airplane, ships, toys, science, farming, potatoes, sports, immigration, population group, to name a few. Museums do not have to have vast budgets and hire hundreds of staff members to be called a museum. There is something very democratic about this. Although most are found in cities, museums can be in any community, regardless of socioeconomic status, and can fulfill important community functions.

Urban areas, which have many assets that can be marshaled into service for youth development, also have enormous numbers of youths. It follows that there are also endless possibilities for partnerships with community-based organizations. I will admit to a bias: cities should not be conceptualized as magnets for social problems; they must be thought of as having concentrations of assets, with new frontier settings being but one type of asset. The presence of marginalized youth within certain sectors of cities lends itself to youth-development programs that have this group as a central focus.

THE FUNCTIONS OF NEW FRONTIER SETTINGS

Historically, many of the new frontier settings named in this book served distinctive functions: they provided access to information, education, and entertainment. Some appealed to the upper and middle classes; for example, museums of art. Children's museums and science museums were unusual. Other settings—libraries, aquariums, planetariums, and zoos—potentially appealed to a wider range of age groups and socioeconomic classes, although low-income groups may not have patronized these places as much as is sometimes thought. Libraries rose in significance along with public education.

The nation's elite established many new frontier settings. This influenced their priorities and how they were shaped. Government rarely sponsored museums. These institutions therefore reflected the values, vision, and priorities of white non-Latinos. More recently, communities of color have increasingly stepped forward and established museums that reflect their social heritage, but these institutions in no way have the same resources and prestige as the mainstream museums.

Libraries and museums may at first appear to be completely different types of institutions; however, on closer examination the similarities are striking. Both strive to encourage lifelong learning; both house and display objects related to history, natural history, and science; both provide access to research and collections; both work with local educational systems to educate youth (Bartholow 1999). For these two settings to collaborate on youth-development initiatives is not a far-fetched idea, and an increasing number of them are doing so.

NINE KEY PRINCIPLES

At this point I want to pause and list a set of guiding principles for use in new frontier settings. These principles will be supported by examples of practice in later chapters. The nine key principles, culled from the literature, can be used in examining youth-development practice and in establishing activities:

1 Youth development must strive to enhance individual and community capacities. One is not possible without the other.
2 Youth development is predicated on youth exercising meaningful decision making over their programs.
3 Youth development must breakdown racial/ethnic, gender, disability, sexual orientation, and class barriers and stereotypes.
4 Youth development builds bridges between community-based organizations (formal and informal).
5 Youth-development activities must transform the environment in which youth live in the process of transforming the lives of participants.
6 Youth development must provide participants with an opportunity to learn and at the same time to have fun.
7 Youth-development activities must provide youth with opportunities to serve their community.
8 Youth development must provide youth with the necessary knowledge and skills that can be converted into meaningful lifelong employment.
9 Youth development must actively integrate as many core elements as possible into all activities.

These principles take into account the context of many unique settings: aquariums, cyberspace, farms, forests, libraries, museums, newspapers, planetariums, and zoos, among other "unusual" places. Such a range presents practitioners with many challenges in applying youth-development principles, interventions, and techniques, but the process can be exciting as well as challenging.

The above principles may not seem dramatically different from what is usually found in programs stressing capacity enhancement; however, each type of new frontier setting brings with it a certain perspective, and that influences how the principles are implemented. An active goal of bringing together youth and adults, for example, can be achieved through having youth participants on boards of directors; another program might have youth advisory committees, where youth and adults share opinions.

MULTIDISCIPLINARY APPROACHES TO THE NEW FRONTIER

The literature has been quick to point out that youth development is not a profession, that it owes its existence to many different professions, and that elements of it can be found in many disciplines. Many professions have contributed to conceptualization of activities, community involvement, better understanding of social-emotional development, cognition, recreational outlets, and so forth. This "sharing of the wealth" can be both an asset and a liability (Hahn and Raley 1999; Morrison, Alcorn, and Nelums 1997).

On the plus side, the youth-development field can draw on many different resources, which is very much in order when taking a broad perspective. Youth-development activities often have elements of social work, recreation, psychology, theology, education, counseling, and business (Bembry 1998). However, not having a "home" as a profession unto itself limits the field's ability to lobby for funding. It is limited in the use it can make of a professional network and the resources of professional societies. Annual meetings of professionals provide an excellent arena for dialogue and creation of initiatives that bring with them political leverage and funding. This lack of a home has profound implications. In many ways, it isolates new frontier settings, and isolation makes youth-development initiatives more difficult to achieve. It severely limits the number and types of partnerships that can be developed across settings and communities.

The National Collaboration for Youth (1997: 2) notes other limitations that come with youth work and youth development not having a commonly accepted base (not necessarily a professional base): "The portrait of credentialing activities . . . is consistent with the observations of others. Youth work education, training and credentialing efforts are fragmented, lacking a coherent vision and widely varying in their utilization. There is great variation in the quality of content, expertise, and instructional approaches among staff development efforts. It is becoming more apparent by the field as a whole that all these initiatives could benefit from exploring commonalties and establishing mutual goals.

That is, youth development can take many different shapes. It depends on who is using the term. But to have a future we must agree on what constitutes a "youth development field of practice."

New frontier settings can play an important and energizing role in expanding the possibilities for youth development. Most youth-service practitioners have more experience in setting up programs and services in after-school settings (U.S. Newswire 2000). Funders, in turn, probably feel most comfortable in funding programs in such settings. However, youth-development programs and staff cannot take the "easy" way out, being comfortable only with certain settings and activities. The challenge is to reach out into new arenas with new ideas and opportunities for youth.

An expansion of the field to include practice in new frontier settings can provide the field with an important "political" boost in lobbying the nation's decision makers, public and private, for support. Further, it can expand the possibilities for collaborative practice involving key community institutions. New frontier settings enjoy having high levels of institutional legitimacy, and these can be tapped in service to youth, their families, and communities. These institutions often have easy access to the popular media, and some even have public relations departments. These connections and facilities can be used to publicize youth-development activities and events.

There is a tremendous need to identify and involve "unfamiliar" settings that are nonstigmatizing and are open to a wide range of age groups (Siegal 2000). There is a wide variety of places that offer tremendous potential and benefits if youth are engaged in activities that not only enhance their capacities but also perform important community service. Such sites include aquariums (Maloney and Hughes 1999), cyberspace (Deitel 1999; Franklin 2000; Jeffries 1996; Meredith 2000; Napier 1999; *Oakland Post* 1997; Ross 2000; Rubin 1998), farms (Buuck 1998; Delgado 2000b; Del Real 2000), forests (Driscol 1998; Ferguson 1999; Ishaya 1999; *Los Angeles Times* 1996; Manale et al. 1998; Shohomish 1995; Weizel 2000), libraries (American Library Association 1999a, 1999b; Meyers 1999), newspapers (Watts 1998), planetariums and museums (Goldberg 1999; Hayes and Schindel 1994; Institute of Museum Services 1996; Muschamp 1999; Museums Australia

1998), and zoos (Mathews 1999). Engagement in activities at such sites can even lead to further formal education and careers.

Geographical location of settings is often overlooked. Geographical accessibility is an important dimension when reaching out to youth, particularly those who do not own cars or have limited access because of public transportation inadequacies. Most new frontier settings are located on public transportation routes, and it is not unusual to find more than one setting within walking distance of another. Geographical accessibility greatly increases a setting's potential for use in youth development.

These settings also broaden the exposure youth have to the general (adult) public and open up new possibilities for entrance into professions and careers (Teichman and Barry 1999); in other words, new frontier settings facilitate the development of new relationships between youth and adults and between youth and settings. These relationships place youth in the position of being helpers through the use of community service (Fazari 1996; Lake 2000; U.S. Newswire 2000). Community service benefits all parties: those who give, those who receive, and those who witness.

New frontier settings have the potential to fulfill a more meaningful and expanded role in society. As well as being settings for youth-development activities and programs, they can undertake community capacity-enhancement initiatives, broker for resources, advocate, and serve as places where residents can come together to meet and exchange ideas and concerns. They can also use their institutional presence to command the attention of the media, thus highlighting the positive role youth can play in society. Jones (1992) notes that new frontier settings lend themselves to involving youth of various age groups, which makes them very attractive for youth development.

Carlson's (1998: 42) observations, although directed at libraries and foster children, is applicable to other types of new frontier settings: "The library is a source of consistency and continuity as kids come, go, and return when a placement doesn't work out. Older ones who used the library when they were younger can find books they read then, and either re-read them as familiar friends, or explore new titles." There are, in fact, few such places where youth of any age can feel welcome. There are even fewer places where youth and adults can share the same space. New frontier settings bring the potential of intergenerational contact and activity.

THE HISTORICAL INVOLVEMENT OF NEW FRONTIER
SETTINGS AND YOUTH DEVELOPMENT

The evolution of new frontier settings into youth-development arenas does not follow a predictable, linear path. Such settings have evolved slowly; they have gradually come to embrace youth-development principles and have even, in some cases, set up youth-development programs. Some, because of already having a youth-centered mission, naturally engaged in youth-development programming (Dunitz 1992). Others, however, did not have a mission specifically focused on youth.

Settings such as libraries have over the last ten to fifteen years taken a much more active role in community affairs, youth programming being but one dimension of this increased interest (Murphy 2001). The American Library Association (2000) has issued a set of guiding principles to foster the involvement of libraries in outreach to undervalued groups such as the poor and the working class, and changes in mission have fostered ventures into youth development.

The 1990s were the period during which youth development initiatives increased in popularity. Some of this resulted from funding initiatives in both private and government sectors; however, part of the increased attention was the result of a wider recognition of the importance of community involvement—and an understanding of the need to foster future patrons and constituencies. An embrace of the importance of marketing and constituency-development translates into greater patronage of the institution and greater political capital—a point well stated by the director of the Queens Borough Public Library: "We think it helps people become library users. It is like retail philosophy. If you don't get someone walking into the store, they are not going to buy anything" (quoted in Murphy 2001: A25). The emergence of this "new public philosophy" and how it views the role of public institutions influenced how public libraries shifted their mission (Buschman 1998). This philosophical approach stresses that public institutions have to serve an active role in helping to transform communities through collaborative efforts—efforts that stress engagement and empowerment of disenfranchised groups.

How can new frontier settings best serve the needs of youth? Knowledge of a community is critical. Gaither's (1992: 63) comments, although addressed to museums, is applicable to other sites: "Knowing one's community means knowing its strengths and weaknesses. Serving one's community means designing programs that are tailored to its needs and that anticipate its future requirements and demands. For small to moderate-sized museums, there exists a clear opportunity to development programs and educational activities that respond very directly to community needs and concerns." Each new frontier setting must endeavor to develop a greater understanding of the community it wishes to serve. This can happen through assets and needs assessments, the extent of which will depend on the setting's resources, its history of relationship with the community, and time limitations. Communities, particularly those in urban areas, can be dynamic, and it may take years before newcomers are recognized. Assessments help institutions to minimize the chance that new groups will be overlooked.

Libraries have played an increasingly active role in developing youth-centered programs (see chapter 11); although they may not be labeled as "youth development," they can easily be considered as part of this movement. The concerted thrust by such community-based organizations has forged ahead with initiatives that historically were thought to be exclusively the domain of social agencies.

Museums are another example. Historically, museums have provided various kinds of programming that was centered on youth-development principles. But as noted in chapter 10, museums have made important strides since the 1980s to reach out to youth (Karp 1992; Lavine 1992). Part of this was the result of funding initiatives; another part of it was undoubtedly because of population shifts, middle-class groups moving out to the suburbs. Schools, probably more than any other social institution, have played a significant role in establishing partnerships with museums. These have ranged from one-shot visits to extensive programming that has involved teacher preparation, internships, workshops, classes, and volunteer opportunities. From a youth-development perspective, school-based special initiatives offer great rewards for youth and their families. These initiatives, when involving families of youth participants, serve to further increase the importance of schools in our communities.

NEW FUNDING INITIATIVES

Major initiatives usually are started when an "incident" captures wide public attention. The media attention that follows such incidents serves as a motivator for institutions to undertake special initiatives. Other major initiatives are started because of the vision of a foundation or other organization. Few things generate as much excitement and attention as a major funding initiative. Initiatives not only support ongoing work but also attract new "players."

Foundations have historically played influential roles in bringing attention and resources to emerging fields of practice (Karp 1992). Foundations are generally well placed to advocate for major initiatives because they can get public support and attention; they also have flexibility in how they can allocate funding. Foundations are in a powerful position to lobby other funders—which often means government—to support initiatives.

A number of major national foundations have taken an interest in new frontier settings for youth development (Weiss and Lopez 2000). Kellogg (Youth Initiatives Program), Ford (Funds for the Communities Future Organization), and Heinz (Youth Places) have made major commitments to youth development. The W. K. Kellogg Foundation's support has generated new frontier programs in museums, farms, credit unions, and news bureaus (Richmond 2000). A major funding initiative by the DeWitt Wallace—Reader's Digest Fund focused on public libraries as settings for youth development (American Public Library Association 1999). The DeWitt Wallace initiative has significantly shaped how library grantees have conceptualized and implemented services to youth. Titled "Public Libraries as Partners in Youth Development," it specifically sets out to help libraries develop activities and programs that support the educational and career development of youth during after-school hours. It is probably the nation's most influential youth-development initiative involving libraries. The Henry Luce Foundation has sponsored forums on furthering collaboration between schools and museums (Institute of Museum Services 1996).

In 1995, the Museum Services Leadership Initiatives were established. They funded fifteen grants supporting museum-school partnerships, and the wide range of activities covered could easily be considered to be youth development. A Kellogg Foundation grant to the Council on Library Resources spurred an initiative titled "Public Libraries, Communities, and Technology." This initiative, although not exclusively focused on youth, did in fact serve youth in many of the fifteen localities supported, and introduced youth-development principles.

New frontier settings have been very creative in seeking out funding sources for their youth-development programming. The unique merging of setting and youth-development programming has been able to reach funding sources—generally in the private sector, and particularly corporations and foundations—with interests in both of these areas. Not that raising funds is easy. Many of the settings contacted in the course of writing this book stated that getting funding was almost a full-time endeavor for senior program personnel, and that task takes energies that otherwise would go into programming.

～

New frontier settings open up a vast new arena for youth-development programming. "New" does not mean that these organizations have been created from scratch: they already exist, and in some cases they exist in multiple numbers in a community. It does mean, however, that they are being opened up to address youth development—and in ways that not only enhance their original mission but that do so in a manner that also serves community. This transformation may be easier in some settings than in others. It is a matter of degree rather than a fundamental decision of yes or no.

Some settings may not possess extensive resources but have leadership and the political will to engage in youth development. In those cases, the process can be viewed as an evolution: the future holds promise. These settings may not be able fully to sponsor an initiative, but they may be able to participate in collaborative initiatives involving other settings. Other new frontier settings have a substantial history in the field of youth development; yet others are relatively new to this field.

Organizational factors are influential in either facilitating engagement in youth development or hindering certain types of new frontier setting from doing so. In the former case, settings sometimes establish sophisticated programs; in the latter case, the organization gravitates toward simpler activities and programs. In this way, new frontier programs have a great deal in common with their community-based youth-development counterparts.
New frontier settings have a particular view of youth development. Often it overlaps with conventional views but it also brings a dimension that is unique to the setting sponsoring the program. Some of the settings do not use the language of youth development; they may not even know that what they are doing is called youth development. For example, the role of informal or experiential education is often central to work undertaken with

youth. Recreational organizations often do this work in a variety of ways such as mentoring, interning, on-the-job-training, or lectures. Although an educational focus on the development of activities is central, it does not mean that other core elements (e.g., social development) are not addressed.

10 / MUSEUMS

THIS CHAPTER specifically focuses on museums, which exhibit particular potential for youth development. Since museums do not fall neatly into distinct categories, programming that involves museums can be thought of as on a continuum, from very focused to broadly focused, involving different activities and different age and gender groups. Youth-development programs and activities can, nevertheless, exist and thrive within museums quite "naturally."

Museums can be found in virtually any community across the United States. Readers must be prepared, however, to broaden their concept of what is a museum. This is an important step in fully exploring the potential of this new frontier setting for youth-development practice.

In this chapter and in chapters 11 and 12 (on libraries and cyberspace) the following outline will be used to compare and contrast functions of several major new frontier settings: (1) Definition and categorization of primary functions; (2) Historical mission; (3) Current mission; (4) Youth-development aspects of programming; and (5) Major youth-development activities. Chapter 13 is arranged similarly, but is first divided into its three main sections: aquariums, zoos, and outdoor adventures. The five aspects touch on process, structure, and mission of new frontier settings, and although they are treated separately, the reader should bear in mind that these elements are interconnected.

DEFINITION AND CATEGORIZATION
OF MUSEUM FUNCTIONS

Museums are very complex organizations. They do not neatly fall into discrete categories such as those of science, art, or children-focused.

According to the International Council of Museums (ICOM), museums (at least, museums who have ICOM membership) can be defined as a "permanent non-profit institution in the service of society and its development which collects, conserves, researches, and interprets for the purposes of study, education and enjoyment, material evidence of people and their environment." This definition is sufficiently broad to encompass a wide range of institutions that may, or may not, have the term *museum* in their titles.

ICOM continues: "Museums enable people to explore collections for inspiration, learning and enjoyment. They are institutions that collect, safeguard and make accessible artifacts and specimens, which they hold in trust for society." Libraries, of course, can maintain permanent exhibition rooms, and under this definition they might qualify as museums, but in general we know what we mean when we say "museum": they function to exhibit objects of cultural or scientific merit and they hire staff with expertise in the particular focus of the museum. Usually they are responsible to some formal accrediting body.

Museums—and I include art galleries under this heading—come in many different types and sizes. Some of the better-known museums are open almost the entire year, have extensive hours, and mount numerous special exhibits. Others may be open only during certain seasons or they may maintain limited hours of operation, and their collections may not be extensive. Youth practitioners therefore need to be flexible in their definition of a museum to better identify settings in their communities. Program staff must also think about whether they have a stereotyped image of who goes to museums. Stereotypes can be difficult to dispel.

HISTORICAL MISSION

Museums have historically fulfilled an important role for society. Access to the material that they collect, conserve, and exhibit serves to inform, educate, and entertain patrons (Baxandall 1991; Greenblatt 1991; Karp 1992). The museum function helps to preserve the past, inform the present, and serve as a foundation from which the future can be built. For those who cannot travel or who do not have sufficient income to purchase items for their homes, access to exhibits opens up a world that would otherwise be closed to them.

Hooper-Greenhill's description (1998: 10) of opinions about museums expressed by people of color in England, obtained through a series of focus groups, has relevance for this country, too:

> The image of museums was common across all ethnic groups. "The Museum" is still the way that museums are perceived; an old building with an imposing entrance, like the British Museum. Typical contents include "Kings and Queens, crowns, suits of armour, weapons, and broken pots and rocks." The atmosphere was described as quiet, reverential and unwelcoming to children. Not surprisingly, this rather unpleasant place was felt to be for intellectuals, and posh people. Art galleries were perceived as even more distant and elitist. There was a real fear that the displays would be too difficult to understand. It is depressing to see that this image is still so entrenched. . . . Curiously, given the strength of negative attitudes, there was a general consensus across all groups that society needed museums. . . . The main roles for museums were to preserve the past, to educate (mainly children), to broaden horizons and increase mutual tolerance, and to offer places to engage emotionally with beautiful things.

According to Gaither (1992) and Karp (1992), museums not only inform but also entertain. But unfortunately, museums will rarely be considered "cool" or "fun" by most youths, regardless of socioeconomic background.

Museums have on occasion displayed controversial art exhibits and have thereby helped communities and society to take a better look at their values and what constitutes "art." First Amendment issues are not foreign to art museums. It is rare year when a news story on a controversial exhibit does not capture national headlines.

In the view of the Institute of Museum Services (1996: 65), "museums are educators. They can be forums for free and open discussion of authentic historic, esthetic, and scientific dilemmas. They can ask good questions, too good ever to be answered completely. In the end, the effectiveness of museums as educators will be measured by what they can make us realize about ourselves." Roberts (1997) notes that the educational function gives museums an important civic role; however, local circumstances strongly influence how active museums are in a community. The historical function of a museum places it in a prominent position in the community; it serves to inform but is also a place where citizens can have a voice—an aspect of museums that is taken up in the next section.

CURRENT MISSION

Museums, according to Gaither (1992), can fill the void created by the failure of other institutions in society such as schools, particularly in undervalued communities. In a similar vein, Karp (1992: 27) writes: "All types of museums have responsibilities to communities. These matters are not just the special preserves of cultural-history of ethnic and minority museums. Art and science museums have the same obligations as others."

Fuller (1992) introduces the concept of "the ecomuseum" to describe the potential that museums have for establishing community-links and serving as agents for positive change in society. Museums, by linking education, culture, and power, relate to the entire life of a community. Terms such as neighborhood museum and street museum have come into use to describe museums as mechanisms for achieving economic, political, and social growth and development at community level. Ecomuseums, says Fuller (1992: 328): "are community learning centers that link the past with the present as a strategy to deal with the future needs of that particular society. Their activities and collections reflect what is important to the community, not necessarily conforming to mainstream values and interpretations."

Museums have, recently, paid increasing attention to the need that they be more accessible to community and youth, particularly to those who historically have not patronized these institutions (Hooper-Greenhill 1997; Lavine 1991; Marzio 1991). In both the United States and other countries, museums have initiated accessibility-enhancement initiatives, reaching out to underserved groups and thus opening up possibilities for youth development to take place in these settings (Dunitz 1992; Gonzalez and Tonelli 1992; MacDonald 1992). Moore (1941), writing more than sixty years ago, argued that youth are critical to the success of museums: "Youth as the backbone of the nation is not a new idea, but youth as the lifeblood of museums is a comparatively recent realization. . . . By far the greatest number of museums are for adults, but each year more of them are opening their doors to young people and through well-organized departments are combining virtual children's museums." Moore's observations, which need not be restricted to museums, are still relevant today.

A 1998 international conference, identifying ways to sustain museums and their collections and the communities they serve, specifically addressed the topic of sustainable communities (ICOM Canada 1998). This conference brought together professionals from the fields of museum work, cultural heritage, and community development. That same year, in Australia, a resource guide was published that focused specifically on museums and galleries, cultural protocols, and communities (Museums Australia, Inc. 1998). This guide set out to help museums better reach and work with culturally diverse communities, particularly those that were indigenous.

Museums do not exist in isolation from other institutions. For example, there has historically been a close relationship between museums and schools in the United States (Institute of Museum Services 1996). This relationship has taken various forms and covers an entire range of curriculum goals, ranging from one-shot field trips to extensive and intensive units. Involvement of teachers in specialized workshops is quite common. However, there has also always been community involvement beyond schools. University-based efforts at bridging gaps between museums and community-based organizations have recently been established. The University of Michigan, for example, has developed the Cultural Heritage Initiative for Community Outreach (CHICO). This initiative addresses how to best engender new methods for sharing cultural materials through the use of digital and collaboration technologies. Interestingly, this initiative utilizes technology as a central feature in bringing about greater participation on the part of community. It also highlights how technology can be a field unto itself and a vehicle for bringing about closer contact and cooperation between new frontier settings and communities. CHICO activities follow six guidelines (Frost 1999: 2):

(1) Enhance, not replace real-world engagement with cultural heritage; (2) Provide contextualization to enrich and build upon the initial artifact by providing background and paths to related works and information; (3) Promote the use of cultural heritage artifacts as an entry into the larger culture of which they are a part; (4) Engage learners in an interactive experience; (5) Encourage learners to create and share their own cultural artifacts inspired and informed by what they have seen in cultural repositories; and (6) Engage the larger community—parents, performers, mentors—in the learning experience.

The CHICO concepts illustrate the potential for museums to overlap with other community institutions. These guidelines can easily be translated into youth-development activities for a wide range of age groups and social domains.

YOUTH-DEVELOPMENT ASPECTS OF PROGRAMMING

The current mission of museums raises endless possibilities for the youth-development field (Karp 1992). Lavine (1992: 138–39) specifically addresses the potential of museums that are not prestigious or well-funded to bring about significant change in communities:

> At present, the most promising innovations in museum partnerships with communities are coming not from the largest, oldest, and best-funded institutions but rather from institutions once viewed as marginal: children's museums, in which interactivity is necessitated by the age of the clientele and the educational goals of the institution; history museums, in which the extraordinary efflorescence of social history has combined with the relative unavailability of materials relating to nonwhite, women, and the poor to require new research, collecting, and exhibition techniques; and ethnic and community-based museums to lie at the heart of their mission.

This evolution to an "education/service" perspective, or mission to engage in active relationships with communities, increases the relevance of museums for all sectors of society. Youth-development programming can occur in any type of museum and does not have to be restricted to ones that are specifically mandated to serve youth. Some would argue that youth-development programming in museums that have historically catered to adults offers the greatest potential for the field of youth development. These settings bring youth into contact with adults, and both benefit.

Pittman-Gelles, Bannerman, and Kendall (1981) note this expansion of museum role into educational institutions providing services to an increasing range of audience. The demographic shifts in population that occurred from the 1940s to the 1960s, with the white middle-class flight to the suburbs, resulted in cities being increasingly populated by residents of color. The mission of museums (most of which are located in cities) thus shifted during this period to include (1) an effort to complement rather than duplicate community services; (2) providing greater relevance and informative programming both within and outside of the museum; (3) outreaching to the broader community; and (4) making museums more stimulating and exciting places to visit. The shift in mission made these museums more receptive to innovative programming that involved youth.

MAJOR YOUTH-DEVELOPMENT ACTIVITIES

There seems to be no limit to youth-development programming in museums, whether they be adult-centered or youth-centered. Museums that subscribe to "active learning" models, with activities that emphasize physical interactions (e.g., using computers, buttons, levers, and other sensory interfaces), are well placed to initiate youth-development programs of various kinds and levels of intensity (Perin 1992). This type of museums usually has a sufficiently strong reputation to attract youth, has space for activities, and personnel who are used to working with youth. These factors facilitate the introduction of a youth-development paradigm and programming.

Gaither (1992: 59) focuses on museums with a specific cultural-heritage mission:

Museums that commit themselves to the criticism and fostering of specific cultural heritages—African American, Hispanic, Native American, Asian—have a unique role to play in such settings since they are at the center of the discussion of their own traditions. Unlike general museums, these institutions treat their cultural heritage neither as a short-term focus nor as an aspect of a larger story. Their heritage is their primary subject matter. The presentations of their own cultural traditions is the foundation on which their identity rests.

An African American museum director echoed this very important point (Kinzer 2001: B2):

In the face of so much negativity, our people, especially young people, need to see positive images. . . . We get kids in here who have been told all their lives that they're going to wind up in prison. When they see our exhibit of African-American inventors, they leave with an "I can" spirit. That helps them move away from distorted images that were created for us.

I suggest that art museums dedicated to the work of people of color strive to combine art with history and similarly address educational and social goals. The solid foundation that these institutions enjoy, using cultural heritage as a basis for activities and programming, allows them to take on key social goals related to youth of color. Systematic effort at increasing self-esteem and providing youth with critical-thinking skills can overcome historical negativity. However, the effort at self-esteem enhancement needs to be given a central role in the activities.

The Mexican Fine Arts Center Museum in Chicago is an excellent example of how an ethnically based museum has pursued a multifaceted approach to youth development because it is in its and the communities best interest to do so (this museum is the subject of a case study in chapter 15). The programming involves the creation of a radio station operated by youth and a museum specifically focused on youth art (Mejias-Rojas 1998). The radio station is not a project usually associated with a museum, but the lessons learned in being involved in it translate into other arenas for the participants.

The Brooklyn Children's Museum, established in 1899, was the world's first museum for children. In 1987, the museum completed a lengthy review of its mission and adopted a strategic plan. Its new mission statement (Dunitz 1992: 247) reads:

> The Brooklyn Children's Museum provides interactive and entertaining experiences in an environment designed for children and their families. It presents exhibitions and other programs which draw upon issues relevant to the interests of its visitors. These exhibits and programs encourage visitors to develop an understanding and respect for themselves, their cultural heritage and their environment, and the heritage and environment of others. The Museum has a commitment to collecting and preserving objects that support its educational functions. The Museum serves families in the greater New York City metropolitan area and reflects the diversity of that community.

The thrust toward being more connected to its community base has resulted in the creation of numerous community-centered programs focused on youth, the museum's primary constituency. The programs have three approaches to youth development: public programs, school programs, and after-school programs (Dunitz 1992). Public programming involves not only youth but their parents, too. One project targets homeless parents with small children who reside in New York City's shelters, stressing parent-child relationship building. School programs stress curriculum development.

The museum's Evi'dents' project focuses on the teaching of natural science to low-income youth of color. The curriculum teaches children about the properties of living things through use of food chains and eating. The project places particular emphasis on teeth and dental care. The Night Journey project focuses on use of dreams and sleeping from a multicultural perspective. This project actively seeks to introduce youth to how dreams are viewed by many of the groups living in the community.

Another of the museum's programs welcomes youths who do not have after-school adult supervision, and a Kids Crew Kids project developed as a result of the after-school initiative. Dunitz (1992: 260) reported: "We believe Kids Crew will serve as a model of institutional commitment to community needs for museums as well as for other cultural, recreational, and educational institutions." Youths can attend from 3 p.m. to 5 p.m., Monday through Friday, and 12:30 p.m. to 4 p.m. on weekends and holidays. Kids have access to the children's resource library, participate in workshops, and receive academic tutoring on work-skill development, reading, and writing. The teen intern program targets youths aged fourteen to eighteen years and provides them with work experience. They work seven to twenty hours per week on collections, exhibitions, education, or administration (Dunitz 1992). They also participate in career and academic workshops and seminars.

〜

The role of museums in society and in the communities they have historically served has slowly but dramatically changed since the nineteenth century. These changes have resulted from a number of significant social and demographic factors. Changes in mission have provided an important impetus for these institutions to offer activities as a primary means of serving communities. An important function of these activities is staff recruitment (in the case of youth-focused activities, working toward future staff recruitment) and developing community support for the institution.

We must be prepared to look at museums from a totally different perspective: they now have a broad mission. The potential of this setting for the field of youth development will be more fully realized once we see museums as being in a "social," service-oriented category, rather than one that is "enlightening." Young people themselves must be prepared to think of museums as places they can visit, learn in, have fun, and work. Not that all museums have the potential or willingness to reexamine their mission; some may prefer to serve the elite.

New frontier settings lend themselves to specialized forms of youth development. Thus an ability to identify a youth's interests and to point him or her in the right direction—for example, toward a museum—will be an important asset for community youth-development programs. They will also thereby perform an important public service.

These early years of the twenty-first century will provide museums with yet greater opportunities to develop activities and services for underrepresented groups. These initiatives will build on museums' strengths and yet allow youth development to occur organically. Hopefully, these initiatives will result in partnerships with community-based organizations that have not had previous collaborative relationships with new frontier settings. Then, when community-based organizations work together in pursuit of youth-development goals, we can comprehensively offer programs that address multiple core elements.

11 / LIBRARIES

LIBRARIES HAVE traditionally held a prominent place in the United States. Where would this society be without free public libraries? Where would this country be right now if it were not for Andrew Carnegie's funding of library construction in the late nineteenth century and the early twentieth? Democracy can only function when information is not the exclusive purview of the elite. There are those who would argue that a community cannot be a true community without easy access to a library (Marks 1998)—that a library is much more than a building providing access to educational materials and that libraries are in fact "sanctuaries" where patrons can be safe from physical, psychological, and social harm.

These institutions do play a critical role in informing communities about events that are significant to a community and society. They are a key aspect of the fabric of a community and have important social roles to perform. However, a library, like other social institutions, can play an active role or an inactive role in the life of the community it seek to serves. In general, though, it is acknowledged that the potential of libraries is under-appreciated and little understood.

Libraries when properly led can play a community role that few if any other institutions can do as well. Their geographical location maximizes access, or should. Their relationship with youth-serving institutions, most notably schools, lends itself to undertaking youth-development initiatives. Their nonstigmatizing role in a community reduces psychological barriers— barriers that, visible or invisible, can be formidable. The physical space of libraries can often be used for community meetings, particularly those that may target groups from different sectors of a community. These settings can be considered "neutral" and therefore safe to attend. Thus libraries as new frontier settings are in a unique position to undertake youth-development initiatives as well as various other forms of community capacity-enhancement projects.

Libraries are in a strategic position to involve families in projects that reinforce the goals they have for their youth members, and to do so in a manner that reflects local customs and priorities. The youth-development field is challenged to develop new partnerships with libraries or to expand current efforts. And as countless number of people in marginalized groups slowly disengage from mainstream society, libraries, for their part, can ill afford to have a narrow definition of their mission.

DEFINITION AND CATEGORIZATION
OF LIBRARY FUNCTIONS

Practically no one who is stopped in the street and asked about their local library's function would have difficulty in identifying the building and talking about what the library does. Sometimes, with a causal observer or one who does not patronize the library, the function may be narrowly described, the focus being on books. Put simply, libraries are thought of as places where one can go and obtain a book (Dahms-Stinson 1998; Feinberg and Rogoff 1998; Martorana 1997). That such a response is a common one is interesting since the library of the twenty-first century is much more than that.

The Council on Library Resources (1996: 3) has reported:

Dramatic developments are taking place in public libraries across the country—developments that are altering how libraries deliver information and interact with communities. As the information revolution sweeps not only the nation, but around the world, public libraries have a unique opportunity to provide resources that were unimaginable a few years ago. The Internet as a communications medium and World Wide Web technology are serving as links to bring people and communities together. But technology alone is not enough. In many regions, cities, and towns, it is the public library that stands as the community's information nexus.

The increased need for libraries to take on a broader social function does not detract from the job they have historically been very good at. This challenge, unfortunately, is not always, on the part of all public libraries, met with enthusiasm and skill.

At risk of being simplistic, I will offer a description of the modern library. Libraries provide residents with access to materials and information on virtually any subject. Sometimes the materials and information are in written format such as books, newspapers, and magazines; at other times, they may be on compact disks or videos. With the advent of recent information technology, the material may be found through access to the Internet. Information is central to the primary functions of a library. The library's importance increases dramatically in communities where, as a result of high unemployment or employment in jobs that do not pay a livable wage, access to information is very limited (Cretinon and Enger 1998; Dotson and Bonitch 1998; McCook and Lippincott 1998; Teasley and Walker-Moses 1998).

Like museums, libraries do not come in any one size or type, although the vast majority are publicly funded through tax dollars. Libraries are much supported by local property taxes. One estimate found that more than 80 percent of library financing is based on local taxes (Martorana 1997). Some libraries specialize in a single subject—for example, art. Other libraries have very limited budgets and cannot provide easy access to computers. Yet other libraries are understaffed and are unable to undertake outreach programming. There are, however, libraries that have sizeable budgets and public support and can undertake highly innovative and sophisticated programming—for example, in shelters and public housing (Dotson and Bonitch 1998; Morris 1998; Teasley and Walker-Moses 1998), through the use of library vans (Cretinon and Egner 1998), and by providing easy access to technology (Marrero and Weinstein 1998). Practitioners must therefore be flexible in their definition of what constitutes a library, and what the functions of this institution are in the community.

HISTORICAL MISSION

Any in-depth examination of the historical function of libraries will reveal that these institutions have been much more than "a book-lending facility." Some libraries took on missions that specifically targeted undervalued sectors of society. In doing so, these libraries emulated "social service" organizations, providing referrals, space for meetings, and helping to support social-action initiatives. These institutions had numerous collaborative partnerships with other key community institutions.

The functions of libraries, according to the Council on Library Resources (1996: 6), have been, as they are now, multifaceted:

> For decades, public libraries have played a wide variety of roles within their communities, but availability of electronic information and interactive communications technologies has enabled them to take on more and increasingly complex roles. Public libraries assume roles that make sense for their local communities. For example, across the nation libraries function as independent learning centers, popular materials centers, community information centers, preschoolers' door to learning, research centers, cultural centers, and homework centers for youth.

When they have sought guidance from the constituencies they serve, and have actively involved them in decision-making roles, libraries have fulfilled functions that have been broad, empowering, and community-centered.

CURRENT MISSION

The current mission of libraries has evolved into one that can be considered comprehensive and encompassing. Given this broadening of mission, they are now settings where communities can come together in search of goal attainment—a function that at one time was considered outside of the domain of a library. These changes are exciting and broaden the potential of libraries to influence the day-to-day activities of communities.

In many ways, no two libraries can be the same, even if they operate at the same level of funding. Efforts to individualize library functions based on the communities they are located in will ensure that this diversity increases. This individualization of libraries is probably nowhere better illustrated than the Queens Borough Public Library in New York City (Murphy 2001). The move of public libraries beyond books to include programming that embraces newcomers to this country, as at the Queens Borough Library, is exciting. It is also not unusual to find that new library construction includes collapsing walls and large auditoriums in order to provide performance stages and sophisticated sound systems. To list but a few other new library activities, there are dance classes, book readings, jewelry making, assistance with tax preparation, after-school care, and talent contests.

The thrust toward these new activities is not without critics, however. One library executive director (Murphy 2001: A25) noted: "New libraries risked turning off some people, but . . . there was no turning back. The secret, several librarians said, is making sure the new continues to promote the old, through things like reading lists and book displays on the special events."

The most progressive and dynamic libraries can easily be viewed as educational, cultural, and community centers. The historical reliance on financial support at the local level increases the likelihood of libraries being responsive to local needs. One excellent example of how libraries have refocused their mission has been their work on stopping gun violence (Tremblay-McGaw 1999).

Libraries can be considered politically "neutral." In this space where patrons can come out of possibly harsh living conditions and be welcomed, library users do not have to have contact with staff. But if, in the patron's quest for information, service is needed, staff can be of assistance. There are few community-based institutions where someone can come in from the street and not be required to register or announce their intentions in order to stay. Further, libraries are free of charge and lend themselves to entire family patronage. These qualities lend themselves to youth-development programming—programming that, incidentally, can also involve families.

Venturella's (1998b) book *Poor People and Library Services* highlights a wide range of library-sponsored programs in a variety of community settings. These programs, some in housing developments, shelters for the homeless, and neighborhood organizations, actively outreached to the marginalized.

While the potential of libraries to transcend a their narrow traditional role is huge, the shifting of roles from provider of information and services to advocacy, reform, literacy, and empowerment has not of course been without critics (Berman 1998; Buschman 1998; Marks 1998; Venturella 1998a). An active reach for programming of any kind (including youth development) may not be well received by other community institutions—negative reactions that may be the result of lack of understanding and information or concern about turf.

The American Library Association has a clear policy on community involvement. In a statement of policy and policy objectives, it highlights the importance of marginalized people having access to libraries (ALA 2000: 1):

The American Library Association promotes equal access to information for all persons, and recognizes the urgent need to respond to the increasing number of poor children, adults, and families in America. These people are affected by a combination of limitations, including illiteracy, illness, social isolation, homelessness, hunger, and discrimination, which hamper the effectiveness of traditional library services. Therefore it is crucial that libraries recognize their role in enabling poor people to participate fully in a democratic society, by utilizing a wide variety of available resources and strategies. Concrete programs of training and development are needed to sensitize and prepare library staff to identify poor people's needs and deliver relevant services. And within the American Library Association the coordinating mechanisms of programs and activities dealing with poor people in various divisions, offices, and units should be strengthened, and support for low-income liaison activities should be enhanced.

This approach is to be implemented (ALA 2000: 1–2) by

1 Promoting the removal of all barriers to library and information services, particularly fees and overdue charges
2 Promoting the publication, production, purchase, and ready accessibility of print and nonprint materials that honestly address the issues of poverty and homelessness, that deal with poor people in a respectful way, and that are of practical use to low-income patrons
3 Promoting full, stable, and ongoing funding for existing legislative programs in support of low-income services and for pro-active library programs that reach beyond traditional service-sites to poor children, adults, and families
4 Promoting training opportunities for libraries, in order to teach effective techniques for generating public funding to upgrade library services to poor people
5 Promoting the incorporation of low-income programs and services into regular library budgets in all types of libraries, rather than the tendency to support these projects solely with "soft money" like private or federal budgets
6 Promoting equity in funding adequate library services for poor people in terms of materials, facilities, and equipment
7 Promoting supplemental support for library resources for and about low-income populations by urging local, state, and federal governments, and the private sector, to provide adequate funding

8 Promoting increased public awareness—through programs, displays, bibliographies, and publicity—of the importance of poverty-related library resources and services in all segments of society

9 Promoting the determination of output measures through the encouragement of community needs assessments, giving special emphasis to assessing the needs of low-income people and involving both anti-poverty advocates and poor people themselves in such assessments

10 Promoting direct representation of poor people and anti-poverty advocates through appointment to local boards and creation of local advisory committees on service to low-income people, such appointments to include library-paid transportation and stipends

11 Promoting training to sensitive library staff to issues affecting poor people and to attitudinal and other barriers that hinder poor people's use of libraries

12 Promoting networking and cooperation between libraries and other agencies, organizations, and advocacy groups in order to develop programs and services that effectively reach poor people

13 Promoting the implementation of an expanded federal low-income housing program, national health insurance, full-employment policy, living minimum wage and welfare payments, affordable day care, and programs likely to reduce, if not eliminate, poverty itself

14 Promoting among library staff the collection of food and clothing donations, volunteering personal time to anti-poverty activities and contributing money to direct-aid organizationst

15 Promoting related efforts concerning minorities and women, since these groups are disproportionately represented among poor people

This fifteen-point statement sets the stage for libraries to play active roles in their communities. The further step, to include youth development in this involvement, is not a big one if local libraries actively embrace this policy. Youth-focused services, for their part, should be flexible in determining how youth will be served; this is necessary in order for libraries to complement rather than duplicate other local initiatives.

Further, each community's history, needs, and assets should be take into account in a library's youth-dev elopment programming. If libraries are to survive and expand, they they will have to meet a wide range of community needs.

YOUTH-DEVELOPMENT ASPECTS OF PROGRAMMING

Feinberg and Rogoff (1998: 50) comment on the leadership that libraries can bring to working with youth and communities:

> With an existing infrastructure of buildings and staff in 16,000 American communities, public libraries are uniquely positioned to take a leadership position in community efforts to improve educational achievement. By building coalitions, reaching out to new and nontraditional audiences, and redesigning services for young children, libraries can participate effectively in society's efforts to produce a literate citizenry and productive workforce.

However, many people—adult as well as young—will question why the new frontier setting of libraries is placed alongside such settings as outdoor-adventure. A DeWitt Wallace–Reader's Digest Fund survey of adolescent perceptions of libraries found that these settings were not considered "cool" (Meyers 1999), and a series of provocative questions was raised as a result of this finding. Meyers asked:

> Are we beginning to see a trend among our young people? Can we afford for teens to respond to the question, "What do you think of when you think of the library?" by answering, "I don't think of the library"? Can we ignore teens who report that some kids they know with home Internet access never use the library? How many teens will get home access to the Internet and drift into the category of hardcore nonusers? Can we provide services, staff, and spaces that will attract teens, and change our image of a morgue run by petty tyrants for nerds, dorks, and dweebs? Our future—and our coolness—might lie in our answers. (43)

However, there has been a dramatic shift in thinking. Libraries now market themselves to specific audiences, one of which is youth, and libraries now provide a wide variety of community-service programs. A survey of programs sponsored by libraries was undertaken by the DeWitt Wallace–Reader's Digest Fund. The results (DeWitt Wallace–Reader's Digest Fund 1999) showed youth-centered programs to be extensive in all regions of the country:

(1) Almost 100 percent (99.6) of all libraries surveyed (1,248) provided various types of reading programs such as book discussions, story telling, summer reading. (2) Almost eight out of ten libraries (82.6 percent) provided cultural programs such as author presentations and readings, musical or dramatic performances, and creative writing workshops. (3) Over 40 percent (42.2) provided community service/leadership programs centered on such topics as friendships, tutoring, volunteering. (4) One-third (32.2 percent) provide computer classes and workshops such as introduction to the Internet, Web page design, software-specific instruction. (4) Almost one-quarter (23.4 percent) provide homework assistance such as a center, hotline, or tutoring. (5) Close to one out of five libraries (19.2 percent) provide career-development programs such as information center, career fairs, vocational demonstrations.

Meyers (1999) notes that access to technology is one of the primary motivators for bringing adolescents into libraries.

The DeWitt Wallace–Reader's Digest Fund survey found that most libraries do not offer reading and cultural programs for adolescents, do not offer homework assistance or career-development programs, and do not target youth in low-income communities. The needs of marginalized youths were generally not being met. It is important that there be initiatives to foster youth development with these young people. Such initiatives will require that libraries be flexible in how they conceptualize their mission, and it will be best if libraries located in the same community do not offer the same services. With careful planning, libraries will be able to offer complementary services and avoid duplication.

MAJOR YOUTH-DEVELOPMENT ACTIVITIES

In 1998 the DeWitt Wallace–Readers Digest Fund established an initiative called "Public Libraries as Partners in Youth Development." The goal (DeWitt Wallace–Reader's Digest Fund 1999: 1): was to

> help libraries throughout the country develop high-quality activities and programs that support the educational and career development of young people during the non-school hours. The initiative draws on the

strengths and qualities that made public libraries so vital to our society over the past 200 years. These include their presence in virtually every community across the nation, free access to all—regardless of age, educational background, income or social status—and their core belief in self-improvement through learning and discovery.

Three-year grants of up to $400,000 to implement youth-development programs were made available, and there were also planning grants.

Young people certainly know how to use computers and the Internet for fun and games. However, these tools can be used to accomplish educational goals (McClelland 1998), and some libraries have developed youth-development initiatives using computers and the Internet as a central focus of activities. Libraries for the Future (Harlem, New York; Newark, New Jersey; Oakland, California) is one such initiative. In an activity called Access Virtual Tours, youth are given worksheets that require them to find information. As McClelland points out, these activities stress that computers and the Internet are not ends in and of themselves, but vehicles to an end. Information and communication are conceptualized as inseparable. Participants are taught to write, edit, format their materials for the Web, participate, interact, and communicate. The library sites also stress collaboration with other community-based organizations. In this library setting, a dynamic learning environment is created. Young people have fun and learn new knowledge and skills in the process.

⌒

After reading this chapter, some readers may never again look at a library in the same way. Although I have always had an appreciation for the potential of libraries to serve marginal communities, until the writing of this book I did not have a full understanding and appreciation of how libraries can help transform communities. The ALA list of service-to-the-poor objectives presented above is outstanding from a human-service and educational perspective.

Libraries can be part of the daily life of a community. They and do not have to play a neutral role. They have evolved over the years to function in ways that historically were not thought to be part of a library's business. This progressive, and some would argue radical, perspective on community places reading and information as a core that can lead to more encompassing roles and services. Active engagement in youth development can fit nicely into the library mission. For some librarians, a small shift in how they view their work would have a profound and dramatic impact on their daily activities. A shift from an emphasis on products to an emphasis on customers would result in the need to undertake inventories and assessments of both assets and needs. Perception of professional role has a profound impact on determining what customers need. If professional roles are conceptualized narrowly, librarians and other professionals will be less responsive to the wider world of what their patrons really need.

12 / CYBERSPACE

THE EVER-EVOLVING role of information technology makes it difficult to examine this setting, and predicting its future is impossible (Ogbu and Mihyo 2000). There is no denying that this field is now important to virtually all aspects of society (Castells 1999). Ayers (2000: 68) eloquently captured a sense of the elusiveness of cyberspace: "By its very nature, cyberspace is space amid other places. It touches them all but is possessed by none." As a new frontier setting, cyberspace does not share much with the other settings discussed in this book, yet it has the potential to influence youth more than the other settings because of the central role it plays in today's economy and workforce preparation. It is not, however, a "setting" in the conventional sense of the term, although, interestingly, a number of scholars have started to think of cyberspace as a community of users (Kollock and Smith 1999a; Smith 1999; Turkle 1999; Wellman and Gulia 1999; Willson 2000).

The term *virtual community* has certainly captured the public's imagination (Wilbur 2000). Mitra (2000: 276) makes a similar point about community:

> The notion of community has become a central construct in thinking about the way in which humans organize their lives. In the electronic age, particularly in the age of the Internet, this organization of human activities has become more complex with the availability of fast, efficient and powerful means of connection that can have a significant impact on the way we organize the communities we live and interact with. . . . It is thus "important" to reconceptualize the "community" as a construct that helps us understand the organization of human activities.

In this early stage of the twenty-first century, the conventional, geographically based definitions of community no longer apply. Nor is the language used to communicate in this new community a conventional one such as English or Spanish.

This broadening of the construct of community attests to the influence that new technologies, particularly the Internet, have had on millions of people worldwide (Barwell and Bowles 2000; Nakamura 2000; Stratton 2000). New technology has made it easier than ever to cross borders. This ease of crossing borders is not without its detractors, however (Sardar 2000). The privileged have an easier time crossing these borders than do those with low income—those less able to "travel." With virtual travel possible for anyone with access to the Internet, those without access to the technology, and the competencies required to make the technology work for them, are yet further isolated.

Information technology is now considered an essential element of most professional jobs in society (Hall 1999). One has only to search the help-wanted ads in a newspaper to see illustration of this fact. There are fewer and fewer jobs—that is, jobs that offer a liveable wage with benefits—that do not require skills in information technology. It is estimated that 60 percent of all jobs today require such skills (Lazarus and Lipper 2000). Use of the Internet is closely associated with salary level. Approximately 20 percent of those earning between $10,000 and $14,999 use the Internet for job-related tasks, whereas 56 percent of those earning $75,000 or more use it in this way (Children's Partnership 2000). Lack of technical skills in this area severely limits employability in virtually all but the service fields. It is estimated that 29 percent of the U.S. real economic growth can be attributed to information technology and Net industries, or 7.8 percent of the nation's gross domestic product (Children's Partnership 2000).

The Committee for Economic Development, writing about the future for the workforce in 1995, identified the rewards and challenges of the structural changes in the nation's economy:

> The new economy is generally good news for workers who have education beyond high school and preparation for careers in managerial, professional, and technical occupations. In some cases, opportunities and rewards for these workers will be further enhanced by experience with new technologies and continued training on the job.

Those who are less prepared, however, are finding a very unwelcoming job market. . . . Higher skill requirements also have made entry-level jobs that provide a first rung on career ladders made difficult to obtain for the least skilled. (1995: 6)

Access to technology in new frontier settings like libraries may be a powerful incentive to getting youth involved. Thus this chapter looks at a wide range of possibilities for the use of information technology. Special attention is given to marginalized youth and marginalized communities.

The so-called digital divide led to the federal government establishing a digital divide Web site (digitaldivide.gov). The divide is keenly apparent in low-income communities, both rural and urban (Sanyal and Schon 1999; Wolpert 1999). The importance of closing this divide and mobilizing community resources is of increasingly critical importance.

DEFINITION AND CATEGORIZATION OF CYBERSPACE FUNCTIONS

By now it is a commonplace to say that the digital revolution is here. The number of households in the United States that were on the Internet increased from 26.2 percent in December 1998 to 41.5 percent in August 2000; 51 percent of homes had computers in August 2000, up from 42.1 percent in December 1998; approximately 116.5 million Americans were able to go on-line at some location in August 2000, compared with 31.9 million in January 1999 (National Telecommunication Information Agency 2000). A national survey conducted in 2000 found that youth aged two to five years old spent on average of twenty-seven minutes per day at a computer, and those aged twelve to seventeen years averaged more than an hour per day (Lewin 2001). In 1999, young people aged two to seventeen years who possessed computers, video games, and a television set spent almost five hours in front of a screen (this compared with 3 hours and 40 minutes for those who did not have a computer or video games) (Lewin 2001).

Information technology has caused a great deal of excitement. Technology has made the world "smaller." The costs of equipment, software, and operation have decreased significantly over the past decade, with information technology becoming available to an ever-increasing number of people. Although there has been a recent bursting of the "Tech" bubble, information technology has been responsible for making many people very rich. This potential for wealth resulted in the talent-search raiding of professional schools such as business and law by Internet firms. "Tech" companies have, to a large extent, shaped the careers of many, many people seeking fame and fortune in the new economy.

It was estimated in 2000 that information-technology jobs paid almost 80 percent more than average wages in the private sector. During the preceding twelve months (1999), the disparity between high-income and low-income sectors in the United States increased by 29 percent (Conhaim 2000). The impact of this new wealth has not been gender-neutral, however. It has been estimated that only 30 percent of computer scientists and programmers are women (Conhaim 2000).

What is cyberspace? Bell (2000: 2) uncovers the complexity involved in answering this type of question:

> Where is cyberspace? We can answer this in a number of ways. We might say that cyberspace exists in the networks of computers, modems, communication links, modes and pathways that connect users into something (or some thing) like the World Wide Web, the Internet, the information superhighway, and so on. We could make cyberspace, in short, as the sum of the hardware that facilitates its practice, Thinking about it cartographically or schematically, we can describe this hardware as a web, a network, a decentralized system—we can use the term rhizomatic to describe its infinite, uncentered, root-like structure.

Cyberspace is all encompassing, and the word can refer to equipment, networks, and a particular perspective on, or orientation to, the world around us.

THE DIGITAL DIVIDE

The origins of the term *digital divide* have been traced back to 1996 and Al Gore, the then vice president. There is controversy about aspects of the divide, as Conhaim (2000: 8) noted:

> A debate is raging about the Digital Divide, which is the gap between "haves" and "have nots" in the fast-moving, globally interlinked, computerized world. How extensive is the gap? What are its parame-

ters? What are its impacts? What can be done about it? And does it exist? The problem as seen by U.S. government officials, community groups, and businesses is that anyone who is not at least literate in digital information technologies or who is without access to on-line communications at home or work is not prepared to be fully engaged in the 21st century economy.

The digital divide is not restricted to the United States. According to the United Nations, the world's wealthiest 20 percent comprise 93 percent of the world's Internet users. South Asia, for example, has 23 percent of the world's population yet fewer than 1 percent of the world's Internet users. Latin America and the Caribbean have fewer than 3 percent of the world's Internet users. North America, however, accounts for 50 percent of users (Conhaim 2000), and as we saw above, the uneven distribution of information technology has raised critical issues (Beamish 1999; Hall 1999; Kollock and Smith 1999a). More than 42 percent of U.S. households have a personal computer, and 26 percent have Internet access. White, non-Latino, households are nearly twice as likely to own a computer as African American or Latino households (Lazarus and Lipper 2000), and 50 percent of children in urban households earning more than $75,000 have Internet access. White, non-Latino households have the highest percentage of access (29.8%), compared with Latino (12.6%) and African American (11.2%) households (Children's Partnership 2000).

For a democratic society, the relationship between income and access to information technology is troubling. It is estimated that by 2005, 45 percent (9.1 million) households with incomes under $15,000 will be wired, and 93 percent (19.8 million) of households making more than $75,000 will be wired (Lipke 2000).

The divide can also be measured in other ways, and one index has been the representation of people of color working in high-technology firms. In the San Francisco Bay Area, African Americans, who make up 8 percent of the labor pool, account for only 4 percent of the workforce at thirty-three Silicon Valley firms; Latinos, who account for 14 percent of the labor pool, supply only 7 percent of the workforce in these companies (Frauenheim 1999). In 1999, there was only one African American executive in 150 publicly traded firms based in Silicon Valley. Representation of people of color on company boards also leaves much to be desired. Among fifty technology firms, there were only five African Americans and one Latino out of 384 board members (Frauenheim 1999).

HISTORICAL FUNCTION

Information technology will continue to have a profound impact on society—one that can be more far-reaching than the introduction of electricity at the beginning of the twentieth century (Marx 1999). The evolution of information technology, having occurred at an extremely rapid pace, has not allowed society to pause and examine its significance. Cyberspace, in its brief history, has always been a haven for the young—regardless of their age. In many ways, the young have been better equipped to take advantage of the limitless potential of this field (Bamberger 1999).

This field is a "natural" for youth development. Many of today's youth are as comfortable with computers and the Internet as my generation was with the telephone and television, and yet the significance of today's changes far outstrips that of the changes that occurred during my young years. In the 1950s, the number of households with television jumped from 10 percent in 1950 to 90 percent in 1955 (Conhaim 2000). Tech. advocates believe that a similar leap will occur in the field of information technology. Few households in this country not now wired will be wired in the near future. Others, however, argue that adaptation will not be as easy as it was with television since the reasons for the digital divide have to do with much more than making equipment less expensive to purchase.

Meanwhile—although access to and competency in using information technology is critical for achieving success in a technology-driven market place (Amsden and Clark 1999; Ross 2000)—access for poor and working-class youth is very limited. Their homes rarely have computers, and their schools, while they may have computers and access to the Internet, often may not have enough equipment for access to be adequate (Amsden and Clark 1999). In addition, institutions such as houses of worship and recreational settings may be affected by both lack of equipment and lack of skills. Of course, "having access" does not necessarily mean that a computer is "connected," especially if it is in a home, as Frauenheim (1999: 3) notes. "Having a computer at home doesn't mean you're connected any more than having a Stairmaster means your fit. . . . I suspect that a lot of these computers are like the Stairmasters—sitting at home, not being used."

Access, according to Mitchell (1999a), can be conceptualized as consisting of three parts: (1) Equipment; (2) User-friendly software; and (3) The motivation to exploit the above. Noting that low-income communities suffer from "radical inequality of access," Mitchell sees no easy solution (1999a: 153):

When access to jobs and services is delivered electronically, those who have good network connections will have an advantage, whereas those with poor service or no service will be disadvantaged and marginalized. So common justice clearly demands that we should strive for equitable access—and, in particular, to ensure that members of low-income communities are not further disadvantaged by exclusion from the digital world. But this goal—although simply stated—probably cannot be achieved in any simple way. The problem turns out to be complex and multilayered, requiring a combination of measures for itsolution.

The Children's Partnership (2000) identified four critical barriers to low-income communities bridging the digital divide: (1) Limited access to local information (21 million); (2) Limited literacy skills (41 million); (3) Primary language being non-English (32 million); and (4) Lack of culturally appropriate content (26 million). It is estimated that at least 50 million people in this country (approximately 20 percent of the population) encounter one or more of these barriers. Multiple barriers translate into the digital disenfranchisement of millions of people.

The importance of having access to local information, in many ways, represents a critical dimension to upward mobility for low-income groups (Shiffer 1999). Information about jobs, educational opportunities, and other matters pertinent to day-to-day living provide residents with a better understanding of local resources and opportunities. The Internet has increased in importance, particularly among middle- and upper-middle-class communities, as a tool for transacting business and obtaining information. Lack of knowledge of local resources therefore effectively limits access to needed resources.

Having limited literacy skills is a serious impediment to the use of information technology. It is estimated that 44 million adults, or approximately 22 percent of the adult population, do not possess the reading and writing skills necessary to function successfully in day-to-day activities (Children's Partnership 2000). Lack of basic skills limits access to information that could play an influential role in helping millions of disadvantaged Americans to better cope with their position in society.

Limited grasp of the English language effectively makes a lot of the information provided on the Internet unusable. It is estimated that 87 percent of the documents on the Internet are in English; however, more than 32 million

Americans have a primary language other than English. As to the fourth barrier on the Children's Partnership list—lack of culturally appropriate content—it will be obvious that the information on the Internet does not reflect the cultural diversity of many of the residents of this country. Racial and ethnic groups of color do not see their cultural heritage reflected on the Internet, and the unique cultural heritages of more than 26 million foreign-born Americans, is, in the main, rendered invisible.

Both opinion makers and practitioners have shared Castells's observations. In new frontier settings, access to information technology is now often given high priority, and is in fact ever-present in any activity sponsored by these settings.

The Children's Partnership (2000) developed a five-point set of recommendations for creation of a "positive information society." Society should (1) be community-driven and meet real community needs; (2) surmount major content barriers for all groups; (3) provide assistance (training and technical support) for users; (4) provide on-line content that is "user-friendly"; and (5) be sustainable. These recommendations should help guide community organizations, political leaders, and other major stakeholders in creating initiatives.

CURRENT FUNCTION

Information technology can be used to connect people or alienate people, and youth are no exception. Mitchell (1999a: 129), however, sees no alternative to working with this medium. He writes:

> The digital revolution, like the agricultural and industrial revolutions before it, opens up new possibilities for urban form and organization and creates powerful pressure for change. . . . If we want to understand the plight of low-income communities in the twenty-first century, and find policies and design strategies to alleviate it, we will have to get the problem firmly in the context of the unfolding digital revolution and its urban consequences.

Information technology can be used to help community-based organizations better serve residents (Ferreira 1999; Shiffer 1999) or as a form of empowerment (Menon. 2000; Shaw and Shaw 1999; Tardieu 1999; Turkle 1999). The concept of "electronic advocacy" is starting to enjoy greater use, and electronic mail is becoming the principle means of communication in efforts aimed at social change.

It would be wrong to argue that this form of youth work is meant to replace traditional forms of engaging and working with youth. Technology increases access to youth and can enhance existing curricula; however, it is no more than a tool in a world that mandates a tool box full of tools in order to succeed. Information technology can bring youth into a program and, up to a certain point, keep them there; however, youth development is far too complex to rely strictly on information technology to help youth in their transition to adulthood. Social aspects (e.g., peer relations) cannot take a backseat in programming.

Increased access to information technology for youth is not free of controversy. The subject of Internet filters, for example, has raised questions about freedom of speech. Internet filters block access to certain sites. These sites are considered to be too sensitive for youth under the age of eighteen. Some filters feature data and other information on sexually transmitted diseases, alternative sexuality, and so forth. It was recently estimated that 16 percent of libraries in Massachusetts that have Internet access used filters on their public-access computers. Of those that used filters, 62 percent use them only in the sections of the library that cater to children (McVeigh 2001). Advocates of free speech argue that the type of information that is filtered is important in the lives of youth and that restricting their access to it constitutes an infringement on freedom of access to information. One critic (McVeigh 2001: B4) went further: "The new federal filtering requirement . . . is nothing less than censorship by the government, and a 'slippery slope,' because if this is successful we will see more requirements and regulations."

Cyberspace in a youth-development perspective must not only prepare youth for a future that will be very much directed by technology but it must do so without balkanizing youth in the process. Although the potential of information technology cannot be denied, its limitations must be identified and addressed if the technology is to make a significant contribution to youth development. Phillip (1999: 45), in fact, sounds a note of warning. He cautions against placing too much emphasis on technology:

Technological innovations like television, automobiles, and computers have changed the ways in which we relate to one another. Shifts in our world structure have fundamentally altered the way we view others and ourselves around us. Instead of bringing us into a "one-world" type of global melting pot (as many have envisioned to be our inevitable future), we have instead Balkanized, fragmenting further the closer we become.

ASPECTS OF PROGRAMMING IN THE DIGITAL AGE

In this next section I show how youth programs can incorporate the new technologies. A recent Rand Corporation study identified the following skills as essential for success in the digital age: problem solving; an ability to evaluate the veracity and utility of information; comprehension of the concept of connectivity; grasp of how computers process, digitize, structure, and store information; and understanding of the meaning of citizenship (Conhaim 2000).

Rathgeber (2000: v), writing about youth in Africa and how ICT (information communications technology) presents youth with unprecedented opportunities, comments on what this field is capable of if youth play a prominent role in shaping its future: "The bright side of economic restructuring and accelerated change is that it also presents youth with new opportunities. . . . One of the most promising areas for youth is information and communications technologies (ICTs). ICTs are for everyone, young and old, but perhaps it is the young who must lead the way." His remarks have application to more than Africa.

Computers have replaced television in the lives of many youths. More adolescents say they can live without their television (28%) than say they can live without their computer (23%) (Howe and Strauss 2000). It was estimated that by the end of the year 2000 there would be 14 million children on-line to complement the 13 million adolescents (aged thirteen to eighteen years) on-line, too (Lipke 2000). Such statistics point to the potential for youth-development activities to use technology of various kinds. Core elements (e.g., moral, social, cognitive) can easily be incorporated into activities using information technology. As will be noted in the next section, these activities can stress collaborative projects and teamwork as a central goal.

When considering programming that involves information technology, it is important to note that computers, with all of their excitement and potential for youth, do have a downside—one that is rarely discussed: excessive use of computers can result in injury. Poor ergonomic habits can have long-term health consequences that are only now being recognized (McGrave 2001).

MAJOR YOUTH-DEVELOPMENT ACTIVITIES

Information technology provides communities, service providers, and advo-cates with a mechanism through which services can be more effectively and efficiently provided. Youth and technology can unite to create an agenda for positive change that ultimately will benefit youth, their families, communi-ties, and society. Use of computers should ideally be sufficiently flexible to respond to particular local circumstances and also allow youth to accom-plish the goals they set out for themselves (Schon 1999). Below I cite four examples that illustrate possibilities and approaches for youth development that involve information technology: the Ella J. Baker House; the Computer Clubhouse; the George Lucas Educational Foundation; and Street-Level Youth Media. My passage on the George Lucas Educational Foundation in turn breaks down into four subsections, so in fact seven projects are described.

As Kahn (2001) observed, the merging of computer literacy with cultural literacy offers youth-development programs great potential for combining two important content areas for reaching marginalized youth. One such example is an after-school program based in Boston's Ella J. Baker House that involves forty middle-school students. The program is a collaboration between the Baker House and Harvard University's W. E. B. DuBois Institute for Afro-American Research.

The fifteen-week course is free. It uses computers and the Internet to help African American youths undertake research on black, Caribbean, and Latin American history. Students not only learn and enhance their technological skills, they also learn typing skills and how to design and build personal Web sites. Participants are required to dress appropriately: no jeans or T-shirts. Black history, instead of being relegated to one month in the year, can be celebrated all 365 days of the year.

The second example, the Computer Clubhouse, is a collaborative project between Boston's Computer Museum, the Museum of Science, and the Massachusetts Institute of Technology's Media Laboratory. It seeks to increase the technical fluency of low-income youth, primarily youth of color (Museum of Science 2001). The way the word fluency is used here, it refers to a high level of mastery. Resnick, Rusk, and Cooke (1999: 266) explain: "Technological fluency means much more than the ability to use technolog-ical tools; that would be equivalent to understanding a few words in a language (like English or French); one must be able to articulate a complex idea or tell an engaging story—that is, be able to 'make things' with language." This concept of fluency encompasses an in-depth understanding and high level of competence that allows an individual to function independently and to be able to act as a consultant for those in need of assistance.

The Computer Clubhouse is open to youth aged ten to eighteen. It subscribes to four principles: (1) Support learning through design experiences; (2) Help youth build on their interests; (3) Cultivate "emergent community" (community involving youth and adults); and (4) Create an environment of respect and trust. These principles, while intended to guide project development and day-to-day activities in the Clubhouse, also speak to the multidimensional goals that must be a part of any information technology-based youth-development activity. It is too easy, when involving technology, to lose sight of the importance of "climate" in setting the stage.

The Computer Clubhouse is a learning community where youth and adult mentors collaborate on projects using technology as a tool to "explore" and "experiment." In the words of the Museum of Science (2001: 8): "The Clubhouse is more than just a high-tech hang-out. It serves as a community where young people not only develop job skills, but also learn important life skills by connecting with their peers and mentors." The Clubhouse undertook extensive connections with community-based organizations and public-housing developments. As a means of encouraging participation, this program allows youth to drop-in whenever the Clubhouse is open. Connections between the program and community are essential in keeping youth connected to their home environment and shaping projects with the potential to impact youth and their community.

Youth participants "become designers and creators—not just consumers—of computer-based products. Participants use leading-edge software to create their own artwork, animations, simulations, multimedia presentations, virtual worlds, musical creations, Web sites, and robotic constructions."

The projects undertaken in the Computer Clubhouse go far beyond what is usually thought of when discussing youth development and information technology. But information technology, as already noted, lends itself well to youth-development activities. The core elements addressed in chapter 5 are easily integrated into activities.

The youth-development work sponsored by the George Lucas Educational Foundation—the example I will describe in greatest detail—does a wonderful job of illustrating how a "new funder" can play an important function in encouraging innovation in this field (Children's Partnership 2000). New funding opportunities are one consequence of the merging of youth and technology. Lazarus and Lipper (2000: 2) explain: "With the advent of a whole new cadre of funders created by the new technology companies and their philanthropies are also interested in finding community and advocacy partners with whom they can work on social development. These companies bring technologic know-how, a willingness to move quickly and an openness to new strategies (or now resources for old strategies) that can benefit undervalued communities." The possibilities for bringing youth and technology together are tremendous: youth are not only consumers of technological products, they are also potential employees in firms creating and marketing this technology.

The George Lucas Educational Foundation, based in Santa Monica, California, was founded in 1991. George Lucas, famed as a filmmaker, established a foundation "dedicated to promoting a vision of inspired learning and teaching—where students are challenged and engaged, have access to interactive technologies, and are supported by inspired teachers and involved parents and communities." Technology has played an influential role in Lucas-directed and Lucas-produced films, and this has spurred the mission of the foundation. The foundation not only funds initiatives but also develops and distributes materials, videos, and reports. The following four Lucas-supported initiatives are fine, multifaceted examples of how learning, use of technology, and youth development can occur. The projects stress project-based learning, collaborative learning, connecting with real audiences, the valuing of youth expertise, and provision of support. These four themes address the core elements identified earlier in this book.

Plugged In Enterprises (PIE) is one of the Lucas initiatives. This program can probably best be described as a "teen-run Web business." Youth participants work as a team and provide technical assistance to "client" groups, creating Web sites for them. Team members develop mock-up pages and obtain reactions from the client. After agreement on how the pages should look, the team enters into a production phase. New members of PIE are paired with a senior member of the team for on-the-job training.

Another Lucas program, I*EARN, stresses active collaboration on projects seeking to "improve the health and well-being of the world." These projects can focus on environmental, political, or social issues that require a team effort. "Collaborative learning," which is central to all aspects, prepares youths to be advocates and collaborators on social-change projects.

ThinkQuest, the third Lucas initiative on my list, is a contest. It is specifically designed to reward collaboration rather than individual competition. Teams of two or three work together to create project sites. The teams can be nationwide in membership, drawing on youths from different parts of the country. in one case, for example, a student from Alaska worked with students from Virginia to create a Web site called The Soundry. These projects focus on use of computer and network resources as vehicles for education.

My fourth Lucas initiative is Latinas en Ciencia. This project, based in Portland, Oregon, seeks to increase the presence of Latinas in science and technology. There is a paucity of Latinas in these areas and many do not see careers in these fields as desirable or feasible. Latinas en Ciencia is a collaborative project between the Oregon Museum of Science and Industry (OMSI), community, and these fields. The project was conceptualized to take a two-pronged collaborative approach. Phase 1 involved OMSI sponsoring a series of symposia focused on better understanding the critical factors at work on girls in the sciences and technology. The symposia also examined how Latino culture impacts girls seeking careers in these fields. Two workshops were also offered through community-based organizations. In phase 2, participants played an active role in sponsoring a day-long conference, "Families and Sciences," for Latino families. Project participants served as hosts and led their families on a tour of the museum, helping siblings and parents in a variety of science-related activities. The success of the conference inspired the museum to sponsor a Latino Family Day once each month.

Leaving the Lucas initiatives, we come to Street-Level Youth Media, the fourth of the organizations that works with youth and information technology. Street-Level Youth Media is a nonprofit, community-based organization based in Chicago, Illinois. The organization is run by artists and adolescents and sponsors three Chicago community drop-in centers. Youth of all ages have access to information-technology equipment, including computers and the Internet, and training and support. They also have access to video-production facilities, editing facilities, and professional artists. The merging of technology and the arts is not unique to this setting, but the manner in which it has been grounded in a youth-development paradigm highlights how activities can blend these two fields together in service to youth and their communities.

Street-Level Youth Media stresses collaborative partnerships with Chicago's public schools. Staff help teachers bring media technology into school curricula and thereby add a dimension that youth enjoy. Street-Level also collaborates with institutions such as the Chicago Historical Society. This project documented oral histories of community elders, and the information was used in a special exhibit sponsored by the historical society. Work on media art produces almost 50 percent of the organization's operating revenue, with the remaining portion coming from grants and donations. Collaboration is an important goal for the program and for participants.

At Street-Level, technology is viewed simply as a vehicle that can enable youth to have their voices heard. A hands-on approach typifies the educational philosophy of the program. The primary goal of the program as stated by a codirector of Street-Level is "to provide youth with experience in terms of all the emerging technologies, and to talk about self-expression and social change, and all the self-esteem and critical thinking skills that you associate with media and media literacy." Technology and the arts are powerful empowering vehicles that can have profound influence on society. Providing youth with a voice can be an incredibly strong motivator for youth to seek change at the community level, and the lessons learned can have life-altering effects. These things would be difficult to achieve without technology and the arts coming together.

⌒

The present-day prominence of information technology can only be expected to increase. No significant sector of society can function without information technology of various kinds. The widespread fears associated with the Y2K bug stands as testament to how much postindustrialized society relies on computers. The influence of technology is so pervasive that major industries (health, for example) cannot function without it. Consequently, it is imperative that the future workforce be equipped to use computers, electronic communications, and the Internet. Competencies in these areas are no longer viewed as a luxury; they are viewed as a necessity in helping youth communicate with each other and be better prepared for transition to the adult world of work.

The importance of information technology for youth is well understood. Youths without competencies in this area will face very limited employment options as they enter adulthood. Families without access to information technology will in all likelihood be marginalized, even within their own communities. Information technology has gone from being a luxury to being an essential element in the economy. However, this transformation has resulted in large-scale disenfranchisement of poor and working-class people. Youth are but one part of this disempowerment, although a critical part because they are the nation's future.

Cyberspace is expensive. As already noted, the cost of equipment is decreasing, but equipment is a relatively small part of the total costs. Training and ongoing support of personnel is expensive, and so is the maintenance of equipment. Programs privileged to be using information technology already are in a propitious position to help prepare American's next generation of programmers and scientists, and they should maximize this potential.

The business potential of cyberspace within low-income communities must not be overlooked. These very same communities represent more than $300 billion in purchasing power, and much of this is untapped by the Internet businesses. Approximately 56 percent of low-income families have a basic cable subscription, for which they pay almost $28 per month (basic service and monthly fee) (Children's Partnership 2000). The potential of youth from this community developing the skills and companies to tap this market makes a strong business case for eliminating the digital divide. The future of cyberspace and how it will transform the future of commerce and the country can only be guessed at. Youth will undoubtedly be part of this future, both as consumers and creators of these changes. Significant barriers, however, will need to be overcome if all youth are to benefit.

13 / AQUARIUMS, ZOOS, AND OUTDOOR ADVENTURES

ONE OF the fascinating aspects of writing about new frontier settings is that many of them are waiting to be found and enlisted in service to youth. Some of these settings can help address aspects of youth development that are often overlooked. There is excitement and wonderment in venturing out into a community and seeing it through new lenses. These lenses show expanded possibilities for youth and allow local circumstances to dictate new settings for youth development.

This chapter, in the spirit of expanding the possibilities, will highlight three types of new frontier settings: aquariums, zoos, and outdoor adventure. They will not be described in detail, but enough information will be provided to encourage some practitioners to venture out and explore the possibilities in their own communities. The definition of aquariums, zoos, and outdoor adventure given is sufficiently flexible to open up possibilities for these types of settings to engage in youth development, and concrete examples of youth-development activities are presented.

COMMON ATTRIBUTES OF THE THREE SETTINGS

Outdoors adventure may seem to have little in common with aquariums and zoos; these three new frontier settings do, however, have much in common. First, all three settings stress the importance of ecology in their mission. An ecological perspective stresses that for there to be a healthy future for the inhabitants of Earth, all people, young and old, must be keenly aware of how today's actions, and inactions, have long-term implications. A second thing these settings have in common is that all three involve youth in active and physical activities. Passive activity is not central to these settings. Technology takes a backseat—a secondary role. "Hands-on" is central.

All three settings place much emphasis on education and self-awareness. Outdoor-adventure settings especially require that youth develop a keener understanding of themselves, but these settings are rarely geographically accessible to youth from low-income communities. Many of the settings may be out of the question for some programs, other than as an all-day field trip. Cost of participation (entrance fee in the case of aquariums and zoos, equipment and transportation in the case of outdoor adventure) severely limits sustained participation by low-income youth. Historically, some settings in this group have relied on youth visiting periodically, maybe several times each year. In including these new frontier settings in youth-development practice, the expansion of "contact period" is to be encouraged.

AQUARIUMS

An opportunity to visit an aquarium, whether on a family outing or a group field trip, is appealing to most people, young or old. At a public aquarium—a place established to expose visitors to the world of sea creatures and their water habitats—people often seem to be transported to an almost magical state of being.

DEFINITION OF AQUARIUM FUNCTIONS

A formal definition of an aquarium is similar to that of a zoo. The Aquarium and Zoological Association (2000: 1) defines "a zoological park or aquarium" as

> a permanent cultural institution which owns and maintains wildlife that represent more than a token collection and, under the direction of a professional staff, provides its collection with appropriate care and exhibits them in an aesthetic manner to the public on a regularly scheduled, predictable basis. They shall further be defined as having as their primary business the exhibition, physical and psychological well-being, conservation, and preservation of the earth's fauna in an educational and scientific manner.

Both aquariums and zoos place a considerable amount of attention on educating the public, and the similarity in mission lends these new frontier settings to collaboration. They form partnerships and coalitions. For example, in cases where two institutions are geographically close, single-fee accessibility may allow patrons to make a day of it and visit both settings.

YOUTH-DEVELOPMENT ASPECTS

Aquariums provide endless possibilities for youth activities and programs involving the sciences. The Tennessee Aquarium and Imax 3D Theater has a volunteer program specifically for youth. After training, youth volunteers are stationed in the aquarium galleries to interpret exhibits––habitats, animals, and plants—for visitors. Volunteers are given duties every other weekend, on Saturdays or Sundays from 9:30 to 2:00 p.m. or 1:30 to 6 p.m. To qualify for the program, volunteers must have successfully completed a year of high school biology.

The National Aquarium in Baltimore, Maryland, has a college internship program. Interns must commit 120 hours in a single semester. Interns work in one of fourteen departments, depending on their interests, abilities, and the needs of the aquarium.

The Baltimore aquarium also has a number of other youth-development programs. The Student Summer Program (SSP) is open to youths who have completed a high school biology course and ninth grade by the beginning of the program. The seven-week training period, which is conducted on Saturdays during the late winter, qualifies youth volunteers to be part-time employees. They work as exhibit guides in the aquarium's galleries, in visitor services, the gift shop, and the membership office.

The Henry Hall Program at Baltimore was established in 1982 to provide students with an opportunity to pursue learning in the environmental and aquatic sciences. The program provides paid internships (for college students), one-year college scholarships, and tuition for summer camps, sailing programs, and youth programs that emphasize the environment and aquatic sciences.

The Vancouver Aquarium Youth Volunteer Team seeks "to build future leaders in conservation, develop career skills, empower youth with knowledge and foster partnerships through direct participation in Aquarium-wide initiatives" (Vancouver Aquarium 1996: 1). Approximately thirty team members, aged fourteen to seventeen, volunteer at the aquarium and the aquarium's community-based initiatives.

ZOOS

We tend to associate zoos with youth, particularly with younger children. There are probably few people who have never visited a zoo, and quite likely the first time for most people was when they were young, either with family or as part of a field trip. One of my favorite field trips in elementary school was to the zoo. Zoos were places where one would spend the better part of a day visiting animals and learning about their natural habitat, diet, and their ecological role.

Today, however, zoos are places where youth can learn about animals and their upkeep on a regular and sustained basis. Instead of being just a destination, a place to visit, they now in some cases offer youths training with a view to future careers. And they can be considered ideal settings for youth development.

Many youths do not have the opportunity to own pets because of cost and time restraints (and for some, it should be mentioned, because of allergies). Especially for such youths, access to a zoo provides a rare opportunity for simultaneous entertainment and education. At a zoo we can learn about relationships between animals, their habits and habitats, and humans. The study of habitats, for example, allows us to learn about environments we are normally not familiar with (e.g., for some, deserts, for others, wetlands), and zoos, with their compressed diversity, provide visitors with an opportunity to focus on their individual habitat (or animal) of choice. Zoos offer youth-development possibilities for a wide variety of approaches and activities, among them opportunities for youth to engage in ecological activism.

DEFINITION OF ZOO FUNCTIONS

Zoos, as we have seen, share their definition with aquariums. Historically, zoos have had royal origins. Kings and queens established the first zoos for their personal edification.

Like aquariums, zoos come in many different shapes and types. Some specialize in certain types of animals. The larger and more established zoos include many different animals, including hard to find ones (e.g., pandas in the National Zoo in Washington, D.C.). But practitioners should not adopt as a standard for "what a zoo should be like" zoos with a national or international reputation.

YOUTH DEVELOPMENT ASPECTS

The case of the Roger Williams Zoo in Rhode Island is an excellent illustration of how well zoo-based programs fit with youth development. Although in "the smallest state in the Union," the Roger Williams Zoo has a perspective that no one could call "small."

Youth activities at this zoo can be structured to take into account age, interests, competencies, time, and a multitude of other factors. Activities can take place throughout the calendar year, with the possibilities for intensive programming during the summer. Youth ALIVE (Achievement through Learning, Involvement, Volunteering and Education) runs from October to June. It recruits sixteen youngsters from Providence and Cranston high schools to participate in this program. Participants (called SALs—Student Activity Leaders) receive training in environmental education, research, and curriculum development. They then teach younger kids, aged six to twelve. SALs are paid $5.65 per hour and are evaluated for a raise after six months. SALs must maintain a grade of C or higher to stay in the program and maintain eligibility for a $5,000 continuing-education scholarship on completion of at least one year in the program and graduation from high school. ALIVE has five goals:

To teach responsible work habits and professional skills

To instill an ability to work in an integrated environment with people from a variety of backgrounds and skill levels

To teach the ability to develop and implement a curriculum that presents environmental issues in a meaningful context with practical applications, making learning fun and nurturing children's interest in science

To instill motivation and guidance to investigate career paths and educational options and attain professional and personal goals

To engender a sense of ownership, awareness, and appreciation of the natural environment as a living laboratory.

To communicate the positive ecological, educational, and social value of the zoo to the community

OUTDOOR ADVENTURE

Marginalized youth often have very limited access to the natural world. Outdoor adventure is about environment and informal education. The group aspect of outdoor adventure is very important since it promotes enhancement of personal and social development through group bonding, cooperation, and cooperative learning (Barrett and Greenaway 1995). Although outdoor adventure may appear to be an individualistic activity, it is best conceptualized as a group experience in a game-like atmosphere (Herbert 1995).

Outdoor adventure usually refers to a wide range of programs that use physical activity as a central organizing theme. Outdoor-adventure programs seek to create situations and obstacles that are likely to occur in day-to-day life. In so doing, these programs seek to increase participants' communication competencies and make youths more cooperative and trusting while members of a group. Outdoor adventure is the context. In this context, participants can grow while enjoying themselves and being productive and creative (Stiehl 2000).

In their *The Role and Value of Outdoor Adventure* (1995: 5), Barrett and Greenaway write:

> In an attempt to understand themselves, others and the changing context of their lives, all young people are engaged, consciously or unconsciously, in an exploration of what it is to be human. This is in essence a spiritual journey, in which young people come to terms with the mysteries of human existence; establish standards and values by which they live and work; identify worthwhile goals and develop the skills and understanding through which these may be achieved. . . . The challenge for all concerned with young people is to empower them to cope effectively with the choices, problems and opportunities which face them, and at the same time to help them develop a real sense of community.

Although Barrett and Greenaway were specifically addressing outdoor adventure, what they say can as easily be applied to the whole of youth development.

Outdoor-adventure activities are structured to engage youth in experiences that provide thrills and excitement (Davis and Sayles 1995; Marx 1988; Wasylyshyn 1988; Scott 1991). Marx (1988: 517) notes that outdoor-adventure programs can play a significant role in helping troubled adolescents:

> Outdoor adventure can be intense, physical, and emotional, just like the teens, For teens with a perceived empty and irrelevant future, outdoor challenges get them thinking about short-term goals. For adolescents living in dysfunctional homes, outdoor adventure teaches them to take better control of their environments. Similarly, especially abused and neglected adolescents, outdoor challenges can teach adolescents to take better command and care of their bodies. Likewise, for the teen who wants to escape a boring environment, an outdoor adventure can offer exciting places and physical thrills.

Outdoor-challenge courses have also been used to add another dimension to community-service projects (Ha 2000). "Outdoor adventure" can also be found in urban areas (Coyle 2000; Herbert 1996) and can bring together youth who are "typical" with those who are "untypical."

One of the most valued techniques used in adventure-style programs is to have youth test their skills on ropes. Ropes-challenge courses have a lengthy history in the youth field (Davis, Ray, and Sayles 1995). These programs can be preventive or therapeutic. Although prevention work using ropes usually takes place in hospitals or treatment centers, therapeutic ropes-challenge courses have found their way into youth-development programs of various kinds.

YOUTH-DEVELOPMENT ASPECTS

Outdoor adventure is unlike any of the other settings identified in this book. The Sierra Club's Galileo Outdoor Adventure Program (GOAP), based in San Francisco, introduces urban youth to adventure programming gradually. GOAP—a semester-long program—starts with a walk across the Golden Gate Bridge, which may not sound like a very big step; since 70 percent of the youths taking part have not done this before, however, it is in fact significant (Coyle 2000). Members of the GOAP club take day hikes to state parks and participate in a ropes course. The semester ends with an eleven-day wilderness expedition in the Sierra Nevada. Later, students learn about the environment and ecology, work on habitat restoration, and undertake coastal clean-ups. Coyle (2000: 2) notes the multifaceted benefits of the program:

> Getting kids into the wilderness allows us to level the playing field. It doesn't matter if you're the smartest or dumbest academically; what matters is if you're been paying attention. The consequence of not putting on long underwear is that you get your butt kicked by nature—not by some authority figure. And there's nothing like the confidence that gets built in the outdoors. I have kids come off a rappel and say, "If I can come down a 60-foot cliff, I can do anything."

In South Central Los Angeles, site of the 1992 Rodney King riots, the Augustus F. Hawkins Natural Park was built and dedicated in 2000 (Brown 2000). Designed by residents and built on land that formerly was occupied by a junkyard, the park brings "wilderness" to the neighborhood. Youth programs centered on the park use both conventional and outdoor approaches. Brown (2000: D9) writes: "Programs will include Saturday morning bus trips to the real mountains, nature talks, tutoring in science homework and a 'survival program'—with ranger Luke McJimpson, who will be living full-time above the nature center, which includes a small wildlife museum. The five jobs available in the park—three full-time and two part-time—have attracted more than 400 applications from the community."

The Topsail Youth Program at San Pedro, California, uses sailing as its central activity in recruiting and engaging youth, but sailing is not the only activity used (Bracken 2000). Youth also hike, swim, and participate in beach picnics. They learn teamwork, problem-solving, decision making, planning, self-reliance, and leadership. The program shares a problem with other new frontier settings: funding. Jim Gladson, the director, says (Bracken 2000: 12): "Many funding sources and youth workers are unfamiliar with the sail training concept, and it can be difficult to convince people of the efficacy of the program." Topsail, which is definitely a youth-development program, is unconventional. Its dilemma highlights the barriers new frontier settings must overcome as they venture into the youth-development field.

Eagle Eye Institute, in Somerville, Massachusetts, involves urban youths in developing their environmental leaderships skills, with the further goal of possible recruitment into the nature-resource professions (Sanchez 2000). The "Learn More About Forests" (LMAF) tree-climbing program is a three-day training for youth aged from ten into early twenties. This program seeks to promote personal growth, environmental stewardship, and community service. Sanchez (2000: 10) writes:

> Working for tree companies in the Boston area, you can work year-round. If you have two legs and walk upright you can get $10 an hour—and if you climb you get $15 or $16 an hour to start. There is incredible opportunity in the arborculture industry. The idea here is to give you a snapshot of it, get you up in the trees a little bit, let you explore, and see if you like it or not. We're here as an open book. We are here for all skill levels. The idea is to have some fun and for you to see what the possibilities are.

Eagle Eye Institute also offers "Learn About Water" and "Learn About Agriculture" programs.

Outdoor adventure is not just for the physically fit or youths who are "typical." Youths with physical disabilities can participate. Adventure programs are flexible and can be adapted to youths with varying degrees of physical, emotional, and cognitive abilities (Herbert 1996), although youths with disabilities often feel discouraged about participating (Nichols and Fines 1995). Concerns about personal safety are often the primary reasons cited as to why they should not take part. Activities such as hunting (Scott 1999) and practice shooting (Paralegia News 2000) are examples of outdoor activities for youths with disabilities. Others are white-water rafting (Wheat 2000), flying (Strasburg 1998), and kayaking (Nichols and Fines 1995). Kayaking provides a good example of how an activity can be modified to accommodate disabilities: a removable upper hull can be used to ease entry and departure; seating has been designed for increased comfort and freedom of movement; floatation can be changed to increase stability; and a sip-and-puff and remote-control rudder system can allow paddlers with lower-body difficulties to steer (Nicjoles and Fines 1995).

∽

In the new frontier settings covered in this chapter, what stands out is the need for the integration of a new vision for education. Stiehl's (2000: 84) vision of education is unique. It is both comprehensive and "different":

I believe that young people possess an inordinate amount of unrealized potential and possibility. The consequences of this state of affairs are tragic, both for our youngsters and our society. The answer to this problem does not lie in education per se. Education is no guarantee of decency, prudence, or wisdom. In fact, more of the same education will only compound problems. We need not education, but education of a certain kind—a kind where knowledge does not supersede feelings and experiences but becomes compatible with them; where young people's feelings, dreams, and imagination will be encouraged, supported, and legitimized; and where their struggles will be respected by caring and knowledgeable leaders and teachers.

Stiehl's vision specifically addresses the use of outdoor-adventure activities. Its lofty goals can also be seen to apply to new frontier settings of other types such as the ones described in chapters 10–13. Readers will have seen how youth-development programming involving aquariums and zoos is not such a stretch (to use an apt word) from that in adventure settings. The three settings focused on in this chapter may not exist in all communities, but if we take a broad view practitioners may find that there are more of them than readily meets the eye. It may require imagination and flexibility to extend into these areas, but the possibilities are there.

14 / ACTIVITIES

WHAT DO youth-development activities look like when practiced in new frontier settings? Are they unique to these new settings or can they be found elsewhere in youth development? Can only staff with very specialized training and background carry out these activities? This chapter will attempt to answer these questions.

With some notable exceptions activities in new frontier settings are not that out of the ordinary. The principles they are based on are similar to those found in conventional settings, but the manner in which activities are operationalized is of course dictated by the settings. And they do require the talents of staff with specialized education and career goals. Consequently, there can be significant differences, and these reflect the nature of the organization sponsoring the activities.

DRAMA

The provision of a socially acceptable outlet for youth to express emotions and creativity is not unique to youth development. Drama is an activity that is highly valued in a sizeable number of new frontier settings, and it is valued for many of the same reasons as in many other youth-serving organizations (Delgado 2000a; Lakes 1996; Maloney and Hughes 1999). Drama, after all, is very much a part of being a youth, and the fact that as an activity it will engage them is not surprising.

Drama is not a monolithic activity. There are many dimensions to it (e.g., role-play, improvisation) that facilitate modification to suit local circumstances. A further point in its favor is that it does not require elaborate or expensive equipment and maintenance of equipment. Unlike some other activities covered in this book, it does not require staff with extensive formal education and training—which is not to say that just anyone can lead this activity. Drama as an activity is within the reach of all youth-development programs, both in new frontier settings and elsewhere. As an activity it can stand alone or complement other activities.

Some new frontier settings particularly lend themselves to the use of drama. Hayes and Schindel (1994: 3) note that drama and museums have a natural working relationship:

> Working through drama is an excellent way to teach fine arts, and therefore it is an unbeatable asset in museum education whatever the focus of the museum. . . . Applying drama techniques in the museum setting can enable us to . . . enter a work of art and experience the artist's motivation first hand, or to . . . respond to historic confrontations and reflect upon them, or to . . . experientially climb inside an atom or the skeleton of a prehistoric creature.

In such participatory ways drama not only becomes a vehicle through which to engage youth but also a way of teaching skills related to organization, team work, writing, brainstorming, and creativity.

The Children's Museum of Seattle, Washington, places a high priority on drama as an activity. Its Experimental Gallery Program specifically targets youth in the state's youth-offender facilities. Youths voluntarily get involved in developing plays and in acting out roles before institutional audiences. The program brings actors from outside the justice system to work with the incarcerated youth. These actors work from an asset perspective as a means of uncovering the participants' talents.

WRITING

Writing skills are essential for both economic and social survival. Training in the art of writing can take place in any setting, even the types that are most restrictive and institutional. Writing skills can be integrated into a wide variety of activities—those that have writing as a primary focus (e.g., activities involving poetry, news articles, personal journals, etc.) as well as those in which it is secondary, in support of a primary activity (e.g., drama).

Youth can use writing in a wide range of settings and to meet any number of needs and goals. Writing does not require huge expenditures of funds and elaborate equipment, and participants can use writing in all social domains.

Those interested in writing as a means of self-expression can do so, or it can be used as a means of communicating with others. It can also be a group activity. Youths can work on assignments as a team.

Activities that creatively integrate multiple core elements are highly sought after in youth-development programs, and the process used in aiding youths to use writing can include emotional goals. That such activities do not require huge expenditures of funds (e.g., for highly sophisticated equipment or highly specialized training) makes them even more attractive. However, it is best if core elements such as emotional and social not be central to the activity; in other words, they should be hidden inside another activity. They will, nevertheless, provide staff with a golden opportunity to explore the activity's emotional and social benefits. A good example is the activity involved in writing a journal: this includes a number of elements. One section of a journal may involve describing an act or experiment in detail; another section may involve the sharing of observations, and yet another may have participants record their feelings. Each of these sections can be modified and addressed in a wide range of ways to take into account the participants' goals, inclinations, and competencies. The importance of writing and the flexibility it allows makes it an attractive activity in new frontier settings.

New frontier settings bring a particular flavor to writing as a program activity. Technical writing or writing for reporting purposes is very different from the type of writing often found in conventional youth-development programs. Technical writing, often associated with scientific exhibits, not only requires participants to have writing skills but also that they be able to use scientific language, and writing for reporting purposes requires the honing of communication skills based on the specific demographics of the audience written for. In some settings this might mean communication in Spanish or other non-English language.

INFORMATION TECHNOLOGY

Many new frontier settings place a lot of emphasis on information technology in carrying out their missions (see chapter 12). In fact it would be near impossible to carry out daily tasks in these settings were it not for information technology. In this situation, technology-related competencies take on an importance almost equal to that attached to setting-specific competencies. Moreover, the use of information technology is an excellent way to attract and keep youth in programs. The use of computers and other telecommunication equipment is a big draw, particularly in situations where participants do not have ready access to such equipment at home or in school.

Access to the Internet and computer use are in fact now often essential elements in youth-development activities, whether for writing, putting one's writing on a Web site, research, or other activity. It is not out of the ordinary to find a team of youths involved in Web site construction. Such an activity can foster group problem-solving skills that can then be used in other social domains.

COMMUNITY SERVICE

Community service has become a prominent, in some cases even central, component of youth development in the last decade. Providing youth with a meaningful chance to help themselves and their communities at the same time has great appeal for the field (London 2000; Youniss and Yates 1997). Service has played an important role in helping youth transition to the world of work and adulthood. This activity takes on added significance when the service targets the communities that participants live in.

Graham (2000: 23) stresses the importance of participants helping to choose the project they will work on. Writing about the Giraffe Heroes Project (sticking your neck out for the public good), a K-12 service-learning/character-education curriculum, he says:

> We've found that the ideal service project is one in which young people are asked to decide what they care about and then design and carry out a project that helps meet that need. Taking major responsibility in their own way generates energy and commitment. And when kids reach their goal, they get a sense of accountability and satisfaction way beyond what they'd get if simply told to show up and put in hours.

Activities related to community service can be found in virtually any new frontier setting actively embracing youth development. Some are much more community centered than others. Some require youth to venture outside of the setting, while others have a community-service component very much based within the setting. The importance of giving back to the community, however, forms an essential aspect of such service.

An example of an internally based effort might be found at an aquarium, where youth staff are sometimes stationed at petting tanks. These youth guides provide patrons with advice on how to handle aquatic animals and information on their natural habitat. Another example might be in a library, a setting where interns have produced and developed videos informing young audiences on how to best access library resources. Internal-based efforts generally stress educational activities. Externally based services may have youth be part of a traveling exhibit or as guest speakers in community organizations. Youth may also volunteer a certain number of hours per week in shelters or after-school programs as part of their requirements for being at a new frontier setting.

New frontier settings sometimes have a combination of internal and external service activities. Such choices depend on the organization's mission and capacities.

ART

Art as a medium or activity has a long and distinguish history in youth work. It is well established. Art can fulfill a multitude of goals and can accommodate a range of settings. Artistic projects involving youth can range from individual assignments to group and community-focused activities such as mural painting.

Expression of creative talent can well find an outlet through the medium of art. The visual arts have generally been well received by youth (Barker 1996; Shames and Gatz 2000). Graffiti is one artistic medium for urban youth, as was noted in chapter 2; another is mural painting—one that, as a program activity, is well understood and appreciated in urban youth development (Delgado 2000a; Delgado and Barton 1998). Such art provides youths with a voice to express their political and cultural sentiments (Barker 1996; Breitbart 1998).

New frontier settings have tapped the artistic creativity of youth through a variety of methods and projects. The creation of Web sites has allowed youths not only to be artistically creative in designing them but also has helped them acquire technical skills. Museums have used youths' artistic skills to design posters announcing programs and exhibits. These posters take on added significance when displayed in community-based settings that target youth. Some aquariums have had youth participants design exhibits that have a focus on youth audiences. The projects entailed doing research on all aspects of the exhibit before the posters could be designed.

Art activities provide settings with flexibility around issues of cost, materials, and time. Among media that can be chosen, photography can be effectively used by youths to mount exhibits, to undertake community mapping, or for other creative impulses. Art can be created on computer. New frontier settings have been known to sell youth artwork at fundraisers and through gift shops. The money generated from these sales has been shared with the artists and used to fund further activities.

MENTORING

Where would youth-development be without mentoring? Mentoring in various forms can be found in virtually any youth-development program, regardless of setting and not only in the United States. The use of mentoring as a method or part of a bigger strategy has quite a history. Taylor and Bressler (2000) do a wonderful job of succinctly tracing the emergence and evolution of mentoring on the world stage. They trace the origins of the term mentoring to ancient Greece, more than twenty-seven hundred years ago. Apprenticeship—a form of mentoring that had career development as a central goal—dates back to the Middle Ages. More recently, mentoring has gained prominence as an effective way to help youth.

Mentoring, in Barron-McKeagney, Woody, and D'Souza's (2000: 40) review of the literature, is defined as "a process aimed at strengthening an individual at risk through a personal relationship with an experienced and caring person. Through shared activities, guidance, information, and encouragement, the individual gains in character and competence and begins setting positive life goals." Mentoring, which is a complex process, provides a youths with an opportunity to be influenced one-on-one by another person, youth or adult. There is good reason for mentoring being so popular. For adults, a mentoring program provides a rare opportunity for them to enter into a structured relationship with youths.

A mentoring relationship in new frontier settings has many of the same qualities and goals as those found in community-based settings. Reciprocity and mutual respect are central to any successful mentoring relationship, regardless of age of the parties involved or the nature of the activities used as a medium for mentoring goals. Both mentors and mentees share in the rewards associated with mentoring; consequently, mentoring programs must never be framed as strictly benefiting only mentees since this can result in a very skewed power differential that is counter to mentoring goals.

Evans and Ave (2000: 41) differentiate the mentoring relationship from other relationships:

> Today, mentoring refers to an enduring relationship between a novice and an older, more experienced individual who provides guidance in a particular domain. The role is different from that of a friend (where relationship is more reciprocal), a teacher (who imparts special skills), or a counselor (who offers personal guidance), although it may contain some elements of all these. Natural mentoring relationships are common in successful business . . . , work . . . , artistic and scientific . . . endeavors. In human services, however, the concept has come to have a more structured, planful meaning.

The mentoring relationship is special. It is unlike any other type of relationship.

There does not have to be a big age difference between mentor and mentee. The process can in fact occur between youth of not dissimilar ages. New frontier settings place high importance on having youth mentor youth. Youth who have participated in youth-development programs and have gone on to college are in heavy demand by new frontier settings. Such a mentor wields significant influence on a mentee. When a mentor is of similar sociodemographic background to the mentee, their influence is considerable. Flexibility in how mentoring is conceptualized is essential and should take into account local circumstances and goals.

Many different activities can be involved in mentoring. The mission of the organization sponsoring the program is usually a major factor in deciding this, but it would not be out of the ordinary in a new frontier setting to find a combination of career exploration, workplace awareness, academic counseling, self-development, and civic responsibility (Jones and Brown 1999). Mentoring lends itself to addressing multiple goals and core elements and can involve special projects in which mentors and mentees spend a considerable amount of time together. There are obvious advantages to a one-to-one relationship, but this is not always possible, sometimes because of a paucity of mentors, and mentoring may take the form of several mentees working closely with a single mentor. In some cases, working in a group is the preferred approach.

LEADERSHIP DEVELOPMENT

There is a special place for leadership-skill development in any program targeting youth. The importance of leadership skills transcends time and settings and is well recognized as critical for the survival of any community or nation. The enhancement or development of leadership skills can be an integral part of a number of activities or it can be the specified goal. When leadership development is integrated into other activities, participants are given opportunities to lead on occasion, to make presentations before a group or at community gatherings, or to assist in processing group dynamics. These skills, although not specifically labeled "leadership," do in fact fall into this category.

To many people, leadership skills are associated with ability to lead large groups of people through difficult, perhaps dangerous, times. Although such a skill is highly desirable, leadership skills do not have to be focused on life-and-death situations. The ability to facilitate a dialogue can well be considered leadership.

When programs specifically mention leadership development in their literature or mission, it usually translates into a set of activities that systematically provide youth with competencies and opportunities within and outside of the program. Sometimes these activities are specifically labeled leadership; however, this does not have to mean that all youths will be leaders. Skills associated with leadership can be exercised in a variety of ways and settings.

It is in fact extremely rare to find a youth-development program that does not make some reference to activities centered on leadership development. Leadership development is an essential element in any definition of youth development and its principles. New frontier settings have embraced leadership development as a central feature of programming. In new frontier settings, however, leadership development has not been conceptualized or operationalized narrowly. Linden and Fertman (1998: 17) define leaders as individuals (both adults and adolescents) who think for themselves, communicate their thoughts and feelings to others, and help others understand and act on their own beliefs; they influence others in an ethical and socially responsible way. For many, leadership is best described as a physical sensation: a need to share ideas, energy, and creativity, and not let personal insecurities . . . be an obstacle. Being a leader means trusting one's instincts, both when doing leadership tasks and being a leader.

Linden and Fertman's (1998) description is one of leaders who are dynamic. It captures how leaders and leadership qualities are thought about in new frontier settings. A leader does not have to be a leader all of the time, and leadership tasks can be performed by individuals whom society usually does not define as meeting "leadership" criteria. Leadership is a state of mind, a presence, and requires competencies with a set of tasks—tasks that incidentally may well vary according to sociocultural context. This broad approach to leadership fits well into a youth-development paradigm.

The teaching of the elements associated with leadership can, like the other activities covered in this chapter, be accomplished through a variety of activities and can also cross into more than one domain. Making a presentation before an audience, for example—a leadership activity already mentioned above—is a leadership skill that can be practiced within the setting or out in the community. Outside presentation is sometimes required by a program. The lessons learned in carrying this out—for example, organizing and delivering a persuasive argument—will be invaluable in other social domains, particularly school.

Every youth participant needs to answer questions such as "How is a leader defined?" "What qualities are involved in leadership?" "How do I measure myself in this area?" True leaders know when they must step forth and when they can let others do so. It is my fundamental belief that all youths have the potential to be leaders and can possess many of the requisite competencies. Circumstances determine when they can and should step forward and play this role. For some, their time as leaders may be more extensive than others, but it is a question of degree, not one of whether or not one is a leader.

Linden and Fertman (1998) refer to these skills as "transactional" leadership. Where "transformative" leadership refers to *being* a leader, transactional leadership deals with the stuff that makes up this type of leadership: it has youths valuing problem solving, making decisions, using standards and principles to guide them, and getting tasks accomplished. Transformational leadership—*being* a leader—has youths valuing the participation and contribution of others, seeking input and advice as part of the decision-making process, taking into account contexts and situations, recognizing the importance of process, generalizing from experiences, sharing power.

New frontier settings have established workshops and created opportunities for all youths to have their "time in the sun." Institutional support for mentors is one way of approaching this. Opportunities for successful graduates of a program are encouraged to return and work at the setting. Their presence leads through example, a powerful motivator and leadership quality. Actions speak louder than words. Leadership is a very complex construct that is very much dependent on content (structure and sociocultural) for its meaning.

CAREER PREPARATION

If one of youth-development's primary goals is to help prepare youths for transition to adulthood, then the world of work must figure in the activities used. Youth development is actually sufficient unto itself without regard to transition to adulthood considerations, but to many people the paradigm is synonymous with preparation for adulthood. For some, youths' pursuit of an education. may simply mean completion of high-school education; for others it means achieving a university-level or postgraduate education. However, regardless of formal educational achievement, learning (formal as well as informal) is highly valued within new frontier settings. Personnel with advanced degrees generally staff these settings; thus, in these programs an emphasis on higher education in preparing youth for careers is not surprising.

Activities that stress continuing of education are commonplace. Some activities do this indirectly. Values-clarification exercises are examples of that are used to help youth better understand their strengths and ambitions. Workshops on various aspects of work within new frontier settings may touch on the kinds of higher educational training required. The merging of the world of work and higher education occurs in a manner that is both experientially meaningful and fun at the same time.

Occasionally there are presentations by representatives from local colleges and universities. These presentations can be low key but impart information on college courses and fields of study. Presenters often look at these sessions as opportunities to recruit youths from families where higher education has not been pursued. Sometimes staff in new frontier settings actively counsel youths on continuing their studies; sometimes staff help youths navigate the admission process.

Some settings work out agreements with local community colleges and universities to grant, free of charge, a number of college credits for youths who have successfully completed a training course. These college credits can, with the right support, induce youths to enroll in the college granting the credit. This will be a win-win situation since the student, the new frontier setting, and the college all benefit. Field trips to colleges and universities to visit special exhibits not only provide youths with content-relevant material on a project but also expose them to a university setting. Sometimes arrangements are made for youths to have a meal in a college cafeteria so that college life may seem less alien to them.

⌣

The activities selected for discussion in this chapter can be found in virtually any youth-development setting. However, when applied to new frontier settings they take on a particular shape, purpose, and character. Sometimes the activities go by names that are unique to the settings, which may require a degree of exploration to find out what is meant by them, but regardless of name their basic goals and purposes are those of youth development.

Many activities sponsored by new frontier settings require youths to have expertise in a particular subject relevant to the mission of the sponsoring setting. Expertise in, for example, aquatic sciences or library science is a core component at an aquarium or a library. Settings shape activities in unique ways—ways that may appear to be unconventional to community-based youth-development programs.

The eight activities singled out for attention in this chapter are not the only ones used in mew frontier settings, but they stand out for the author in their popularity and the role they play in helping these settings carry out youth-development missions. Some settings place greater emphasis on one type more than others, but it is rare for them not to be present. Most of the activities, with the possible exception of information technology, are not expensive or high-maintenance. They provide great flexibility in how they can be carried out and they easily address multiple core elements. In keeping with the mission of new frontier settings—their organizational structure and funding sources—these settings have a unique way of carrying out these activities.

15 / EXAMPLES OF PROGRAMS

PRECEDING CHAPTERS have outlined the diversity in youth development: there is truly a multitude of activities and settings. However, by and large these chapters have not provided great detail, and it is critical that we gain an in-depth appreciation and understanding of how youth-development programs take shape in new frontier settings (Networks for Youth Development 1998b).

On one level, it is very encouraging to see how widespread in the United States the use of youth development is. Some organizations actively sponsor youth-development activities without even realizing that that is what they are doing—engaging in youth-development practice (the implications this has for the field is discussed in the epilogue). On the other hand, much of what is referred to as youth development is nothing more than conventional social sciences disguised as youth development. The evolution of the paradigm and practice has been rapid, and this has been accomplished without benefit of being a "profession." Consequently, practitioners must be ever vigilant about is referred to as youth development. A focus of this chapter will be to provide concrete examples of how youth-development activities are operationalized in new frontier settings and how they are different from (as well as similar to) those used in more conventional settings.

Youth development is not restricted to any particular setting, although carrying out its goals is much easier in a youth-focused setting. Empowerment of youth is one example of an activity that it is much easier to foster in a youth-centered organization than one that is adult-centered—for obvious reasons. In the latter, youth may find resistance to them exercising decision-making powers, whereas in a youth-centered organization support for such activity can be explicitly stated as a program goal.

The three case studies given in this chapter present a variety of new frontier settings, ranging across selected geographical sections of the country and different age groups and including a gender-specific program. The cases examined illustrate how key demographic factors, settings, and activities influence the course of youth-development programming. Although I would have liked to include more case studies, because of space considerations I have held the number at three, nevertheless selecting programs that illustrate a wide range of possibilities. Each of these cases taps the potential of youth development to bring significant changes within several social domains.

A case study is best undertaken with the use of a framework. Patton (1987) developed a framework for qualitative research in organizational settings that has influenced the framework I used. Patton's framework consists of seven dimensions: (1) Describing the program setting (physical and human environment); (2) Program activities and participant behaviors; (3) Informal interactions and unplanned activities; (4) The language of program participants; (5) Unobtrusive measures; (6) Program documents; and (7) Observing what does not happen. The framework used in this book emphasizes the gathering of information that will be useful readers who want to replicate parts of a program. New frontier programs are in fact impossible to replicate fully because so much of their shape, content, and form is influenced by local circumstances, but essential features are clearly replicable. It is easy for practitioners to feel doubts as to whether they are doing the right thing when planning a program. It is even easy to be overwhelmed by the complexities of youth-development programming in general. I hope that this chapter will help to alleviate some of that anxiety.

Each section in this chapter emphasizes aspects that I believe are critical to communicating to the reader the full story of new frontier settings. Each new frontier setting is described under seven headings: Rationale for its inclusion in this chapter; Context—factors leading to the creation of the program; Program description—details about how the program is organized and operated; Funding—amount and sources; Program staff—description of professional background and youth-development experience; Challenges in delivery of activities—the key obstacles that needed to be addressed in planning and implementing the program; Lessons learned—words of wisdom from each program for those contemplating establishing a similar program.

Not all the case illustrations share the same level of detail and richness (the nature of case studies allows for flexibility as to extent of detail). Nevertheless, each study opens up a new world for youth-development practice and shows what is possible in the field, and each addresses multiple core elements.

METHODOLOGY AND CASE SELECTION

Any venture into developing a better understanding and appreciation of youth development requires the use of a methodology that seeks to capture key theoretical points. It should also provide a vivid and, hopefully, contextualized picture of programming. The quest to accomplish these two goals invariably leads to the use of case studies that represent "best practices" in the field. These goals necessitate the use of a qualitative method that provides all significant parties to have their voices heard and recorded. This is not to say that quantitative methods do not have their place, and a significant place, but the strengths of qualitative methods make this approach the obvious one to use in this book.

The application of theory to practice is a challenge in any helping profession. Consequently, the facilitation of this application to real-life examples must be stressed in any book that professes to be practice-directed. Case studies provide readers with the rare opportunity to see how practice occurs in otherwise inaccessible settings.

The selection of the case studies used in this chapter followed a deliberate pattern that consisted of five sequential stages: (1) Identification; (2) Initial contact; (3) Obtaining written materials; (4) Telephone interviews; and (5) Field visits. The first four stages provided sufficient material to make a determination whether the setting added to the understanding of how new frontier settings can actively engage in youth-development practice. The identification phase consisted of a variety of methods ranging from use of the Internet, review of the literature (scholarly and popular), recommendations from colleagues, and the author's personal knowledge.

Youth perceptions of their situation and environment provide much-needed information for youth-development programs. These perceptions, which are sometimes better expressed as "stories" of situations youth have found themselves in, shape what they believe they can get out of participation in a program. Figueira-McDonough (1998: 126–27) comments on how rarely youth, particularly those who are marginal, have a voice in shaping programs. He advocates the use of qualitative research methods in all facets of investigations, from needs/asset assessments to evaluation: "The voices of the powerless do not enter in the dialogue of traditional quantitative inquiry. Qualitative methods . . . are particularly useful in providing detailed descriptions of phenomenon, adding questions of population for which there is little prior inquiry and suggesting new insights and understandings."

The use of qualitative methods, particularly ethnographic, lends itself to uncovering experiences, or stories, that are often not heard (Burawoy 1991a, 1991b; Kanuha 2000; Layder 1993; Spradley 1979). Nor are the relevant stories always those told by teenagers: youth-development programs have historically been open to hiring staff who were once members of a program, and by bringing them back as staff, a perspective is gained that often is not otherwise seen.

LIMITATIONS OF METHODOLOGY

By highlighting the limitations of my methodology (all research methodologies have limitations) I hope to help the reader to interpret the results in a manner that is prudent and cautious. First, comprehensive geographical representation, a critical aspect of any effort to generalize findings, is sorely lacking. It was not possible to have wide geographical representation of new frontier settings. The case selections are drawn from large urban areas of the country, the northeast being overrepresented. This was the result of limited funding for travel to settings. Also, urban areas had a greater number of new frontier settings, making interviews easier to conduct. My familiarity with urban settings made this venture into the field that much easier.

It is not possible to generalize from the case studies presented in this chapter to other new frontier settings. That was never the intent. Lack of suitability for generalizing is often looked upon as a serious limitation in research, particularly studies that are quantitative-oriented. The purpose here, however, was to examine a selected group of settings, describe them, and raise issues and make observations, suggestions, and recommendations for future approaches.

A quantitative-based research method would have provided what can best be described as an overview. It would not provide in-depth examinations of programs or stories that capture salient points for discussion. This lack of generalizability can be considered a limitation, but one it is worth accepting in order to develop new insights into youth-development.

A further word about my methodology: while my quest to provide detailed information was in some cases richly fulfilled, in others it was not. Some settings had a wealth of documentation, allowing for in-depth examination, and a willingness to take time away from their busy schedules to accommodate intensive interviews; and some settings in addition had experienced minimal staff turnover since inception of their program and consequently I was able to conduct interviews with the program originators. Other organizations unfortunately did not have a richly documented past had no tradition of participating in scholarly ventures. Some also had experienced significant staff turnover. Scheduling demands made it impossible for staff to give long interviews and I was not able to thoroughly explore their work and perceptions. Such cases were not discarded; I have used them to illustrate key points, activities, and approaches, but they did not lend themselves to in-depth case study. This is no reflection on their capacities to reach and engage youth.

THE SITES SELECTED FOR CASE STUDY

The three cases selected cover three major geographical regions of the country: (1) New England (Massachusetts); (2) the South (Florida); and (3) the Midwest (Illinois). Two of the sites were museums, but very different from each other (the Mexican Fine Arts Center Museum, Chicago, and the Miami Science Museum). The third case is an aquarium (the New England Aquarium, Boston). Why two museums? One of the museums is Mexican and reflects a growing trend in the United States toward race/ethnic-specific museums. The other museum illustrates the increasing importance of science in youth-development programs.

THE MIAMI MUSEUM OF SCIENCE

RATIONALE FOR SELECTION: Given my work and experience in Miami, Florida, it would have been inconceivable for me to overlook this city as a site for case study (anyone who has ever visited Miami, with or without children, will understand). But Miami was selected for a variety of reasons: (1) Its geographical location (representing a southern region of the country); (2) Its racial and ethnic composition (a high degree of diversity and rapidly changing ethnic and racial composition); (3) Its rich array of new frontier settings; (4) Its high national social visibility as a city; (5) Its distinct demographic trends (increasing numbers of young newcomers of color); (6) The age-profile of its residents (high percentage of youth); and (7) The presence of the Museum of Science, which has a complex set of interrelated youth-development programs. This museum was a natural for inclusion in this book.

CONTEXT: To say that Miami is a diverse city is an understatement. The city has a population of approximately 375,000, with Latinos representing the largest ethnic group (approximately two-thirds, or 63% of the population). Miami is one of the few "large" cities in the United States with a majority of Latinos. African Americans account for almost 27 percent of the city's population. Miami might be said to be synonymous with diversity of population, an image that holds both nationally and internally in this cosmopolitan city.

The Miami Museum of Science's mission statement reads:

> The Museum promotes science literacy and serves as a catalyst for continued science exploration by providing science education in a stimulating, enjoyable, non-threatening environment. The Museum plays a leadership role in informing and exciting South Florida's residents and visitors about all areas of science including, but not limited to, the physical and natural sciences, astronomy, technology, and the area's unique ecology. The Museum continues to assess the scientific and technological needs and interests of our broadly based community and service these needs through focused, on site and outreach initiatives. The Museum acts as a community resource on the issues of science, health, technology, and the environment through timely dissemination of information and provision of learning opportunities for the public and other organizations, agencies, and institutions. The Museum cultivates support in the private, corporate, government, and academic sectors.

This mission clearly sets the foundation for youth-development work involving the sciences.

Program descriptions: The two programs highlighted in this section— IMPACT (Integrated Marine Program and College Training) Upward Bound and SECME RISE (Raising Interest in Science and Engineering) emphasize a multifaceted approach to youth development. The RISE program, which has both a boys' and a girls' component, supplies us with an example of gendered programming. All three programs are predicated on the premise that students, particularly those from low-income and first-generation families, learn complex curricula by participating in interactive learning experiences that draw on knowledge derived, in part, from students' personal experiences (IMPACT 1998).

IMPACT Upward Bound: IMPACT is based on the national Upward Bound model. IMPACT is the first museum-based science and math center funded under the Upward Bound model. The Museum of Science in 1999 received a grant from the U.S. Department of Education to fund this program. Although students do not board overnight as is required in other Upward Bound programs, there are occasional overnight activities (a full-scale overnight component was not feasible because of financial and group-composition considerations). For example, a College Summit program for seniors consists of a four-day comprehensive meeting that prepares students for the college application process. Participants host writing sessions, have meetings with university counselors, and discuss financial aid, and so forth. By the end of the summit, students have their college essays written, a list of schools they will apply to, and a list of recommendations to improve their chances of getting into college. The program focuses on helping youths learn how to navigate ethnic barriers by being able to see, at the museum, a different world than the one they see at home and in school.

IMPACT has three basic components: (1) After-school tutoring; (2) Saturday classes; and (3) A summer program. During the academic year science and math tutoring is available to participants and the computer lab is open for research and homework. The students select two or three activities from the following: English, newsletter, photography Web design, digital wizard, butterfly garden, science theater, and college prep. All students must complete college-preparation activities. These include scholarship information, field trips, guest speakers, counselors, and classroom activities. Every Wednesday there is a math seminar for 9th to 12th graders.

Counseling is another component of the program. The program coordinator meets with youth individually at least once a year. Group sessions are held every Saturday, addressing topics such as life skills and behaviors. The purpose of these sessions is to explore home, school, and personal issues. During the summer, the program extends beyond after-school and Saturdays. For the summer program, youth are broken up by grades to take part in different activities. They participate in both classroom and field experience. Each group must complete a research project and has to put together a power-point presentation. Part of the field experience is to try to have youths be able to see what they are learning about in their classroom. Much of the focus is on experiential learning, which moves away from the "lecture" format that youths are accustomed to in a school setting.

The summer program combination of classroom and field experience focuses on the marine environment. Students are divided into teams to study local coastal habitats. At the end of the summer, the students have a chance to use computer skills by putting on a power-point presentation of their findings. The learning process is complemented by a lecture series that allows students to become aware of science research methods, use of technology, and the variety of science-related career options available to them. Furthermore, IMPACT makes high use of its geographical location by taking the students on field research excursions out of Biscayne Bay.

IMPACT is exemplary in how it has managed to function under the Upward Bound model taking into account its unique location, the Miami Museum of Science. While focusing on helping first-generation students go through the college-preparation process, in accord with other Upward Bound programs, IMPACT simultaneously manages to use its geographical location, target population, and resources to carry out innovative youth development.

SECME RISE: In 1996, the Miami Science Museum received a grant from the National Science Foundation to implement Girls RISE, a six-week summer experience for middle-school girls. The program was developed in response to data reflecting the low representation of women in the sciences and of girls taking science during their middle-school years. Through program participation, middle-school girls were exposed to technology by doing activities such as on-line research. Furthermore, the girls also received hands-on experiences (i.e., building bridges). After completing Girls RISE, the Miami Science Museum went back to the National Science Foundation to seek funding for SECME RISE (Raising Interest in Science and Engineering). The museum obtained a three-year grant to implement this program.

SECME RISE is an example of gender-specific youth-development work. It seeks to increase middle-school girls' self-esteem and confidence in mathematics and science, reducing the attrition in advanced-level mathematics and science courses that occurs as girls make the shift from middle school to high school. SECME RISE partners with Miami-Dade County Public Schools and SECME, Inc. SECME is a precollege program whose goal is to increase the number of underrepresented students who are prepared to enter and complete studies in science, mathematics, engineering, and technology.

SECME RISE targets all fifty-two middle schools in Miami-Dade County. Each year, eighteen middle schools select girls to be part of the summer academies (there are two four-week academies). The girls are either sixth or seventh graders (an arrangement made in order that participants can go back to their schools and serve as mentors in the SECME clubs). In 1999 they targeted schools that had SECME clubs that were not necessarily well-established. For the third year, the remainder schools (some of which do not have SECME clubs at all) will be targeted. Aside from providing summer academies, SECME RISE works with teachers in the middle schools to examine gender-equity issues and provide technology-enhancement opportunities.

SECME RISE conducts two four-week summer academies. Each academy has twenty-four participants. These are broken up into four teams. The programming integrates the use of technology as they gain knowledge in science, math, and engineering. Four mentors work with the girls during the academies. These mentors are either second- or third-year university students majoring in science or engineering. Mentors in 2000 were graduates of the Coral High School Magnet Program. That year also included four girls picked from the preceding summer to return and serve as peer mentors. At the end of the academy, the participating girls receive a $300 stipend if they have not missed a single day. The academy concludes with a family day—the last Saturday of the academy—an opportunity for parents to see what their daughters have accomplished in the course of the four weeks.

Girls are given the opportunity to create two Web pages: an individual Web page and a team Web page. Through these projects girls are able to learn the technical aspects of constructing a Web page as well as the details involved in putting the content together for their pages. The Web sites include links to other sites that the girls feel it is important to have included. Also they do an egg-drop activity (in the summer of 2000 they went to a fire station to do the egg drop and were able to speak with a female fire fighter). Guest speakers and off-site experiences are designed specifically to address gender inequities.

Another summer activity includes guest women speakers from the science and engineering fields. "One of the informal activities is to continuously bring to the surface the idea that they are girls and can surmount to anything," states Mara Hernandez, SECME RISE staff. The guest speakers are brought in to serve as role models for the participants. Projects follow a hands-on approach. In teams, the girls design and build model bridges. Through this experience, they learn the detailed processes engineers go through to build full-size structures. Another project involves the computer programming of Lego robots.

FUNDING: The Museum of Science, like many new frontier settings, has struggled to maintain the financial resources to continue to work with youth. Initially, IMPACT was a program targeting middle-school students and was funded by the Toyota USA Foundation. In 1999, the Miami Museum of Science became the first to be awarded a grant by the Department of Education as an Upward Bound site. Given the new funding and regulations, the program now targets high-school youth, while maintaining its original goal of encouraging youth to pursue careers in the sciences and technology.

As was the case for IMPACT Upward Bound, SECME RISE was born out of an earlier program that still focused on gender-specific science, math, and technology education. SECME RISE is currently in its second year of its three-year National Science Foundation grant. They hope to be able to secure funding to continue further.

PROGRAM STAFF: The staffing of the Miami Museum of Science youth-development programs is diverse in background. As is the case some other new frontier settings, the staff for IMPACT Upward Bound and SECME RISE do not have backgrounds in youth development. Summer academy staffs, referred to as mentors, are university students who are majoring in math, science, or engineering. One of the main criteria for hiring is that they show genuine interest in helping middle-school girls develop interest in the subjects. The mentors are usually motivated to work for the program as a result of their own experiences as women (often women of color) pursuing majors in science and engineers. Some mentors returning in the summers to work for the program highlight their dedication to the goal of SECME RISE.

Some IMPACT Upward Bound staff are recruited from the nearby Rosensteil School of Marine and Atmospheric Sciences. Not from youth-development backgrounds, most are interested in pursuing careers in the sciences, not youth development—although, interestingly, Jennifer Schooley, who started her work with youth as a mentor, is now project director, in charge of running the program; she has been with the Museum of Science in this capacity since 1996. One of the main starting points for hiring is that mentors be energetic and excited about working with young people.

CHALLENGES IN DELIVERY OF ACTIVITIES: Anyone even faintly familiar with the challenges of instituting and carrying out collaborative programs involving schools will not be surprised by the challenges inherent in the Miami Science Museum's youth projects. Miami-Dade is the fourth largest school district in the country. Efforts to reach out to all sectors of this school system necessitate considerable outreach and follow-through for program staff. Each project faces unique challenges.

Several of the Miami Museum of Science programs are school-based. This allows the museum to offer activities throughout the city without having to establish settings. Unfortunately, involving multiple schools, principals, and teachers necessitates numerous meetings and extensive communication efforts with these different schools. Schoolteachers in these projects play active roles in carrying out activities involving youth and the sciences. Commitments from principals are required to allow teachers to participate. Much time and effort goes into maintaining these collaborative partnerships.

The emergence of new communities of color as a result of immigration and high birth rates can be very challenging for new frontier settings, but the diversity of participants can create a climate of excitement in a program. Youths may come out of groups where families hold traditional values, particularly for girls. These families may not see a girl's future tied into academics and professional careers; they see a future as wife and mother. In such instances, a lot of work needs to be put in with the families of potential participants. This process can entail countless numbers of home visits to convince parents of safety and the potential rewards.

LESSONS LEARNED: The lessons learned by the Miami Museum of Science have direct applicability to other new frontier settings. Although the undertaking of multiple initiatives makes the Miami Museum of Science unique, each of the programs individually has much to teach the field.

The conceptualization of youth development across the lifespan is important, though never easily accomplished. A commitment to providing activities to a wide range in age groups necessitates paying close attention to development needs and other age-appropriate considerations. Hiring and supporting staff to carry out these activities is no small achievement. Having space to accommodate a wide range of age groups also often seems to require a small miracle. However, activities across the lifespan offer many benefits: for administrators, for example, there is the potential for having future staff graduate from their programs; and for participants, there is the opportunity to stay with the program until they are ready to move on to other adventures and challenges, rather than having to leave because they no longer qualify because of age. Staff also benefit because it provides them with opportunities to work with different age groups as their careers evolve. And communities benefit because of the stability youth development provides over the life of many generations.

THE NEW ENGLAND AQUARIUM

RATIONALE FOR SELECTION: Aquariums have not received the attention they deserve: they have high potential for youth-development programming. They provide youth with an opportunity to combine science and entertainment and also offer careers in aquatics. The New England Aquarium has what arguably is one of the most carefully thought-out aquarium-based youth-development programs in the country. It is firmly based on a desire to broaden the institution's appeal to urban communities. In addition, the site's location provides this small collection of case studies with some needed geographical variety.

CONTEXT: There is greater recognition on the part of the aquariums located in urban areas that cities are increasingly diverse. The future of aquariums rests with their ability to attract a diverse audience. Sometimes this requires innovative efforts at outreach and program development, as can be seen in the New England Aquarium case example. The aquarium's mission statement reads:

> The Aquarium's new mission incorporates a renewed commitment to serving an increasingly diverse audience, demanding that we serve as a responsive community resource, that attracts and involves the broadest possible audience. More than ever, we have a role to play in introducing visitors, particularly those in our inner city, to the important creatures and habitats with which we share the planet, and the need to understand and care for them. This also provides important opportunities for the public to learn about important scientific issues and concepts firsthand through direct experiences with live animals, exhibits, and educational programs.

The New England Aquarium is an excellent example of how new frontier settings have established youth-development programs to help them achieve their goals (see chapters 9–13). Readers will see many parallels between the aquarium and the Miami Museum of Science. The similarities go beyond the shared interest in science; they are compatible in philosophy as well as having similarity in programs and activities. Both have taken youth development as a central focus of their mission and have been highly innovative in how they have conceptualized this paradigm. The New England Aquarium mission statement goes on:

These programs serve two broad institutional goals: diversifying our work force [and] developing the next generation of aquatic scientists and environmental leaders. As part of this initiative, Aquarium youth programs have undergone extensive evaluation and revision to build a strong "career" ladder beginning with hands-on-science activities and volunteering opportunities for middle-school youth and continuing with service learning, internship, and job programs for youths aged 14 and older.

PROGRAM DESCRIPTIONS: The New England Aquarium youth programs target youth nine years of age and older and fall into three general types: (1) Hands-on science activities; (2) Volunteer opportunities; and (3) Internships and job opportunities. Note the wide age range.

Hands-on-science activities: the Science League: This program was influenced by the youth athletic leagues and represents the collective efforts of eight New England science museums and Hampshire College, Massachusetts. Youth are placed into regional teams of two to three museums and meet every three or four months for overnight activities, the gatherings being sponsored by a host museum. Each of the three regional groups focuses on one of three aquatic ecosystems: ocean, river, or pond. An oceans project was led by the New England Aquarium and the Children's Museum of Boston.

Summer Harbor Discoveries: This program focuses on children and youths in grades 4 to 9. It provides an intensive day-camp experience with a focus on environmental science and conservation. Field trips are made to the Harbor Islands and other Boston localities and sessions have targeted particular aquatic themes such as a whale watch. Programs last one to two weeks, the activities including visits to the New England Aquarium galleries, behind-the-scenes tours, a boating experience. and an overnight camping trip. Projects have been done on wetlands, coastlines, and aquatic careers.

Five hundred youngsters participate in the Harbor Discoveries program; 250 scholarships are available. The program operates in partnership with the City of Boston and the Massachusetts Environmental Trust. Staff are mostly college graduates with teaching and/or science backgrounds. A number of college and adolescent interns assist with the program.

The ASK Program: For ages nine to fourteen. Participants visit the aquarium once a week for a year. In the fall, students research a subject related to aquatics and create a book on the subject. In the spring, participants have the opportunity to translate their research into the creation of activities; they create boxed activities that are then left in the activity center for others to use. The program operates in partnership with Citizen Schools. Out of this partnership came the Blue Planet Youth Alliance (BPYA), a Web-based network, developed and maintained by youth, for youth, for the purposes of communication and environmental action. In its first year (2000), members of BPYA developed of a trash-can initiative, made a collection of environmental surveys, tested water quality in the Charles River, and created a school recycling project.

To expand the educational experience of after-school programs, the New England Aquarium has developed a series of curriculum kits. Aquarium staff provide an introduction to the kit, then after-school, on-site-staff use the kit with students. The aquarium also offers outreach programs, taking live animals, exhibits, and creative drama to schools, camps, and community centers. Classroom programs and assembly programs are also offered.

Outward Bound Environmental Leadership Programs: In the Outward Bound two-week summer program, students meet in small groups They explore habitats and wildlife in Boston Harbor and study the effects of water and weather and uses of the ocean's resources. They also study seamanship and navigation and take part in physical activities such as ropes and camping. The program is a partnership between the New England Aquarium and the Thompson Island Outward Bound Education Center.

Volunteer opportunities: The aquarium's principal opening for youths to volunteer is in the New England Aquarium Junior Guide Program. Youths aged fourteen to fifteen years work as interpreters of exhibits and special programs. Volunteers are required to complete a modified version of the Aquarium Guide Training class and are mentored by staff and volunteer educators. Older youths (eighteen or older) can participate in the Aquarium's Aquatic Volunteer program,. This requires a commitment of at least one full day per week (8 a.m. to 6 p.m.). Volunteers with biology, marine science, or animal science are preferred. Placements are made in the Temperate Gallery, the Freshwater Gallery, the Cold Marine Gallery, the Tropical Gallery, the Education Center Wet Lab, and the Tidepool and Shore Birds. Volunteers are given task-related titles such as water-quality analyst volunteer; animal-records assistant; administrative/clerical volunteer; marine mammal volunteer–sea otters; vet services lab assistant; interviewer-handler, penguins; holding-area volunteer, penguins; graphics-design volunteer; teacher resource center volunteer; hospital outreach program volunteer; New England aquaculture volunteer–lobster-rearing facility and jellyfish culturing facility; associate keeper; rescue and rehabilitation volunteer; aquarium medical center assistant; aviculture associate: shorebirds and puffins volunteer; and travel-program volunteer. Each of these volunteer positions has a detailed description of responsibilities, qualifications needed, and time-commitment requirements. Some involve heavy lifting; some require availability on particular days of the week.

Internships and job opportunities: More intensive involvement in the New England Aquarium can be obtained through a series of internships and similar employment options. Positions available are as teen program interns, teen ambassadors, and in the college internship program.

Teen program interns: Teen program interns are youths fourteen to eighteen years of age who qualify for the mayor's summer-jobs programs. This requires that they commit twenty-five hours a week to the aquarium. Participants are required to complete the aquarium's guide-training class. They work for the education department and behind the scenes in the aquarium's galleries. In addition they are required to participate in a career skill-development course and complete a major team project. Part of one summer project was completion of a mural depicting aquatic life.

Teen ambassadors: Teen Ambassadors is a high-school internship program that involves youth as roving educators in Boston communities. Participants receive training in marine science, outreach, and interpretation skills. This work-based program also involves leadership and career-development workshops. Teen ambassadors are required to complete a nine-hour volunteer training course in addition to attending leadership and career-centered workshops. An "independence" project entails youths designing and presenting before a public audience. In the past, projects were titled "Giant Ocean Tank Talk," "Sea Otter Presentation," and "Penguin Interview." The program is undertaken in collaboration with Boston community-based organizations. These partnerships further the New England Aquarium's reaching out to communities of color and audiences that are not typical patrons of the institution. Teen ambassadors are also able to participate in the teen internship program. One of the initiative partners (Bunker Hill Community College) grants students three semester credits on completion of aquarium guide training and twenty hours of advanced gallery training.

The college-internship program: The New England Aquarium has an internship program specifically tailored for college-level students.

Interns must commit to a minimum of one hundred hours in a semester (approximately two days a week). They can be assigned to the aquarium's administration, education, conservation, communications, or design departments. Interns are selected based on application/resumé and an interview.

FUNDING: The New England Aquarium has a variety of private and public funding. The Teen Ambassadors Program is supported through a grant from the Arthur F. Blancard/Mellon Trust. The Teen Intern Program is funded through a city government grant. The Outward Bound Environmental Leadership Program is funded by a federal grant. Many of the other programs are funded through the collection of aquarium entrance fees.

PROGRAM STAFF: Youth-development staff at the New England Aquarium are from a variety of educational and professional backgrounds. The programs bring together individuals with training and experience in science, education, and social-service work. Although most have extensive experience in working with youths, of varied of ages, no one on the staff has specific training in youth development.

CHALLENGES IN DELIVERY OF ACTIVITIES: The New England Aquarium is located on Boston public transportation routes. However, its location at Boston Harbor—ideal from an aquarium perspective—is not near major residential centers or of easy access for youth. Activity programming has to be flexible to reach the city's many ethnic/racial neighborhoods. The aquarium's numerous partnerships are valuable in offering programs both at home and away. Private funding has also made scholarships available for youths in financial need.

As at other new frontier settings, recruitment of staff from diverse backgrounds is a perpetual challenge. One method of increasing the diversity of staff at the New England Aquarium has been to invest in youth participants and provide them with opportunities to participate long term. Programs, internships, and the provision of opportunities for paid employment is an effective (though time-consuming) way to recruit a diverse staff. Staff need to have both youth-related and scientific competencies in order to be effective.

As the programs for youth have expanded and evolved, public interest in the aquarium has increased; this, in turn, requires an increase in staff to handle the expansion. Developing the necessary infrastructure is an ongoing challenge.

LESSONS LEARNED: The New England Aquarium has a very ambitious and unusual mission. In order to run a new frontier setting on such a scale, youth-development work has to have a real presence within the institution; it needs internal instrumental and expressive support. Coupled with an ability and willingness to venture out into surrounding communities, this increases the institution's ability to deliver services across a wide geographical area.

Flexibility in structuring services is desirable; however, the administrative and logistical challenges in operating such programs are serious considerations. Partnerships, while they provide relatively easy access to youth, are labor intensive; they require the hiring of personnel with excellent interpersonal skills. At times staff may be called on to meet with school administrators; at other times they may have to meet with grassroots community leaders and service providers. These partnerships require constant monitoring and are subject to setbacks because of changing personnel.

"Success breeds success." Having a highly visible and successful youth-development program at the aquarium has many advantages. Having activities on site, at the setting, infuses youth-development philosophy throughout the aquarium. This visibility makes the development office more cognizant of the importance of youth, and this translates into yet greater efforts at approaching funding sources for youth-development programming.

A major strength of the New England Aquarium is the ongoing effort to promote a "build your career ladder" attitude within the organization. Programs are structured so that children can come in as early as three years of age and continue on through the variety of youth programs—summer-camp counseling, high school and college internships, all the way to full-time paid staff. This environment provides youth with excellent short-term and long-term opportunities for learning and, if they wish, eventual employment. Building a career ladder within the organization creates an atmosphere in which staff are fully invested in the organization. This leads to staff stability, which is especially crucial when trying to keep youth involved over a long period of time. Successful youth development is never a "one-shot" deal.

THE MEXICAN FINE ARTS CENTER MUSEUM

RATIONALE FOR SELECTION: Museums—especially ethnic/racial ones—offer the field of youth development unique opportunities for group-specific initiatives that stress cultural heritage. Working with Latinos, primarily Mexican American youths, Chicago's Mexican Fine Arts Center Museum is a good example. It is undertaking unique forms of youth development.

It seems we sometimes lose track of the Midwest when discussing innovative programs. The coasts, East and West, get a disproportionate amount of attention from scholars and the national media. However, the case of the Mexican Fine Arts Center Museum youth initiatives clearly illustrates that innovative youth development is taking place in the center of the country.

CONTEXT: The prominence of ethnic/racial-specific museums in this country is increased by the need of these institutions to address a multitude of needs within their respective communities. In addition to the needs related economic viability of residents, there is an equally if not more prominent need—the rediscovery of a cultural history that better reflects the contributions of people of color within this society and the history of the world. The achievement of this goal is critical for any community, but particularly more so for the youth of the community.

The Mexican Fine Arts Center and Museum (MFACM) has taken a broad and highly innovative approach to serving the Mexican community of Chicago. The museum's director and founder Carlos Tortolero stated this approach eloquently (Hardman 1998: 57): "We're an art museum, but we're more than about art. . . . Art and culture are vehicles in which we show everybody the beauty and greatness of our culture and in doing that we're telling people, You have to respect us. Things have to change." Museums must go beyond their historical missions and seek to achieve positive changes within the communities they serve (Duncan 1991; Marzio 1991). In Tortolero's words, "museums have to be responsible institutions."

MFACM is located in the Pilsen/Little Village community—the largest Mexican community in the Midwest. Many people ask why MFACM has not moved downtown. Why does it remain in a working-class community? The museum believes it needs to remain accessible to its community, and this means not only with regard to location but also to not having an admission fee (Chicago's only museum to do this).

MFACM was established in 1987, with a meager budget of $900. By the turn of the century the museum had expanded tremendously, and in 2000 it had a budget of $4 million, an endowment of $1 million, and employed a full-time staff of thirty-two. It had a permanent collection of twenty-four hundred pieces. The museum was the first (and is still the only) Latino institution in the United States to achieve full accreditation from the

American Association of Museums. It is the largest Mexican or Latino arts institution in the country (Mejias-Rentas 1998).

MFACM's purpose as outlined in its mission statement is "to simulate and preserve the knowledge and appreciation of the Mexican culture as it manifests itself in and outside of Mexico." The museum defines Mexican culture as a culture without borders and therefore unifies the artistic contributions of Mexicans in Mexico and the United States (Livingston and Beardsley 1991; Ybarra-Frausto 1991). MFACM addresses four goals: "To sponsor special events and exhibits that exemplify the rich variety in visual and performing arts found in the Mexican culture; To develop, preserve, and conserve a significant permanent collection of Mexican art; To encourage the professional development of Mexican artists; and, To offer educational programs."

Although youth development is not mentioned specifically in the mission statement, youth-development work is fully integrated into MFACM activity. The museum's Yollocalli Youth Museum, Radio Arte 90.5 FM, and community education programs bring a welcome Latino dimension to youth development.

PROGRAM DESCRIPTION 1: The Yollocalli Youth Museum is not a conventional art museum. It describes itself as "an arts education and career training program which educates students in different artistic mediums while introducing them to diverse professions in the arts." Artist-teachers encourage participants (aged from thirteen to nineteen) actively to explore their artistic talents through a variety of courses. The program "encourages students to learn the skills and processes inherent across art disciplines and professions. Our teaching artists provide . . . optimum individual attention and instruction. We also maintain a cooperative environment that provides young people with many opportunities to learn in collaboration with one another." Yollocalli is not a drop-in center. Each session, students enroll in the courses that best suit their schedules, interests and career objectives.

Courses offered are in (1) Visual arts—comprehensive training in fundamental concepts of arts and design; (2) Creative writing—students develop their own voice, learning to write and perform poetry, short fiction, and memoir; (3) Interdisciplinary arts—interwoven instruction in various art disciplines, fostering experimentation; (4) Performing arts—includes theater, storytelling, and other performance arts, teaching voice and body expression that informs and interacts with an audience; and (5) Communication arts and technology—providing access to technology and computer skills and thus helping to bridge the digital divide. The courses are described in more detail below.

In 2000, the youth museum launched the Community Initiative Internship Project, which expands programming to people up to the age of twenty-four. This project was developed to help the museum maintain its community-based approach. Assistant director MariCarmen Moreno told me, "There is a tendency to lose sight of the goal of maintaining a community-based approach to the day to day work. . . . The interns will hopefully be able to keep us grounded on our goal." The interns work on recruitment of students and artist instructors, advise on development of future projects, and are given management experience, but their primary job is to develop community projects that take the arts into Chicago's various Latino communities. Interns write proposals for the projects and then spearhead implementation.

The youth museum also assists with professional development. Youths learn how to research employment and higher-education opportunities, prepare portfolios, and polish interview skills. They can also develop entrepreneurial skills such as negotiating commissions, contracts, and sales of artwork and are introduced to administrative professions in the arts such as fund-raising, public relations, and being a curator of exhibits. Some students get the opportunity to work with the Visual Arts Department at the Mexican American Fine Arts Center Museum. The Yollocalli Youth Museum serves 60 to 70 students each semester and about 150 to 170 during the summer.

The youth museum has formed successful partnerships with other arts organizations, among them the Goodman Theater, the Little Black Pearl Workshop, Gallery 37, and the Chicago Symphony Orchestra. "These partnerships," said director Tortolero, "enable us to expand our programming capability and offer students unique learning opportunities that reach across artistic boundaries." A collaborative project with the Little Black Pearl Workshop (an African American youth arts organization) focused on the impact that empowerment-zone programs had on students' lives. The resulting series of photographs was made into a book entitled Empower Zone. Published by Aperture, a leading photography publishing house, it is being distributed nationwide.

Here I want to describe the courses offered by Yollocalli in more detail.

1. Visual arts: This program exposes youth to fundamental concepts of art and design. Youth get to use a variety of materials and media. They use not only conventional approaches but also digital imaging. Courses on drawing,

painting, design, printing, assemblage, sculpture, and photography are available. Visual arts projects have included work on murals, logo and poster design, Venetian glass mosaics, Retablos, functional art (tableware, furniture, and musical instruments), production of a print and poetry anthology and other print portfolios.

2. Creative writing: Participants draw on personal experience in writing, for example, poetry, short fiction, and memoirs. Students also learn how to publish their work.

3. Interdisciplinary arts: Examples of work produced through working in the various disciplines have been an anthology, chapbooks, and brochures (bringing together the literary and visual arts); musical instruments, based on learning music theory; compact disks, and cover art. Students have to be willing to experiment.

4. Performing arts: Courses in theater, storytelling, and performance art expose students to vocal work, movement, and improvisation. They also do scriptwriting and adaptation and research; set, lighting, and costume design; and production promotion.

5. Communication arts and technology: As in other new frontier settings, the use of technology is ever-present at Yollocalli; however, at the youth museum in addition to being used for everyday tasks, it is also used as a graphic design tool. Students "create and manipulate images, text and sound to give ideas and information visual form." In design courses, students explore typography, layout, color manipulation, Web authoring, and signage/logo development. The Communication Arts Technology Center is equipped with IBM Pentium II computers, flatbed scanners, high-resolution color printers, and Internet accessibility.

PROGRAM DESCRIPTION 2: Radio Arte 90 FM must be one of the very few radio stations in the United States to be operated by a new frontier setting, and almost certainly the only one run by a setting that is, to boot, a museum. In addition, Radio Arte is said to be the country's only youth-operated urban-community radio station. Its central goal is

to provide students with a well-rounded educational experience in various media; to provide students with the latest technological skills;

to empower the youth of the community by creating a place where they can have a sense of ownership and develop skills that can lead to professional careers; to teach youth that they are an integral part of the community and, as such, have social responsibilities that include being role models for their peers; and to expose youth to the beauty and richness of their living history, thereby stressing that the arts are an integral component of the human experience.

Radio Arte targets youths aged fifteen to twenty-one in the Pilsen and Little Village communities. Radio Arte makes an effort to include youths otherwise excluded from participating in programs; that is, in its recruitment strategies Radio Arte targets "nontraditional" youth—a wide range that would not, for example, exclude teenage mothers and school dropouts.

A two-year training program prepares participants for all aspects of operating a radio station. The mission is specifically focused on the Latino community. Yolanda Rodriguez, the station manager, says that Radio Arte is "more than just getting kids behind the microphone project.... Most [radio-training programs] tend to focus solely on broadcasting, ours focuses also on management and production."

The training program consists of three distinct stages.

Phase 1 is a three-month theory course that covers creative writing, journalism, voice training, FCC regulations, and radio programming. Phase 2 provides hands-on instruction in basic production and on-air equipment. During this phase students begin to learn about developing a radio program. Phase 3 provides students with an opportunity to design, develop, and maintain their own on-air program for one year.

A major feature is that participants serve on committees during the second and third phase of the program. These committees are what make it a youth-operated radio station. Rodriguez says, "A lot of what we do is experimental. Our philosophy is creative freedom. We don't give them [the students] a model to follow. These are the tools, what can you do with them?" The seven committees fall into two major types. These are (1) Regular programming—community service (English and Spanish public-service announcements); English news (production of morning and evening newscasts); and Spanish news (production of morning and evening newscasts); and (2) Special pro-gramming—Radio Vida (health and social issues); Armonia: a collaboration with the Chicago Symphony Orchestra documenting style segments on Latin American composers and American contemporary recording artists and young composers; Youth metro (social issues from a teen perspective;

includes a print magazine to complement the radio segments); and Web site (putting the station, live, on the Internet).

Students from the program have been successfully employed as producers and broadcasters by commercial Chicago radio stations, but Radio Arte does not limit itself to strictly radio-oriented topics. It has also sponsored artists from Mexico, allowing students to experience the marketing, planning, and development aspects involved in putting on a concert. Radio Arte also increases students' awareness about community issues. It combats negative stereotypes about Latino youth and their community. Rodriguez says, "I think this radio station is important because of the way young people in general have been portrayed. Everything you see on TV or print is very stereotypical and very negative, unfortunately, it is more so with young people of color" (Hernandez 2000). Radio Arte strives to increase student awareness about community issues. Students develop decision-making and leadership competencies and a greater commitment to the Latino community and civic society.

Student Jessica Valdinia, a nineteen-year-old, said of the impact that Radio Arte can have on youth, "There are things I couldn't have learned anywhere else. I have a good taste of what the real world is like the pressures, the responsibilities, the deadlines. I know I want a job that requires me to think and figure things out like this. And I'd rather be in charge. I'm not going for being a nursing assistant when I could be the head doctor. I definitely got that from here."

PROGRAM DESCRIPTION 3: The Mexican Fine Arts Center and Museum maintains an active and diverse community-education program. Its mission statement reads, "The Museum's education department helps interpret the Museum's permanent collection and special exhibitions from a First Voice perspective with interpretive text, lectures, artist talks and demonstrations, exhibition-related family art activities, and guided tours which are presented in English and/or Spanish and tailored to various age groups."

Family Days is a program that targets families through special workshops. Families are provided a tour of the museum's main gallery and learn about the techniques and skills used to create the art on display. Families are also able to participate in creating their own works of art. Arte Ambulante (Art on the Go) is a hands-on art activity—a vehicle to learn about Mexican culture. "From mask-making to Metepec sons, papel picado to papier-mâché, these workshops help students explore Mexican art and culture while developing artistic skills, enhancing their critical thinking, and fostering art appreciation. Art on the Go attracts students of all ages, teachers, adult, and community groups."

FUNDING: The Mexican Fine Arts Center Museum has a total budget of $4 million. MFACM—unlike new frontier settings that receive their funding from a single source, as some do—funds its youth initiatives from "a lot of pockets." The museum receives funding from foundations and corporations such as the John D. and Catherine MacArthur Foundation, Kraft Foods, the Academy for the Arts, Public Radio Broadcasting, and the GAP Foundation. MFACM also receives funding from the City of Chicago's Department of Planning's empowerment zone. The museum finds it imperative to seek funding from sources that do not compromise MFACM's community-based approach to youth development.

PROGRAM STAFF: The staff at Yollocalli Youth Museum and Radio Arte do not have backgrounds in youth development. As at other new frontier settings, the staff has varying educational and professional backgrounds. In the case of Radio Arte, two staff members, the program director and the community outreach manager, were youth participants at one point. The Yollocalli Youth Museum primarily seeks artists from the community to teach and serve as role models for *participants*. Although none of the staff has specific training in the field, their day-to-day work with youth clearly lies along the lines of youth development in new frontier settings.

CHALLENGES IN DELIVERY OF ACTIVITIES: Staffing remains a challenge at the Mexican Fine Arts Center and Museum. In new frontier settings, a high priority on community involvement always brings with it numerous challenges, and senior management and program staff have to devote much time and energy to cultivating relationships; moreover, chief executives with the inclination and talent to be community-involved rarely head new frontier settings, particularly those like museums. However, in a setting like the Mexican Fine Arts Center and Museum that has an ethnic or racial population group as a central feature of its mission statement, things are different. The hiring of staff who are Latino is still there, but it is made easier because of the central mission of the organization.

Staffing programs with Latinos has been addressed through a multifaceted approach. It has been, however, in ways that often push the MFACM to the "outside of the box." The very unconventionality of their approaches has in itself presented challenges to the delivery of activities. The challenge can be seen as being twofold. First, a mission that extends outside traditional realms of youth work requires funding that does not compromise that mission. Second, because such a new frontier setting is not common, the museum has to feel comfortable being in a position where it is setting the pace.

Moreno, assistant director of the youth museum, told me, "It's a challenge learning how to develop this organization. . . .There aren't many programs like us." Tortolero, the MFACM executive director, is aware of both the challenges and advantages involved in remaining an internally driven organization, rather than one externally driven by funding sources. "If you believe in youth," he says, "the money will be allocated internally, not because it's a fad. . . . We believe in youth," Tortolero remains cautious in following accountability trends that focus more on outcomes than on process. "Everyone is trying to guarantee things . . . how do you guarantee things. . . . If you can change a life here and there it's great." The Yollocalli Youth Museum currently has a small staff. Funding limitations do not make it possible to hire all the staff needed to get the work done. This translates into long hours for the staff. The museum is seeking to alleviate this through the Community Initiative Internship Program. Like other new frontier settings, Radio Arte and Yollocalli are learning as they grow. The youth museum now has a new location, but Moreno remembers "there was a time when classes were being held out on the hallway." The current challenges make it crucial for MFACM to continue building an infrastructure that will facilitate expansion.

LESSONS LEARNED: Having arts as a central theme in programming brings advantages and disadvantages to youth-development programs in new frontier settings. Much of the success attained by MFACM can be attributed to its local situation—its commitment to youth and the community it serves—but its strategies, highlighted below, can be applied to other new frontier settings.

MFACM has taken on a leadership role in the community and it has remained faithful to its mission. MFACM has made it a point to open dialogue in the community (Mexican and Mexican American) around issues of race by bringing forward its Afro-Mestizo heritage. Furthermore, it has challenged society's view of museums as institutions for the elite by refusing to abandon its home in a working-class community.

Again "outside the box," MFACM, with its youth initiatives, MFACM has worked with a youth-strength perspective. Youth empowerment is central to the work of Radio Arte and the Yollocalli Youth Museum. "Best people to talk about young people are young people," says Tortolero as he tells of the time when a participant from Radio Arte advocated that the station increase their power to 73 watts. Rodriguez, the station manager, maintains that youth should play an intricate role in the development of a program's mission. "Involving young people is critical, it gives them a sense of ownership."

The three cases studies clearly show the potential of new frontier settings to make an important contribution to the field of youth development. A few highlights stand out: (1) In the case of girls from cultural backgrounds where higher education was not possible, intense work had to be accomplished with their parents to allow them to participate. (2) Knowledge of math and science necessitates an in-depth understanding and competence in order to carry out programming in science museums. (3) People-related skills are not lost in the process of becoming more "scientific"; a merging of the sciences and more conventional youth-development competencies occurs in new frontier settings. (4) Multiple approaches to youth development can and often do exist within one institution; these approaches were in many instances complementary and the result of strategic thinking on the part of the institution's leadership; (5) in some instances, an age continuum was created to take youth from an early age into adulthood.(6) Families played more of a role in some settings than others, but even in settings where families were on the periphery of activities, there was acknowledgement that more needed to be done to bring them into the setting.

Highly specialized new frontier settings require that youth, too, have specialized skills. The importance of youth continuing their education in college was often a message in these settings, sometimes explicit, sometimes implicit. Having graduates of the program return served to send to youth the message, "You, too, can do it."

16 / THE RECRUITMENT AND ENGAGEMENT OF YOUTH IN NEW FRONTIER SETTINGS

I T SEEMS like no two days are ever alike for a youth-development program. This variability can be very attractive to some practitioners, overwhelming to others. Like it or not, however, we all need help. This chapter therefore addresses a question rarely posed in the professional literature on youth development: How do staff in new frontier settings recruit and engage youth in programming? (see Almen 2000; Hahn 1999; McLaughlin, Irby, and Langman 1994; National Collaboration for Youth 1996; Zeldin and Camino 1999). Every effort will be made to provide case examples and detailed descriptions of typical situations involving staff and youth (Networks for Youth Development 1997). Readers as a result will get a rare glimpse into the variety of approaches used.

Few would argue that any program could exist without a carefully thought out plan to recruit and engage youth in day-to-day operation. The ability to attract and keep youth actively engaged in programs is critical to the ultimate survival of organizations, new frontier or otherwise. There are, however, no standard approaches or activities that will work effectively in every type of setting. New frontier settings engage in many of the same approaches to youth recruitment and retention as their community-based counterparts. However, they often have a unique twist to them that lends itself to their particular mission and daily operation. Information or insight into their strategies will be of particular use to readers who wish to explore new avenues.

In recruitment of youth, one of the most important challenges new frontier settings face is the reputation they have in their community. Often they have to change their public persona in order to attract youth. If an organization's reputation is significantly negative, this can often be traced to historical experiences between marginalized communities and the institutions sponsoring the youth-development initiative. To change a reputation is no small feat for a major organization such as a museums.

THE IMPORTANCE OF RECRUITMENT

In the field of human services and education, the manner of recruitment is never left just to chance. This phase in any program must be carefully thought out, examined, and modified to maximize use of resources (time, money, effort). In the case of new frontier settings, how do the efforts differ from those in "ordinary" youth-development organizations? Do lessons learned in these new settings lend themselves to other types of youth-development setting? The answers to these questions provide rich material for discussion in the field of youth development. Further, the answers have implications for how to best develop recruiting efforts to take into account the kind of youth-development program being offered. Although answers to these questions will be influenced by local circumstances, general patterns do emerge that reflect the unique position of new frontier settings in society.

RECRUITMENT STRATEGIES

Recruitment strategies are often influenced by the historical preferences of an organization. Some organizations simple refrain from active recruiting, although that is increasingly rare, or display a proclivity for certain approaches like public-service announcements. Other organizations may embrace recruitment strategies that are labor intensive and involve active outreach to the community. Yet others prefer a combination of approaches, direct (face-to-face) and indirect (by telephone, mail, posters, and so forth).

One labor-intensive approach is streetwork—otherwise known as "detached youthwork." Streetwork has a long and distinguished history in this and other countries, most notably England (Thompson 1999). This form of outreach often entails having a youthworker venture into the community, spend a considerable period of time where youth congregate, and develop a relationship with them in the hope of getting them to enter a program. The approach is particularly needed when reaching for youths who have histori-cally been suspicious of the organization, or who have a history of not responding to conventional outreach. This is important work; however, it is very labor intensive and requires a major commitment from the organization sponsoring the youthworker. Some organizations without a tradition in this area, or with limited funds, will not take this approach. New frontier settings have generally not gone the route of streetworker. In fact, recruitment strategies used by new frontier settings have much in common with mainstream settings. Word-of-mouth is often what leads to success, as is evident when participants bring their friends and relatives to the program in the hopes of enrolling them (Almen 2000). Referral from other community-based organizations is another form of word-of-mouth, although what more usually facilitates referrals is sharing of printed materials with these organizations or the holding of information meetings.

While the latter two recruiting methods are not unique to new frontier settings, other forms do take on distinct characteristics when found in such settings: examples are volunteering, interning, employment, and special activities or initiatives (even these can of course be found in other types of youth-development programs). Each of these approaches to recruiting youth is based upon a high level of competence and commitment. Some organizations actively use all or some of these approaches, the mix depending upon mission and resource availability.

VOLUNTEERING

Volunteers in youth organizations are usually adults; in a typical youth-development organization, youths either are participants or employees. However, new frontier settings have been able to expand volunteer programs that have historically catered to adults to also include youths and have involved various age-groups. This is no small feat, The use of specific initiatives to get volunteers to staff programs is an approach usually foreign to youth organizations.

Not all new frontier settings have active volunteer programs. Youth-volunteer programs provide all of the same challenges associated with those involving adults, plus some of their own. "What is age-appropriate?" considerations play an important role in these types of programs: youth are often in school or have school-related duties during a major portion of the work week.

In California, the Stockton Public Library's Book Buddy program matches volunteers with young children to share a book (ALA 2000a). The volunteers must be at least fifteen years of age. The Queens Library in New York City has a Latchkey Enrichment Program that involves youth and adults as volunteers in working with young children. Minimum-age requirements differ from setting to setting and also within programs. The San Diego Zoo has a minimum-age requirement for volunteers of eighteen years. Commitments, too, may differ along with the "rewards" given to volunteers who carry out their duties successfully. Some new frontier settings place specific limitations on what volunteers can take part in; others limit the day or time period when volunteers can participate. Probably no two new frontier settings are alike.

The Boston Museum of Science has an active volunteer program, open to anyone fourteen years of age or older, that requires a minimum commitment of four to six months. Volunteers

> Work with hands-on materials and share in the enthusiasm with our youngest audience in the Discovery Center. Help the Museum run smoothly and contribute to the energy behind the scenes. Introduce visitors to computers and the world of the web. Give adults and children a special look at the Museum as a Greeter. Encourage visitors to explore objects and ideas in our Exhibit Halls. Welcome and provide information to guests as they arrive. Work in the Human Body Connection and share knowledge of human biology.

This Boston program integrates volunteers into virtually all aspects of the organization's operation, a level of integration so high as to make this setting stand out.

The Science Museum in Ithaca, New York, actively recruits volunteers in its monthly newsletter, personalizing the process by providing activity-specific detail and the name of the person to contact (Sciencenter 2000: 1):

> We are looking for someone to work on the monthly science activity for kids that is published in the Ithaca Journal. Talk to Ron Lis or Llma Levine. . . . More Bluecoats are needed to staff the exhibit floor and assist visitors during the busy summer months. Help is needed both on weekdays and weekends. Robert Ayres will provide training. Chris Bissen and Mike Katz need a volunteer to do data entry on a regular basis. Mike would also like to have someone who can help with research and grant writing. Greeters are needed for the front desk. See Barbara Thorp or Ron Lis for details. Training will be provided. The weeds are winning. Do you have a green thumb? Or do you just love plants? You can help us maintain the landscape plantings. See Eric Poysa. (Tools will be provided.) Volunteers are needed to help staff

events. See Debbie Levin if you can help. Showtime ideas are always welcome. Please let Debbie Levin have your suggestions for topics and presenters.

At the Miami Museum of Science, volunteers (aged thirteen-plus) are offered opportunities to

> Assist staff perform science demos for school groups and visitors. Explain the ways behind our science exhibits. Lend a technical hand with lights and sounds during our stage shows. Guide groups through ancient cultures in SMITHSONIAN EXPEDITIONS (Age requirements: 18+). Research artifacts and assist with exhibit installations and breakdowns (Age requirement: 21+). Staff informational booths at fairs and shows. Perform administrative duties. Be a part of our special event team. Assist customers in our Museum store. Be a part of our educational camps.

Volunteers are required to attend a three-hour orientation, participate in training provided by each department, and make a commitment of seventy-five hours over a six-month period. An interview helps to determine the volunteer's interest and commitment.

In California, the Monterey Bay Aquarium has developed a two-track volunteer program. Their Student Guide Program focuses on youths aged fourteen to seventeen; another program requires volunteers to be at least eighteen. The Volunteer Resources Department links volunteers to aquarium projects and provides ongoing support. The Children's Museum of Seattle, Washington, requires volunteers to commit to at least eight hours per month and for a period of no less than three months. Volunteers must be at least fourteen years of age and be actively in school.

New frontier settings generally make extensive use of volunteers to supplement staff or to run particular programs. Volunteers, not surprisingly, are often in a propitious position to enter programs sponsored by these institutions or to be employed by them when a position becomes available. Although for some youths—for example, those who must earn money to support themselves or their families—it may be difficult to avail themselves of these opportunities, other options, fortunately, are available to them in many new frontier settings.

INTERNSHIPS

Internship has a rich and distinguished history in a variety of professions and settings. Interns (sometimes paid, sometimes unpaid) are somewhere between a volunteer and a staff member. The internship helps the intern to learn the job by doing. Internships are a common learning activity in the human-service and educational fields. In the new-frontier area, settings as diverse as Microsoft and the U.S. Forest Service have launched internship programs.

While the application process can vary from setting to setting, it invariably requires that students fill out an application, obtain letters of recommendation, and attend a personal interview. The screening process is very important. Many internships involve educational credits and have an established curriculum, involving advisors and other requirements. However, internships can also be established by governmental and community settings.

Microsoft's Certified Solution Provider Internship Program specifically sets out to identify, train, and eventually hire students to work for the company. The U.S. Forest Service internship program provides participants with skills and awareness of the outdoors, with possible future employment in this arena. The National Aeronautical and Science Administration (NASA) offers internships that are highly specialized. The Structured Intern Program (SIP)—a three-week, unpaid internship for high-school and college students—is held at the Mechanical Engineering Branch of the Goddard Space Flight Center in Greenbelt, Maryland. Interns spend 120 hours immersed in the use of computers in mechanical engineering. Interns must be in grades 8 through 12 or be an undergraduate student in an engineering program. Interns are responsible for all transportation, housing, and food costs.

The Boston Museum of Science uses its Web site to attract both volunteers and interns. Interns can be in high school, college, or graduate school. The Museum's Career Pathway program specifically focuses on high-school students. These interns must first have been a volunteer. The museum's web page notes: "An internship at the Museum of Science is one of the best ways to get hands-on experience in a specific area of interest or field of study. Interns focus on their assigned duties and also learn about other areas and opportunities in the Museum." Many of the internships—which range in time commitment from three to twelve months—are paid. Others are unpaid, but students can receive academic credit. Interns can be involved in "preparing and evaluating educational materials," says the Web page. "Some assist in training and supervising volunteers. Others help children explore the wonders of science, catalog Museum collections, research and develop materials to supplement existing exhibits, assist with the writing and editing of print projects, and much more!"

The Monterey Bay Aquarium offers summer internships in visitor presentation (deliver educational and interpretive presentations); as seasonal interpreters (help train aquarium guides in marine science and interpretation; interpret exhibits to the public, and develop materials); and as husbandry operations aquarists (provide assistance in daily exhibit maintenance and animal care). The Metropolitan Museum of Fine Art in New York City has a summer high-school apprenticeship program (four days a week, 9 a.m. to 5 p.m.). Summer interns must have completed either their junior or senior year of high school. Another program lasts an entire academic year; for these the interns must be in their senior year. Summer interns get an honorarium of $1,200; those interning in either the fall or spring semesters get $500 per semester. Each intern assists with general departmental duties.

Job experience plays an important role in better orienting youth to career options. Internships also help organizations to fulfill an educational mission and perform a public service. They are also an excellent way to mentor and recruit future staff.

But some settings have very specific requirements for interns. The Denver Botanic Gardens, for example, which offers a ten-week internship in applied horticulture, requires that interns be currently enrolled in college or graduate school. Those in college must have at least one-year completed and a minimum of a 2.5 grade point average (scale of 4.0). Priority is given to residents of, or students in, the states of Arizona, Colorado, Kansas, Montana, Nebraska, New Mexico, Oklahoma, South Dakota, Utah, and Wyoming. Geographical factors are rare, but as this example shows, they can play a role in the selection of interns.

EMPLOYMENT

It is not unusual for a new frontier setting to hire a youth for summer employment or even during the regular school year. However, this will rarely occur for a youth with no prior involvement with the setting. Youths with histories of volunteering, interning, or involvement with special projects might be identified as candidates to return and work for the setting. This employment strategy has a lot of appeal for youths.

Employment can be used as a strategy to prolong youth involvement past a contracted period of time; for example to retain a program participant or to convert a volunteer into a paid helper. Youths with such a background bring a lot of legitimacy to the setting that hires them. Program participants can see how success has helped someone who started as a participant: a real-life example is standing before them. And the employing setting benefits because it is hiring a known quantity, thus saving time in orienting new staff. Such hiring is likely to reduce staff turnover. This kind of situation becomes a win-win for all parties.

New frontier settings thus have an established labor pool from which to tap during busy periods in their schedules. The Miami Museum of Science, for example, generally hires ten youths for the summer—all of them youths who have a history of involvement with the setting. New frontier settings, like their community-based counterparts, always seem to be on a quest to diversify their staff and organization. The other recruitment mechanisms outlined in this chapter often serve as a "feeder" for staff. Unfortunately, the specialized nature of some of the new frontier settings necessitates that youth continue their education to college and graduate school. The ability to keep them actively involved in programs while they obtain their formal education and return on completing their studies is an important goal in these settings.

SPECIAL INITIATIVES

Special initiatives are institutional efforts, often uniquely tailored to a particular situation, that may, if successful, lead to institutionalization. They can be used by youth-development settings to create increased opportunities for recruitment of program participants. Special-initiative funding lends itself well to public-awareness campaigns and to in-depth planning and allocation of resources. For example, money might be allocated to paying youths to work on a campaign. Because such initiatives are self-contained, they work well in obtaining special grant funding—a strategy that seems to be well appreciated by settings.

Youth participation under such a scheme can last for months. Because it entails frequent attendance, this provides staff with an extraordinary chance to integrate a range of core elements into program activities. These initiatives invariably have a vocational element to them, with the natural spin-off that competencies are transferred to the world of work.

Unlike in other youth-development settings, which often can afford to be broad and flexible, special initiatives at new frontier settings are time limited; they have very specific expectations regarding competencies. This naturally lends itself to evaluation efforts. Nevertheless, extensive screening of potential participants is essential in order to program activities successfully. Candidates must be willing to commit time and effort in order to maximize the benefits of participation. Requirements for participation in special initiatives may vary considerably between settings because of local circumstances.

Recruitment to club membership is a special form of recruitment. It is often sponsored under a special initiative. Although it is recruitment in a different sense to sense to staff recruitment, it nevertheless often requires a degree of commitment. "Clubs," however, are a flexible format and are sometimes open to youths dropping in: there may be no commitment to participation in ongoing activities (although this is often encouraged); others might be highly programmed. Somewhere between the two extremes seems ideal, although much can be said for projecting a definite policy. Allowing youth to "test the waters" before making a commitment is one road to youth making a long-term commitment. For some, a long-term commitment to a program other than school may be a totally new experience. Having participants make a seriously thought-out decision has the possible added benefit of reduced dropout rates.

Some clubs have a specific mission that is attractive to youth. The Museum of Fine Art in Boston offers youth a free drop-in-activity program (between ages six and twelve) at specified times (Monday through Thursday, 3:30 to 4:45 p.m.). Participants can explore the museum's collections through such vehicles as art projects, drama, poetry, and music. Long-term commitment is not required. The Science Center at Ithaca, New York, uses a clubhouse theme. Sciencenter (2000: 3) invites participants as follows:

> The tech clubhouse is a place to learn about computers and different kinds of software. . . . The tech clubhouse is only for teens, who may use the tech clubhouse for basic learning, projects, homework, or just exploring how the world of computers work. A lot of the software may consist of typing, web page designing, internet exploring, and whatever else your creative mind can think up. When you come in to the tech clubhouse, there will be mentors to help you out. All of the differ-

ent types of software can do shows, pictures, graphing, etc. The tech clubhouse is a great place for doing homework as well. The software is capable of helping you put together professional and attractive word documents for English or history class, and the software might also be useful for graphing in math class. Almost anything can be done with the computers and software available at the tech clubhouse. . . . An example of a Tech Clubhouse project is "activeworlds.com." At this web site teens can create a Sciencenter virtual world with 3D animation skills acquired at the Tech Clubhouse.

Special initiatives provide new frontier settings with a chance to package into a program with a youth-development focus what they do best. These initiatives can cover a range of time periods from a week to months, depending on program goals and availability of external funding. These initiatives allow new frontier settings to undertake more elaborate goals and to intensify their efforts. Special initiatives have a natural life—a clear start and finish. This factor allows settings to establish a program knowing that if it is not successful they do not have to offer it again.

THE ENGAGEMENT PROCESS

New frontier settings, with some notable exceptions, are not typically drop-in places for youths in search of a safe environment or an activity to relieve their boredom. Many new frontier settings have the flavor of a job, and in some cases (e.g., paid internships) they are a source of employment and education. Participation—as volunteer, intern, employee, or part of some form of club—requires long-term commitments in order to enroll in a program. There is flexibility, however: each of these levels of participation requires a different degree of commitment. However, involvement provides the sponsoring setting an opportunity to establish and implement elaborate goals for change.

Participation predicated on consistent attendance is a tremendous benefit in programming; however, some youths cannot or will not be able to make and keep the commitment. This raises the question of who is to benefit from new frontier settings. A flexible level of commitment opens up possibilities for engaging youths who may be afraid of a long-term relationship or who, in the face of the vicissitudes in their lives, cannot attend on a consistent basis. Important decisions need to be made up-front concerning who is expected to benefit the most from participation. Programs cannot be all things to everyone. A clear and specific focus is imperative in order to maximize any intervention effort.

There are usually similarities between new frontier settings and educational programs. In both there is a curriculum, which sometimes is well established and predicated on achievement of certain competencies before movement is made to another task or activity. Such a program does not lend itself to participants dropping in and dropping out. Such programs are also based on requirement of a level of cognitive competence before youths can enroll. Completion of a certain grade level of education may satisfy this requirement.

The approaches outlined in this chapter present a series of challenges to the organizations sponsoring them. They are labor-intensive and require deliberate thought about the "target" population. A successful volunteer program, for example, necessitates having a staff member responsible for all aspects of the program. Recruitment, screening, orientation, training, supervision of progress, the writing of reports, validation, and the writing of letters of recommendation are tasks for a director or coordinator of volunteers. All this is labor intensive, an aspect that is often not fully appreciated. A volunteer or internship program has all of the elements and challenges associated with any initiative.

⤳

This chapter has touched on the most significant approaches new frontier settings use to reach out to and engage youth. The nation's shortage of skilled workers will only intensify efforts on the part of new frontier settings to develop new and improved ways of identifying and engaging youth. I would not be surprised to see information-technology businesses, in search of a viable workforce, soon entering the field of youth development in unprecedented numbers. If they do, it will raise countless issues for the field.

New frontier settings have an advantage over conventional youth-development programs in reaching out to prospective participants. They offer possibilities of engaging in activities that for most people are out of their reach. But they also have disadvantages. They may not be within easy geographical reach and they may have to convince youths that they are welcome. The approaches identified in this chapter can be implemented in countless combinations and with varying degrees of intensity. A multifaceted approach seems to offer the greatest potential for reaching out to and keeping potential participants.

PART 3

WHERE DO WE GO FROM HERE?

Part 3 consists solely of an epilogue. It provides this book with a final opportunity to help shape future directions and debates about youth development and new frontier settings. The evolution of youth development will no doubt continue, with the next two decades witnessing dramatically new opportunities and interpretations of the field. Youth development will no doubt face incredible challenges, not all of which will have been foreseen or mentioned in this book. The paradigm will be judged by how well it has changed the lives of youth, and this will require of programs an ability to prove that beneficial changes have resulted from participation. The epilogue delineates a series of tensions in the field that must be successfully addressed if the potential of youth development is to be fully realized.

EPILOGUE

THE TWENTY-FIRST century requires bold initiatives on how best to reach and engage youths in the coming generations' transitions to adulthood. Particularly we need to reach youths who are undervalued. The transition to adulthood can either be facilitated or thwarted by society. A smooth transition will result in citizens who are capable and willing to make contributions to the general welfare; it will serve as a foundation for social, economic, political, and technological advance. An unsuccessful transition will create a group of marginalized citizens unable and unwilling to be productive. It will no doubt cause a great deal of anxiety in society and increase the economic costs associated with "failures" such as incarceration, substance abuse, and so on. The costs, by today's standards, will appear to be staggering.

It would be easy to end this book with a chapter devoted to recommendations for future research, but I cannot do that. I prefer to highlight the key issues and tensions inherent in the field. By getting them out in the open, I hope to facilitate the field's addressing them. It seems as though there is never a "right" time to tackle issues or problems. Sometimes even raising them causes trouble, some critics arguing that more damage than good is the result. But ignoring issues will never start us on the path to resolving them, and this epilogue addresses what I see to be the twelve key issues in the field. Some of them stress the need for a reconceptualization of how new frontier and community-based settings can best maximize their resources and be partners in programming. Others reflect a bias of mine: the need for the field to pause and examine what is meant by youth-development practice (the purest among us argue that it is everything and anything). Finally, this epilogue raises a number of ideas that are being talked about in the field. I hope by discussing them here to help readers not get lost in the vastness of youth development.

TWELVE KEY ISSUES AND TENSIONS

1. Can and should new frontier staff be considered youth-development staff? It is staff members who bring youth-development goals and activities to life. They do this day in and day out, and a program is only as good as its staff. In fact the best-laid plans for services will fail if the proper staff are not there to implement them. The staff not only implement the mission of an organization, they also embody it, and a good staff not only needs organizational support, it deserves it.

There is no disputing that new frontier settings have a role in the field of youth development, even if typically their staff profile is dissimilar to that of their community-based counterparts.

New frontier settings generally have unusual staffing patterns. They primarily employ individuals with specialties in particular disciplines. The staff may first be, for example, scientists, librarians, journalists, or curators. With some exceptions. such staff do not have backgrounds in youth development. They arrived in their roles by accident, and perhaps the opportunity awakened a dormant interest in working with youth. They were in the right place at the right time. This staffing pattern, unlike that found in conventional youth-development programs, where staff have experiential or educational credentials, can prove challenging. The nature of their work can result in their isolation from the rest of the organization. These staff members, set aside to work with young people, have to relate to their youth clientele and to parents and community-based organizations; their colleagues in the organization, not having youth initiatives to run, can concentrate on their chosen field. Thus youth-development staff in new frontier settings must have both excellent communication skills and brokering skills. They must also of course be adept at engaging youth. In fact their adult interactions tend to be secondary to youth engagement.

At the same time, new frontier staff have different needs from those of their community-based colleagues. They not only have those common to all youth-development staff, they have needs special to their disciplines. Keeping abreast of developments in their discipline is crucial to their being able to transmit their knowledge to youths, as well as to interact with colleagues in their own discipline.

Nevertheless, all that said, a coming together of new frontier settings and community-based settings is essential.

2. To encourage collaboration, how much flexibility in programming is essential in youth-development programs? Are new frontier settings an alternative or a supplement to community youth-development programs? Those in new frontier settings may well answer that their settings are youth-development settings. Those in more conventional youth-development programs may answer that although similarities are evident, new frontier settings may appeal to some youth, but not all youth. A strict approach to programming—one that for example demands commitment from participants—is not for every youth; nor should it be.

Flexibility about drop-in attendance should be a cornerstone of any youth-development program. We must hope eventually to engage such participants in a more lasting commitment. Youths who are marginalized or live in chaotic circumstances rarely possess the ability to make informed judgments about what is best for them; they may not have long-term views of their future, and such youths, although possessing the cognitive capacities to engage in new frontier settings, cannot do so. So what happens to them? Community youth development has always and will continue to be there for them. It maintains an open door. It does not screening them out. New frontier settings would do well to provide youths with a similar opportunity, allowing them to participate during an early exploration period (several days or weeks) before asking for a long-term commitment. In addition to the opportunity this offers participants—to make an informed judgment—these settings will develop a reputation for being flexible and nonthreatening. Another route into new frontier settings can be via referral from community youth-development programs. In this way, participants may be in a better position to make a commitment. The resources available in new frontier settings can be quite extensive—if compared with community youth-development programs—and a partnership arrangement can expand the list of activities that community youth-development programs can offer, and after completion of an internship, volunteer assignment, or special program participants can return to their original youth-development program.

3. Is there a need for cross-fertilization of youth-development staff, or separation of them? Many new frontier settings have been successful in actively attracting staff for their special initiatives involving youth. Some of these settings have been able to use internships as a vehicle for bringing new staff into programs. Others have been fortunate in hiring personnel with sufficient flexibility, talent, and interests to move them over into positions stressing

youth-development activities. These individuals come with technical expertise in their chosen area and have the right attitude and personality to make them effective in working with youth.

Murphy (1995: 5) notes that the importance of staff development and training is multifaceted and far-reaching:

> Youth workers have a variety of professional development needs. Although their needs are not mutually exclusive, they do raise a question as to whether a single approach to training can meet so many different needs. Certainly, training must be offered through a variety of styles and forms to suit the particular goals. Although training should always equip participants with skills for more effective practice, it is much more than telling people what to do and how to do it. Training is an ongoing process of growth, one that meets the needs of the worker's own development in addition to imparting knowledge and practical skill.

It is important to conceptualize staff development in as broad and flexible manner possible. Staff development can involve formal education (university-sponsored courses), visiting other settings, consultation, workshops, supervision, internships, networking, and self-styled and self-initiated learning (Murphy 1995b). This flexibility allows each organizations to create staff development based on their own priorities, resources, and circumstances.

New frontier settings sometimes have to make difficult decisions about how best to support their youth-development staff. Since funding for attendance at conferences is always in limited supply, where do new frontier settings send their people when considering staff-enrichment conferences? Do they send them to conferences targeting their particular setting (museums, zoos, libraries, etc.)? Do they send them, in the case of scientists, to conferences focused on specialties? Or do they send them to conferences focused on youth development? Similar decisions sometimes have to be made about in-service (at-home) training.

Related questions are to what extent are youth-development staff to be encouraged to venture out of their setting to interact with community-based staff? To what extent is this type of relationship considered optimal for programming and to what extent is it valued? These questions are but the tip of the iceberg.

4. Terms mean different things to different people. It would be irresponsible to end this book without another comment on a need for a consensus definition of youth development. The reader is no doubt ready to put this book

down and run out to do some youth development. But wait one more minute, please. At risk of belaboring the point, I have to say that such a definition would be very beneficial to the field. It will not only benefit conventional youth-development programs but new frontier settings as well. Of course, we cannot force a definition onto the field: the dynamic nature of youth development inveighs against a consensus definition, and it is appropriate that the paradigm be full of energy and paradoxes—and even, since we work in the area of youth, have an identity crisis.

However, the practical side of me says that as long as we allow this paradigm to free-float, the greater the chance we put the field at-risk for criticism, or worse, extinction. This statement may seem harsh, but after more than fifteen years in this field I cannot help but think and feel this way. The battle essentially is between those who want the field to coalesce into a profession and those who would leave it vague. Maybe the best we can hope for is that some form of truce will allow the field to move forward. Not having a clearly defined discipline is making it difficult for some organizations to work in the field, and it is only a matter of time before we have to pay the piper. Bringing new frontier settings into a field of practice that does not have a clear definition of itself raises the eyebrows of practitioners who also happen to be, say, scientists. Precision of terms, concepts, and constructs is well understood in scientific circles.

Once a definition of youth development is embraced, we can try to better understand the dynamics that make this practice work. This would no doubt have greater meaning and value for some youths than others. This, too, is an important question. Which youths are to benefit the most? If we believe that youth development is a universal concept and that services must be made available to all youths—the argument being that all youths are essentially vulnerable because of their power differentiation with adults—that will dictate one course of action. If we believe that services should be only for the most needy youths, it dictates a different course of action. Is there a middle course? This issue of universal versus targeted initiatives is a subject of debate in England (Bradford 1997). A consensus definition of youth development, however, cannot but help bring new frontier settings and other youth-development settings closer together and make the field more receptive to different approaches.

5. What limits, if any, should be placed on the empowerment of youth? It seems like the concept of empowerment has been around for a long time. Its appearance in the professional literature can be traced back to the 1970s. Empowerment as a concept can easily be embraced by the political Left and

the Right. The Rev. Jesse Jackson praises its potential and Jack Kemp praises its potential. Are both talking about the same empowerment? They are not, and youth development offers youths themselves a tremendous opportunity to meaningfully participate in the debate.

The politicization of the youth-development field raises important practice and ethical issues. The evolution of youth development from a focus on individuals to a broader context involving families and communities has challenged the field in more than one way. The way the concept of empowerment has evolved within the field, too, has gone from individual, to family, to community. This evolutionary process has resulted in the acknowledgement of youth having the rights associated with decision making and the need to address social and economic justice in this society. In some circles, *empowerment* is a term with little meaning other than being "politically correct."

To what extent should the field of youth development embrace a concept of empowerment that actively seeks to identify social- and economic-justice issues and tries to bring about social change? Are marginalized youth (youth of color, low-income, gay, lesbian, challenged youth, etc.) to have true power of decision making, with appropriate responsibilities, or are they to play a secondary role in determining how youth-development programs are conceptualized and implemented? These questions are—as well being central—very touchy, particularly for adults who run these organizations, who staff and fund them. Adultism is alive and well. However, this *ism* is one among other *isms*—those of race, class, gender, abilities, sexual orientation, and so forth.

Empowerment cannot be practiced in one setting without there being a spill-over effect on other settings and domains. In the employment domain, there are three key requirements: right attitude, knowledge, and skills. The latter two cannot be effective unless youth have the attitude that they have rights that must be exercised in the course of their lives. Participation in youth-development programs does not mean that they waive this right.

Empowerment is well-established in the field of youth development. New frontier settings, however, have significant strides to make before this perspective takes hold. This is to be expected since new frontier settings have only recently started to embrace greater participatory practices. Only recently have they sought to broaden their audiences through community studies and outreach. But it is be unfair to single out new frontier settings: there are those who argue that youth-development programs within adult-centered organizations, too, have a long way to go before fully embracing empowerment.

6. To what extent do youth programs have to specialize in youth? Can they reach out to include families and other groups? We live in a highly individualized society, and this plays an influential role in how programs are shaped. A focus on individual participants and their accomplishments often not only plays a critical role in evaluation of a program or service but it may also be the total focus of interventions. The more specialized a program, the easier it is to sell the program to the public.

The thrust toward contextualizing youth development has however resulted in broadening interventions to include families, peers, and communities. Families and communities have become a vehicle for change and a target for it as well. But this may lead to some confusion. A school-based program, for example, is well understood to mean that everything takes place within a school setting. A school-based program that reaches out to families and community, however, may confuse people as to its primary purpose, which in fact is still youth. Can youth-development practice continue to expand to encompass more than just youths and still be true to the concept? There are, after all, limits to this practice. This shift is not away from youth but toward encompassing a broader arena. It has, however, presented serious challenges to practitioners and funders alike. Evaluators, too, have been challenged to more fully document process and outcome results.

New frontier settings staff may experience particular challenges in venturing into the community. If an institution such as a museum, aquarium, or library does not have a history of involving peers, families, and communities, its conceptualization of youth development may not be as broad as that of a community-based counterpart. Does this make their version of youth development of less worth?

7. Can youth development lead to family and community development? Youths possess a tremendous amount of energy, imagination, and willingness to take on challenges. They have a joy for life that is often missing in adults. And they bring a lot to the table concerning positive change. Funding for youth development is therefore an excellent investment in society. The payoffs far outweigh the risks since everyone benefits from youth being healthy and able to make contributions to their community and society.

But although there is relatively little debate about the need for a youth-development paradigm and programs that stress development of youth, expanding a paradigm to include families and communities raises numerous issues. There are issues about feasibility—social, economical, and political. There are questions about staff capacity to engage in all four systems—individual, family, peer, and community. Often, the moment a program reaches out beyond what is considered to be its turf, there is a backlash, questioning its purpose. In addition, venturing out into new areas can bring new perspectives, negative as well as positive. The former may result in significant setbacks and open the institution to criticism.

Is it wise to expand the paradigm of youth development beyond youth? Part 1 of this book advocates a youth-development perspective that encompasses all of the key social domains youth come into contact with. But the question must be asked: Is it, given the uphill climb that youth-development programs face in reaching youth who are marginal, and their limited budgets, wise—or even fair—to also expect them to change families, peers, communities? There is no shame in trying; it is a noble goal, and anything short of trying is to sell the mission short. But a warning is in order. Trying to be all things to all people when change is at the center of a mission is bound to seriously limit what can be accomplished without undue political consequence. Any institution that wishes fully to explore the potential of youth as agents of change must be prepared for adverse reactions from many major stakeholders. Failure to be so prepared will be to do a disservice to the field.

8. How important is it to involve schools in carrying out youth-development principles? The role of schools in youth development needs to be raised and discussed. Part 1 (particularly chapter 5) addressed the importance of schools in the development of youth. Schools are mandated to meet critical goals in this society, among them moral and civic goals as well as cognitive ones, and schools have been widely discussed in this country, particularly following tragedies such as the one at Columbine High School. Few people—parents, youth, politician, or academics—would say schools are doing an excellent job with youth. The extent of education reform attests to the worries we have.

However, most of the criticism is focused on a narrow area of development—cognition. It is almost as if we believe that a well-educated person is someone with competencies in writing, reading, math, and science—someone who can successfully pass a standardized test. Our concept of education must be broadened. Education must include the other core elements identified throughout this book.

Although many in the field argue that youth development is alive and well in after-school programs, schools as a distinct entity are generally not part of the discussion of where youth development is being practiced and thriving. But schools represent a tremendous potential for using youth-development principles, strategies, and activities. They represent a formidable challenge to the field of youth development. Youths spend most of their daytime hours in schools. Consequently, schools are probably the "last frontier" in the expansion of youth development.

As we have seen, it is not unusual for new frontier settings to establish partnerships with schools. However, these efforts generally have been conceptualized to address a cognitive core element. Invariably, new frontier settings send in an instructor to teach on a particular subject matter, or classes visit the settings to learn about the subject. These efforts rarely, if ever, involve families. Collaboration between new frontier settings, schools, and communities are very much needed.

9. Who should call themselves youth-development specialists? Programs that capture the essence of youth development may be developed by the best theoreticians and planners in the world, but it falls to staff to carry the planned programs out. Sometimes we tend to forget this point. Organizations, funders, and policymakers cannot ignore the importance of hiring and retaining staff with the competencies to carry out the youth-development mission. Staff are the energy of an organization. They bring to life its mission, goals, objectives, strategies, and activities.

The lack of properly recognized professional identity makes it difficult to recruit staff with the requisite competencies and values that are often shaped through professional education. It is also much more difficult to plan, implement, and evaluate programs when there is no consistency in language across organizations (Murphy 1995b). The field of youth development will soon have to make a momentous decision about to what extent it should be a credentialed field of practice (see chapter 3). If there is a concerted shift toward controlling who qualifies as a youth-development specialist, it will come at a great price—a price that may be too great to pay in the long run. Do we wish to continue to open the field to include talented, committed, and capable staff who do not have initials after their names?

10. To what extent can new frontier settings that are adult-centered successfully address youth? The subject of undue adult influence on youth development is one that typically is overlooked in staff youth-development workshops. This may well be because adults, not youths, invariably plan and attend these workshops. Although the literature on youth participation is clear that youth decision-making powers must be fostered or enhanced

whenever possible, the subject does not get the attention it deserves. The subject is not questioned in youth-focused settings (e.g., children's museums and children's libraries); however, the question needs to be posed in settings such as art museums, zoos, and newspapers and settings that can serve youth but do not have a specific mandate to do so in their mission statement. These settings might modify their mission or mode of operation to highlight youth-development activity.

This applies not only to new frontier settings. Conventional youth-serving organizations, including those that embrace youth development, need to address the role of adults and their sharing of power with youth (some of the implications of youth empowerment have already been addressed above). The sharing and eventual transfer of power does not mean that adults say yes to whatever youth propose; adults still have an important role to play in helping youths understand the meaning of decision making and the responsibilities that go with it. This responsibility goes beyond the individual and may involve the organization and the community they serve.

11. Can and should new frontier settings and conventional youth-development settings work together? Any effort at bringing these two worlds together must be encouraged. Youth, particularly those that are marginalized, need an immense amount of attention and resources. Organizations working by themselves or at cross-purposes are not the answer. If we are accept that new frontier settings are a form of youth development (there is still debate over this) or a subgroup of youth development, can these two worlds come together as partners? Opportunities for the two arenas to interact and dialogue are rare. There has to be an acknowledgement that these two arenas are fulfilling important functions within the youth-development field. One is not better than the other. They are different yet complementary, and there should not be competition for funding between the two.

Private-sector funding generally plays a more influential role in new frontier settings than it does with community-based organizations. If funding opportunities bring the two to compete, collaboration will be difficult, and perhaps impossible. The ultimate losers will be youth, their families, and communities. Joint proposals that stress the strengths of each setting are a good way to go, for obvious reasons. Collaborative partnerships serve to minimize competition and maximize available resources: no one setting can possibly address all of the needs of youth, and a collaborative partnership between two or more settings increases the options.

12. How political do we make youth development? The term *political* is highly

charged; it can mean many different things to different people. I have little doubt that this paradigm is highly politicized now, but unfortunately, few are willing to acknowledge this and to be open to talk about its implications for the field. When youth development is contextualized, youth must be prepared to discuss topics such as ablism, classism, racism, sexism, homophobia, and so forth. These subjects, deeply grounded as they are in the fabric of society and in the lives of many youths (particularly those who fit a designated profile), are highly sensitive. They are usually avoided as topics for discussion at any cost. Few adults want to talk about them.

When youth development systematically and deliberately addresses these topics (as it sometimes does), it brings forth a reaction from family and other authorities. Reactions range from displeasure to outright anger. The former can result in youth not being allowed to attend programs because of parental fears that they are being "radicalized." The latter can have dramatic political repercussions.

One dimension of politicization is getting youth to play an active role in voter registration and get out the vote campaigns (Storrie 1997). This type of activity is probably more frightening to adults than any other. The prospect of youth getting family and neighbors to register to vote and getting them actually to vote has tremendous implications for communities with many marginalized adults. Further, it has tremendous potential for youth to be socialized into voting as they enter adulthood. Politicians who do not share an empowerment agenda, one devoted to social and economic justice, will no doubt actively work against programs stressing this approach.

The above issues and tensions need our attention. They have not been selected because they are either those the easiest or the most difficult to do something about but as the ones that, if carried out successfully, would have the most positive and profound impact on the field of youth development. It may not be possible to carry out all of them, but totally to ignore them because they are not "politically feasible" would be a big mistake. The lives of youth are involved, and so is the future of the nation.

I sincerely hope that this epilogue does not discourage anyone from youth-development practice. No field of practice is without tensions, and this chapter has attempted to be straightforward about those in youth development. To ignore them would be irresponsible. The tensions are what makes practice so difficult, challenging, and rewarding when successfully dealt with. Youth participants are often keenly aware of tensions within a program, or between staff, community, families, and school. We must not to sweep them under the rug. The role modeling alone can have immediate and long-lasting affects on young people: all too rarely are they "brought into the secrets."

The reader will no doubt think of countless other tensions that should have been listed in this epilogue. The tensions I selected are here because they are the ones I believe have the greatest potential to set the field back from achieving its noble goals of achieving equality, social and economic justice, and partnerships between adults and youth and programs and community.

The writing of this book was relatively easy. The writing of books on criminal justice and memorial murals (Delgado in press a,b), which signify the consequences to youth when society turns its back on them, were much more difficult to write. My subject matter here stresses the positive side of youth development. I wish to convey that the role of taking a positive perspective not only facilitates practice but also scholarship. The field of youth development has the potential to bring together practitioners from various disciplines, as well as youth and adults.

This possibility is increased when examining new frontier settings. These places employ scientists, journalists, zoologists, librarians . . . professions that do not jump out at us as possible colleagues and collaborators. But the expansion of this field to include these and others cannot but help youth development increase its influence. It will, however, force us to look at the language that we use to discuss youth development, and force us to expand our vocabulary. Vocabulary, in this instance, refers to new concepts that bridge the divide between the worlds of new frontier settings and community youth-development settings. It necessitates that we again take a new look at the youth-development paradigm. This paradigm has shifted over the past decade or so and may continue to do so into the next decade. We should welcome this change. Youths and their families and communities cannot help but benefit from this development. A paradigm that is dynamic is less likely to become obsolete. And a dynamic paradigm requires that we consistently discuss, debate, and innovate in order that we properly contextualize our work.

REFERENCES

Academy for Educational Development (AED). 1997. *Girls Programing in New York City: A Summary Report.* AED.

Acuff, D. S., and R. H. Reiher. 1997. *What Kids Buy and Why: The Psychology of Marketing to Kids.* New York: Free Press.

Adams, A. C. 2000. Outrageous leadership: The work is the circus and you are the ringmasters. *CYD Journal: Community Youth Development* 1:42–43.

Administration on Children, Youth, and Families. 1997. *Understanding Youth Development: Promoting Positive Pathways for Growth.* Washington, D.C.: U.S. Department of Health and Human Services.

Almen, R. 2000. What one "Yooper" has learned about youth involvement. *Focal Point* 14:14–15.

American Library Association. 2000. *Library Services for the Poor.* Washington, D.C.: ALA.

——. 2000a. *Connect for Kids @ the Library.* Washington, D.C.: ALA.

——. 1999a. *Public Libraries as Partners in Youth Development.* Washingtion, D.C.: ALA.

——. 1999b. *Programs for School-age Youth in Public Libraries.* Washington, D.C.: ALA.

American Youth Policy Forum (AYPF). 1995. *Contract with America's Youth: Toward a National Youth Development Agenda.* Washington, D.C.: AYPF.

Amsden, A. H., and J. C. Clark. 1999. Software entrepreneurship among the urban poor: Could Bill Gates have succeeded if he were Black? . . . Or impoverished? In Schon, Sanyal, and Mitchell, *High Technology and Low-income Communities,* 213–229.

Ander, C. 1996. The sociomoral development of young children at the East End Children's workshop: A Phoenix Foundation pilot project. Paper presented at the Save the Children Child Care Technical Assistance Conference, Atlanta, Georgia, March 28–31.

Anderson, E. 1999. *Code of the Street.* New York: Norton.

Arnstein, S. R. 1969. A ladder of citizen participation. *Journal of the American Institute of Planners* 35:216–224.

Armistead, P. J., and M. B. Wexler. 1998. Community development and youth development: The potential of convergence. *New Designs for Youth Development* 14:27–33.

Astroth, K. 2000. Measuring your vibrancy index: A simple self-assessment tool. CYD *Journal: Community Youth Development* 1:30–35.

Atkinson, H. 1997. *Ministry with Youth in Crisis.* Birmingham, Ala.: Religious Education Press.

Austin, J., and M. N. Willard. 1989. Angels of history, demons of culture. Introduction to *Generations of Youth: Youth Cultures and History in Twentieth-century America,* ed. J. Austin and M. N. Willard, 1–20. New York: New York University Press.

Avenilla, F., and S. Singley. 2001. Neighborhood effects on child and adolescent development: Assessing today's knowledge for tomorrow's villages. In Booth and Crouter, *Does It Take a Village?* 229–243.

Ayers, E. L. 2000. A historian in cyber space: A place, it turns out, best understood by Alexis de Tocqueville. *American Heritage* 51:68–74.

Baines, T. R., and J. R. Selta. 1999. *Raising the Rest of the Neighborhood: Reclaiming Children and Youth* 8:25–30.

Bamberger, J. 1999. Action knowledge and symbolic knowledge: The computer as mediator. In Schon, Sanyal, and Mitchell, *High Technology and Low-income Communities,* 235–261.

Ban, T., et al. 1999. ROCA: A multicultural way of life. *New Designs for Youth Development.* 19:13–18.

Bandura, A. 1979. Self-efficacy: Toward a unifying theory of behavioral change. *Psychological Review* 84:191–215.

Banks, S. 1997. The dilemmas of intervention. In J. Roche and S. Tucker, *Youth in Society,* 218–226.

Barboza, D. 2000. Rampant obesity, a deblitating reality for the urban poor. *New York Times,* December 26, D5.

———. 1997. Beverage makers pursue teen market to extremes. *Journal Record,* August 26, 2.

Barker, C. 1996. *YaYa: Young New Orleans Artists and Their Storytelling Chairs.* Baton Rouge: Louisiana State University Press.

Barker, G., F. Knaul, N. Cassaniga, and A. Schrader, eds. 2000. *Empowerment in Especially Difficult Circumstances.* New York: Intermediate Technology Publications.

Barkman, S. J., and K. L. Machtmes. 2000. Measuring the impact of youth development programs: The four-fold youth development model. *CYD Journal: Community Youth Development* 1:40–47.

Barrett, J., and R. Greenaway. 1995. *Why Adventure? The Role and Value of Outdoor Adventure in Young People's Personal and Social Development.* Scotland: Foundation for Outdoor Adventure.

Barron-McKeagney, T., J. D. Woody, and H. J. D'Souza. 2000. Mentoring at-risk Chicano children and their parents: The role of community: Theory and practice. *Journal of Community Practice* 8:3756.

Bartholow, C. 1999. The Brooklyn expedition: A case study in collaboration. *Museum News* 78:36–41.

Barton, W. H., M. Watkins, and R. Jarjoura. 1997. Youths and communities: Toward comprehensive strategies for youth development. *Social Work* 42:483–493.

Batavick, L. 1997. Community-based family support and youth development: two movements, one philosophy. *Child Welfare* 76:639–664.

Battistich, V., E. Schaps, M. Watson, D. Solomon, and C. Lewis. 2000. Effects of the Child Development Project on students' drug use and other problem behaviors. *Journal of Primary Prevention* 21:75–79.

Barwell, G., and K. Bowles. 2000. Border crossings: The Internet and the dislocation of citizenship. In Bell and Kennedy, *The Cybercultures Reader* 702–711.

Baxandall, M. 1991. Exhibiting intension: Some preconditions of the visual display of culturally purposeful objects. In Karp and Lavine, *Exhibiting Cultures,* 33–41.

Bazemore, G., and T. W. Clinton. 1997. Developing delinquent youths: A reintegrative model for rehabilitation and a new role of the juvenile justice system. *Child Welfare* 76:665–716.

Beamish, A. 1999. Approaches to community computing: Bringing technology to low-income groups. In Schon, Sanyal, and Mitchell, *High Technology and Low-income Communities,* 349–368.

Beck, E. L. 1999. Prevention and intervention programming: Lessons from an after-school program. *Urban Review* 31:107–124.

Beedy, J. P., and T. Zierk. 2000. Lessons from the field: Taking a proactive approach to developing character through sports. *CYD Journal: Community Youth Development* 1:6–13.

Belkin, L. 2000. The making of an 8-year-old woman: How do we understand early puberty? Through the prisim of our times. *New York Times,* December 24, magazine: 38–43.

Bell, D. 2000. Cybercultures reader: A user's guide. In Bell and Kennedy, *Cybercultures Reader*, 1–12.

Bell, D., and B. M. Kennedy, eds. 2000. *The Cybercultures Reader*. London: Routledge.

Bell, J. 1996. A key to developing positive youth-adult relationships. *Humanics*.

Belle, D. 1999. *The After-school Lives of Children: Alone and with Others While Parent's Work*. Mahwah, N.J.: Erlbaum.

Bembry, R. 1998. A youth development strategy: Principles to practice in re-creation for the 21st century. *Journal of Park and Recreation Administration* 17:15–34.

Benard, B. 1997a. Fostering resiliency in urban schools. In B. Williams, ed. *Closing the Achievement Gap*. Alexandria, Virg.: ASCD.

——. 1997b. Resiliency research: A foundation for youth development. *Resiliency in Action* (winter):13–18.

——. 1993a. Fostering resiliency in kids. *Educational Leadership* 51:44–48.

——. 1993b. Resiliency paradigm validates craft knowledge, *Western Center News* 6:6–7.

——. 1993c. Resiliency requires changing hearts and minds. *Western Center News* 6:4–5.

——. 1987. Protective factors research: What we can learn from resilient children. *Practice Forum* 7:3–10.

Benson, P. L. 1999. *Beyond the "Village" Rhetoric*. Minneapolis, Minn.: Search Institute.

Benson, P. L., M. J. Donahue, and A. Erickson. 1990. Adolescence and religion: A review of the literature for 1970 to 1986. In L. L. Monty and D. O. Moberg, eds., *Research in the Social Scientific Study of Religion: A Research Annual* 1:153–181. Greenwich, Conn.: Jai Press.

Benson, P. L., P. C. Scales, N. Leffert, and E. C. Roehlkepartain. 1999. *A fragile foundation: The State of Developmental Assets among American Youth*. Minneapolis, Minn.: Search Institute.

Berg, R. J. 1999. Demographic trends and the issues they raise. *Global Meeting of Generations* [newsletter], 1–15.

Berman, S. 1998. Foreword to Venturella, *Poor People and Library Services*, 1–14.

Besharov, D. J., ed. 1999. *America's Disconnected Youth: Toward a Preventive Strategy*. Washington, D.C. : Child Welfare League of America.

Besharov, D. J., and K. N. Gardiner. 1999. Preventing youthful disconnectedness. Introduction to *America's Disconnected Youth*, ed. Besharov.

Betley, M. 1995. Multiple choices: Reaching out to youth. *American Theatre* 12:64–66.

Beyth-Marom, R., and Fischoff, B. 1993. Adolescents' decisions about risks: A cognitive perspective. In Schulenberg, Maggs, and Hurrelmann, *Health Risks and Developmental Transitions*, 110–135.

Billy, J. O. G. 2001. Better ways to do contextual analysis: Lessons from Duncan and Raudenbush. In Booth and Crouter, *Does It Take a Village?* 137–147.

Blum, R. W. 1998. Healthy youth development as a model for youth health promotion. *Journal of Adolescent Health* 22:368–375.

———. 1995. Enhancing resilience: Toward a new model of adolescent health. In AYPF, *Contract with America's Youth*, 10–11.

Blum, R. W., et al. 2000. The effects of race/ethnicity, income, and family structure on adolescent risk behaviors. *American Journal of Public Health* 90:1879–1884.

Blyth, D. A. 2001. Community approaches to improving outcomes for urban children, youth, and families. In Booth and Crouter, *Does It Take a Village?* 223–227.

BMRB International. 1996. *Cultural Diversity: Attitudes of Ethnic Minority Populations Towards Museums and Galleries*. London: Museums and Galleries Commission.

Bocarro, J., and A. Richards. 1998. Experiential research at-risk: The challenge of shifting traditional research. *Journal of Experiential Education* 21:102–122.

Bogenschneider, K. 1996. An ecological risk/protective theory for building prevention programs, policies, and community capacity to support youth. *Family Relations Journal of Applied Family and Child Studies* 45:127–138.

Bond, L. A. 2000. Prevention's adolescent identity struggle. *Journal of Primary Prevention* 21:11–14.

Booth, A., and A. C. Crouter, eds. 2001. *Does It Take a Village? Community Effects on Children, Adolescents, and Families*. Mahwah, N.J.: Erlbaum.

Bourdieu, P. 1986. The forms of capital. In J. Richarson, ed. *Handbook of Theory and Research for the Sociology of Education*, 241–258. New York: Greenwood Press.

Bouvier, L. F., and L. Grant. 1994. *How Many Americans? Population, Immigration, and the Environment*. San Francisco: Sierra Club Books.

Boyd, W. L., and R. C. Schouse. 1997. The problems and promise of urban schools. In Walberg, Reyes, and Weissberg, *Children and Youth*, 141–165.

Boyle, P. 2000a. Boy Scouts' holy war over homosexuals. *Youth Today* 9, no. 1: 16–18.

———. 2000b. How other agencies avoid gay flaps. *Youth Today* 9, no. 3: 17.

———. 2000c. Gay youth find a crusader. *Youth Today* 9, no. 2: 50–51.

——. 2000d. Can young voters be stirred from slumber? *Youth Today* 9, no. 4: 56, 40–43.

Boyle, P., and I. De Pommereau. 1999. An arranged marriage shows promise: Community schools grow as youth workers, educators learn to get along. A key: Happy principals. *Youth Today* 8, no. 1: 42–44.

Bracken, A. 2000. Youth work snapshots: Topsail youth program. *Youth Today* 9:12.

Bradford, S. 1997. The management of "growing up" Youth work in community settings. In Roche and Tucker, *Youth in Society,* 245–254.

Braverman, M. T., et al. 1994. For children facing adversity: How youth programs can promote resilience. *California Agriculture* 48:30–35.

Breitbart, M. M. 1998. Dana's mystical tunnel: Young people's designs for survival and change in the city. In Skelton and Valentine, *Cool Places,* 305–327.

Brettschneider, W. D., and R. Helm. 1997. The physical self: From motivation to well-being. In K. R. Fox, ed., *Identity, Sport, and Youth Development.* Champaign, Ill.: Human Kinetics.

Bronfenbrenner, U. 1986. Ecology of the family is a context for human development research perspectives. *Developmental Psychology* 22:723–742.

Brofenbrenner, U., and T. A. White. 1993. *What Is Youth Development? Youth and Nationhood: An International Challenge.* San Francisco: International Foundations.

Brookins, G. K., A. C. Petersen, and L. M. Brooks. 1997. Youth and families in the inner-city: Influencing positive outcomes. In Walberg, Reyes, and Weissberg, *Children and Youth,* 45–66.

Brown, B. B., M. M. Dolcini, and A. Leventhal. 1997. Transformations in peer-relationships at adolescence: Implications for health-related behavior. In Schulenberg, Maggs, and Hurrelmann, *Health Risks and Developmental Transitions,* 161–189.

Brown, B. V., and C. Emig. 1999. Prevalence, patterns, and outcomes. In Besharov, *America's Disconnected Youth,* 101–115.

Brown, C. G. 1995. Devising a national youth development strategy. In AYPF, *Contract with America's Youth,* 14–15.

Brown, D. W. 1995. *When Strangers Cooperate: Using Social Conventions to Govern Ourselves.* New York: Free Press.

Brown, P. L. 1999. A park offers nature, not just hopes. *New York Times,* December 28, D1, D5.

Brown, M., L. Camino, H. Hobson, and C. Knox. 2000. Community youth development: A challenge to social injustice. *CYD Journal: Community Youth Development* 1:32–39.

Burawoy, M. 1991a. Reconstructing social theories. In Burawoy et al., *Ethnography Unbound*, 1–8.

———. 1991b. The extended case method. In Burawoy et al., *Ethnography Unbound*, 291–300.

Burawoy, M., et al., eds. 1991. *Ethnography Unbound: Power and Resistance in the Modern Metropolis*. Berkeley: University of California Press.

Burgess, J. 2000. Youth involvement can be the key to community development. *CYD Journal: Community Youth Development* 1:38–41.

———. 1998. Spheres of community change: Youth as a bridge. *New Designs for Youth Development* 14:6–9.

Burke, E. 1979. *A Participatory Approach to Urban Planning*. New York: Human Sciences Press.

Burton, L. M. 2001. One step forward and two steps back: Neighborhoods, adolescent development, and unmeasured variables. In Booth and Crouter, *Does It Take a Village?* 149–159.

Buschman, J. 1998. History and theory of information poverty. In Venturella, *Poor People and Library Services*, 16–28.

Buuck, M. M. 1998. 4-H Club off new year. *Times-Picayune* (Louisiana), August 20, 1G.

Cable World. 1999. Marketing to today's kids. *Cable World* 11 (November 1): 2a.

Cairns, R. B., and B. D. Cairns. 1994. *Lifelines and Risks: Pathways of Youth in Our Time*. New York: Cambridge University Press.

Camino, L. 2000. Putting youth-adult partnerships to work for community change: Lessons from volunteers across the country. *CYD Journal: Community Youth Development* 1:27–31.

Canada, G. 1998. Raising boys in America. *New Designs for Youth Development* 14:18–21.

Capowich, G. E. 1995. Implementing positive youth development in juvenile justice. In AYPF, *Contract with America's Youth*, 54–55.

Cappell, M. L. 1995. Sista-2-sista: A self-empowerment program. *Journal of Physical Education, Recreation, and Dance* 66:43–45.

Carlson, P. 1998. "Reading can give you a dream." In Venturella, *Poor People and Library Services*, 36–43.

Carnegie Council on Adolescent Development. 1994. *Consultation on Afterschool Programs*. New York: Carnegie Corporation of New York.

———. 1992. *A Matter of Time: Risk and Opportunity*. New York: Carnegie Corporation of New York.

———. 1989. *Turning Points: Preparing American Youth for the 21st Century*. New York: Carnegie Corporation of New York.

Castells, M. 1999. The information city is a dual city: Can it be reversed? In Schon, Sanyal, and Mitchell, *High Technology and Low-income Communities,* 25–41.

Catalano, R. F., M. L. Berglund, J. A. M. Ryan, and J. D. Hawkins. 1998. *Positive Youth Development in the United States: Research Findings on Evaluations of Positive Youth Development Programs.* Seattle: Social Development Research Group, University of Washington, School of Social Work.

Center for Youth Development (CYD). 2000. *Calculating the Return on Investment: What Could Be.* Washington, D.C.: CYD.

Cervantes, J. M., and O. Ramirez. 1992. Spirituality and family dynamics in psychotherapy with Latino children. In Vargas and Koss-Chioino, *Working with Culture,* 103–128.

Chahin, J. 2000. The contrast between the pathological attributes and the status/aspirations of Mexican American youth. In Montero-Sieburth and Villarruel, *Making Invisible Latino Adolescents Visible,* 107–130.

Chaimers, M. 2000. Lessons in strengths-based youth involvement: Minding the mays, the dos and the possibilities. *Focal Point* 14:24–27.

Chalk, R., and D. A. Phillips. 1996. *Youth Development and Neighborhood Influences: Challenges and Opportunities.* Washington, D.C.: National Academy Press.

Chaplan, M. Z., R. P. Weissberg, J. S. Graber, P. J. Siva, K. Grady, and C. Jacoby. 1992. Social competence promotion with inner-city and suburban young adolescents: Effects on social adjustment and alcohol use. *Journal of Consulting and Clinical Psychology* 60:56–63.

Chappel, M. L. 1998. A generation at risk: A societal dilemma. *Journal of California Law Enforcement* 32:1–6.

Checkoway, B. 1998. Involving young people in neighborhood development. *Children and Youth Services Review* 20:765–795.

——. 1994. *Involving Young People in Neighborhood Development.* Washington, D.C.: Center for Youth Development and Policy Research, Academy for Educational Development.

Children's Partnership. 2000. *Online Content for Low-income and Underserved Americans: The Digital Divide's New Frontier.* Santa Monica, Calif.: Children's Partnership.

Choi, J. K. 2000. Valuing the voice of our young people. *Focal Point* 14:9–10.

Cline, R. 1998/99. Youth speak out. *Assets* (winter): 10.

Cohen, M., and M. H. Greenberg. 2000. *Tapping TANF for Youth: When and How Welfare Funds Can Support Youth Development, Education, and Employment Initiatives.* Washington, D.C.: Center for Law and Social Policy.

Coie, J. D., N. E. Watt, S. G. West, J. D. Hawkins, J. R. Asarnow, H. J. Markman, S. L. Ramey, M. B. Shure, and B. Long. 1993. The science of prevention: A conceptual framework and some directions for a national research program. *American Psychologist* 48:1013–1022.

Coleman, J., L. Catan, and C. Dennison. 1997. You're the last person I'd talk to. In Roche and Tucker, *Youth in Society*, 227–234.

Coleman, J. S. 1990. *Foundations of Social Theory.* Cambridge: Harvard University Press.

———. 1988. Social capital in the creation of human capital. *Journal of Sociology* 94:S95-S120.

Collins, M. E. In press. Transition to adulthood for vulnerable youth: A review of research and implications for Policy. *Social Service Review.*

Comer, J. R. 1988. Educating poor minority children. *Scientific American* 259:42–48.

Commerce Business Daily. 2000. Constructing communities to promote youth development. *Commerce Business Daily,* Feburary 3, PSA-2526.

Committee for Economic Development (CED). 1997. *Connecting Inner-city Youth to the World of Work.* New York: CED.

———. 1995. *Rebuilding Inner-city Communities: A New Approach to This Nation's Urban Crisis.* New York: CED.

Conhaim, W. W. 2000. The Digital divide. *Link-Up* 17:1–8.

Connell, J. P., J. L. Aber, and G. Walker. 1999. How do urban communities affect youth? Using social science research to inform the design and evaluation of comprehensive community initiatives. *New Approaches to Evaluating Community Initiatives* 1:1–21.

Connell, J. P., and A. C. Kubisch. 2001. Community approaches to improving outcomes for urban children, youth, and families: Current trends and future directions. In Booth and Crouter, *Does It Take a Village?* 177–201.

Cooper, M., and H. Chalfant. 1984. *Subway Art.* New York: Holt, Reinhart & Winston.

Corsaro, W., and D. Eder. 1990. Children peer cultures. *Annual Review of Sociology* 16:197–220.

Corwin, M. 2000. *And Still We Rise: The Trials and Triumphs of Twelve Gifted Inner-city High School Students.* New York: Morrow.

Council on Library Resources (CLR). 1996. *Public Libraries, Communities, and Technology: Twelve Case Studies.* Washington, D.C.: CLR.

Cowen, E. L., P. A. Wyman, W. C. Work, and M. R. Iker. 1995. A preventive intervention for enhancing resilience among highly stressed urban children. *Journal of Primary Prevention* 15:247–260.

Coyle, J. 2000. More wilderness for more children: Club program gives disadvantaged youth new chances to learn about nature. *Sierra Club* (July/August): 1–4.

Cretinon, D., and C. Egner. 1998. Libraries in the street. In Venturelle, *Poor People and Library Services*, 92–108.

Crockett, L. J. 1997. Cultural, historical, and subcultural contexts of adolescence: Implications for health and development. In Schulenberg, Maggs, and Hurrelmann, *Health Risks and Developmental Transitions*, 23–53.

Curnan, S. P. 2000a. Aligning strategies and outcomes to advance social change: What CYD innovators need to know and do. *CYD Journal: Community Youth Development* 1:42–43.

———. 2000b. Social justice and "The power of belief." *CYD Journal: Community Youth Development* 1:52.

Curnan, S. P., and L. A. LaCava. 2000. *CYD Management zone: Evaluation as a management and learning tool. CYD Journal: Community Youth Development* 1:48–50.

Currie, D. H. 1994. "Going green": Mythologies of consumption in adolescent magazines. *Youth and Society* 26:92–117.

Dahms-Stinson, N. 1998. Arts and humanities programs for children and youth at risk. *Missouri Library World* 3:21.

Davis, D., J. Ray, and C. Sayles. 1995. Ropes course training for youth in a rural setting: "At first I though it was going to be boring. . . . " *Child and Adolescent Social Work Journal* 12: 445–463.

Davis, M. 2000. *Magical Urbanism: Latinos Reinvent the US City*. New York: Verso.

Decker, J. L. 1994. The state of rap: Time and place in hip hop nationalism. In Ross and Rose, *Microphone Fiends,* 99–121.

Deitel, B. 1999. A base in cyberspace: Today's "military brats" still move around a lot, but with the "Net," they leave fewer friendships behind. *Courier-Journal* (Louisville, Ky.), July 25, 1h.

DeJesus, E. 2000. *Undervalued and Overlooked*. Gaithersburg, Md.: Youth Development and Research Fund.

Delgado, M. In press a. *Where Are All of the Young Men and Women of Color? Capacity Enhancement Practice in the Criminal Justice Arena*. New York: Columbia University Press.

———. In press b. *Death at an Early Age and the Urban Scene: The Case for Memorial Murals and Community Healing*. Westport, Conn.: Praeger.

———. 2000a. *New Arenas for Community Social Work Practice with Urban Youth: The Use of the Arts, Humanities, and Sports.* New York: Columbia University Press.

———. 2000b. *Community Social Work Practice Within an Urban Context: The Potential of a Capacity Enhancement Perspective.* New York: Oxford University Press.

———. 1999. *Social Work Practice in Nontraditional Urban Settings.* New York: Oxford University Press.

Delgado, M., and K. Barton. 1998. Murals in Latino communities: Social indicators of community strengths. *Social Work* 43:346–356.

Del Real, T. S. 2000. City farmers: 4-H kids may live in Denver, but their hearts are in the outdoors. *Rocky Mountain News*, January 27, 6D.

Denner, J., D. Kerby, and K. Coyle. 2000. How communities can promote positive youth development: Responses from 49 professionals. *CYD Journal: Community Youth Development* 1:31–35.

DeWitt Wallace–Reader's Digest Fund. 1999. *Public Libraries as Partners in Youth Development.* New York: DeWitt Wallace–Reader's Digest Fund.

Deyhle, D. 1998. From breakdancing to heavy metal: Navajo youth, resistance, and identity. *Youth and Society* 30:3–31.

Dimick, B. 1995. Marketing youth services. *Library Trends* 43:463–473.

Discount Store News. 1999. Cameras tap youth market. *Discount Store News*, November 11, 38, 43.

DNR. 1999. Target marketing to teens should increase in next decade. DNR (September 27): 29, 42.

Dominguez, S. 2000. Community youth development policy. Boston: Unpublished MS. 35 pages.

Donohue, B., J. Keith, and S. Kaagan. 1999. Community asset development for youth: A strength-based approach to preventing substance abuse and violence. *ICYF Annual Report, 1998–1999.* East Lansing: Institute for Children, Youth, and Families at Michigan State University.

Dosher, A. 1996. Community youth development practice fields. *New Designs for Youth Development* 12:11–13.

Dotson, M., and Y. Bonitch. 1998. Libraries and the poor: What's the connection? In Venturella, *Poor People and Library Services*, 126–135.

Drake, I. N., S. Ling, and D. M. Hughes. 2000. Youth are the future of America. *Focal Point* 14:32–34.

Dreyfus, E. A. 1972. *Youth: Search for Meaning.* Columbus, Ohio: Merrill.

Driscol, A. 1998. Group inventories Marblehead trees. *Boston Globe*, August 2, 2.

Dryfoos, J. 1991. Adolescents at risk: A summation of work in the field programs and policies. *Journal of Adolescent Health* 12:630–637.

Duncan, C. 1991. Art museums and the ritual of citizenship. In Karp and Lavine, *Exhibiting Cultures*, 88–103.

Duncan, G. J., and S. W. Raudenbush. 1999. *Neighborhood and Adolescent Development: How Can We Determine Links?* Ann Arbor: University of Michigan.

Dunitz, M. 1992. The soul of a museum: Commitment to community at the Brooklyn Children's Museum. In Karp, Kreamer, and Lavine, *Museums and Communities*, 242–261.

Earls, F. 1993. Health promotion for minority adolescents: Cultural considerations. In Millstein, Petersen, and Nightingale, *Promoting the Health of Adolescents*, 58–72.

Earls, F., R. B. Cairns, and J. A. Mercy. 1993. The control of violence and the promotion of nonviolence in adolescents. In Millstein, Petersen, and Nightingale, *Promoting the Health of Adolescents*, 285–304.

Eccles, J. S. 1991. Control vs. autonomy during early adolescence. *Journal of Social Issues* 47:53–68.

Edelman, M. W. 2000. Help from everyone. *HOPE* 24:34–37.

Edginton, C. R., and W. deOlivera. 1995. A model of youth work orientations. *Humanics* (spring): 3–7.

Einerson, M. J. 1998. Fame, fortune, and failure: Young girls' moral language surrounding popular culture. *Youth and Society* 30:241–257.

Elias, M. J., R. P. Weissberg, J. D. Hawkins, C. L. Perry, J. E. Zins, K. A. Dodge, P. C. Kendall, and D. C. Gottfredson. 1994. The school-based promotion of social competence: Theory, research, practice and policy. In R. J. Haggerty, N. Garmezy, M. Rutter, and L. Sherrod, eds., *Stress, Risk, and Resilience in Children and Adolescence: Processes, Mechanisms, and Interactions*, 269–315. New York: Cambridge University Press.

Erkut, S., L. A. Szalacha, C. C. Coll, and O. Alarcon. 2000. Puerto Rican early adolescents' self-esteem patterns. *Journal of Research on Adolescence* 10:339–364.

Escobar, D. A., and L. A. Escobar. 1996. Health education for youth of the 21st century. *Education* 116:495–502.

European Cosmetic Markets. 1994. Youth marketing: Focusing on a moving target. *European Cosmetic Markets* 11 (November): 443.

Evans, I. M., and K. T. Ave. 2000. Mentoring children and youth: Principles, issues, and policy implications for community programmes in New Zealand. *New Zealand Journal of Psychology* 29:41–56.

Everson, T. 1994. Resilience and skill building: A spiritual perspective. *Journal of Emotional and Behavior Problems* 3:25–29.

Exchange, The. 1998. Translating youth development into action. News from FYSB and the Youth Services Field, *The Exchange*, December, 1–12.

Family Youth Services Bureau. 1998. *Compendium of Critical Issues and Innovative Approaches in Youth Services*. Washington, D.C.: Administration on Children, Youth, and Families, U.S. Department of Health and Human Services.

Farmer, G. C., P. C. Krochalk, and M. Silverman. 1998. Selected factors associated with demonstrating success in health education programs. In Henderson, Champlin, and Evashwick, *Promoting Teen Health*, 199–209.

Fassler, I. 1998. The voices of children and youth in the democratic process. *New Designs for Youth Development* 14:36–40.

Fazari, L. 1996. It's camp confidence; Outward-Bound kids teaching kids. *Toronto Sun*, May 10, 92.

Feely, K. 1995. Thinking about youth in families and communities. In AYPF, *Contract with America's Youth*, 28–29.

Feetham, S. 1997. Families and health in the urban enviornment: Implications for programs, research and policy. In Walberg, Reyes, and Weissberg, *Children and Youth*, 321–359.

Feinberg, S., and C. Rogoff. 1998. Diversity takes children to a friendly family place. *American Libraries* 29:50–52.

Fellin, P. 2001. *The Community and the Social Worker*, 3rd ed. Ithasca, Ill.: Peacock.

Ferguson, G. 1999. *Shouting at the Sky: Troubled Teens and the Promise of the Wild*. New York: St. Martin's Press.

Ferreira, J., Jr. 1999. Information technology that chabge relationships between low-income communities and the public and nonprofit agencies to serve them. In Schon, Sanyal, and Mitchell, *High Technology and Low-income Communities*, 163–189.

Ferrell, J. 1997. Youth, crime, and cultural space: Losing a generation: Probing the myth and reality of youth and violence. *Social Justice* 24:21–39.

——. 1993. *Crimes of Style: Urban Graffiti and the Politics of Community*. Boston: Northeastern University Press.

Figueira-McDonough, J. 1998. Environment and interpretation: Voices of young people in poor inner-city neighborhoods. *Youth and Society* 30:123–162.

Find/SVP Market Research Reports. 1998. Teens market: Use of language when marketing to teens, *Find/SVP Market Research Reports*, November: 36.

Fine, G. A. 1989. Mobilizing fun: Provisioning resources in leisure worlds. *Sports Sociology Journal* 6:319–334.

Fine, G. A., and Mechling, J. 1993. Child saving and children's cultures at century's end. In Heath and Laughlin, *Identity and Inner-city Youth*, 120–146.

Fink, D. B. 2000. *Making a Place for Kids with Disabilities.* Westport, Conn.: Praeger.

Finn, J. L., and B. Checkoway. 1998. Young people as competent community builders: A challenge to social work. *Social Work* 43:335–345.

Fitzpatrick, K., and M. LaGory. 2000. *The Ecology of Risk in the Urban Landscape: Unhealthy Places.* New York: Routledge.

Florida Tobacco Control Clearinghouse (FTCC). 1999. *What Constitutes a Youth Development Program?* Tallahassee, Fla.: FTCC.

Foner, N. 1987a. New immigrants and changing patterns in New York City. Introduction to *New Immigrants in New York*, ed. Foner, 1–33.

––, ed. 1987b. *New Immigrants in New York.* New York: Columbia University Press.

Footwear News. 1999. Youth brigade. *Footwear News* 55: 16.

Frank, G. 1998. Nutrition for teens. In Henderson, Champlin, and Evashwick, *Promoting Teen Health*, 28–45.

Franklin, M. C. 2000. Computer age. *Boston Globe,* February 13, H5, H8.

Frauenheim, E. 1999. New efforts bring poor and minority users into tech revolution. *Tech Week,* November 1, 1–7.

Freedman, M. 1993. *The Kindness of Strangers: Adult Mentors, Urban Youth, and the New Voluntarism.* San Francisco: Jossey-Bass.

French, S., and J. Swain. 1997. Youth disabled people. In J. Roche and S. Tucker, *Youth in Society*, 199–206.

Frost, C. O. 1999. *Museums and the Web 1999.* Pittsburgh, Pa.: Archives and Museum Infomatics.

Furstenberg, F. F., T. D. Cook, J. Eccles, G. H. Elder Jr., and A. Sameroff. 1999. *Managing to Make It: Urban Families and Adolescent Success.* Chicago: University of Chicago Press.

Gabriel, R. M., T. Hopson, M. Haskins, and K. E. Powell. 1996. Building relationships and resilience in the prevention of youth violence. *American Journal of Preventive Medicine* 12, 48–55.

Gaither, E. B. 1992. "Hey! That's mine": Thoughts on pluralism and American museums. In Karp, Kreamer, and D. Lavine, *Museums and Communities*, 56–64.

Galambos, N. L., and M. F. Ehrenberg. 1997. The family as health risk and opportunity: A focus on divorce and working families. In Schulenberg, Maggs, and Hurrelmann, *Health Risks and Developmental Transitions*, 139–160.

Gambone, M. A., and A. J. A. Arbreton. 1997. *Safe Havens: The Contributions of Youth Organizations to Healthy Adolescent Development.* Philadelphia: Public/Private Ventures.

Garbarino, J., N. Dubrow, K. Kostelny, and C. Pardo. 1992. *Children in Danger: Coping with the Consequences of Community Violence.* San Francisco: Jossey-Bass.

Garbarino, J., and N. Jacobson. 1978. Youth helping youth in cases of maltreatment of adolescents. *Child Welfare* 57:505–510.

Gardiner, J. W. 1994. Foreword to *Urban Sanctuaries,* ed. McLaughlin, Irby, and Langman, ix–xii.

Gardner, H. 1983. *Frames of Mind: The Theory of Multiple Intelligences.* New York: Basic Books.

Garmezy, N. 1984. Stress-resistant children: The search for protective factors. In J. E. Stevenson, ed., *Recent Research in Developmental Psychopathology,* 212–233. *Journal of Child Psychology and Psychiatry,* book supplement no. 4. New York: Oxford University Press.

Garnier, H. E., and J. A. Stein. 1998. Values and the family: Risk and protective factors of adolescent problem behaviors. *Youth and Society* 30:89–120.

Garr, R. 1995. *Reinvesting in America.* Reading, Mass.: Addison-Wesley.

Garratt, D. 1997. Youth cultures and sub-cultures. In J. Roche and S. Tucker, *Youth in Society,* 143–150.

Gaunt, K. D. 1998. Dancin' in the streets to a Black girls's beat: Music, gender, and the "ins and outs" of double-dutch. In J. Austin and M. N. Willard, eds., *Generations of Youth: Youth Cultures and History in Twentieth-century America,* 272–292. New York: New York University Press.

Gebreselassie, T., and B. Politz. 2000. *Youth Development and . . . Series: A Series of Annotated Quotations and Excerpts from Selected Research on Youth.* 2nd ed. Washington, D.C.: Center for Youth Development and Policy Research, Academy for Educational Development.

George, S. S. 1999. On the Web, a world of hope is spun for teens. *Washington Post,* November 26, A01.

Gerzon-Kessler, A. 2000. Sports: A forum for collaboration, connection, and community. *CYD Journal: Community Youth Development* 1:20–23.

Giarratano-Russell, S. 1998. Overview of teen health. In Henderson, Champlin, and Evashwick, *Promoting Teen Health,* 1–6.

Gibbs, J. C., G. B. Potter, and A. P. Goldstein. 1995. *The EQUIP Program: Teaching Youth to Think and Act Responsibly Through a Peer-helping Approach.* Champaign, Ill.: Research Press.

Gilligan, C. 1982. *In a Different Voice.* Cambridge: Harvard University Press.

Gilligan, C., J. V. Ward, J. M. Taylor, and B. Bardige. 1988. *Mapping the Moral Domain.* Cambridge: Harvard University Press.

Giordano, P. C., S. A. Cernkovich, and A. DeMaris. 1993. The family and peer-relations of Black adolescents. *Journal of Marriage and the Family* 55:277–287.

Giroux, H. A. 1998. *Channel Surfing: Racism, the Media, and the Destruction of Today's Youth.* New York: St. Martin's Press.

Goetz, T. 1997. Why New York taco stands are Chinese. *New York Times*, October 19, magazine: 59.

Glover, J. 1995. Promoting youth development in a therapeutic milieu. In AYPF, *Contract with America's Youth*, 22–23.

Golberg, V. 1999. Outreach, the wandering museum's specialty. *New York Times*, January 10, AR41, AR43.

Goleman, D. 1995. *Emotional Intelligence: Why It Can Matter More than IQ.* New York: Bantam Books.

Gomez-Pena, G. 1992. The other vanguard. In Karp, Kreamer, and Lavine, *Museums and Communities*, 65–75.

Gonzalez, A. M., and E. A. Tonelli. 1992. Companeros and partners: The CARA project. In Karp, Kreamer, and Lavine, *Museums and Communities*, 262–284.

Gordon, K. A., and W. C. Coscarelli. 1996. Recognizing and fostering resilience. *Performance Improvement* 35:14–17.

Graham, J. 2000. Stick your neck out: Building leaders at the Giraffe Heroes Project. *CYD Journal: Community Youth Development* 1:20–25.

Green, M. B. 1998. Youth violence in the city: The role of educational interventions. *Health Education and Behavior* 23:175–193.

Greenberg, M. 2001. Developmental and ecological considerations in implementing community action strategies for children and youth. In A. Booth and A. C. Crouter, eds., *Does It Take a Village?* 211–221.

Greenblatt, S. 1991. Resonance and wonder. In Karp and Lavine, *Exhibiting Cultures*, 42–56.

Greenhouse, S. 2001. Problems seen for teenagers who hold jobs. *New York Times*, January 29, A1, A22.

Gregory, L. W. 1995. The "turnaround" process: Factors influencing the school success of urban youth. *Journal of Adolescence* 10:136–154.

Griffin, C. 1997. Representations of the young. In J. Roche and S. Tucker, *Youth in Society*, 17–25.

Grimmett, D. 1998. Physical activity and fitness. In Henderson, Champlin, and Evashwick, *Promoting Teen Health*, 22–27.

Guest, H. E. 1995. A national youth agenda: Returning the community interest to the community. In AYPF, *Contract with American's Youth,* 26–27.

Gurak, L. J. 1999. The promise and the peril of social action in cyberspace: Ethos, delivery, and the protests over MarketPlace and the Clipper chip. In M. A. Smith and P. Kolloack, eds., *Communities in Cyberspace,* 243–263. London: Routledge.

Ha, J. 2000. Improving a challenge course scout finds reward in community service. *Hartford Courant,* October 4, p. 7.

Hahn, A. 2000. A nation of residual youth policies. *Youth Today* 9:54.

———. 1999a. Research challenges assumptions about youth work. *Youth Today* 8:54.

———. 1999b. Extending the time of learning. In Besharov, *America's Disconnected Youth,* 233–265.

———. 1995. The central role of "age" in youth development policy. In AYPF, *Contract with America's Youth,* 24–25.

Hahn, A., and G. Raley. 1999. *Youth Development: On the Path Towards Professionalization.* Washington, D.C.: National Assembly.

———. 1997. Youth development: A profession in the making. *Youth Today* 4:2–97.

Halbfinger, D. M. 1997. Political role of immigrants is still lagging. *New York Times,* December 1, A21.

Hall, P. 1999. Changing geographies: Technology and income. In Schon, Sanyal, and Mitchell, *High Technology and Low-income Communities,* 43–69.

Halpern, S. J., G. Cusack, R. Raley, R. O'Brien, and J. Wills. 1995. *Contract with America's Youth: Toward a National Youth Development Agenda.* Washington, D.C.: American Youth Policy Forum.

Hansot, E. 1993. Misperceptions of gender and youth: Learning together, learning apart. In Heath and McLaughlin, *Identity and Inner-city Youth,* 196–209.

Hardman, C. M. 1998. Taking Mexican art beyond borders: Chicago's Mexican Fine Arts Center Museum. *Americas* 50:56–57.

Harmon, B. 1999. Youth Alive puts a young man on the right track. *Tampa Tribune,* October 2, 3.

Hart, D., R. Atkins, and D. Ford. 1998. Urban America as a context for the development of moral identity in adolescence. *Journal of Social Issues* 54:513–530.

Harter, S. 1987. The perceived competence scale of children. *Child Development* 33:87–97.

Hartup, M. W. 1993. Adolescents and their friends. In B. Laursen, ed., *Close Friendships in Adolescence,* 3–22. San Francisco: Jossey-Bass.

Haslip-Viera, G., and S. L. Baver, eds. 1996. *Latinos in New York: Communities in Transition.* Terre Haute, Ind.: University of Notre Dame Press.

Hatch, T., H. Goodrich, C. Unger, and G. H. Wiatrowski. 1994. On the edge of school: Creating a new context for students' development. In Villarruel and Lerner, *Promoting Community-based Programs,* 51–63.

Haveman, R., and B. Wolfe. 1994. *Succeeding Generations on the Effects of Investments in Children.* New York: Sage.

Havighurst, R. J., R. F. DeHaan, W. J. Dieterich, H. Hackamack, L. Johnson, and R. D. King. 1952. *A Community Youth development Program.* Chicago: University of Chicago Press.

Hayes, J., and D. Schindel. 1994. *Pioneer Journeys: Drama in Museum Education.* Charlottesville, Virg.: New Plays.

Hayes-Bautista, D. E., W. O. Schink, and J. Chapa. 1988. *The Burden of Support: Young Latinos in an Aging Society.* Stanford, Calif.: Stanford University Press.

Heath, S. B. 1994. The project of learning from the inner-city youth perspective. In Villarruel and Lerner, *Promoting Community-based Programs,* 25–34.

Heath, S. B., and M. W. McLaughlin. 1993a. Ethnicity and gender in theory and practice. In Heath and McLaughlin, *Identity and Inner-city Youth,* 13–35.

—, eds. 1993b. *Identity and Inner-city Youth: Beyond Ethnicity and Gender.* New York: Teachers College Press.

Hein, K. 2000. Joing creative forces with adolescents. *CYD Journal: Community Youth Development* 1:44–47.

——. 1999. Young people as assets: A foundation view. *Social Policy* 30:20–29.

Hellison, D. R., and N. J. Cutforth. 1997. Extended day program for urban children and youth: From theory to practice. In H. J. Walberg, O. Reyes, and R. P. Weissberg, eds., *Children and Youth: Interdisciplinary Perspectives,* 223–249. Thousand Oaks, Calif: Sage.

Hellison, D. R., N. J. Cutforth, J. Kallusky, T. Martinek, M. Parker, and J. Stiehl. 2000. *Youth Development and Physical Activity: Linking Universities and Communities.* Champaign, Ill.: Human Kinetics.

Henderson, A. 1998. In context: The future for adolescent health. In Henderson, Champlin, and Evashwick, *Promoting Teen Health,* 252–256.

Henderson, A., S. Champlin, and W. Evashwick, eds. 1998. *Promoting Teen Health: Linking Schools, Health Organziations, and Community.* Thousand Oaks, Calif.: Sage.

Henderson, K. A., and K. King. 1998. Recreation programming for adolescent girls: Rationale and foundations. *Journal of Park and Recreation Administration* 16:1–15.

Herbert, J. T. 1996. Use of adventure-based counseling programs with persons with disabilities. *Journal of Rehabilitation* 62:3–12.

Hernandez, R., M. Siles, and R. I. Rochin. 2000. Latino youth: Coverting challenges to opportunities. In Montero-Sieburth and Villarruel, *Making Invisible Latino Adolescents Visible*, 1–28.

Hernandez, R., and S. Torres-Saillant. 1996. Dominicans in New York: Men, women, and prospects. In G. Haslip-Viera and S. L. Baver, eds., *Latinos in New York: Communities in Transition*, 30–56. Terra Haute, Ind.: University of Notre Dame Press.

Hile, J. L. 2000. A chance to tell their stories. HOPE 24:24–27, 69.

Hill, H. M., F. I. Soriano, S. A. Chen, and T. D. LaFromboise. 1994. Sociological factors in the etiology and prevention of violence among ethnic minority youth. In L. D. Eron, J. H. Gentry, and P. Sclegel, eds., *Reason to Hope: A Psychosocial Perspective on Violence and Youth*, 59–100. Washington, D.C.: American Psychological Association.

Hill, J. D. 2000. Dickies tv only looks young. *AdWeek Southeast* 21 (January 10): 5.

Hill, P. T. 1999. Focus high schools. In Besharov, ed., *America's Disconnected Youth*, 213–232.

Hingson, R., and J. Howland. 1993. Promoting safety in adolescents. In Millstein, Petersen, and Nightingale, *Promoting the Health of Adolescents*, 305–327.

Hirzy, E. C. 1996. *True Needs, True Partners: Museums and Schools Transforming Education*. Washington, D.C.: Institute of Museum Services.

Honig, A. S. 2000. Musings on primary prevention for the 21st century. *Journal of Primary Prevention* 21:21–23.

Honig, M., Kahne, J., and M. W. McLaughlin. 1998. Theory of action in research and practice. *New Designs for Youth Development* 14:10–11, 41–43.

Hooper-Greenhill, E. 1998. Review of cultural diversity: Attitudes of ethnic minority populations towards museums and galleries. *GEM News* 69:10–11.

———. 1997. Towards plural perspectives. In Hooper-Greenhill, *Cultural Diversity*, 1–11.

Howe, N., and Strauss, W. 2000. *Millenials Rising: The Next Great Generation*. New York: Vintage Books.

Howes, C. 1987. *Peer Interaction of Young Children*. Monographs of the Society for Research in Child Development. Monographs 53 (1, serial no. 217).

Hudson, S. D. 1997. Helping youth grow (youth development). *Journal of Physical Education, Recreation, and Dance* 68:16–18.

Huebner, A. J. 1998. Examing "empowerment": A how-to-guide for the youth development professional. *Journal of Extension* 36:1–6.

Hughes, D. M. 2000. Hope: The life source. *CYD Journal: Community Youth Development* 1:12–17.

Hughes, D. M., and Curnan, S. P. 2000. Community youth development: A framework for action. *CYD Journal: Community Youth Development* 1:7–13.

Hughes, D. M., and N. Nichols. 1995. Changing the paradigm to community youth development. In AYPF, *Contract with America's Youth*, 30–32.

Husock, H. 1993. Bringing back the settlement house: Settlements see poor people as citizens not clients. *Public Welfare*, 16–25.

ICOM Canada. 1998. Museums and sustainable communities. *Bulletin* 8:1–14.

IMPACT. 1998. *An Upward Bound Math and Science Proposal.* Miami, Fla.: Miami Museum of Science.

Institute of Museum Services. 1996. *True Needs, True Partners: Museums and Schools Transforming Education.* Washington, D.C.: Institute of Museum Services.

Ishaya, V. 1999. Youth and beyond: Repressed voices. *New Designs for Youth Development* 15:6–9.

Jarvis, S. V., L. Shear, and D. M. Hughes. 1997. Community youth development: Learning the new story. *Child Welfare* 76:719–741.

Jason, L. A., M. D. Engstrom, S. B. Pokorny, G. Tegart, and C. J. Curie. 2000. Putting the community back into prevention: Think locally, act globally. *Journal of Primary Prevention* 21:25–29.

Jeffries, S. 1996. Street of shame: Television. *Guardian* (London), March 20, T13.

Jenkins, R. 1995. Youth development in the information age. In AYPF, *Contract with America's Youth*, 50–51.

Jones, J. P. 1992. The colonial legacy and the community: The Gallery 33 project. In Karp, Kreamer, and Lavine, *Museums and Communities,* 221–261.

Jones, N., and R. Brown. 1999. *The Value of Youth Mentoring Programs.* Washington, D.C.: National Governor's Association, February 21.

Jones-Correa, M. 1998. *Between Two Nations: The Political Predicament of Latinos in New York City.* Ithaca, N.Y.: Cornell University Press.

Kahn, J., and K. Baily. 1999. The role of social capital in youth development: The case of "I have a dream" program. *Educational Evaluation and Policy Analysis* 21:321–343.

Kahn, J. P. 2001. Making the dream digital: Class links young African-Americans, history. *Boston Globe,* January 15, B5, B11.

Kanuha, V. K. 2000. "Being" native versus "Going Native": Conducting social work research as an insider. *Social Work* 45:439–447.

Karp. I. 1992. Museums and communities: The politics of public culture. Introduction to *Museums and Communities*, ed. Karp, Kreamer, and Lavine, 1–17.

Karp. I., C. M. Kreamer, and S. D. Lavine, eds. 1992. *Museums and Communities: The Politics of Public Culture*. Washington, D.C.: Smithsonian Institution Press.

Karp, I., and S. D. Lavine, eds. 1991. *Exhibiting Cultures,: The Poetics and Politics of Museum Display* 33–41. Washington, D.C.: Smithsonian Institution Press.

Kaufman, B. A. 1994. Day by day: Playing and learning. *International Journal of Play Therapy* 3:11–21.

Kessler, R. 2000. Nourishing soul in adolescents: Integrating heart, spirit, and community in youth work. *CYD Journal: Community Youth Development* 1:6–11.

Kellogg Foundation. 1999. *Youth Philanthropy: A Framework of Best Practice.* Battle Creek, Mich.: Kellogg Foundation.

———. 1998. *Safe Passages Through Adolescence: Communities Protecting the Health and Hopes of Youth*. Battle Creek, Mich.: Kellogg Foundation.

Kinzer, S. 2001. A struggle to be seen: Museums on Black culture are springing up all over, but must still fight for money and a future. *New York Times*, February 22, B1, B2.

Kiple, M. D., ed. 1999. *Risks and Opportunities: Synthesis of Studies on Adolescence*. Washington, D.C.: National Research Council Institute on Medicine.

Kirby, D., and K. Coyle. 1997. Youth development programs. *Children and Youth Services Review* 19:437–454.

Knox, V., C. Miller, and L. A. Gennetian. 2000. *Reforming Welfare and Rewarding Work: A Summary of the Final Report on the Minnesota Family Investment Program*. Minnesota: Manpower Demonstration Research Corporation.

Kohn, A. 1991. Caring kids. *Phi Delta Kappa* 72:496–506.

Kolasky, B. 1997. Issue of the week: Demographic shiftIntellectualCapital.com, August 21, 1–4.

Kolata, G. 2001. Doubters fault earlier puberty. *New York Times*, February 20, A1, A16.

Kollock, P., and M. A. Smith. 1999. Communities in cyberspace: In M. A. Smith and P. Kollock, eds., *Communities in Cyberspace*, 3–25. London: Routledge.

Konard, R. 1999. In the driver's seat automakers' focus shifting to youth. *Fort Worth Star-Telegram*, November 12, bus. sec., 1.

Konopka, G. 1973. Requirements for healthy development of adolescent youth. *Adolescence* 31:1–26.

Korbin, J. E. 2001. Taking neighborhood seriously. In A. Booth and A. C. Crouter, eds., *Does It Take a Village?* 79–86.

Koss-Chioino, J. D., and L. A. Vargas. 1999. *Working with Latino Youth: Culture, Development, and Context.* San Francisco: Jossey-Bass.

Krueger, R. A. 1988. *Focus Groups: A Practical Guide for Applied Research.* Newbury Park, Calif.: Sage.

Kurth-Schai, R. A. 1988. The role of youth in society: A reconceptualization. As cited in W. R. Penuel. 1995, *Adult Guidance in Youth development Revisited: Identity Construction in Youth Organizations.* Worcester, Mass.: Clark University.

Kurtz, P. D. 1997. Clients as resources: Empowering school social work practice with students, families, and communities. *Social Work in Education* 19:211–218.

Kyle, J. E. 1996. Addressing the needs of youth in America's cities and towns. *Nation's Cities Weekly,* May 27, 9.

Kysela, G. M., et al. 1996. The child and family resiliency research program. *Alberta Journal of Educational Research* 42:406–409.

LaBelle, T. 1981. An introduction to the nonformal education of children and youth. *Comparative Education Review* 25:313–329.

LaCava, L. A. 2000. Evaluation as a management and learning tool: Balancing the call to prove with the need to improve CYD practice. *CYD Journal: Community Youth Development* 1:48–49.

Lachter, R. B., K. A. Komro, S. Veblen-Mortenson, C. L. Perry, and C. L. Williams,. 1999. High school students' efforts to reduce alcohol use in their communities: Project Northland's youth development component. *Journal of Health Education* 30:330–342.

Lagerloaf, J. 2000. The pied piper of healing. HOPE 25:38–42.

Lake, L. 2000. Kids design special bears to comfort hurting children. *Tampa Tribune,* January 19, 4.

Lakes, R. D. 1996. *Youth Development and Critical Education: The Promise of Democratic Action.* Albany: State University of New York Press.

Lambert, B. L. 2000. Forty percent in New York City are foreign born, study says. *New York Times,* July 24, A18.

Lammers, J. C. 1991. Attitudes, motives, and demographic predictors of volunteer commitment and service duration. *Journal of Social Service Research* 14:125–140.

LaMonaca, J. 2000. Being our own advocates: Youth and young adults as partners in planning, evaluation, and policy making. *Focal Point* 14:5–6.

Langman, J., and McLaughlin, M. W. 1993. Collaborate or go it alone? Tough decision for youth policy. In Heath and McLaughlin, *Identity and Inner-city Youth,* 147–175.

Larson, R. W. 2000. Toward a psychology of positive youth development. *American Psychologist* 55:170–183.

Lavine, S. D. 1992. Audience, ownership, and authority: Designing relations between museums and communities. In Karp, Kreamer, and Lavine, *Museums and Communities,* 137–157.

———. 1991. Art museums, national identity, and the status of minority cultures: The case of Hispanic art in the United States. In Karp and Lavine, *Exhibiting Cultures,* 79–87.

Lavine, S. D., and Karp. I. 1991. Museums and multiculturalism. Introduction to *Exhibiting Cultures,* ed. Karp and Lavine, 1–9.

Lawrence, D. H. 1998. Positive youth development promotes pathways of growth. *Common Ground* 15:9.

Layder, D. 1993. *New Strategies in Social Research.* Cambridge, England: Polity Press.

Lazarus, W., and L. Lipper. 2000. Creating a children's policy agenda in the digital world: Strategies for advocates. *Next Generation* (July): 1–6.

Leadbeater, B. J., and N. Way. 1996. *Urban Girls: Resisting Stereotypes, Creating Identities.* New York: New York University Press.

Lee, B. A,. 2001. Taking neighborhood seriously. In A. Booth and A. C. Crouter, eds., *Does It Take a Village?* 31–40.

Leffert, N., R. N. Saito, D. A. Blyth, and C. H. Kroenke. 1996. *Making the Case: Measuring the Impact of Youth Development Programs.* Minneapolis, Minn.: Search Institute.

Leming, J. S. 1997. *Values and Character Education in Public Schools: Should the Schools Teach Moral and Civic Virtue?* Carbondale: Southern Illinois University.

Lerman, R. I. 1999. Improving links between high schools and careers. In Besharov, *America's Disconnected Youth,* 185–212.

Lerner, R. M. 1995. *America's Youth in Crisis: Challenges and Options for Programs and Policies.* Thousand Oaks, Calif.: Sage.

Lerner, R. M., C. W. Ostrom and M. A. Freel. 1997. Preventing health-compromising behaviors among youth and promoting their positive development: A developmental contextual perspective. In Schulenberg, Maggs, and Hurrelmann, *Health Risks and Developmental Transitions,* 498–521.

Leukefeld, C. G., and M. Staton. 2000. The future of prevention: An imperfect essay. *Journal of Primary Prevention* 21:35–41.

Leventhal, H., and P. Keeshan. 1993. Promoting healthful diet and physical activity. In Millstein, Petersen, and Nightingale, *Promoting the Health of Adolescents*, 260–284.

Lewin, T. 2001. Children's computer use grows, but gaps persist, study says. *New York Times*, January 22, A11.

Liederman, D. S. 1995. Don't forget young people in foster care! In *Contract with America's Youth*, 52–53.

Linetzky, M. 2000. Youth development: Putting theory into practice. *Focal Point* 14:11–14.

Linn, D. 1998. *Preparing Students for the Twenty-first Century.* Washington, D.C.: National Governor's Association.

Lipke, D. J. 2000. Dead end ahead? *American Demographics* 22: 50–51.

Lipsitz, G. 1994. *We Know What Time It Is: Race, Class, and Youth Culture in the Nineties*, 17–28. New York: Routledge.

Little, R. 1993. *What's Working for Today's Youth: The Issues, the Programs, and the Lessons.* East Lansing: Michigan State University.

Littman, M. 1998. Youths will be served. *Prepared Foods* 167:21.

Livingston, J., and J. Beardsley. 1991. The poetics and politics of Hispanic art: A new perspective. In Karp and Lavine, eds., *Exhibiting Cultures,* 104–120.

Lloyd-Kolkin, D. 1998. Baile de vida: The dance of life. In Henderson, Champlin, and Evashwick, *Promoting Teen Health*, 219–223.

Logan, P. 1997. Workshops focus on youth development. *Albuquerque Journal,* April 26, B8.

London, J. 2000. The experience of youth in focus. *Focal Point* 14:35–36.

Lopez, B., L. Nerrenberg and M. Valdez. 2000. Migrant adolescents: Barriers and opportunities. In Montero-Sieburth and Villarruel, *Making Invisible Latino Adolescents Visible*, 289–307.

Los Angeles Times. 1996. Environment. *Los Angeles Times*, September 8, B2.

LoSciuto, L., M. A. Freeman, E. Harrington, B. Altman, and A. Lanphear. 1997. An outcome evaluation of the Woodrock Youth Development Project. *Journal of Early Adolescence* 17:51–66.

Loury, L. D. 1999. Family background, church attendance, and school achievement. In Besharov, *America's Disconnected Youth*, 117–132.

Lunquist, J. 1998. Peer-education . . . a little help from my friends. In Henderson, Champlin, and Evashwick, *Promoting Teen Health*, 215–218.

McCabe, R. H. 1999. 21st century challenges. *Presidency* 2:14–19.

McClary, S. 1994. Same as it ever was: Youth culture and music. In A. Ross and T. Rose, eds., *Microphone Fiends,* 29–40.

McClelland, J. 1998. It takes more than computers: Libraries in the information age. *News Tech*:1–3.

McCook, K., and K. Lippincott. 1998. Library services to farm workers in West Central Florida. In Venturella, *Poor People and Library Services,* 154–164.

McDonald, G. F. 1992. Change and challenge: Museums in the information society. In Karp, Kreamer, and Lavine, *Museums and Communities,* 158–181.

McGrave, S. 2001. Creating a generation of slouchers. *New York Times,* January 4, E1, E9.

McKeggie, K. 2000. El Arco Iris youth power program. *Planning* 66:14–17.

McKenna, T. 2000. Imbedding positive youth development. *Youth Today* 9:54.

McKnight, J. L. 1995. *The Careless Society: Community and Its Counterfeits.* New York: Basic Books.

McLaughlin, M. W. 1993. Embedded identities: Enabling balance in urban contexts. In Heath and McLaughlin, *Identity and Inner-city Youth,* 36–68.

McLaughlin, M. W., and S. B. Heath. 1993. Casting the self: Frames for identity and dilemmas for policy. In Heath and McLaughlin, *Identity and Inner-city Youth,* 210–239.

McLaughlin, M. W., M. A. Irby, and J. Langman. 1994. *Urban Sanctuaries: Neighborhood Organizations in the Lives and Futures of Inner-city Youth.* San Francisco: Jossey-Bass.

McLearn, K. T., and S. V. LaFrance. 1999. Listening to young, inner-city African American males. In Besharov, *America's Disconnected Youth,* 133–150.

McNeal, J. U. 1999. *The Kids Market: Myths and Realities.* Los Angeles, Calif.: Paramount Market Publishing.

———. 1992. *Kids as Customers: A Handbook of Marketing to Children.* San Francisco: Jossey-Bass.

McVeigh, E. C. 2001. On different pages. *Boston Globe,* January 23, B1, B4.

McWhirter, J. J., B. T. McWhirter, A. M. McWhirter, and E. H. McWhirter. 1993. *At-risk Youth: A Comprehensive Response.* Pacific Grove, Calif.: Brooks/Cole.

Maggs, J. L., J. Schulenberg, and K. Hurrelmann. 1997. Developmental transitions during adolescence: Health promotion implications. In Schulenberg, Maggs, and Hurrelmann, eds., *Health Risks and Developmental Transitions,* 522–546.

Males, M. A. 1998. *Framing Youth: Ten Myths about the Next Generation.* Monroe, Maine: Common Courage Press.

———. 1996. *The Scapegoat Generation: America's War on Adolescents.* Monroe, Maine: Common Courage Press.

Mallon, G. P. 1997. Basic premises, guiding principles and competent practices for a positive youth development approach to working with gay, lesbian, and bisexual youths in out-of-home care. *Child Welfare* 76:591–609.

Maloney, L., and C. Hughes, eds. 1999. *Case Studies in Museum, Zoo, and Aquarium Theater.* Washington, D.C.: American Association of Museums.

Manale, Y., C. Nelson, F. Davis, and B. Martin. 1998. Kids work hard to preserve woodlands. *New Designs for Youth Development* 14:37–38.

Marks, W. 1998. Hosmer branch library. In Venturella, *Poor People and Library Services,* 109–116.

Marrero, L., and S. Weinstein. 1998. The Free Library of Philadelphia Technology Demonstration Project. In Venturella, *Poor People and Library Services,* 80–90.

Marshall, H., and P. Stenner. 1997) Friends and lovers. In J. Roche and S. Tucker, *Youth in Society,* 183–189.

Marshall, J. 2000. Theater of life: A Chicago playwright teaches teens to recognize the power of their own stories. *HOPE* 22:64–68.

Martin, L., and C. Ascher. 1994. Developing math and science materials for school age child care programs. In Villarruel and Lerner, *Promoting Community-based Programs,* 11–23.

Martinek, T. 2000. Challenges. Epilogue to *Youth Development and Physical Education: Linking Universities and Communities,* ed. D. Hellison, N. Cutforth, J. Kallusky, T. Martinek, M. Parker, and J. Stiehl, 245–248. Champaign, Ill.: Human Kinetics.

Martinez, A. L. 1999. Cambios: A Spanish-language approach to youth development. *SIECUS Report* 27 (June 1): 9–10.

Martorana, J. 1997. Libraries: More than just books. *Long Island Business News,* May 12, 1–2.

Marzio, P. C. 1991. Minorities and fine-arts museums in the United States. In Karp and Lavine, *Exhibiting Cultures,* 121–127.

Marx, J. D. 1988. An outdoor adventure counseling program for adolescents. *Social Work* 33:517–520.

Marx, L. 1999. Information technology in historical perspective. In Schon, Sanyal, and Mitchell, *High Technology and Low-income Communities,* 131–148.

Masten, A. 1994. Resilience in individual development: Successful adaptation despite risk and adversity. In M. C. Wang and E. W. Gordon, eds., *Educational Resilience in Inner-city America: Challenges and Prospects,* 3–25. Hillsdale, N.J.: Erlbaum.

Mathews, C. S. 1999. The future for theater in zoos, aquariums, and museums. In L. Maloney and C. Hughes, eds., *Case Studies in Museum, Zoo, and Aquarium Theater,* 101–108. Washington, D.C.: American Association of Museums.

Matysik, G. J. 2000. Involving adolescents in participatory research. *CYD Journal: Community Youth Development* 1:15–19.

Meier, D. 2000. Schools that seek solutions. HOPE 24:18–21.

Mejias-Rentas, A. 1998. Young at art. *Hispanic* 11:36–42.

Mele, C. 1999. Cyberspace and disadvantaged communities: The Internet as a tool for collective action. In M. A. Smith and P. Kollock, eds., *Communities in Cyberspace*, 290–310.

Mendez-Negrete, J. 2000. "Dime con quien andas": Notions of Chicano and Mexican American Families. *Families in Society: The Journal of Contemporary Human Services* 81:42–48.

Menon, G. M. 2000. The 79-cent campaign: The use of on-line mailing lists for electronic advocacy. *Journal of Community Practice* 8:73–81.

Mercogliano, C. 1996. Fixing a desk, mending a mind. *SKOLE: The Journal of Alternative Education* 13:93–107.

Meredith, R. 2000. They hope to move up by learning to log on. *New York Times*, March 13, A11.

Merighi, J. R., and M. D. Grimes. 2000. Coming out to families in a multicultural context. *Families in Society: The Journal of Contemporary Human Services* 81:32–41.

Merrill, S. A. 1999. Roselawn: A community regaining its youth. *Clearing House* 73 (November 1): 101–105.

Meyer, A. L. 1999. The subjective impressions of sixth grade urban adolescents concerning their ability to achieve personal goals. *Journal of Primary Prevention* 19:315–349.

Meyer, A. L., and Lausell, L. 1996. The value of including a higher power in efforts to prevent violence and promote optimal outcomes during adolescence: In R. L. Hampton and P. Jenkins, eds., *Preventing Violence in America: Issues in Children's and Families' Lives*, 115–132.

Meyers, C. 1998. Outdoors the place to grow youth programs provide options. *Denver Post*, November 29, C-07.

Meyers, E. 1999. The coolness factor: Ten libraries listen to youth. *American Libraries* 30:42–45.

Michigan State University. 2000. *Age-appropriate Educational Approaches to Youth Development*. East Lansing: Michigan State University 4-H Youth Development.

——. 1997. *Five-to-eight-year-olds: Youth Development Programs for School-aged Children*. East Lansing: Michigan State University.

Miller, C. 1996. Broadway increases marketing to reach younger theater crowd. *Marketing News* 30, September 9, 1.

Millstein, S. G. 1993. A view of health from the adolescent's perspective. In Millstein, Petersen, and Nightingale, *Promoting the Health of Adolescents*, 97–118.

Millstein, S. G., A. C. Petersen, and E. O. Nightingale. 1993. Adolescent health promotion: Rationale, goals, and objectives. In Millstein, Petersen, and Nightingale, *Promoting the Health of Adolescents*, 3–10.

Millstein, S. G., A. C. Petersen, and E. O. Nightingale, eds. 1993. *Promoting the Health of Adolescents: New Directions for the Twenty-first Century.* New York: Oxford University Press.

Minority Markets Alert. 1999. Street promotions blend grassroots techniques with music and style. *Minority Markets Alert* 11:1.

Mitchell, W. J. 1999a. Equitable access to the online world. In Schon, Sanyal, and Mitchell, *High Technology and Low-income Communities*, 153–163.

——. 1999b. The city of bits hypothesis. In Schon, Sanyal, and Mitchell, *High Technology and Low-income Communities*, 105–129.

Milton S. Eisenhower Foundation. 1990. *Youth Investment and Community Reconstruction: Street Lessons on Drugs and Crime for the Nineties.* Washington, D.C.: Eisenhower Foundation.

Mitra, A. 2000. Virtual community: Looking for India on the Internet. In Bell and Kennedy, *The Cybercultures Reader*, 676–694.

Montero-Sieburth, M. 2000. Demystifying the images of Latinos: Boston-based case studies. In Montero-Sieburth and Villarruel, *Making Invisible Latino Adolescents Visible*, 155–201.

Montero-Sieburth, M., and F. A. Villarruel, eds. 2000. *Making Invisible Latino Adolescents Visible: A Critical Approach to Latino Diversity.* New York: Palmer Press.

Moore, D. 2000. Healing our spirits through native spirituality. *CYD Journal: Community Youth Development* 1:40–45.

Moore, E. M. 1941. *Youth in Museums.* Philadelphia: University of Pennsylvania Press.

Moore, K., and D. Glei. 1995. Taking the plunge: An examination of positive youth development. *Journal of Adolescent Research* 10:15–40.

Moore, K. A. 1998. Criteria for indicators of child well-being. In R. M. Hauser, B. V. Brown, and W. R. Prosser, eds., *Indicators of Children's Well-being.* New York: Sage.

Mora, R. 2000. The multicultural literacies of precollege Latino students. In Montero-Sieburth and Villarruel, *Making Invisible Latino Adolescents Visible*, 131–153.

Morley, E., and S. B. Rossman. 1997. *Helping At-risk Youth: Lessons from Community-based Initiatives.* Washington, D.C.: Urban Institute.

Morris, S. 1998. Denver Public Library reads aloud to young children. In Venturella, *Poor People and Library Services*, 62–69.

Morrison, J. D., S. Alcorn, and M. Nelums. 1997. Empowering community-based programs for youth development: Is social work education interested. *Journal of Social Work Education* 33:321–333.

Msimuko, A. K., and P. P. W. Achola, eds. 1985. *The University and the Challenge of Youth Development: Proceedings of the 6th Conference of the Professors World Peace Academy*, Zambia, Africa.

Mueller, W. 1994. *Understanding Today's Youth Culture: For Parents, Teachers, and Youth Leaders*. Wheaton, Ill.: Tyndale House.

Mundy, J. 1996. Tipping the scales from risk to resiliency. *Parks and Recreation* 31:78–86.

Muraskin, L. D. 1993. *Understanding Evaluation: The Way to Better Prevention Programs*. Washington, D.C.: U.S. Department of Education.

Murdock, S. H. 1995. *An America Challenged: Population Change and the Future of the United States*. Boulder, Colo.: Westview Press.

Murphy, D. E. 2001. Moving beyond "shh" (and books) at libraries. *New York Times*, March 7, A1, A20.

Murphy, R. 1995a. *Training for Youth Workers: An Assessment Guide for Community-based Youth-serving Organizations to Promote Youth Development*. Washington, D.C.: Center for Youth Development and Policy Research, Academy for Educational Development.

———. 1995b. *Definitions, Language, and Concepts for Strengthening the Field of Youth Development Work*. Washington, D.C.: Center for Youth Development and Policy Research, Academy for Educational Development.

Muschamp, H. 1999. Culture's power houses: The museum becomes an engine of urban redesign. *New York Times*, April 21, E1, E6.

Museum of Science. 2001. The computer clubhouse: A view from the inside. *Boston Museum of Science* (winter): 7–9.

Museums Australia, Inc. 1998. *Taking the Time: Museums and Galleries, Cultural Protocols, and Communities*. Queensland, Australia: Museums Australia.

Nakamura, L. 2000. Race in/for cyberspace: Identity tourism and racial passing on the Internet. In Bell and Kennedy, *The Cybercultures Reader*, 712–720.

Napier, J. 1999. Youth program innovators attracting attention, talent. *Ottawa Citizen*, June 21, B6.

National Assembly. 1998. *Clients on Board: Profiles of Effective Governance*. Washington, D.C.: National Assembly.

———. 1997. *The New Community Collaboration Manual*. Washington, D.C.: National Assembly.

———. 1994. *Building Youth Resiliency*. Washington, D.C.: National Assembly.

National Center for Policy Analysis. 1997. *Policy Digest: Second Baby Boom's Demographic Impact*. February: 1–4.

National Clearinghouse for Families and Youth. 1998. *Youth Development*. Silver Spring, Md.: National Clearinghouse for Families and Youth.

National Collaboration for Youth (NCY). 1999. *Public Policy Statements of the National Collaboration for Youth, 1999*. Washington, D.C.: NCY.

———. 1998. *Positions for Youth: Public Policy Statements of the National Collaboration for Youth, 1998*. Washington, D.C.: NCY.

———. 1997. *Credentialing Activities in the Youth Development Field*. Washington, D.C.: NCY.

———. 1996. *Something to Say "Yes" To! Careers in Youth Development*. Washington, D.C.: NCY.

National Network for Youth. 1997. *Guiding Principles*. Washington, D.C.: National Network for Youth.

National Research Council. 1993. *Losing Generations: Adolescents in High-risk Settings*. Washington, D.C.: National Research Council.

National School-to-Work Learning and Information Center. 1996. *Incorporating a Youth Development Perspective into School-to-work Systems*. Washington, D.C.: National School-to-Work Learning and Information Center.

National Technical Information Service. 1971. *Youth Development Program Models*. Washington, D.C.: U.S. Department of Commerce.

National Telecommunications and Information Agency. 2000. *Falling Through the NET: Toward Digital Inclusion*. Washington, D.C.: U.S. Department of Commerce.

National Youth Development Information Center (NYDIC). 2000. *Talking About "Youth Development."* Washington, D.C.: NYDIC.

———. 1999. *What Works: Essential Elements of Effective Youth Development Programs*. Washington, D.C.: NYDIC.

———. 1998. *Definitions of Youth Development (and Related Terms)*. Washington, D.C.: NYDIC.

Networks for Youth Development (NYD). 1998a. *The Handbook of Positive Youth Outcomes*. New York: NYD.

———. 1998b. *A Guided Tour of Youth Development*. New York: NYD.

———. 1997. *Core Competencies for Youth Work*. New York: NYD.

Newman, R. P., S. M. Smith, and R. Murphy. 1998. *A Matter of Money: The Cost and Financing of Youth Development*. Washington, D.C.: Academy for Educational Development.

Newson, R. 1998/99. Youth speak out. *Assets* (winter): 11.

Ngai, N. P., and C. K. Cheung. 1997. Participation in youth center activities: A sequential specificity approach. *Youth and Society* 29:238–253.

Nichols, D., and L. Fines. 1995. Self-concept, attitude, and satisfaction benefits of outdoor adventure activities: The case for recreational kayaking. *Journal of Leisurability* 22:1–8.

Nichols, M. 2000. Charter schools: CBOs' risky pot o' gold. *Youth Today* 9:42–44.

Nicholson, H. J. 1991. *Gender Issues in Youth Development Programs.* New York: Carnegie Council on Adolescent Development.

Nisbet, J. 1992. *Natural Supports in School, at Work, and in the Community for People with Severe Disabilities.* Baltimore, Md. Brookes.

Nixon, R. 1997. What is positive youth development? *Child Welfare* 76:571–575.

Noack, P., and B. Kracke. 1997. Social change and adolescent well-being: Healthy country, healthy teens. In Schulenberg, Maggs, and Hurrelmann, *Health Risks and Developmental Transitions,* 54–84.

Nobles, W., and L. Goddard. 1992. An African-centered model of prevention for African-American youth at risk. In L. Goddard, ed., *African-American Youth at High-risk Work Group: An African-centered Model for Prevention for African-American Youth at High risk.* Rockville, Md.: U.S. Department of Health and Human Services.

Noddings, N. 1992. *The Challenge to Care in Schools.* New York: Teachers College Press.

Oakland Post. 1997. Bonds donates $10,000 to Youth Technology Center. *Oakland Post,* April 9, 12.

O'Donnell, J., E. A. Michalak, and E. B. Ames. 1997. Inner-city youths helping children: After-school programs to promote bonding and reduce risk. *Social Work in Education* 19:231–241.

Oetting, E. R., and F. Beauvais. 1987. Peer cluster theory, socialization characteristics, and adolescent drug use: A path analysis. *Journal of Counseling Psychology* 34:205–213.

Ogbu, J. U. 1997. Understanding the school performance or urban blacks: Some essential background knowledge. In Walberg, Reyes, and Weissberg, *Children and Youth,* 190–222.

Ogbu, O., and P. Mihyo, eds. 2000. *African Youth on the Information Highway: Participation and Leadership in Community Development.* Ottawa, Canada: International Development Research Centre.

Olasky, M. 1996. *Renewing American Compassion.* New York: Free Press.

Opiano-Misdom, J., and J. D. Luca. 1997. *Street Trends: How Today's Alternative Youth Cultures Are Creating Tomorrow's Mainstream Markets.* New York: Harperbusiness.

Orenstein, P. 1994. *Schoolgirls: Young Women, Self-esteem, and the Confidence Gap.* New York: Doubleday.

Ortiz Hendricks, C., and G. Rudlich. 2000. A community building perspective in social work education. *Journal of Community Practice* 8:21–36.

Osher, D., and B. Mejia. 1999. Overcoming barriers to intercultural relationships: A culturally competent agenda. *Reaching Today's Youth* 3:48–52.

Ostrom, C. W., R. M. Lerner and M. A. Freel. 1995. Building the capacity of youth and families through university-community collaborations: The development-in-context evaluation (DICE) model. *Journal of Adolescent Research* 10:427–448.

Owens, T. R., and C. Wang. 1997. *Community-based Learning: A Foundation for Meaningful Educational Reform.* Portland, Ore.: Northwest Regional Educational Laboratory.

Paraplegia News. 2000. Sports and recreation. *Paraplegia News* 54:36–40.

Parker, M. 2000. The way it could be. In D. Hellison, N. Cutforth, J. Kallusky, T. Martinek, M. Parker, and J. Stiehl, eds., *Youth Development and Physical Activity: Linking Universities and Communities,* 17–27. Champaign, Ill.: Human Kinetics.

Parks, S. D. 2000. *Big Questions, Worthy Dreams: Mentoring Young Adults in Their Search for Meaning, Purpose, and Faith.* San Francisco: Jossey-Bass.

Pate, H. R., and A. M. Bondi. 1992. Religious beliefs and practice: An integral aspect of multicultural awareness. *Counselor Education and Supervision* 32:108–115.

Patrick, H., A. M. Ryan, C. Alfed-Liro, J. A. Fredricks, L. Z. Hruda, and J. S. Eccles. 1999. Adolescents' commitment to developing talent: The role of peers in continuing motivation for sports and the arts. *Journal of Youth and Adolescence* 28:741–750.

Patterson, J., and R. W. Blum. 1996. Risk and resilience among children and youth with disabilities. *Archives of Pediatric Adolescent Medicine* 150:692–698.

Patton, M. Q. 1987. *How to Use Qualitative Methods in Evaluation.* Newbury Park, Calif.: Sage.

Pearce, S. 1997. Making other people. In Hooper-Greenhill, *Cultural Diversity,* 15–31.

Pedro-Carroll, J. 1997. The children of divorce intervention program: Fostering resilient outcomes for school-aged children. In G. W. Albee and T. P. Gullotta, eds., *Primary Prevention Works. Issues in Children's and Families' Lives,* 213–218. Thousand Oaks, Calif.: Sage.

Penuel, W. R. 1995. *Adult Guidance in Youth Development Revisited: Identity Construction in Youth Organizations.* Worcester, Mass.: Clark University.

Perin, C. 1992. The communicative circle: Museums as communities. In Karp, Kreamer, and Lavine, *Museums and Communities,* 182–220.

Perkins, D. F. 1997. *A Method of Presenting Key Concepts Regarding Positive Youth Development to Community Audiences.* Newsletter, Children, Youth, and Families Education and Research Network.

Perkins, D. F., and F. A. Villarruel. 2000. An ecological, risk-factor examination of Latino adolescents' engagement in sexual activity. In Montero-Sieburth and Villarruel, *Making Invisible Latino Adolescents Visible,* 83–106.

Perlmutter, F. D., D. Bailey, and E. E. Netting. 2000. *Managing Human Resources in the Human Services: Supervisory Challenges.* New York: Oxford University Press.

Perry, C. L., S. H. Kelder, and K. A. Komro. 1993. The social world of adolescents: Families, peers, schools, and the community. In Millstein, Petersen, and Nightingale, *Promoting the Health of Adolescents,* 73–96.

Peterson, A. C., N. Leffert, B. Graham, J. Alwin, and S. Ding. 1997. Promoting mental health during the transition into adolescence. In Schulenberg, Maggs, and Hurrelmann, *Health Risks and Developmental Transitions,* 471–497.

Phillios, S. A. 1999. *Wallbangin': Graffiti and Gangs in L.A.* Chicago: University of Chicago Press.

Phinney, J. S. 1990. Ethnic identity in adolescence and adults: Review of research. *Psychological Bulletin* 108:499–514.

Phinney, J. S., and E. L. Kohatsu. 1997. Ethnic and racial identity development and mental health. In Schulenberg, Maggs, and Hurrelmann, eds., *Health Risks and Developmental Transitions,* 420–443.

Pipher, M. 1994. *Reviving Ophelia.* New York: Ballantine.

Pittman, B., C. Bannerman, and A. Kendall, eds. 1981. *Museums, Magic, and Children: Youth education in Museums.* Washington, D.C.: Association of Science-Technology Centers.

Pittman, K. 2000a. Youth development's imagination failure. *Youth Today* 9:63.

——. 2000b. Balancing the equation: Communities supporting youth, youth supporting communities. *CYD Journal: Community Youth Development* 1:32–36.

——. 1999a. Beyond participation. *Youth Today* 8:55.

——. 1999b. Affordable, accessible, appropriate. *Youth Today* 8:55.

——. 1991. *A New Vision: Promoting Youth Development.* Washington, D.C.: Academy for Educational Development.

Pittman, K., and M. Irby. 1998. Youth development field. The cost of being certain. In W. Rhodes and K. Hoey, eds., *Overcoming Childhood Misfortune: Children Who Beat the Odds.* Westport, Conn.: Praeger.

Pittman, K., and S. Zeldin. 1995. *Premises, Principles and Practice: Defining the Why, What, and How of Promoting Youth Development Through Organizational Practice*. Washington, D.C.: Center for Youth Development and Policy Research, Academy for Educational Development.

———. 1994. From deterence to development: Shifting the focus of youth programs fro African-American males. In R. B. Mincy, ed., *Nurturing Young Black Males: Challenges to Agencies, Programs, and Social Policy*, 45–58. Washington, D.C.: Urban Institute.

Poertner, J., and J. Ronnau. 1992. A strengths approach to children with emotional disabilities. In D. S. Saleebey, ed., *The Strengths Perspective to Social Work Practice*, 111–121. New York: Longman.

Pointsett, A. 1996. *The Role of Sports in Youth Development: A Report of a Meeting Convened by the Carneige Corporation of New York*. New York: Carnegie Corporation.

Posner, J., and D. Vandell. 1994. Low income children's afterschool care: Are there beneficial effects of afterschool programs? *Child Development* 65:440–457.

Pouncy, H. 1999. The "hallwalkers." In Besharov, *America's Disconnected Youth*, 151–184.

Price, H. 1999. Epilogue. In Besharov, *America's Disconnected Youth*, 295–305.

Project Map, Inc. 1997. *Youth Program Models Development*. Washington, D.C.: Project Map.

Purdum, T. S. 2000. Shift in the mix alters the face of California. *New York Times*, July 4, A1, A12.

Putnam, R. 1993. The prosperous community: Social capital and community life. *American Prospect* (spring): 35–42.

Quinn, J. 1999. Where need meets opportunity: Youth development programs for early teens. *The Future of Children* 9:96–116.

Rak, C. F., and L. E. Patterson. 1996. Promoting resilience in at-risk children. *Journal of Counseling and Development* 74:368–373.

Ramey, S. L., and C. T. Ramey. 1997. The role of universities in child development. In Walberg, Reyes, and Weissberg, *Children and Youth*, 13–44.

Ramsey, R. S., and R. W. Ramsey. 1983. Management and measurement for total youth development. *Adolescence* 18:307–316.

Rathgeber, E. M. 2000. Foreword to *African Youth on the Information Highway: Participation and Leadership in Community Development*, ed. O. Ogbu and P. Mihyo, v–vii. Ottawa, Canada: International Development Research Centre.

Rattini, K. B. 1998. Alpine tower experience challenges students to climb high, surpass goals: Team building and trust as some top achievements. *St. Louis Post-Dispatch*, May 11, 6.

Rauner, D. M. 2000. *"They Still Pick Me Up When I Fail": The Role of Caring in Youth Development and Community Life.* New York: Columbia University Press.

Redding, S. 1997. Urban myth: The family in hard times. In Walberg, Reyes, and Weissberg, *Children and Youth,* 92–115.

Reed-Victor, E., and J. H. Stronge. 1997. Building resiliency: Constructive directions for homeless education. *Journal of Children and Poverty* 3:67–91.

Reis, S. M., T. P. Herbet, E. I. Diaz, L. R. Maxfield, and M. E. Ratley. 1995. *Case Studies of Talented Students Who Achieve and Underachieve in an Urban High School.* Storrs, Conn.: National Research Center on the Gifted and Talented.

Resnick, M., N. Rusk, and S. Cooke. 1999. The Computer Clubhouse: Technologic fluency in the inner city. In Schon, Sanyal, and Mitchell, *High Technology and Low-income Communities,* 263–285.

Richardson, G., and C. J. Nixon. 1997. A curriculum for resiliency. *Principal* 77:26–28.

Richmond, J. 2000. New partnerships and new systems: Supporting young people's growth and job readiness. *CYD Journal: Community Youth Development* 1:20–25.

Roberts, K. 1983. *Youth and Leisure.* Boston: Allen & Unwin.

Roberts, L. C. 1997. *From Knowledge to Narrative: Educators and the Changing Museum.* Washington, D.C.: Smithsonian Institution Press.

Robinson, B. 2000a. Wow, we have computers . . . now what? *Youth Today* 9:52–54.

——. 2000b. Computers mean business for teens. *Youth Today* 9:54.

——. 2000c. Hard drive delivers bytes to kids. *Youth Today* 9:53.

——. 2000d. Computer clubhouse gets computers out of the way. *Youth Today* 9:53.

Robinson, M. 1995. Towards a new paradigm of community development. *Community Development Journal,* 30, 21–30.

Roche, J,, and S. Tucker, eds. 1997. *Youth in Society.* Thousand Oaks, Calif.: Sage.

Roehlkepartian, E. C., and P. C. Scales. 1995. *Youth Development in Congregations: An Exploration of the Potential and Barriers.* Minneapolis, Minn.: Search Institute.

Rollin, M. 2000a. Youth policy approaches: Where we've come from_ where we're going. *CYD Journal: Community Youth Development* 1:47–51.

——. 2000b. Religion, CYD, and policy: An imperfect union. *CYD Journal: Community Youth Development* 1:52–53.

Rook, A. 1998. Youth development programs combat negative press on kids. *Youth Today* 8:49–50.

Rose, S. M. 2000. Reflections on empowerment-based practice. *Social Work* 45:403–412.

Ross, A., and T. Rose, eds., *Microphone Fiends: Youth Music and Youth Culture*, 29–40. New York: Routledge.

Ross, J., P. Saavedra, G. Shur, F. Winters, and R. Felner. 1992. The effectiveness of an afterschool program for primary grade latchkey students in precursors of substance abuse. *Journal of Community Psychology*, special issue: 22–38.

Ross, L., and M. Coleman. 2000. Urban community action planning inspires teenagers to transform their community and their identity. *Journal of Community Practice* 7:29–45.

Ross, S. A. 2000. Clinton wants poor to use Internet. AP Online, Document ID 20000404120000104, April 4.

Roth, J., J. Brooks-Gunn, L. Murray, and W. Foster. 1998. Promoting healthy adolescents: Synthesis of youth development program evaluations. *Journal of Research on Adolescence* 8, no. 4: 423–459.

Roth, J., L. F. Murray, J. Brooks-Gunn, and W. H. Foster. 1999. Youth development programs. In Besharov, *America's Disconnected Youth*, 267–294.

Rubien, B. 1998. Transforming the environment, youths. *Washington Post*, June 18, MO1.

Russo, L. 1998. Seen and heard: Marketing to kids means a lot of looking and listening. *Beverage World* 117 (September 30): 1.

Rutter, M. 1993. Resilience: Some conceptual considerations. *Journal of Adolescent Health* 14:626–631.

——. 1987. Psychosocial reslience and protective mechanisms. *American Journal of Orthopsychiatry* 37:317–331.

Sagawa, S. 1998. *Ten Years of Youth Service to America*. Washington, D.C.: American Youth Policy Forum.

Sagor, R. 1996. Building resiliency in students. *Educational Leadership* 54:38–43.

Sallis, J. F. 1993. Promoting healthful diet and physical activity. In Millstein, Petersen, and Nightingale, *Promoting the Health of Adolescents*, 209–241.

Salovey, P., and J. D. Mayer. 1990. Emotional intelligence. *Imagination, Cognition, and Personality* 9:185–211.

Sameroff, A., and M. Chandler. 1975. Reproductive risk and the continuum of caretaking causality. In F. Horowitz, ed., *Review of Child Development*, 187–244. Chicago: University of Chicago Press.

Sampson, R. J. 2001. How do communities undergird or undermine human development? Relevant contexts and social mechanisms. In A. Booth and A. C. Crouter, eds., *Does It Take a Village?* 3–30.

Sanchez, A. 2000. The power of nature: Using trees to build community. *CYD Journal: Community Youth Development* 1:7–13.

Sanford, G. 1999. Breaking the silence: Supporting gay, lesbian, bisexual, transgender, and questioning youth. *New Designs for Youth Development* 15, 19–24.

Santiagi, A. M. 2000. The impact of growing up poor or welfare-dependent on the economic status of young adults. In Montero-Sieburth and Villarruel, *Making Invisible Latino Adolescents Visible*, 29–60.

Sanyal, B., and D. A. Schon. 1999. Information technology and urban poverty: The role of public policy. In Schon, Sanyal, and Mitchell, *High Technology and Low-income Communities*, 105–129.

Sardor, Z. 2000. ALT.CIVILIZATIONS.FAQ: Cyberspace as the darker side of the west. In Bell and Kennedy, *The Cybercultures Reader*, 732–752.

Savin-Williams, R. C., and T. J. Berndt. 1990. Friendships and peer-relations. In S. S. Feldman and G. R. Elliot, eds., *At the Threshold: The Developing Adolescent*, 277–307. Cambridge: Harvard University Press.

Scales, P. C., and N. Leffert. 1999. *Developmental Assets: A Synthesis of the Scientific Research on Adolescent Development*. Minneapolis: Search Institute.

Schilling, T., and T. Martinek. 2000. Learning through leading in the Project Effort Youth Leader Corps. *CYD Journal: Community Youth Development* 1:24–30.

Schinke, S., M. Orlandi, and K. Cole. 1992. Boys and Girls clubs in public housing developments: Prevention services for youth at-risk. *Journal of Community Psychology*, special issue: 118–128.

Schon, D. A. 1999. Introduction to *High Technology and Low-income Communities*, ed. Schon, Sanyal, and Mitchell, 1–22.

Schon, D. A., B. Sanyal, and M. J. Mitchell, eds. 1999. *High Technology and Low-income Communities: Prospects for the Positive Use of Advanced Information Technology*. Cambridge: MIT Press.

Schulenberg, J., J. L. Maggs, and K. Hurrelmann, eds., *Health Risks and Developmental Transitions During Adolescence*, 444–468. New York: Cambridge University Press.

Schustack, M. W., C. King, M. A. Gallego, and O. A. Vasquez. 1994. A computer-oriented after-school activity: Children's learning in the fifth dimension and la clase magica. In Villarruel and Lerner, *Promoting Community-based Programs*, 35–50.

Sciencenter [Ithaca N.Y. Science Center]. 2000. *Volunteer Voice* 7 [newsletter], no. 7: 1–4.

Scott, R. 1999. Disabled hunters' land of opportunity. *Progressive Farmer* 114:84.

Scott-Jones, D. 1996. Urban children in family context: Ethnic variations. Paper presented at the 104th Convention of the American Psychological Association, Toronto, Canada.

Search Institute. 1998. *Helping Youth Thrive: How Youth Organizations Can—and Do—Build Developmental Assets.* Minneapolis, Minn.: Search Institute.

———. 1997. *The Asset Approach: Giving Kids What They Need to Succeed.* Minneapolis, Minn.: Search Institute.

Seefeldt, G. A., and E. C. Roehlkepartain. 1995. Building assets: What congregations can do. Minneapolis, Minn.: Search Institute.

Seidman, E., and S. E. French. 1997. Normative school transitions among urban adolescents: When, where, and how to intervene. In Walberg, Reyes, and Weissberg, *Children and Youth,* 166–189.

Sengstock, M. C., and M. Hwalek. 1999. Issues to be considered in evaluating programs for children and youth. *New Designs for Youth Development* 15:8–12.

Shames, S., and C. Gatz. 2000. *Empower Zone: Youth Photography from the Empowerment Zones/Enterprise Community Initiative.* New York: Aperture.

Shartin, E. 2001. Body-image class boosts confidence. *Boston Sunday Globe,* January 28, E7, E8.

Shaw, A., and Shaw, M. 1992. Social empowerment through community networks. In Schon, Sanyal, and Mitchell, *High Technology and Low-income Communities,* 315–335.

Shear, L. 2000. Learning large: Reclaiming the sacred in youth work. *CYD Journal: Community Youth Development* 1:24–29.

Sheehy, A. M., Jr., E. Oldham, M. Zanghi, D. Ansell, P. Correia III, and R. Copeland. 2000. *Promising Practices: Supporting Transition of Youth Served by the Foster Care System.* Baltimore, Md.: Annie E. Casey Foundation.

Shelton, C. M. 1989. *Morality and the Adolescent: A Pastoral Psychology Approach.* New York: Crossroads.

Shiffer, M. J. 1999. Planning support systems for low-income communities. In Schon, Sanyal, and Mitchell, *High Technology and Low-income Communities,* 191–211.

Shih, T. A. 1998. Finding the niche: Friendship formation of immigrant adolescents. *Youth and Society* 30:209–240.

Shohomish, L. 1995. Youth program builds trails. *Seattle Times,* September 4, B2.

Siegal, N. 2000. Hope is artists' medium in a Bronx neighborhood. *New York Times,* December 27, B1, B5.

Sipe, C. L., and P. Ma. 1998. *Support for Youth: A Profile of Three Communities.* Philadelphia: Public/Private Ventures.

Skelton, T., and G. Valentine, eds. 1998. *Cool Places: Geographies of Youth Cultures.* New York: Routledge.

Smale, S., and A. Supple. 2001. Communities as systems: Is a community more than the sum of its parts? In A. Booth and A. C. Crouter, eds., *Does It Take a Village?* 161–174.

Smilowitz, B. 2000. The youth movement: Claiming our piece of the pie. *CYD Journal: Community Youth Development* 1:42–45.

Smith, M. A. 1999. Invisible crowds in cyberspace: Mapping the social structure of the usernet. In M. A. Smith and P. Kollock, eds., *Communities in Cyberspace,* 195–219. London: Routledge.

Smith, R. C. 1996. Mexicans in New York: Memberships and incorporation in a new immigrant community. In G. Haslip-Viera and S. L. Baver, eds., *Latinos in New York: Communities in Transition,* 57–103. Terre Haute, Ind.: University of Notre Dame Press.

Smokowski, P. R. 1998. Prevention and intervention strategies for promoting resilience in disadvantaged children. *Social Service Review* 72:337–364.

Solomon, B., and H. Gardner. 2000. The origins of good work: Getting kids, parents, and coaches on the same page. *CYD Journal: Community Youth Development* 1:36–41.

Sonenshein, R. 1998. Making the rules: Youth participation and Los Angeles charter reform. *New Designs for Youth Development* 14:39–40.

South, S. J. 2001. Issues in the analysis of neighborhoods, families, and children. In A. Booth and A. C. Crouter, eds., *Does It Take a Village?* 87–93.

Spencer, M. B. 2001. Resiliency and fragility factors associated with the contextual experiences of low-resource urban African-American male youth and families. In A. Booth and A. C. Crouter, eds., *Does It Take a Village?* 51–77.

Spradley, J. P. 1979. *The Ethnographic Interview.* New York: Holt, Rinehart and Winston.

Stanton-Salazar, R. D. 2000. The development of coping strategies among urban Latino youth: A focus on help-seeking orientations as network-related behavior. In Montero-Sieburth and Villarruel, *Making Invisible Latino Adolescents Visible,* 203–238.

Stark, R., and W. S. Bainbridge. 1997. *Religion, Devine, and Social Control.* New York: Routledge.

Stevenson, H. C., J. Reed, P. Bodison, and A. Bishop. 1997. Racism stress management: Racial socialization beliefs and the experiences of depression and anger in African American youth. *Youth and Society* 29:197–122.

Stevenson, L. 2000. Bringing youth to the table in systems of care. *Focal Point* 14:16–18.

Stiehl, J. 2000. Outdoor and adventure programs. In D. Hellison, N. Cutforth, J. Kallusky, T. Martinek, M. Parker, and J. Stiehl, eds., *Youth Development and Physical Activity: Linking Universities and Communities*, 67–85. Champaign, Il: Human Kinetics.

Storrie, T. 1997. Citizens or what? In J. Roche and S. Tucker, *Youth in Society*, 59–67.

Strasburg, J. 1998. Showing disabled youths the sky's the limit: Challenge Air teaches fliers that feats difficult even for the fully abled people can be done. *Corpus Christi Caller-Times*, September 13, 3.

Stratton, J. 2000. Cyberspace and globalization of culture. In Bell and Kennedy, *The Cybercultures Reader*, 721–731.

Sugarman, B. 1973. *The School and Moral Development*. New York: Harper & Row.

Sullivan, M. L. 2001. Hyperghettos and hypermasculinity: The phenomenology of exclusion. In A. Booth and A. C. Crouter, eds., *Does It Take a Village?* 95–101.

Tardieu, B. 1999. Computer as community memory: How people in very poor neighborhoods made a computer their own. In Schon, Sanyal, and Mitchell, *High Technology and Low-income Communities*, 287–313.

Tasker, M. 1999. "You like Tupac, Mary?" *Families in Society: The Journal of Contemporary Human Services* 80:216–218.

Taylor, A. S., and J. Bressler. 2000. *Mentoring across Generations: Partnerships for Positive Youth Development*. New York: Kluwer Academic/Plenum.

Taylor, C. S. 1996. *Growing Up Behind Bars: Confinement, Youth Development, and Crime*. East Lansing: Michigan State University.

Taylor, R. B. 2001. On Mount and Fayette: Implications for comprehensive youth development approaches. In A. Booth and A. C. Crouter, eds., *Does It Take a Village?* 203–210.

Tchen, J. K. W. 1992. Creating a dialogic museum: The Chinatown history museum experiment. In Karp, Kreamer, and Lavine, *Museums and Communities*, 285–326.

Teasley, M. D., and D. Walker-Moses. 1998. On-site library centers. In Venturella, *Poor People and Library Services*, 136–151.

Teichman, S., and H. Barry. 1999. Educating global leaders. *New Designs for Youth Development* 15:16–22.

Terry, J. P. 2000. Hold that thought. *CYD Journal: Community Youth Development* 1:5.

Thompson, J. K. 1999. *Caring on the Streets: A Study of Detached Youthworkers*. New York: Haworth Press.

Thornton, S. 1996. *Club Cultures: Music, Media, and Subcultural Capital.* Hanover, Conn: Wesleyan University Press.

Thurlow, N. 2000. Connecting with inner courage. *CYD Journal: Community Youth Development* 1:18–23.

Tierney, J. 1997. New York's parallel lives. *New York Times,* October 19, magazine: 51–53.

Tolan, P. H., and D. Gorman-Smith. 1997. Families and the development of urban children. In Walberg, Reyes, and Weissberg, *Children and Youth,* 67–91.

Torres-Saillant, S., and R. Hernandez. 1998. *The New Americans: The Dominican Americans.* Westport, Conn: Greenwood Press.

Townsel, K. T. 1997. Mentoring African American youth. *Preventing School Failure* 41:125–127.

Tremblay-McGaw, R. 1999. Part of the solution: Librarians work to stop gun violence. *American Libraries* 30:56–58.

Turkle, S. 1999. Commodity and community in personal computing. In Schon, Sanyal, and Mitchell, *High Technology and Low-income Communities,* 337–347.

Uggen, C., and J. Janikula. 1999. Voluntarism and arrest in the transition to adulthood. *Social Forces* 78:331–362.

Uhl, A. 2000. The future of primary prevention. *Journal of Primary Prevention* 21:43–45.

Urresta, L. 1996. Marketing to the soccer-mad. *Fortune* 134 (December 9): 46.

U.S. Department of Education. 2000. *Internet Access in U.S. Public Schools and Classrooms, 1994–1999.* Washington, D.C.: U.S. Department of Education.

U.S. Newswire. 2000. Report finds community support critical on youth development programs. March 8, 11:05.

Valentine, G., T. Skelton, and D. Chambers. 1998. Cool places: An introduction to youth and youth cultures. In Skelton and Valentine, *Cool Places,* 1–32.

Vancouver Aquarium. 1996. *Youth Volunteer Team* [newsletter]. Vancouver, Canada: Vancouver Aquarium.

Van Linden, J. A., and C. I. Fertman. 1998. *Youth Leadership: A Guide to Understanding Leadership Development in Adolescents.* San Francisco: Jossey-Bass.

Vargas, M., and N. A. Busch-Rossnagel. 2000. Authority plus affection: Latino parenting during adolescence. In Montero-Sieburth and Villarruel, *Making Invisible Latino Adolescents Visible,* 265–287.

Vargas, L. A., and J. D. Koss-Chioino, eds. 1992. *Working with Culture: Psychotherapeutic Interventions with Ethnic Minority Children and Adolescents,* 103–128. San Francisco: Jossey-Bass.

Vecchio, G. D. 1997. *Creating Ever-cool: A Marketer's Guide to a Kid's Heart.* New York: Pelican.

Venturella, K. M. 1998a. Libraries and poverty. In Venturella, *Poor People and Library Services*, 29–34.

Venturella, K. M., ed. 1998b. *Poor People and Library Services*. Jefferson, N.C.: McFarland.

Villarruel, F. A., and R. M. Lerner. 1994a. Development and context and the contexts of learning. In Villarruel and Lerner, *Promoting Community-based Programs for Socialization and Learning*, 3–10.

––, eds. 1994b. *Promoting Community-based Programs for Socialization and Learning*. San Francisco: Jossey-Bass.

Villines, C. 2000. Listening to voices. *Focal Point* 14:22–23.

Wahl, E. 1995. Youth development: A journey of strength, power and love. In AYPF, *Contract with America's Youth*, 18–19.

Walberg, H. J., O. Reyes, and R. P. Weissberg. 1997a. Introduction to and overview of *Children and Youth*, 3–10.

––, eds. 1997b. *Children and Youth: Interdisciplinary Perspectives*. Thousand Oaks, Calif.: Sage.

Walberg, H. J., O. Reyes, R. P. Weissberg, and C. B. Kuster. 1997. Strengthening the families, education and health or urban children and youth. Afterword to *Children and Youth*, 363–368.

Walker, J., and T. Dunham. 1994. *Understanding Youth Development Work*. Saint Paul: Minnesota Extension Service, University of Minnesota College of Education.

Wallace, J. M., Jr., and D. R. Williams. 1997. Religion and adolescent health-compromising behavior. In Schulenberg, Maggs, and Hurrelmann, *Health Risks and Developmental Transitions*, 444–468.

Walser, W. 1998. Clamor and community in the music of Public Enemy. In J. Austin and M. N. Willard, eds., *Generations of Youth: Youth Cultures and History in Twentieth-century America*, 293–310. New York: New York University Press.

Walsh, J. 1999. More than a ramp. *New Designs for Youth Development* 15:25–29.

Wang, M. C., G. D. Haertel, and H. J. Walberg. 1997. Fostering educational resilience in inner-city schools. In Walberg, Reyes, and Weissberg, *Children and Youth*, 119–140.

Wasylyshyn, V. 1988. Outdoor adventures encourage youths to S.T.A.Y. in school. *Children Today* 17:16–21.

Watkins, M., and E. Iverson. 1998. Youth development principles and field practicum opportunities. In R. R. Greene and M. Watkins, eds., *Serving Diverse Constituencies: Applying the Ecological Perspective*, 167–197. New York: Aldine de Gruyter.

Watts, T. 1998. Harlem youths have voice in their community newspaper. *New York Amsterdam News*, January 14, 27.

Way, N. 1998. *Everyday Courage: The Lives and Stories of Urban Teenagers*. New York: New York University Press.

Wehlage, G. 1989. *Reducing the Risk: Schools as Communities of Support*. Philadelphia, Penn.: Palmer Press.

Weil, M. O. 1996. Community-building: Building community practice. *Social Work* 41:481–499.

Weinberger, D. R. 2001. A brain too young for good judgement. *New York Times*, March 10, A27.

Weiss, H. B., and M. E. Lopez. 2000. New strategies in foundation grantmaking for children and youth. *CYD Journal: Community Youth Development* 1:53–59.

Weissberg, R. F., M. Caplan, and R. L. Harwood. 1991. Promoting competent young people in competence-enhancing environments: A systems-based perspective on primary prevention. *Journal of Consulting and Clinical Psychology* 59:830–841.

Weissberg, R. P., M. Caplan, and P. J. Sivo. 1989. A new conceptual framework for establishing school-based competence promotion programs. In L. A. Bond and B. E. Compas, eds., *Primary Prevention in the Schools*, 177–200. Newbury Park, Calif.: Sage.

Weissberg, R. P., and M. T. Greenberg. 1997. School and community competence—enhancement and prevention programs. In W. Damon, I. E. Siegeld, and K. A. Renninger, eds., *Handbook of Child Psychology,* vol. 5: *Child Psychology*, 45–66. New York: Wiley.

Weizel, R. 2000. "Teenagers build confidence at wilderness school." *Boston Globe,* January 9, J6.

Wellman, B., and M. Gulia. 1999. Virtual communities as communities: Net surfers don't ride alone. In M. A. Smith and P. Kollock, eds., *Communities in Cyberspace*, 167–194.

Werner, E. E. 1990. Protective factors and individual resilience. In S. J. Meisels and J. P. Shonkoff, eds., *Handbook of Early Childhood Intervention*, 97–116. New York: Cambridge University Press.

——. 1989. High-risk children in young adulthood. A longitudinal study from birth to 32 years. *American Journal of Orthopsychiatry* 59:72–81.

Werner, E. E., and R. S. Smith. 1992. *Overcoming the Odds*. Ithaca, N.Y.: Cornell University Press.

——. 1982. *Vulnerable but Not Invincible: A Longitudinal Study of Children and Youth*. New York: McGraw-Hill.

——. 1977. *Kauai's Children Come of Age*. Honolulu: University of Hawaii Press.

Weston, R., and H. E. A. Tinsley. 1999. Widerness adventure therapy for at-risk youth. *Parks and Recreation* 34:30–42.

Wheat, A. 2000. Running the rapids of risk. *Parks and Recreation* 35:78–81.

Wigfield, A., and J. Eccles. 1994. Children's competence beliefs, achievement values, and general self-esteem: Changes across elementary and middle school. *Journal of Early Adolescence* 14:107–138.

Wilbur, S. P. 2000. An archaeology of cyberspaces: Virtuality, community, identity. In Bell and Kennedy, *The Cybercultures Reader*, 45–55.

Wilgoren, J. 2000. Swell of minority students is predicted at colleges. *New York Times*, May 24, A14.

Willard, W. 1989. Séance, tricknowlogy, skateboarding, and the space of youth. In J. Austin and M. N. Willard, eds., *Generations of Youth: Youth Cultures and History in Twentieth-century America*, 327–346. New York: New York University Press.

Willson, M. 2000. Community in the abstract: A political and ethical dilemma. In Bell and Kennedy, *The Cybercultures Reader*, 644–657.

Wison, W. J. 1999. The plight of the inner-city back male. In Besharov, *America's Disconnected Youth*, 31–48.

Women's Wear Daily. 2000. Youth brand mantra: To be inventive. *Women's Wear Daily*, February 11, 179, S2.

World Sources Online. 1999. Challenges facing youth development: National and global perspectives. *Independent*, November 19, EB 19991119460000029 10:18.

W. T. Grant Consortium on the School-Based Promotion of Social Competence. 1992. In J. D. Hawkins, R. F. Catalano, and Associates, eds., *Communities That Care*, 129–148. San Francisco: Jossey-Bass.

Wulff, H. 1995. Introducing youth culture in its own right: the state of the art and new possibilities. Introduction to *Youth Cultures: A Cross-cultural Perspective*, ed. V. Amit-Talai and H. Wulff, 1–18. London: Routledge.

Wuthnow, R. 1995. *Learning to Care: Elementary Kindness in an Age of Indifference.* New York: Oxford University Press.

Ybarra-Frausto, T. 1991. The Chicano movement/The movement of Chicano art. In Karp and Lavine, *Exhibiting Cultures*, 128–150.

Yourniss, J. 1980. *Parents and Peers in Social Development.* Chicago: University of Chicago Press.

Yourniss, J., and J. Smollar. 1985. *Adolescents' Relations with Mothers, Fathers, and Friends.* Chicago: University of Chicago Press.

Yourniss, J., and M. Yates. 1997. *Community Service and Social Responsibility in Youth.* Chicago: University of Chicago Press.

Youth Markets Alert. 1999. Kids want r-e-s-p-e-c-t. *Youth Markets Alert* 11:6.

Zabel, D. 1999. Selling to generation y, virtual workers, and boomer grandparents. *Reference and User Services Quarterly* 39:10–15.

Zeldin, S. 1995a. Community-university collaboration for youth development: From theory to practice. *Journal of Adolescent Research* 10:449–469.

———. 1995b. *Making Research Relevant to Community Mobilization Efforts for Youth Development: A Project and Conference Summary.* Washington, D.C.: Center for Youth Development and Policy Research, Academy for Educational Development.

Zeldin, S., and L. Camino. 1999. Youth leadership: Linking research and program theory to exemplary practice. *New Designs for Youth Development* 15:10–15.

Zeldin, S., M. Kimball, and L. Price. 1995. *What Are the Day-to-day Experiences that Promote Youth Development? An Annotated Bibliography of Research on Adolescents and Their Families.* Washington, D.C.: Center for Youth Development and Policy Research, Academy for Educational Development.

Zollo, P. 1999. *Wise Up to Teens: Insights into Marketing and Advertising to Teenagers.* New York: New Strategies.

Zuck, R. B., and W. S. Benson. 1978. *Youth Education in the Church.* Chicago: Moody Press.

INDEX OF NAMES

INDEX OF SUBJECTS